PENGUIN
SELECTIVE MEMORY: ST

Shobha Dé is a Mumbai-based writer.

BY THE SAME AUTHOR

Socialite Evenings
Starry Nights
Sultry Days
Sisters
Strange Obsession
Snapshots
Second Thoughts
Uncertain Liaisons: Sex, Strife and Togetherness in
    Urban India (Co-edited with Khushwant Singh)
Shooting from the Hip
Small Betrayals
Surviving Men

SHOBHA DÉ

SELECTIVE
MEMORY

Stories From My Life

PENGUIN BOOKS

Penguin Books India (P) Ltd., 210 Chiranjiv Tower, 43 Nehru Place, New Delhi 110 019,
India
Penguin Books Ltd., 27 Wrights Lane, London W8 5TZ, UK
Penguin Books USA Inc., 375 Hudson Street, New York, NY 10014, USA
Penguin Books Australia Ltd., Ringwood, Victoria, Australia
Penguin Books Canada Ltd., 10 Alcorn Avenue, Suite 300, Toronto, Ontario M4V 3B2,
Canada
Penguin Books (NZ) Ltd., 182-190 Wairau Road, Auckland 10, New Zealand

First published by Penguin Books India (P) Ltd. 1998

10 9 8 7 6 5 4 3 2 1

Typeset in Sabon by Digital Technologies and Printing Solutions, New Delhi

*To Lord C... from whom there can be no secrets
and
my beloved family, from whom I've still kept a few.*

Contents

Prologue

A late night phone call. Early 1997.

'I think you should write your autobiography now that you're about to turn fifty.'

That was David Davidar.

'I'm not sure. I don't think it's the right moment to do it.' That was me.

'There's no right time or wrong time to put your life on the line.' David.

'Isn't there?' Me.

I thought people wrote their memoirs at seventy. Nice number, seventy. It's all behind you. Good times and bad. You want to chronicle it before memory itself fades.

People also write their memoirs at twenty. Nice number again. Twenty. It's all ahead of you. Good and bad. You can't wait to get it all down before life itself hurtles past and memories seem redundant.

'Fifty is in between,' I said hesitantly. 'I don't know. I'm not sure. Fifty is so . . . non-committal and boring. I hate mid-points.'

'Look, I think you should do it. Now.' David.

'I'm scared.' Me.

'Of course you are. It is the scariest experience for anybody in the world. People are terrified at the thought of writing about themselves. They find all kinds of excuses. They lie. They make up. They invent. They rub out.' David.

'I know. That's why I don't want to do it.' Me.

'Think of it as a column. A really really long one. That's what your life has been for twenty-five years—an unending column.' David.

Has.it? Just that? A column?

Maybe.

And then I started to think. Fifty. Funny, I didn't feel it. Fifty. Such finality in that word. Fifty. Stocktaking time. Fifty. Flashback time. Fifty. Ugh. Fifty. Wow. I repeated fifty, fifty times over. It had to sink in. Register. I needed that sense of fifty to fix it. Was I really going to turn fifty a few months from that phone call? And did I want to write the damn book?

I guess I did.

'Please go away,' I pleaded with the unwritten manuscript, even as I prepared to write it.

'Leave me alone,' I beseeched as images exploded in my head.

I knew what it was leading up to.

I was readying myself to turn into a monster. It was going to happen the moment I took up my standard writing pad, scribbled the date on the first page, muttered a short prayer to 'Ganesha' and wrote the first words. Something awful would happen to me. It always did. And for the next year, I'd become insufferable.

For a woman, a book in progress is like a secret lover she has to hide from her family. Steal time to go back to. Dream about. Luxuriate in. Fantasize about. It's a guilty secret she can't share with anybody. There is a sense of regret—you can't make love to a book or talk to it. And yet, the secret thrill of each encounter provides a high. The book makes you feel desirable, sexy, beautiful, interesting. It's better than the best sex.

The summer of '97. I knew I was getting there. Critical mass time was rapidly approaching. I knew I'd resent all intrusions—family excursions, visitors, phone calls, social obligations, school trips, shopping expeditions, TV programmes, books, magazines—anything that required my time and attention.

The worst aspect of writing, whether it's a memoir or a racy novel, is that you can't share the experience with any one. It can be hellishly lonely sometimes. A feeling of such isolation, you ask yourself why you are punishing yourself like this. What for? There have to be better options.

I don't know how others are affected by the process but I become an intensely obsessive and irritatingly preoccupied person. I feel resentful of each second taken away from the writing ritual. My existence is consumed by the act itself. It gets to a point where the pressure is physical, not merely mental. An unbearable pain reverberates through the entire body. The mind starts racing faster than the fingers can keep up. That in turn becomes a cause for frustration. A sense of desperation and urgency dominates every waking hour. I can't concentrate on anything, not even crucial conversations. So much concentration takes its toll.

It's hard to keep one's mind focused on domestic trivia while longing to write those extra pages one has abandoned because of the quarterly pest-control date or an ill-timed PTA meeting. It's even harder to feign interest in family matters, a spouse's routine conversation, a child's prattle, while longing to get back to writing.

Family members complain of neglect, and friends, understanding and simpatico in the initial months, drift away and look to others with more time and concern. I feel the need for a speedbreaker. But there's no way to slow down or stop. A day becomes 'good' when the writing has gone well. A 'lightness of being' takes over. It turns 'bad' if the natural rhythm has missed its beat. That's when blackness envelops one. It's worse, far worse than the worst menstrual cramps. The mind doubles up in pain and there's no relief for that except the next round of productive writing . . . but you aren't sure when that's likely to occur—that evening, the next morning, a week later, maybe two months down the line.

At the 1998 Winter Olympics, I watched the sole Indian representative Shiva Keshavan preparing for the luge—his special event. As he careened down the narrow icy passage on his back, I said to myself, 'My God. That's me. I'm moving so fast, whatever happens now, it's out of my control.'

There was just one thing to do. Lie back and enjoy the ride.

David was right. Partially so.

Selective Memory was not an easy book to write. But it wasn't that tough either.

Once I'd put my foot into it, I rather enjoyed myself. Lots and lots of writing. Yes. No notes. No dates. No aides-memoirs. No diaries. No clippings. Not even a particularly retentive memory. Just a myriad echoes and images. Mostly colourful, generally pleasant. Looking back wasn't such a bitch after all, or it could be that turning fifty had a lot to do with my changed perspective. At fifty, nothing is at stake. Nothing and nobody matters all that much—not even old adversaries. Enmity itself gets diluted. Poison disappears. Co-existence becomes the key. People cease to affect you with the same intensity.

At fifty, one cuts the fat, trims non-essentials and starts sifting. David's words came back to me constantly: 'You have the ability to pick out that one characteristic that defines an individual, and bury it in amber. Tap into it. Use it—and you've got your book.' Perhaps. But once I'd started, it was the process and not the fate of the book that began to matter. Like everything else, I attributed my altered thinking to the prospect of turning fifty.

When my father decided to hold a Satya-Narayan puja at his residence to mark the event, I went along with the plan without any particular sentiment. He'd done it for my older sisters, Mandakini and Kunda, for their fiftieths, skipped it for my brother's, respecting Ashok's sentiments about pujas in general being a waste, and now he was enthusiastically organizing the final one for his youngest child.

As my husband and I took our places in front of the light-eyed, bare-chested, fair-skinned brahmin, my husband wearing a silk dhoti and I a traditional nine-yard Paithani saree, my mind was not on the shlokas the priest would soon be reciting monotonously, or on the elaborate Maharashtrian feast that would follow. I was distractedly thinking of mundane matters—the column I had to write the next day, the clothes that were to be picked up from the laundry, my daughter Arundhati's new gym shoes which I'd promised her before school reopened. It was difficult to stay focused on what, for me, was nothing more than incomprehensible mumbo-jumbo. Gradually, however, I began to notice the details surrounding the puja, all the planning and thought that had gone into making this evening auspicious, the pride with which my father (playing solo host for the first time at a religious function in his home, without my mother by his side) had made sure all the ritualistic silver vessels were brought out, brilliantly polished and beautifully displayed around the compact shrine created for the occasion. I saw my sister Kunda's complete involvement as she supervised the proceedings, filling in for our late mother.

Dressed in a resplendent kanjeevaram, Kunda had instinctively and effortlessly slipped into the vacated role, and once or twice when I caught a flash of her purple saree as she swept in and out of the room, I thought I saw my 'Aie'—not someone like her. Not a daughter who resembled her, but Mother herself. I sensed Aie's unmistakable presence and gradually, my mind eliminated the trivia crowding it and started to concentrate on the katha being narrated by the priest. It no longer mattered that his words meant nothing to me. I looked at the fresh flowers, the lotuses and roses, the small mound of tulsi leaves, the gleaming thalis and diyas, the tiny figure of Krishna. I breathed in the gentle fragrance of sandalwood, the sharper one of camphor, the aroma of freshly-made prasad wafting in from the kitchen, and the puja became a part of a piece. I closed my eyes. I thought of my father's phone call a month earlier—suppressed excitement in his voice, a strange sense of urgency, secrecy. 'My dear . . . can you come and see me today?'

'Something urgent?' I was mildly irritated at being interrupted. The book again.

'Yes. It is.'

'But . . . what! Can't it wait? I have a deadline. I'm writing.'

'Half an hour. Fifteen minutes. No more.'

'Okay, I'll be there at lunchtime.'

Close to 2 p.m. the phone rang.

'You aren't here yet.'

'I'm sorry. I got caught up. I'll come later . . .'

'You said lunchtime.'

'I know. I'm really sorry. I'll be there around 5 p.m.'

'No. That won't be convenient. Why not now?'

'What is it?'

'I can't tell you over the phone.'

'Well . . . all right. Expect me in ten minutes.'

'Don't disappoint me. And don't be late.'

6

'No, I won't.'

I walked into his neat, well-lit flat. He met me at the door, took my elbow and escorted me into his bedroom.

'Sit down.' He indicated the chair meant for visitors.

'I want to give you your fiftieth birthday present today.' He went towards his cupboard—the steel almirah, not the wooden one.

'No-o-o, baba. I don't want it now. Please give it to me on my birthday.' He turned around. 'I'd like you to have it. Today. Right now. It's my decision.'

'Why?'

'In case . . . in case . . . something happens to me . . . I wouldn't want the gift to lie unclaimed. I wouldn't want it to cause any confusion or embarrassment. I got it for you. It has a special significance. This year India completes fifty years. You begin yours. When you see what I have, you'll understand my reason for handing it over, like this.'

'Please, baba. I don't want you to give it to me just yet. And don't even say something might happen to you. Nothing will. You'll be here and we'll celebrate together.'

'I am a ninety-year-old man. It would be foolish to say nothing's going to happen. Maybe nothing will. But if for any reason I am no more, this gift will lose its charm. You were born in free India. You will not know what that moment of freedom meant to people of my generation. So, don't argue with me. Take it. And keep it safely.'

He opened the cupboard.

I continued to protest.

'Look, in case you are worried about your health, leave a note with the gift.'

He wasn't listening.

He took out a slim, hand-made paper envelope. I recognized his beautiful handwriting on it. He handed it to me and asked mischievously, 'Can you guess what's inside?'

I ran my fingers lightly over the envelope. There was something fairly hard in there.

'Give up?' he continued, with a gleam in his eyes.

'Give up,' I admitted.

He took back the envelope, opened it carefully and removed a small, neat packet which he handed to me.

It was from the Government of India mint. A gold coin commemorating fifty years of independence. Beautiful. And so appropriate.

'Purest of gold. Twenty-four carat. Look. Read. It's certified. Not easy to get, either. I had to try from several different sources. Great demand for it. One day it will become a collector's item,' my father declared proudly.

I took the coin out of its packaging and stared at it for a long time. It looked like a miniature sun on my palm. I was far too moved by the gesture to say anything. It really was perfect, even in its execution. For a change, the government design department hadn't gone horribly wrong. There was nothing ostentatious about the coin. And I could only marvel at my father's imagination. Another man might have handed over a sum of money and said, 'Buy yourself something.' But here we were, sharing such a deeply moving moment—and I couldn't think of a thing to say, not even 'thank you'. We admired its impeccable finish, turned it around a few times in our hands. I imagined my mother's presence beside me..This was so much 'her' room, with her things still all around—her hand mirror, her dressing-table, her toiletries, the towel rack with her 'home sarees' on it. Finally, I bent down and touched his feet. We did not embrace. The old awkwardness was still there. 'God bless you, my dear,' he said, a small catch in his voice. And then, out of sheer embarrassment, we resumed our 'normal' conversation—the chances of the Congress party in the elections, why the United Front government fell. How Inder Gujral could have made a difference but didn't.

I placed the envelope in my handbag.

'Put it away carefully,' my father said as he must have countless times when I was a child. The tone was exactly the same, too. I behaved like an adolescent myself, nodding obediently while receiving baba's instructions. It was time to leave and return to my own home. At which point I experienced a familiar sense of confusion. My home? Wasn't this, my father's house, also my home? More 'my home' than the one I lived in? Or at least equally so? I went back feeling slightly disturbed, mainly by the poignancy of his gesture. The thought that he'd felt he might not be there for my fiftieth birthday even though it was just round the corner . . . A feeling of my own mortality swept over me. For the first time. It had never before featured on my agenda. I hadn't planned for it. My father was expressing his worry about not being present on my birthday. How could I be sure I'd be around myself? I could hear Kunda's words: 'Don't be morbid.' Was it morbid to consider your own mortality? At fifty? Clearly not. I had arrived at a turning point.

With a start I came back to the present. The religious ceremony was coming to an end.

On the way home, my thoughts drifted back to the day on which I had first considered death. Whether the book had been responsible for getting me there or not, the writing of it had made me stop in my tracks and look back on areas of my life I'd almost forgotten. I'd been so busy living in the present, the past had been all but obliterated. I'd had no time for it. No real interest in it. My attitude had consistently been forward looking. I'd arrived at fifty in a flurry, with a surge that was still propelling me at breakneck speed towards my tomorrows. Fifty. So different from forty. But I was the same determined little girl crouching at the starting blocks, waiting to hear the sharp crack of the umpire's pistol-shot before my favourite event—the hundred metres sprint.

I wasn't frightened. Not at all. Just as I'd only recently overcome my life-long fear of the dark and no longer needed a night-lamp in the room. I felt ready for the remaining stretch. I was willing to give it my best shot—never mind how I placed. The victory stand had ceased to be important. I used to desperately want to be there on it—and only in one position, the top place I frequently succeeded in getting to. The top—comforting, comfortable, and oh-so-familiar. I'd been spoilt. I'd started to believe it was the only spot for me. Foolish, vain, arrogant. It didn't matter any more. It wasn't resignation or fatigue prompting me to acknowledge this. Rather, it was sweet acceptance.

I'd never felt better about myself, never so comfortable in my skin, never as much at peace. Where was the restlessness, the impatience, the irritation? Rapidly receding. Far too rapidly for comfort. I panicked. But just a little. Soon, I wouldn't be able to recognize myself. Soon, people who once knew me would say, 'Who is this woman? Do we know her? Do we even want to?' And then I'd hear those awful words whispered behind my back or uttered sweetly to my face: 'Know something? You've mellowed. Really. You have. It's so nice.'

'Nice? No, it isn't,' I'd shoot back.

Mellow? Who needs mellow? I'm not 'nice', you dumb clucks. Nor mellow. Merely older. I can't be a brat at fifty. It's obscene. Fortunately, a few remnants of that other woman are still intact. I found myself squaring my shoulders, sticking my chin out and thinking, 'So what? I've changed. I'm entitled to. Those who're looking for the familiar me will just have to settle for this one—or lump it. For, this one is here to stay.

Prologue*

And frankly, I'm rather enjoying being her.'

If nothing else, *Selective Memory* aided and abetted the transformation. Kick-started the process, as it were. Forced me to glance over my shoulder. Look back, sift, discard, reinforce, assess, re-assess, come to terms, recognize, accept—above all, accept. It was not easy. Not easy at all. But having endured the experience, I feel that much stronger. It wasn't as painful as I'd imagined. I didn't 'suffer'. It's the exhilaration of forced remembering that I'll cherish. In my preoccupation with the present I'd lost touch with my past. The book served as an excuse, an alibi and a prod. There was no escape.

The makeover isn't over yet. But the book is. One part of it, at any rate. Like any seasoned conspirator, I can hear a small voice from its pages saying, 'You think you're through? You really think this is it? Do you believe you'll be let off this easily? Not on your life. Not so fast, Dé. Not so fast. Remember your own lines: "no short-cuts on this route"?' I do remember. Unfortunately so.

I'm still seeking sanction—an old habit. Indulge me.

Glancing Back

Unfortunately for my mother I was not the second son she'd prayed for. My birth could not possibly have been a day of celebration for the family especially since my maternal grandmother was around to remind everybody that a third daughter had arrived as an additional liability and it had been rather reckless of my parents to have gone in for a fourth child with no guarantee that it would be male. Whether or not my mother had really and truly been moved to tears of dejection at the nurse's announcement of my sex, my grandmother had made sure she felt wretched and guilty about it. As she began to cry bitter tears at the sight of me, her mother had slapped her own forehead hard in an unambiguous gesture of disgust and disappointment. It was my father who had rejoiced with all his heart. His reasons, he explains candidly, were aesthetic.

'I had never seen such a perfectly formed infant, with regular features, a clear skin, and tapering fingers. You were a joy to behold. I scolded your mother for her foolish tears. I held you up for her to examine and said, "Look at her. Just look. Isn't she a beauty? God has been so kind to us. We have a healthy, good-looking daughter—why are you weeping?"'

Unconvinced by his argument, my mother shed some more tears, to placate my grandmother, I suspect, and display solidarity under the circumstances.

Dr Rajguru, the obstetrician who delivered me in a

converted military bungalow in Satara, was paid Rs 30 as his professional fees. Another hundred was spent for a week's stay and miscellaneous post-delivery charges. About the same time the wives of my father's peon and orderly each delivered bouncing boys—they were clearly one up on 'Raosaheb' (my father). As the special magistrate at that time, my father was preoccupied with the plague epidemic raging in Satara. A dead rat had been found in a barrel of water in the courtyard and sent for dissection. The report was expected shortly. He paid scant attention to their triumphant cries of 'Mulga' (boy), 'Mulga', followed by gleeful references to poor Raosaheb's 'Mulgi' (girl).

Despite the gloom, I went home in style. The first car I rode in was a sleek blue Buick. I was seven days old. And the car, a borrowed one. My father was a few months away from forty and the only one, besides my sister Kunda, to be delighted with the newest Rajadhyaksha baby. Poor Kunda, at six, had no idea that it was only the birth of a son that called for celebration in my mother's family. She'd been told that my eldest sister Mandakini had had an auspicious kumkum hand impression imprinted on her back, to commemorate my brother Ashok's birth. Innocently, she'd demanded the same privilege at mine, to which my grandmother had witheringly snapped, 'What? You want kumkum on your back? Go and fetch some cow-dung instead. Do you realize there are three daughters in the family now? Three. Weren't two enough?' Kunda had shrunk into the dark recesses of the sprawling bungalow, not daring to coo over her baby sister for fear of attracting her grandmother's scorn and, worse, her wrath.

Fortunately for me, my mother's initial feeling of being let down was transformed into warmth and love soon after. My father had declared me 'lucky' for the family. And she was gradually converted. Whether or not I was a mascot, many major changes did follow my birth. My father applied for a job at the Centre in Delhi—and got it. This meant we were out of the districts and into the real world. I was two years old when we moved to the capital where my father had been appointed as an assistant solicitor to the government of India. For my siblings, this was a decidedly traumatic and ill-timed move. From Marathi-medium schools in the mofussils they were air-dropped into an English and Hindi dominated environment without knowing a word of either language. Mandakini at thirteen was battling her own awkward adolescent demons. The other two at ten and eight were expected to follow lessons in science, history, geography and English literature at a school (Delhi Public School) which boasted very high standards. There was no question of hiring tutors as my father still had old debts to settle—all of thirty-odd rupees.

Unaccustomed to Delhi winters, the three of them would shiver in the early morning chill, waiting for the school bus to pick them up. They'd sit through their classes in complete incomprehension, often blindly copying down 'patterns' on the blackboard or taking notes phonetically in Marathi. And yet, a year or two later, these same children were topping their class, and continued to do so till two of them got their Senior Cambridge certificates with aggregates of over ninety per cent.

Meanwhile, I stayed home, a pampered, mollycoddled child who clung to Mother's saree pallu and insisted on accompanying my parents to official government functions. My conduct annoyed the others and they taunted my mother about her obvious favouritism. I didn't go to primary school till the age of seven, preferring to stay back, close to Mother, who by then was more relaxed about raising her brood and

14

needed me as much as I needed to be with her. During the seethingly hot Delhi summers, I'd stretch my body over hers as she relaxed under a fan in an easy chair and napped lightly, the fragrance of damp khus wafting from the chiks covering the windows of our government-colony residence. Absently, her fingers would probe my nostrils and ears looking for obstinate remnants of grime that hadn't been scrubbed away during bath-time.

It must have irritated my brother and sister to observe such preferential treatment they themselves had been denied as kids. Often, I refused to get out of bed till my father came into the room and carried me piggy back to the dining table. I refused to get out of my parents' bedroom too, till we moved again, this time to Mumbai. I was ten then.

I have vivid recollections of my years in Delhi, living next to Khan Market and wandering around the crowded bazaar with my father. There was one regular stopover, a small photo-studio where I insisted on getting my pictures taken. I still have those grainy black-and-white prints and when I look at my self-conscious poses, the expression surprisingly serious in most, I wonder whether the long relationship I later developed with the camera was foretold in that tiny studio in Delhi.

I was also the child who made the maximum number of demands on my parents. Happily, these weren't shot down. Often, my requests were indulged, even when they were unreasonable. I used to go to nursery school riding on the rod of a bicycle pedalled by a domestic. My snack-box requirements were not just expensive but fussy too. I liked Keventer's pastries, and bananas sliced just so. These I refused to eat with a regular stainless steel fork, preferring a delicate pastry one especially purchased for me. I was equally particular about my school-bag, napkin and pencil box.

Where did I pick up these finicky habits from? Nobody else in my family dared to voice such desires—not to my father at any rate, unless the person was prepared to listen to a fifteen-minute speech extolling the virtues of austerity. Yet, I got away with this and more.

I was the only child whose birthdays were celebrated. At age two (en route to Delhi and staying at the family home in Central Mumbai), I had very definite ideas on what exactly I wanted to do on my big day. Predictably enough, I opted for a pink theme—and pink it was. Uncles and cousins were despatched to search out pink booties, a pink frilly frock, pink socks and a pink cake with pink candles. The cousin given the responsibility of finding matching shoes nearly gave up but persevered enough to produce a red pair instead.

My sister tells me I was an insufferable brat at that age, constantly whining and clinging to my mother. I was the only one who threw tantrums when our parents were going out, the only one who was not punished for a show of temper or ever left behind. My foot-stomping worked—it was easier to have me tag along than risk foisting me on the others who had exams to deal with and mounds of homework to complete.

My days in Man Nagar (rechristened Ravindra Nagar now), were spent with the neighbour's children, wandering through the sprawling colony in search of adventure. Our big nights were during the 'Ram Lila', when, after an early dinner, we'd excitedly head for the nearby grounds to watch the Ramayana unfold on a makeshift stage. We'd sit transfixed on a hastily cleared patch of the maidan, waiting breathlessly for the finale—the fireworks display and the traditional burning of Ravana's effigy on the last day.

Each time I visit Delhi I make it a point to go to Khan Market. Most of the old stores from my childhood have disappeared, a few are reassuringly still there—Empire Stores, Shoes and Stores, Fakirchand's, and somehow, the smells are still the same. Walking through the long corridors, my senses are overtaken by aromas and tastes I associate with a particularly happy phase of my childhood. Strangely enough, I don't react to the memory of Delhi winters at all. Of course I can recall the early morning chill as I shivered under two razais despite the proximity of a tiny electric heater. But other than that memory and the feel of heavy cardigans against my skin, I remember very little.

It's the summers that have stayed. Long, still afternoons spent in darkened rooms filled with 'government furniture'—numbered clunky desks, chairs, sofa-sets, beds. Ugly, thick navy blue curtains to keep the glare away, earthenware matkas containing water that tasted of wet mud, the patch of lawn outside where we slept covered lightly with thin cotton sheets, unexpected hail and sand storms, even clouds of marauding locusts moving rapidly through the colony and blanking out the sun with their dense formations as they swept past our home and into distant wheat fields. The slightly acrid aftertaste of ripe, juicy, glossy jamuns, the long, snakey summer cucumbers eaten with salt and red chilly powder, raw mangoes plucked from low trees heavy with fruit, secret hideouts in the bushes where friends met regularly for 'club meetings', cycling round the colony on hired bikes, grazed shins, countless bruises and always, the calm, cool presence of Mother at home as she relaxed in her favourite armchair reading popular Marathi magazines while reprimanding the Garhwali domestics who worked for us.

The move to Mumbai couldn't have been better timed. I was ten and ready for the world. Even at ten, Delhi seemed too small and slow a town to me. I knew nothing about Mumbai, remembered nothing. And yet, when my father's transfer orders came, I felt we were finally going 'home'. This was rather surprising. Our upbringing had not been fiercely 'Maharashtrian'. Anything but. I did not know a single Marathi-speaking person. The people who visited our home were my father's colleagues—a Parsi, a Gujarati, a Bengali and a UP-wallah. My brother's friends from school weren't Maharashtrians. Nor did we have a single Maharashtrian neighbour. By now, I was speaking more Hindi than Marathi, more English than Hindi. I had never tasted bhelpuri. I didn't know gol-guppas were called paani puri in Mumbai. Or that hardly anybody lived in low-slung government colonies there. I had no recollection of having seen the sea, having felt salty breeze in my hair; palm trees didn't exist for me; the only mangoes I'd enjoyed were langdas not aapoos (Alphonso); double-decker buses were associated with the London of picture postcards, not Mumbai. And yet . . . and yet . . . we were going home.

My mother was elated. She'd be reunited with her sisters and mother. My father was pleased—this was a major step up in life for him. He was going to his new posting on promotion as a joint secretary in the ministry of law, heading the first ever law wing of the Centre to be established in Mumbai.

While the family waited to be assigned quarters in distant Ghatkopar, we lived with my father's brothers' families in a modest-sized flat in Girgaum. I remember the astonishing rains as our train pulled up at Bombay Central station. Sheets and sheets of sharp, strong, steady rain lashed against my skin as we stepped out of the old station and looked for a ghoda-gaadi. I still can't get over the brooding beauty of the Mumbai monsoon. It continues to remain my first and lasting impression of the city.

School and college admissions were obviously a priority.

All of us managed to get in easily. Once again, the timing couldn't have been worse for my sisters and brother. Kunda's Senior Cambridge exams were a few months away. She had to study quite on her own since one of the science subjects she'd opted for in Delhi Public School was not being taught at her new one—Queen Mary High School—where I was enrolled as well. For Mandakini, too, it was once again a case of horrendous mistiming. After acquiring a degree from Miranda House in Delhi, she found herself at sea in Mumbai, unsure of her future plans and uncertain about her feelings for this alien city she no longer identified with. Leaving close college friends behind to begin a new chapter must have been hard for her and it showed. If anything, my brother Ashok had it slightly better. He was already enrolled at the IIT (Kharagpur), which meant that Mumbai became nothing more than a vacation home for him.

Ghatkopar in 1958 was not the bustling suburb it is today. It was considered a remote outpost completely lacking in basic infrastructure. In order to make it to school on time, we had to leave home at a ghastly hour (6 a.m.). This meant we had to be up and bathed by 5.30 with our mother packing lunch for the family and getting the bath water ready for all of us on an old stove (there was no gas connection, the only alternative being a primitive woodfire). By the time we got home at 8 p.m. or later, we were too tired to even exchange polite conversation with one another. Mercifully, this phase was short-lived. My father moved out of our transit flat into the one allotted to him opposite Churchgate station. This was the best move ever—and it changed my life.

Strange how location even within the same city often determines the course one's life takes and the choices one makes. Had we remained stuck in Ghatkopar I would have grown into yet another suburban kid. But I was spared that fate. Instead we shifted to a smart address, a comparatively posh area and one of the liveliest streets in Mumbai—the old Queen's road (since renamed) which ran from Eros Cinema (a magnificent Art Deco building) all the way down to a busy junction where yet another, equally busy commercial artery began, leading up to the grand Opera House. I loved my new home. More than the flat itself, I flipped for the area. This was downtown Mumbai—fashionable, affluent and sexy. This was where the action was—lots of it. Fancy stores, theatres, cafés, bistros, five-star hotels, offices, colleges, the mock-Gothic High Court, the university, pavement stalls, gymkhanas . . . I had found my kind of environment, my kind of people, my kind of fun.

I fitted right in from day one. I swiftly got to know my way around—all the various bus routes, convenient trains that took me from Churchgate to Grant Road in ten minutes flat, taxis that plied short distances for seventy-five paise, endless espressos at Napoli that didn't cost more than five rupees, favourite songs on the jukebox at no more than twenty-five paise a request, boys and girls in trendy clothes—bell-bottoms, guru shirts, beads, clogs. I was in heaven. I began enjoying my new school, making new friends, dressing and talking differently. I grew up in a tearing hurry and the rapidity with which I changed caught my family slightly off-guard. No longer was I the kid sister hanging around Mother's knees and baby-talking cutely. I'd graduated to being a precocious pre-teen with far too much attitude.

My appearance had altered too. I swaggered around in my school tunic, wearing the sash daringly low over my hips, I teased my hair into a crazy bouffant (frowned on fiercely by the Scottish missionary teachers at school), I chewed gum incessantly and used far too much slang in my speech. I also took to advising my older sisters. When Mandakini brought home her first 'earnings' (she did a short stint as a tourist guide with the Maharashtra State Tourist Board), I provided a useful tip: 'Take my advice—buy yourself a lipstick.' And she did. She hasn't stopped wearing lipstick since.

Compared to them, I grew up fast, very fast. Today, they insist it was I who introduced them to a life they didn't know existed—pop music, stolen cigarettes smoked furtively in the small balcony outside our room, occasional swigs of beer, western-style dancing, trendy hair-styles and fashions, waxing of unwanted hair, high heels, mascara, Hollywood magazines, racy books . . . so much forbidden fruit in one single basket. It had a lot to do with sharing the same physical space. Perhaps if I'd had a separate room to myself I might have safeguarded my privacy a little. Since there was none to begin with, the smarter option was to co-opt my sisters and get them on the same side. That would reduce the chances of being squealed on as we'd be locked in a safe conspiracy of silence. It didn't always work this way, but it was better than suspicion and warfare. Nothing I did remained a secret for too long, anyway. Soon, I stopped trying to hide any aspect of my life from them, hoping this tactic would lead to eventual boredom and disassociation. It didn't.

I know my mother was always curious about what was going on in our room with the doors shut (but never locked). That was one of my father's house rules—no barricading yourself behind closed doors, which meant we had to wait for our parents to fall asleep before we did anything even remotely wicked. I suppose that was part of the thrill, given the long list of 'don'ts'. I was not allowed to wear sleeveless blouses, cut my hair in a fringe, use make-up, listen to the western station of All India Radio, dance (even by myself), wear perfume, jeans or grown-up outfits or behave in any manner that might attract attention. Perhaps my father had his reasons. I remember a few unsavoury and puzzling incidents in Delhi when I was less than ten years old, and my father's colleagues came visiting. I can still see the expression in the eyes of one particular man when he asked me to lead him to the washbasin to clean his hands. While I waited, holding a hand-towel, this man who was in his mid-forties made a crude pass, pretending it was an accidental touch. But I recognized it for what it was and fled. Seeing my expression my mother asked me what had happened. I narrated the incident and watched her face crumple with horror and disgust. She whispered something to my father, who abruptly declared the dinner over. The man was never invited back.

My parents became very protective of me after that, monitoring my movements and ensuring I was never left alone. I see all that now. But at the time my 'freedom' was being curbed and I was irritated and straining at the leash. The sort of school I was in had students who led far more 'westernized' lives with less constraints and strictures. They were 'allowed' to do far more things in their spare hours. They went to movies in groups, picnics on weekends, even to hill-stations with friends. At our home we had to adhere to strict timings and couldn't dream of going anywhere unaccompanied by a family member. But if there was one aspect of my life as a schoolgirl that was restricted, there was another aspect of it in which I was allowed to flower. My father recently reminded me about the way in which I'd become an 'accidental athlete'. At a sports meet organized by Central government officers in Mumbai, I ran my first race in the juniors' category—and won it easily. The prize was a large tray laden with 'useful' household objects donated by various companies ('the best prize you ever won,' says my father). That evening I brought home, among other things, a smart thermos.

The race was forgotten but not the track. I must have enjoyed the experience sufficiently to test my speed during subsequent trials at school. Spotted by a canny house captain (the lovely Laila Talyarkhan) who took me under her wing, I started running as fast as my feet would carry me. I won every event I participated in. The lovely Laila seemed pleased (it meant additional 'house points' for Joan of Arc, our 'house'). Her own sister Diana was a fleet-footed athlete. The generous, warm and kind Talyarkhan family 'adopted' me as a fringe member and I'm certain my attraction to athletics was more because I found acceptance within their home than my desire to excel and win trophies.

When I was selected to be on the athletics team for the state of Maharashtra and compete in the national meet in Patiala (I was already the holder of state level records in long jump and sprint events), it took my father less than a second to say a firm 'no'. That 'no' resolved a lot of dilemmas for me. I stopped participating in competitive sports, and almost completely gave up my training in athletics, which was being provided gratis by one of the best coaches in India, Ullal Rao, because he believed I had the potential to make it big. It was after a great deal of argument that I'd been allowed to avail of this special concession Rao was making. Three mornings a week I'd be up at 5.30 a.m., wearing trainers (donated), carrying spikes (donated), and holding a javelin (borrowed), as I walked a kilometre to the maidan near Metro Cinema where Rao conducted his camps. This left me very little time for anything else. I'd be dead beat after playing on the school netball team, swimming for the glory of my 'house' (I was no good at this since I was scared of water and remain so even today) and keeping in shape for the big moment—the inter-school athletics championships which I won at all the levels I ever competed in. I had to wear shorts for this, much to my father's disapproval. But so long as they were worn solely on the field and out of his sight, it was all right. It was when I took to wearing them at home (while he was at the office) and got caught, that trouble erupted.

After he nixed my participation in the nationals, I sulked silently for months and switched to basketball and hockey. Once again, I made it to the state-level team. The finals were being held in Bangalore. I begged and pleaded with him to let me go. He agreed—on one condition. My sister Kunda had to accompany me as a chaperone. He'd pay for her train fare and stay. I was sixteen and in college then. Fine, no problem. We set out happily enough, with me trying to hide what looked like a largish boil on my forearm. That was no boil, as it turned out, but an abscess that had spread deep under the skin. It burst during the train journey itself, squirting pus and blood all over my clothes. Without my sister Kunda to look after me, I would have been demoralized and frightened. With her care and encouragement I played the crucial match (we lost) and came back feeling like a wounded warrior with a large dressing on my arm. It reminded my mother of another occasion when I'd been escorted home from a sports meet, my head partially shaved and a huge bandanna-like bandage wrapped around my skull. She'd nearly fainted at the sight. I'd received a deep cut from a rusty barrel that had been part of an obstacle race. I'd never attempted a decathlon after that.

Strangely enough, when I look at some of those old photographs (my former school teacher, Violet Minchin, recently sent over a pile she had discovered while clearing her attic), I cannot remember the gruelling hours spent in training. Nor can I recall the moment of triumph, standing at the number one position on the victory stand, being handed the championship shield in a stadium full of applause, coming home with my arms filled with glittering silver trophies. I wonder why my mind is so blank about what these glorious moments meant to me back then. Surely that's what the effort was for, that's why the dawn training, strict diet, disciplined practice and regimented hours? Or was it? Maybe I enjoyed the physical process for itself and my efforts had nothing whatsoever to do with the triumphs that followed. Maybe the thrill actually lay in the pleasure I received from jumping, sprinting, throwing. I switched to other sports and other passions pretty abruptly. One day I was a champion athlete, the next I was playing basketball. No looking back, no nostalgia, no regrets. From solitary wins it had become group accolades. And it made no difference.

While writing this I tried to recreate those heady years when I'd hear one section of the stadium chanting 'Sho-bha, Sho-bha' as I laced my spikes, crouched at the starting blocks and waited to take off at the sharp sound of the starter's pistol shot. I can visualize it all with complete detachment. Like an old movie starring someone familiar. It's hard to think of that person as a young me. I am unable to get under her skin or identify with her glory. Ironically enough, my entire collection (a pretty impressive one) of silver cups was stolen sometime in the Seventies. Nobody knows what happened to the steel trunk in which they'd been stored. I suspect a newly hired domestic sold them for a pittance. I do have the certificates somewhere. And a few gold and silver medals. They're no longer of any importance to me—if they ever were. My children examine the photographs with some amusement. 'Mother—is that really you? Were you that good?' I nod absently. Yes, I suppose I was that good. But it was over thirty years ago. And who cares now?

It's the same when I chance upon assorted certificates of merit I won at Shankar's weekly art competitions. I was rather good at painting. Not brilliant. But I did enjoy it very much at one point in my life. It was Kunda who had recognized my interest and bought me a handsome wooden easel, oil paints and brushes from her meagre medical internship stipend. I set up my 'studio' excitedly in our large, well lit and airy balcony at Maskati Court. The first ambitious canvas I painted, alas, didn't meet with my father's approval. It was a nude. A rather voluptuous one at that. Embarrassed and shocked by its position on a second-floor balcony where it was drying in full view of interested office-goers, my father ordered it to be removed. 'Paint flowers, trees, birds, mountains, scenic themes. Not these types of vulgar, 'shameless pictures,' he admonished. I got the message. I stopped painting. I still doodle from time to time and my loving children encourage me to go back to something I once enjoyed. I'm not sure I want to any more. My own mediocrity will repulse me. On the other hand, I had liked the act of putting paint to canvas or paper, howsoever clumsily I'd done it. I know I would have remained nothing more than an enthusiastic weekend painter—but what enthusiasm!

I suppose I enjoyed my school years. But my memories of them are mixed. I do recall my last and final year as being particularly awful. Compelled as I was to opt for science subjects (zero aptitude, sub-zero application), I hated every moment of the time spent on trigonometry, physics and maths during the crucial eleventh standard. It showed in my performance. I hit a low in every sphere, academics and otherwise. I was never a 'good' girl at school. Now I also felt like a dud. Feeling oppressed and pushed into a corner, my worst traits emerged. Defiance led to disobedience which resulted in dire consequences (a temporary rustication for an April Fool's joke that the headmistress was convinced I'd master minded) that left me demoralized and disillusioned. The 'joke' (a silly one involving a fake fire drill) has since gone down in the school's history books with generations of Queen Marians giggling over that one day in 1964 when the unauthorized clanging of a fire-alarm bell sent shock waves through the airy classrooms and a few notorious heads rolled—notably, mine.

Given this backdrop it surprised me greatly when I was invited back to my old school in 1995—this time as the chief guest presiding over the annual Speech Day function. As I stood on that familiar stage surveying a hall filled with wide-eyed young girls, I had a catch in my throat. It was hard to believe the authorities had 'forgiven' me for that ancient prank and considered me worthy enough of the honour.

Yes, when I look back on my school years, my feelings are decidedly mixed. Had I not excelled on the sports field, I might have gone through school like so many other anonymous, nameless students—just another roll-number. I don't feel a sense of attachment. There is no nostalgia either. Truth be told, I couldn't wait to get out.

St. Xavier's, the college I went to, was all that Queen Mary was not. A happy, relaxed institution in which I flowered—literally. I wore asters in my hair on the first day at college. And continued to stick seasonal blooms above my right ear all through those four years. Flowers became my trademark, colour co-ordinated and carefully picked to complement my wardrobe. I was rarely seen without them. Campus life was a four-year picnic—exactly as my father had feared.

What my father would have really liked for me was a 'serious' career in a profession he understood and respected. So many years of writing later, I'm still not sure whether he perceives what I do with any appreciation. He tried hard to nudge me in the general direction of competitive exams—he'd tried and failed with Mandakini, but she at least had a law

27

degree in addition to a master's in economics. I had just a worthless piece of paper—a second-class BA in psychology and sociology. He and I both knew it didn't mean a thing. I was a bona fide graduate, nothing more. One of countless others waving similar pieces of paper in an overcrowded job market. It wouldn't have got me too far and I didn't try my luck with it either. He tried to get me to do my master's, even though he realized how worthless that exercise would be. I stalled for time, faking a keen interest in studying various options but making it clear that the IAS/IFS exam wasn't one of them. I'm sure I'd have flunked at level one itself. My father would express his disappointment with me in various ways. Even my handwriting came in for censure. He would say, 'Your handwriting, my dear, is nothing but an untidy scrawl. See the size of the letters—will anybody reading this be able to tell an "o" from an "a" or an "l"? Good handwriting is the key to success. You should improve yours if you want to get anywhere in life.'

It's ironical that of his four children, the one with the worst handwriting chose to make a career out of the written word—in my case, the hand-written one. My untidy scrawl hasn't improved with the years, but I fervently hope the contents have, though I can't be sure. A couple of years ago I found an old diary (circa '62). I was fourteen and cheeky as is evident from the entries which bear an uncanny resemblance to 'Neeta's Natter' (the popular *Stardust* column with its breathless prose and frequent exclamation marks).

With a career in government clearly ruled out, I hung around trying to keep out of my father's way. But often I'd get caught—either sneaking out of the house or sneaking in. My friends were all 'undesirables' I couldn't bring home, with the exception of one or two. My phone calls could be easily overheard (and were). The only escape was to make myself scarce and pretend to be busy looking around for suitable employment. It was difficult levelling gazes with my father when I could so clearly see his impatience. It was even more difficult placing my mother in a situation where she'd be forced to take sides. Dinner-table conversation became very stiff and stilted at this point. There was nothing he said that sounded right to me.

Now, as a parent of young people myself, I can see things from my father's point of view. I'm certain I'm repeating the patterns myself. My children insist I'm suspicious of all their friends and actively hate them. It's true I'm not the 'Hello beta. How are you, darling?' kind of mom. I rarely welcome strangers into our home. It takes me a long time to accept stubble-faced, earring-wearing young men in tattered jeans—and I don't care whether they're from the top university in the world, with a string of impressive degrees to their names. I tell myself I'm being horrible. But I don't change. The young visitors seem clearly intimidated. One of them dubbed me the 'Evil Empress' (E^2 for short), another gave my daughter a cactus saying, 'It reminds me of your mother.' It is those who behave with complete naturalness and are themselves who eventually get accepted and absorbed into the family fold. Once there, they stay.

When we were growing up there was no question of friends 'dropping by' or staying for meals. By the same token, we were rarely permitted to go over to other peoples' homes. However, during my early years at Maskati Court, I didn't miss companionship at all, it was enough for me that Kunda was there to share my life with. The one outing we both looked forward to and were allowed to go for was the YWCA annual fête. We walked the distance there and back, our steps and hearts light at the prospect of untold adventure. The first time I dared to defy my father and go out in a sleeveless blouse

29

was to this fair. The blouse was made out of thin embroidered cotton and I loved it. By now, I'd also acquired a pair of white high-heeled, closed shoes. Out-fitted thus, I thought I was stepping out in style. Just then some pimply-faced 'building boys' spotted me and began to snigger. Kunda glared. I blushed. 'She thinks she's so grown-up . . . but she can't walk straight on high heels,' I overheard them saying. Ignoring the taunt, I carried on walking, assuming my most disdainful expression. I vowed to myself I'd master the art of striding confidently on high heels—the taller the better. Today, I feel stunted and clumsy wearing flats.

Sometimes my children ask me, 'Mother, did you tell your parents everything? No secrets? Did you ever lie?' I fib and say, 'I confessed all. And I certainly expect you to do the same.' They raise their eyebrows in disbelief and say, 'Oh sure.' The truth is, I did lie. But never dangerously. Never to the extent of compromising either them or me. They were small lies that didn't really matter. But all along, when I did resort to even minor untruths, it was two words that haunted me. Two words that I felt like running away from as a child. They became a punishment in themselves, instruments of torture. 'Character building,' my father would thunder, 'youth is meant for character building.' Each time he reminded me of my goal I'd shrink and recoil. Who needs to be reminded about character building at fifteen? Or even forty?

Lessons in character building were provided on a daily basis. But they didn't stop me from pinching four annas for an hour of bicycling on racers, experimenting with menthol cigarettes, cutting my own hair (a disastrous 'Sadhna' style fringe) since I wasn't allowed to go to a salon, or exchanging love letters with gangly pre-adolescents who couldn't spell. I'm certain these clandestine activities were known to my mother. But she never let me down by squealing to my father. Neither did Kunda, who, of course, knew everything.

When I was much older and a young mother myself, I recalled my father's words and heard them emerging from my own mouth. On one level I was filled with horror: was that really me uttering the two words I'd so loathed during my childhood? And, was I actually emulating my father who always demonstrated the virtues he was extolling through deed and example? Or merely lecturing? Were my words empty and hollow even if they were sincere and well meant? The picture hadn't really changed . . . only the characters articulating the scripted lines had.

I must have created a lot of problems for my parents as an adolescent (and even later). Journalists often ask me whether I was a rebel. And I hotly deny ever having been one. I don't remember going through angry, defiant, rebellious outbursts. I truly don't. Instead, I recall being somewhat baffled by adult reactions to areas of my life that seemed perfectly acceptable to me. Very reasonable, too. It's true I'd sulk, but overt displays of rebellion were not my style.

Maybe I didn't conform to norms laid down by those in authority. But I was not a rude or difficult child. Not especially. I did not set out to break rules or shock anybody. I did what came naturally to me without worrying too much about the consequences. Like travelling ticketless in local trains and bluffing my way past the ticket-collector or pinching restaurant menus as souvenirs. Or racing down Marine Lines on a hired bike, hanging on to the rail of a double-decker bus for extra speed. All this gave rise to a great deal of stress at home and I was dealt with strictly by an irate father. The menu cards in particular shocked him deeply. 'This is theft,' he admonished, 'not mischief.'

I was instructed to go back to each and every restaurant

31

I'd picked up the cards from and return them with an apology. As for the hired bikes, there were two aspects to his rage—one, the sight of his teenage daughter running around in a pair of very tight, very short shorts (black khadi with bright yellow elephants); two, the recklessness of the act. Unfortunately for me, I was caught red-handed one time as I spotted him walking home—and he spotted me. At that mad moment I was more terror-stricken at the prospect of facing him than of the imminent death I risked by letting go of the handle bar of the bike in my panic. Frankly, between the two options, I preferred getting run over.

The image I harbour of a rebel is a negative one. Of a person who determinedly shatters known rules of conduct and upsets everybody around by being impossible and obstinate. I did swim against the tide but while I was doing so, my own sights were on getting to the other shore, not on the turbulence I may have been leaving in my wake.

In sharp contrast to my own indifferent academic achievements, my siblings excelled at school and college. My brother Ashok scored a hundred out of hundred in four out of six subjects for his Senior Cambridge exams. My sister Kunda won a gold medal while qualifying as an ophthalmic surgeon. My other sister Mandakini acquired three degrees before she became a banker. As for me—I got by. That's all. My focus was not on studies, and about the only time I reached for my books was a week or two before the exams. This created a lot of tension in the family, since my siblings were exemplary students whose report cards would have made any parent proud. It was more my casual attitude to grades rather than the grades themselves that caused problems. I was perfectly happy with my above-average performance. I didn't long to be in the top three, five or ten. I knew exactly how much work I was putting in and didn't expect any miracles to take place. My parents were equally puzzled by my lack of academic ambition. Constant lecturing didn't help, nor did angry outbursts or scornful remarks. How did it matter whether or not I got ninety-five per cent like my brother and sister in maths? Whether my performance in physics and chemistry was far from impressive? I was doing well in athletics—academics really did not figure. Not in my list of priorities.

At Queen Mary it was compulsory for even those selected for the Senior Cambridge exams to appear later for SSC. We looked down on what was considered a formality, a form of torture that we were forced to endure. I appeared for mine burning with high fever. Outside the examination centre waited my anxious parents and Kunda, armed with medicine to keep the temperature down and my brow cool. I managed what is called a 'high second class'. Another certificate to add to a useless collection.

The fact that I was nowhere as clever as my siblings did not cause me any anxiety. I didn't lose sleep over my average report cards. I didn't envy those who did far better. Nor did I feel inferior by comparison. Perhaps had I shown a little shame, remorse or contrition, my father would have felt less hostile. It didn't occur to me to pretend or make promises I had no intention of keeping. Studies did not interest me—that was that. There was a life right outside the classroom that I vastly preferred. And I wanted to make the most of it.

My attendance at college was dismal. The professors failed to recognize me during my rare appearances at lectures. The degree course (psychology and sociology) was a waste of time. But it kept Father off my back. So long as he thought I was gainfully occupied, he left me alone.

It was during this time that I first began to interact with persons of the opposite gender. The experience was new and exciting. I was discovering that it was possible to be friends without a romantic involvement to ruin it all. The set I knew was self-consciously 'intellectual', with the mandatory public-school snobbery. It was Sartre and Satyajit Ray for breakfast, Camus and Kamladevi Chhattopadhya for lunch, Nietzche and Nirad C. Chaudhuri for dinner. All this wisdom filtered through a haze of marijuana and rum—we hung out at smoky cafés, sang Joan Baez ballads, wore 'Om' printed guru shirts and love beads and flowers in our hair, and generally felt wonderful about ourselves, our lives, our tastes, our superiority.

Freud was big in this circle. So was Jung. We analysed one another to death. We were the masters of the universe—great looking, well read, well informed . . . and conceited boors to boot. Too good for our college. Too good for the other hicks in class. Too good for our parents, home, country.

It was too good to last. It didn't. The group split up after much heartbreak. Freud didn't help at all. We wrote stream-of-consciousness letters to one another. We agonized over our 'id'—the libido which worked overtime, took care of itself. The party ended as we asked ourselves the one question that dominated our self-obsessed generation: 'Where have all the flowers gone?' Nobody came up with a credible answer. I still don't know where all those lovely pink asters and lilies disappeared. Sometimes I miss their fragrance. But only sometimes.

Boyfriends? Yes. Two. Wonderful chaps—caring, attentive and intense. One a good raconteur, the other, a great letter-writer. My father detested both. Everybody was relieved when the relationships ended. 'Not marriage material,' my sisters sighed. I agreed.

I'd watched Kunda bent low over enormous medical

tomes, often studying all night with cups of coffee to keep her awake. This is not for me, I'd decided. She had a calling. She was working towards a specific goal. She earned that gold medal. She slogged for it.

'It's your attitude,' my father scolded. 'You have the aptitude and grasp. But no application. How can you excel with such a lackadaisical approach?'

Of course I couldn't. I didn't want to, either—not if it meant I'd be pushed into appearing for a competitive exam by a father who felt sufficiently encouraged by my results (even if they weren't first rate) to send out for the forms.

Besides, by then I was already modelling. And enjoying the independence it brought me.

Walking Tall

As in most other areas of my life, modelling too was a happy accident that took place when I was seventeen or eighteen years old. I was pretty enough, I suppose. But not particularly striking, as I remember. Two unrelated incidents brought me into what was considered a slightly disreputable career in those days.

While at a fashion show (my father, a senior bureaucrat, received such invitations routinely) being held in the ballroom of the Taj Mahal Hotel, I was approached by a soft-spoken, well-bred gentleman (Shashi Banker was the name, if I recollect correctly), who asked whether I'd ever considered modelling and if not, would I want to give it a try. I said I would, but without any real excitement or enthusiasm. I was seventeen then. I didn't think of seeking my parents' permission. For one, I didn't believe I stood much of a chance. For another, I thought I'd break it to them only when I had to—after getting a specific assignment. That happened sooner than I'd imagined. Within a week of meeting the gentleman, I was asked to present myself for an audition, which was to be held in the Madame Pompadour salon at the Taj. The name itself was intimidating. Besides, I'd heard that the English lady who ran what must have been India's first and certainly finest boutique was imperious and forbidding.

The audition clashed with an inter-collegiate basketball

match the same afternoon, and I didn't want to miss the game. By the time I showed up at Mrs Courtney's ('Madame Pompadour' was her professional name) elegant salon, I was already twenty minutes late and looked like a scruffy urchin, with mud on my knees. She looked disdainfully at me and said sharply, 'You are late. This won't do. Now . . . let's see you walk. And remember, if you possibly can, that you aren't on a football ground or a hockey field here.'

The room was full of recognizable, perfectly groomed models, the leading names of the day. I could sense their disbelief and mild disgust—I didn't look like one of them. I couldn't possibly be an aspiring model. I put the basketball I was carrying in one corner and strode towards Mrs Courtney.

'Turn around,' she commanded. 'What's your height?'

I told her. 'Chin up. Head up. Glide . . . don't march.' I tried again. My mind was actually on the next match. I didn't care whether or not I was selected. If it worked out, great. If it didn't, what the hell—there was always basketball and hockey.

'Measurements,' said Mrs Courtney to a quaking assistant. I guess that meant I was in. We walked some more—this time in a sequence. The other girls were very good at it. They walked with their hips. I used my knees. Nobody bothered to talk to me. Not even when it was time to leave.

'Fitting and rehearsals next week,' said Mrs Courtney, her voice cracked and a trifle shrill, her blond topknot bobbing while she spoke.

We were given our individual schedules.

'Don't be late, girl,' she cautioned, 'one more time and you're out.'

I nodded. This was going to be a new experience altogether and I was already looking forward to it . . . to its 'newness'. I didn't consider either the glamour or the money an important part of my decision to give modelling a shot. For me the thrill lay in doing something I hadn't done before. The chance to break the monotony of my young life, which at that point revolved around attending two boring lectures at college (to qualify me at the end of the term for appearing for my exams) and playing basketball in the college quadrangle after that. Modelling presented a different challenge. I couldn't believe anybody could think I had it in me to float down a fashion ramp in all those wonderful, elegant clothes. I was too much of a jock and too indifferent about my appearance—after my initial forays as a young girl into the forbidden world of make-up. I wasn't good with cosmetics, didn't paint my nails, and stuck to nondescript clothes when I wasn't in sports gear—shorts and a T-shirt.

This world was so distant from my own and therefore so exciting. Just entering that salon with its flowery fragrance that reeked of money and good taste transported me into another, entirely unknown sphere, where women discussed shaving versus waxing, false nails, false eyelashes, false hair switches . . . and falsies, with a concentrated, almost ferocious passion. Like nothing else mattered in their pampered lives but the next bouffant.

Getting to do the show was step number one. Breaking the news to my parents was the next, far more formidable problem. I took the easy way out—I didn't tell them, hoping I'd be able to pull it off without their ever finding out. After all, they weren't fashion-show goers themselves. Nor were their acquaintances. My disappearances were easy enough to explain—I did have rigorous sports schedules. I did stay out fairly late on college days. I did play several matches. Besides, I was beginning to enjoy this absurd thing that had happened to me. My walk was changing. My knees were cleaner, I tried not to scrape my shins during games, I applied cold cream on my elbows. I even thought of reshaping my eyebrows (I didn't). This was fun.

The others in the show were old troupers, with the emphasis on 'old'. There was a tall, painfully thin Anglo-Indian woman who looked like she was well into her thirties, hard-faced, rough-talking and strangely attractive, with a cleft chin like Michael Douglas'. She lived in filthy paying-guest digs on Colaba Causeway and seemed a part-time hooker, going by the number of business calls she received and the assortment of dubious-looking men who came around to collect her after rehearsals.

I was treated like the baby of the team and teased mercilessly. Mrs Courtney, who constantly smoked cigarettes stuck into a long black cigarette-holder, struck terror in my heart each time her sharp, bright eyes fixed themselves on me, and a volley of instructions would usually follow: 'Chin up. Tummy in. Back straight. Watch those knees. Don't trip over your own feet, girl. When was the last time you ran a comb through your wild hair?'

Since I had no previous ramp experience, she gave me just three minor entries in the show—but I was overwhelmed even by those. The thought of performing in public on a stage paralysed me. I watched the other models, their self-absorption, their concentration on make-up, figures, accessories . . . and wondered what the hell I was doing with my hair like steel, sprayed pancake, caterpillar-like false eyelashes weighing down my eyelids, and clothes that I'd never choose to wear, given the option. The whole thing was fake, unnatural and comical. And I was a part of it.

That first walk down the brightly-lit ramp was an unending journey to a destination that would soon become familiar to me. But that night I had no idea where those forty-odd strides were taking me, as I wobbled uncertainly on heels that were too tall and too thin (just like the models in the show). My three entries were far from spectacular. I couldn't have turned too many heads that night. Even so, other assignments soon followed.

And that was when I had to come clean and tell my mother about the shows. I had the support of one of my sisters, Kunda. And that was it. But then, hers was an unconditional love that encouraged me to go ahead and do whatever I wanted to, no questions asked. It wasn't for nothing that the family blamed her when things went wrong or when I found myself in a a messy situation (mainly, low grades or perky boyfriends). 'It's because of you that she defied all of us,' they'd reprimand a person who honestly didn't think I was doing anything that terrible. To this day, her attitude towards me remains consistently uncritical and loving. Maybe it has something to do with the fact that my mother had placed a two-month-old infant—me—in the lap of a curious six-year-old Kunda and told her, 'She's your baby—look after her.' The solemn-faced little girl had taken those instructions literally. From that moment onwards Kunda raised me as her own child, playing surrogate mother well after her own daughter, Lakshmi, was born.

As soon as I came clean about my modelling to the rest of the family, all hell broke loose. My mother was caught in the crossfire instantly. 'Who allowed her to accept these shows?' My father thundered. It was my mother's turn to take the rap and mutter softly, 'It isn't as bad as you imagine. She hasn't done anything wrong . . . the people she's working with are quite decent.' My father did not wish to listen. He wasn't ready to be convinced. And that's how it stayed even five years later. He disapproved. Period. He didn't want his daughter to be in a field he considered cheap and disreputable. That's how it probably is even today, were I to ask him whether he has changed his mind about the modelling business.

I never did succeed in getting over my original stage fright. Ramp modelling was something I forced myself to do since it provided an opportunity to travel, even though the money per show was paltry (Rs 150 as compared to the Rs 15,000 being paid these days). The atmosphere backstage was frenzied and tense, with the same level of chaos and confusion I notice each time I go to a show now. The competitiveness and hierarchies of this insecure profession were also in evidence, especially if a former beauty contestant was participating. I remember Persis Khambatta's insistence on opening and closing a show in Ahmedabad during the time she was the reigning queen of the catwalk after winning the Miss India title. I also remember Zeenat Aman's charming but firm insistence on preferential treatment after she won her title. There were also the fights for the best outfits, jewellery, and publicity pictures, even though it was still an awfully amateurish world where we had to apply our own make-up, go to a beauty salon to have our hair done and often provide our own accessories (and risk having them stolen backstage).

It was time to invest in a smart vanity case like the other girls. But I didn't have the money to buy one. My sisters chipped in again and I got not one but two cases to carry my belongings in: a black leather one resembling a hat box, and a standard-shaped one in a black-and-white cane weave. Carrying them around made me feel more of a professional even if I didn't have too many cosmetics to transport. I made do with regular poster paints, improvising and mixing colours, coming up with a formula that didn't crack on the skin. I got quite good at it, just as I taught myself to pile my hair in those ridiculously high bouffants without resorting to 'back combing'. Hair-sprays then were nothing more than sticky lacquer that glued strands together so effectively, it needed a hair brush with iron bristles to separate them.

The 'stigma' my father was so afraid of, turned out to be an exaggerated fear for the most part. Perhaps a few of his colleagues did pass the odd snide remark, perhaps his judgemental and ultra-conservative brothers questioned him about my decision, but after the first few months, when he himself realized there was no real disgrace in what I'd undertaken, he calmed down sufficiently enough to pretend he didn't know what I was doing in my spare hours . . . so long as I kept my mother informed. It was a taboo topic that was never raised or discussed, even after a series of press campaigns began to appear in national publications and my face was on the cover of the two leading women's magazines, *Femina* and *Eve's Weekly*.

My father did express strong disapproval over my pose, outfit and brief interview for *Femina*—understandably so. I was clad in a smart blouse . . . made out of handmade paper. The picture, shot by veteran TOI lensman Balkrishan, had me staring goggle-eyed at a paper parrot, while the blurb inside quoted me saying my sole ambition in life was to get married and have lots of children. Oh well, I guess I've fulfilled that all right. But my father was disappointed and disgusted by my lack of drive.

'What sort of an ambition is this?' he said scornfully. 'Young girls dream about becoming doctors, lawyers, engineers. Everybody and anybody can get married—and does. You cannot describe that as an ambition. Is it some sort of an achievement? Something to boast about?'

I guess not. But I sure as hell didn't want to be a doctor, lawyer or engineer. I didn't want to be anything at all, except a happy, carefree young person. My lack of clearly defined goals used to distress my father a great deal, and modelling certainly didn't help.

'It's not a career for decent girls. It's not a career at all. You'll get the wrong values, you'll meet the wrong people. I do not approve of this line,' he'd stated categorically enough. And now, with the publication of the *Femina* cover, it was out in the open—Shri Govind Hari Rajadhyaksha's youngest daughter was a model. And she was featured in a paper shirt. Got that? A paper shirt. Ridiculous suspicions were confirmed. I didn't like the cover either. But at that stage I was pleased enough that I'd made it to one.

Even at that stage, modelling wasn't something I regarded too seriously. When a photographer friend of my brother began clicking informal pictures of me each time he came to the house, I thought the man needed a guinea pig—who better than a friend's kid sister? Ashvin Gatha was quite a character—an 'orphan' (he loved describing himself like that) with a colourful history, he was self-taught and enthusiastic. Talented too, considering he rose rapidly to become the chief photographer at the *Eve's Weekly* group of publications, besides making it big as an adman with an unconventional approach. Years later, he left India and went on to a successful career as a freelance photographer for an international photo agency, contributing specialized spreads to magazines as disparate as *Penthouse* and *National Geographic*. At the time, he was bursting with ideas and in a tearing hurry to create an impact in India—the country of his birth which he was a stranger to after leaving it as a child and being raised by his uncle's family in Singapore. Ashvin and I did some memorable features together, including a dramatic cover for *Eve's Weekly* in which I wore strands of fake pearls. It still rates amongst my favourite shoots.

My initiation into fashion and ad photography was through Ashvin and since he was my brother's friend, and a familiar figure at home, this made it slightly easy for me. More importantly, Ashvin knew my father, who by then had acquired a formidable reputation in the ad world—it was well known that interested clients would have to deal with his wrath if the photographers offended his strict sense of propriety. In any case, my own inhibitions were protection enough. Besides, I too had my own code of conduct which, paradoxically enough, matched my father's. There was no question of posing for any pictures that were less than 'decent' (even by my family's prudish standards).

Earlier this year Avantika, my nineteen-year-old daughter, received her first call from an ad agency, and the lady contacting her was none other than dear old 'Ernie', who thirty years ago had made an identical call to my home. When my daughter went across to the agency to meet Ernie, she was amused to hear some of the stories Ernie had to tell about my shoots. 'We had to seek not just your mother's sister's permission, but also her father's. Often the pictures were shot at her home under the watchful eyes of the entire family. When we booked a studio, your mother came properly chaperoned by one of her sisters, who made sure all of us abided by the rules.'

Easy enough to chuckle over so many years later. But when I look back, I wonder why the agencies put up with it. Perhaps there weren't that many 'faces' at the time. And I fit a certain classic mould—the stereotypical 'Indian' one at a time when the field was dominated by modern looking Anglo-Indian and Parsi girls who wore their mini-skirts with panache. I had neither the legs nor the daring for anything half as adventurous. I stuck to sarees and salwar-kameezes—clothes I felt comfortable in.

There were two or three exceptions to the 'solo pictures, no male models' rules. I did a 'Made for Each Other' press campaign and a promotional brochure for the Taj Mahal group of hotels. Both were pleasant experiences—for me. But they displeased my father enormously. The only two ad films I featured in were shot by film-makers who, at that point, were making waves in the ad world but were unknowns outside—Shyam Benegal and Zafar Hai. The Benegal film was for a soap (Godrej) and was shot in black and white. He set it up in an old bungalow near Bombay Central Station and I remember it as a wearying experience. The endless wait between lighting each shot, the tedium between takes, the long hours spent on getting a few seconds' worth of usable film—no, this wasn't for me at all. I disliked the layers of make-up required for films, as well as the tiring process involving dozens of technicians and cumbersome props. It was boring and mechanical compared to a photographic shoot—where each frame was different and swift. Where the only people in the studio were the photographer, his assistant, and perhaps the art director from the agency. Once the concept was finalized, all it took was an afternoon to wrap it up.

Editorial shoots for magazines were more complicated but also far more satisfying. They gave one the chance to improvise and innovate since they didn't come with a specific brief. Most models agreed to pose for them even though no payment was involved. For one, these pictures provided a great deal of exposure, besides being fun. They gave the photographer and model enough scope to experiment with lighting, make-up, hair styles and looks. Then, as now, the main inspiration came from foreign fashion magazines and photographic journals. In other words, we stole shamelessly. There was nothing 'original' about our fashion spreads—all we did was pore over *Vogue*, *Elle*, *Harper's* and *Queen*, and copy like crazy.

Only one photographer tried to inject some originality

into his approach and that was 'Balsie' (who left India to work in Hong Kong where he died a few years ago). Balsie (short for Balsara) was passionate about his work. We did a magazine shoot together in '68, and when I look at his pictures I see a freshness, a great visual sense and a spirit of adventure that is largely missing from the cold, static, self-conscious posing and posturing of the current crop of lensmen with their hi-tech gadgetry and high-flying attitudes. The pictures for that assignment were shot all over India with three models and a generous budget. It eventually led to the suicide of the poor man who'd forked out the money for it—at the insistence of a very pushy woman who'd talked him into a sponsorship deal.

I was the youngest of the three women chosen and had to model exquisite Benarasi sarees while the other two had entire wardrobes created for themselves. One of the models saw this shoot as an opportunity to acquire a free trousseau, while for the other (a wealthy married socialite) it was an ego-trip and an opportunity to display her splendid body.

Our first stop was Delhi, where the pushy fashion editor had booked us into the Oberoi Hotel. I was to share a room with one of the models, while the pushy lady occupied a grand suite along with her husband, son, and the son's nanny. My roommate had plans that didn't include me. In fact, she made it clear that she'd appreciate it very much if I picked up my toothbrush and disappeared for the night.

'I'm entertaining a friend,' she smiled broadly, while picking up the phone, calling room-service and asking for a dozen cognac tumblers. 'My friend is a foreigner—a business contact,' she said, 'we'll be entertaining a few friends here . . . so . . . why don't you share Mrs X's room?'

I said 'okay' and called up Mrs X who said she didn't particularly mind or care, but she had plans of her own, too.

She'd be out to dinner. A late night. A really, really late night. Would I . . . take her calls . . . and . . . and . . . say she was in the loo . . . or in the adjoining room . . . or something like that? Just in case her husband phoned . . . ? I said 'okay' again.

The next morning when I went back to 'my' room, I saw it was filled with empty glasses, and the ashtrays were overflowing with cigarette butts. Stale smoke filled the air. The beds were mussed up. There were towels draped over the settee. The bathroom was a complete mess. 'What happened?' I asked the tall, dusky woman lying in bed with a pillow over her head. 'Oh . . .' she slurred, 'didn't I tell you? My business partner had come over . . . and we had a private party.'

We were leaving for Agra. I started putting my things together. The woman stretched out, reached for the phone and asked for housekeeping. 'Darling,' she cooed, 'I need a dozen napkins. Urgently.' The man who came to the room to deliver them seemed familiar. Yes, of course, I'd seen him the previous evening when he'd arrived with the cognac snifters. The woman got out of bed and staggered towards him. 'So sweet of you,' she gushed, planting a kiss on his cheek. 'Now help me pack . . . come on . . . it's nearly time to leave.'

The two of them rinsed out the crystal cognac snifters in the bathroom, dried them carefully and wrapped each one individually in the napkins. She pulled out a smaller bag from inside her large suitcase. 'Here . . . put them in here,' she instructed. They packed the snifters into the smaller case, taking care to ensure each piece had a buffer around it. The woman folded a hotel towel in two and placed it over the crystal ware. 'There,' she said with a satisfied air, 'now they won't break.'

She hugged and kissed the hotel guy, giggled a lot and whispered something into his ear. He looked sharply in my direction, smiled and whispered something back into hers.

'Don't worry . . . no problem,' he declared, before leaving the room. The woman smiled at me, 'Nice—no? I needed twelve of these for my new house.' I nodded silently. This was the first of many lessons I was to learn on that trip. My room-mate had 'business partners' in each hotel. I rarely got to sleep in my own bed. And by the end of those ten days, I'd become familiar enough over the phone with the other woman's husband to actually greet him cheerfully each time he called to enquire about his wife's whereabouts—before fibbing glibly about her absence.

By the time we got back to Mumbai, one woman had accomplished a major feat—her trousseau was complete. The other had decided she'd had enough of her sham of a marriage and was ready to move on. That left me—one beautiful Benarasi brocade saree richer (yes, that's all I got for my efforts) and definitely a great deal wiser. Even so, it was years later that the details registered. Was I just dumb? How come I didn't know what was going on? Put it down to lack of experience. Nothing like this existed in the world I was raised in. Unprepared and frankly indifferent, I was neither shocked nor disgusted. I may have been far too focused on my own young life to want to get drawn into the depressing, degrading lifestyle of the far older people I interacted with. It didn't matter sufficiently to me that one of those women was nothing but a petty thief, while the other was blatantly cheating on her husband.

The pushy entrepreneur who'd organized all this was even worse—she'd successfully bullied a naïve, trusting looms-owner to part with huge sums of money in return for paltry prestige and publicity. The poor sucker had sanctioned funds without consulting his brothers who were also his business partners. The fabulous sarees from the legendary looms of Benaras were supposed to be on loan for the shoot.

Instead, the fashion editor had decided to keep them all and let the owner whistle for their return. She had no intention of giving those heirlooms back. The other two models had walked away with outfits specifically tailored for them which were of no use to anybody else. I was the fool who had to be content with precisely one saree (which I still possess), reluctantly given up by the pushy lady from her hoard.

A few months after this debacle, the owner called up and asked to see me at my home. A highly agitated man walked in and started barraging me with questions. He looked terribly distraught and could barely string one intelligible sentence together. He spoke no English and even his Hindi was heavily accented. He wanted to know how much I'd been paid and how many sarees had been given to me. I told him truthfully that I'd been paid zip and precisely one saree represented my total 'payment'. He seemed stunned, then he clutched his head and wept. Actually wept. His despair was overwhelming. I didn't know what I was supposed to do.

'That woman has destroyed me . . . cheated me . . . my family wants to disown me,' he cried.

He went on to give me details of how he'd been taken for a ride and how helpless he was against the woman. 'She will not return my sarees—each one is a museum piece. Priceless. She said she'd given five to you. And that she couldn't find the rest. What am I going to do? My brothers are harassing me to get them back.'

Shamed by his outburst, I rushed into my room and brought his saree. 'Please take it,' I pleaded, 'I don't want it.' He looked sadly at the beautiful black-and-gold saree in my hands. 'I don't need this one. I want the others. This saree is the least expensive out of the lot you wore. I can always have another one made . . . keep it. But please help me get those back . . . or else my family will throw me out of the business.'

Which is exactly what happened. With the sarees missing and enormous hotel bills to settle, the poor man found himself out in the cold. Unable to take the humiliation, he took his own life instead. As for me. . . well . . . that saree is there somewhere . . . I can't bear to wear it. The other two models are doing fine as well. The one with the readymade trousseau is still married to the same man. And the husband whose voice I'd become so familiar with, is now dead.

There was a lot of growing up to do, and I guess I did it in double-quick time. I saw beauty queens with dirty toenails and ramp mannequins with oily pigtails. And then I saw myself—someone in between, amused by the world I had perforce become a part of, and yet not belonging to it. I remained on its fringes, watching, laughing and learning. It was possible then (as I'm sure it must be even now) to work in that artificial, almost unreal, environment without losing one's perspective or sense of humour. While the other girls concentrated on becoming swans, I chose to be a clown. I refused to take lipstick seriously or treat hair-spray with reverence. I was in the thick of it, making some money and having a ball—but for all the wrong reasons. Backstage pranks, *Mad* magazine-style jokes and schoolgirlish horsing around must have seemed absurdly out of place in an atmosphere where most of the others reserved every ounce of energy for the perfect flounce and flourish on stage. The other models were more focused on their priorities, which I guess were to cash in on the glamour and bag a prosperous husband. Which is precisely what most of them did succeed in doing.

Whatever the motivation of the others in the modelling business, it was hard for me to take it seriously. I didn't see myself as a sleek, sexy, soignée creature of collective fantasy. If anything, I kept wondering what the hell I was doing in that business, when I didn't possess what I thought were the prerequisites for such a high-visibility job: I wasn't in love with myself, and I didn't believe I was particularly effective on stage, wracked as I was with self-consciousness and self-doubt. For anything to work, one has to believe in it—I didn't believe I was cut out for modelling even as I went from one big show to the next, draped in gaudy 'ramp sarees', making sure my expression matched that of all the other girls who'd worked so hard on theirs.

Shows are nothing but entertaining 'tamashas' now, and that's exactly what they were even then. Textile mills with an image to project were the chief sponsors. And the organizers who undertook this projection were as amateurish as all of us walking the ramp on heels too high, hair too stiff, lipstick too pale. Nobody knew any better. There was no satellite television to get our cues from, only old *Vogue* magazines and our version of 'their' fashion shows. Given the Indian enthusiasm for improvisation, we added a little song here, a small dance there, to make the show what it was not meant to be—a two-hour 'nautanki' with bits of ballet, bharatanatyam and bhangra thrown in. The girls who could shake a leg but suffered from a serious lack of looks, were given these choreographed items to perform between sequences.

One of them was a strange American who'd decided to go Indian with a vengeance. She did that with all the zeal of a neo-convert—low nape bun, bindi, sarees, kaajal, and an armful of colourful bangles. Despite her short stature and thick legs, she soon acquired star status which annoyed her taller, slimmer rivals. She was mysterious, too, and rather bewitching. Disinclined as she was to discuss her antecedents, nobody quite knew where she'd come from, though it was rumoured she'd left a broken-hearted kathak guru in some remote North Indian town, in order to make a new life for

51

herself in Mumbai.

There was no dearth of admirers in her adopted city, as fellow models noticed. Prominent admen would wait anxiously at the greenroom door after a show, while she hastily wrapped herself in a simple cotton saree, creamed the pancake off her face, grabbed her bag and left without participating in the traditional post-show camaraderie. At rehearsals she'd keep to herself, writing endless letters or burying her nose in fat books.

One day she disappeared and the admen she'd left behind gathered to mourn their loss. Who was she really? I still don't know. There have been sightings galore in and around Paris. There was talk that she'd married a French film director many years her senior. But nobody is sure. She vanished as suddenly as she'd appeared on the scene . . . leaving the ladies who organized these shows short of a charming opening act that involved simple pirouettes and awkward high-kicks familiar enough to any young girl in the West who has taken ballet lessons over the summer.

It was photographic modelling that really interested me. And I grew into it seamlessly. Even though mine is not the easiest face to capture on camera, the high cheekbones helped when everything else failed. I taught myself to make the most of my better features and the results were rewarding enough to get me some of the top assignments. The few that turned out to be memorable were shot by photographers I'd established a good rapport with—people like Ashvin Gatha. These men became buddies with whom I felt entirely comfortable. While my first shoot was with an old-fashioned Maharashtrian photographer, R.R. Prabhu, who made me resemble a stiff store mannequin clad in an over-starched voile saree, with plastic lotuses stuck in my lacquered hair, the others were ready to take chances with different lighting, different looks. I felt a part of the overall process. I believed I had something to contribute to the success of a campaign. And I got drawn into the technical aspects of the assignment—the lighting, make-up, props and approach. Jehangir Gazdar and Wilas Bhende were legends in the field. Some of my best campaigns were shot by them. D.L. Oberoi ('Obi') came later. They were thorough professionals, these men, with exceptionally high standards. Models were treated like ladies, not commodities.

This modest level of involvement took away the tedium from what is essentially a very boring, repetitive, mechanical profession. And I knew, somewhere deep down inside, that this wasn't going to last. I wasn't particularly proud of what I was doing, which was spending hours and hours in front of a camera, figuring out a new angle, new pose, new expression. I'd lose interest after the first hour and start counting the minutes to pack-up time. I found it impossible to tell a stranger I was a model. If somebody from my father's generation asked what I was doing, I'd say evasively that I was still studying . . . taking courses . . . still thinking about my future. I guess I felt embarrassed and ashamed of the job description. Maybe I knew exactly what would run through those people's heads at the mention of the 'm-word'. (Girls may have come a long way in other areas, but when it comes to modelling the basic prejudices remain the same.) I didn't respect the business, even if I enjoyed its fruits. I didn't care for the so-called 'fame' it brought me either. I suspected its authenticity, which may have been just as well. Had I taken any of that literally, I might have been leading a completely different life today.

A bright editor I met in Goa recently asked why I hadn't thought of going into a parallel field, given that I'd spent over five years modelling. 'How come you didn't move on to a glamour-related job, say films, or how come you didn't think of opening a modelling agency, choreographing shows, grooming other girls?'

The truth is, I was sickened by it all. And bored out of my mind by the end of it. It was such a relief to leave that narcissistic, shallow world behind and move on. I couldn't wait for another career option to present itself, and I'm fortunate that it did when it did. The question to ask would be, if it was such a deadening experience, why did I endure it for as long as I did? The short answer is: money. I was earning the equivalent of a full-fledged salary from a part-time profession and I liked the feeling of independence it gave me. I learnt the value of it too, since I had to work for it. After the first year I began handling my own affairs, negotiating contracts, collecting dues, keeping track of late payments. It was a learning process in itself, which taught me never to take the next buck for granted. And more importantly, to hang on to the one in hand. Since I was living with my parents, I had no real expenses to take care of, other than those my modelling demanded. A huge chunk of my earnings went on cab fares, the rest was spent on updating the essentials of the trade—make-up, costume jewellery, high heels. These days, of course, it's a far more professional game where all the models have to do is present themselves for a shoot without worrying about details which aren't their responsibility any longer—there are stylists to take care of them.

Modelling also provided opportunities to travel at someone else's expense—and that was another magnet which kept me hanging in there. About the most bizarre assignment I put my foot into involved shooting a crazed maharaja's ancestral collection of spectacular jewellery. The other model picked for it, and I, were told these pictures weren't for publication—the bearded maharaja was only interested in cataloguing them for posterity. It was his way of documenting his dynasty's amazing history. That was the official version. The photographer and the two of us were to be flown to his palace in a private four-seater aircraft. The fee was nominal, but in this case the fee wasn't the attraction. It was the chance to fly across the Bay of Bengal to see the legendary jewels for ourselves. We weren't disappointed. And that's an understatement. What we saw cannot possibly be imagined . . . except perhaps by Steven Spielberg's art directors.

The magnificent palace was impressive by any standards, but the jewels themselves were staggering in their pricelessness. Their owner was pretty staggering too, even if he did resemble Rasputin, with his flowing beard and straggly pony-tail. The man's eyes were like glowing coals. It was rumoured he was a sadist and a maniac. Tales were whispered about his former wife, dead mistresses and current live-in girlfriend whom nobody ever caught a glimpse of. On our first day, he took us around his private zoo where he kept dozens of exotic species, rather in the manner of Michael Jackson's menagerie. As we sat sipping tea in the garden, his pet peacock turned up for a piece of cake, wearing a diamond anklet. Right outside the palace walls clouds of pink flamingoes circled the shallow backwaters, while we contemplated our unreal selves in these unreal surroundings and stared out of the corner of our eyes at the strange man in flowing robes who was talking softly to the photographer about exactly which mind-boggling baubles he wanted photographed over the next two days.

For me, the assignment was nothing more than a two-day paid picnic. The mad maharaja may have owned impossible-to-price jewels, but when it came to paying the models he turned miserly and came up with an unprincely sum of five thousand rupees. We were assigned two suites in one wing of the palace, with veiled maids at our beck and call. All this would have been rather nice had it been less sinister. I felt uncomfortable after the first couple of hours, as if the two of us (my friend and I) were being constantly watched. The palace was crawling with his retainers, some of them armed with primitive shotguns. It was only after the grand tour of the jewellery hall was completed that we understood why the maharaja and his men seemed so jittery.

The gigantic hall resembled something out of *Indiana Jones* or *Alladin*. But why look that far? Our own mythological costume dramas will do. Without exaggeration, the entire length of the grand hall with all its gilt, velvet and chandeliered splendour, was taken up by enormous wooden caskets filled to the brim with stones the size of mini-boulders and moon-rocks—sapphires, emeralds, rubies, topazes . . . and this was only a part of the collection—the less valuable part. The photographer examined each specimen carefully before making his selection. My friend turned to me and said, 'If I were to pocket a few dozen, would anybody notice?' I silently pointed to the men with the obsolete weapons watching us. She laughed and said a trifle unconvincingly, 'I was only joking.'

We saw strands and strands of Basra pearls, gold ornaments, silver by the kilo . . . and this was only a segment of the real business ahead, which was the photographing of jewellery that had no price tag. Some of it obviously went back several generations, since the maharaja talked fondly about a great-great-grandfather's favourite necklace—seven strands of solitaires, each stone the size of an almond. I was much too ignorant about any kind of expensive jewellery, which was why I was less impressed than I might have been otherwise. Yes, it looked terribly pretty and must have cost a fortune, but who wanted to wear something as heavy and ostentatious?

Apparently, there were several very keen buyers abroad. After we had finished photographing select pieces, the maharaja whispered to the lensman that he required superior prints and he didn't trust Indian technology enough . . . so . . . would he kindly hand over all the film to His Highness, so as to have the lot processed in Switzerland? I don't know what sort of deal was finally struck. But I do know that we, the models, never got to see the results. Not a single picture.

Years later, the photographer mentioned that he'd given away all the exposed rolls to the client. It was obvious that the maharaja had wanted to find buyers overseas and smuggle the stuff out as discreetly as possible. He needed the pictures to create an exclusive catalogue for European dealers to look at. It was definitely a smart move and I don't really care that we were made a part of his grand scheme. For us it was just another photography job for which we got paid.

I would have left it there, had my fellow model not spilled the beans when we met after a gap of two decades. 'Do you know what the horrible maharaja tried?' she asked, after a couple of stiff whiskies. 'He came home and met my mother a week or two after we returned. He'd brought a lot of mithai with him and I was wondering what he wanted when he took my mother aside and said, "Your daughter is clever and smart. Would you mind very much if she made a few trips to Europe . . . at my expense, of course? I need her services for some very simple work. She has to hand over a few packages to my friends in Paris. I'm very busy at present and can't do so myself. Don't worry, I'll take care of everything . . . tickets and all that. I'll also give her some pocket money."'

Even though my friend's folks were simple people, they knew a conman when they met one. Her mother declined politely, without consulting her model-daughter, who at the time was greedy and naïve enough to have said an instant 'yes'. We laughed over the averted 'danger' as she described the incident graphically—the Rasputin-like figure walking into her humble suburban home with an offer he was sure she wouldn't refuse, and her old mother, unfazed by the presence of royalty, telling him, in effect, to bugger off and leave them alone.

Today the tall, dusky beauty is a successful entrepreneur who lives abroad and hobnobs with international aristocracy. I asked her if she'd ever spotted any one of those magnificent chokers, rings, bracelets or necklaces on a countess or a marquise seated by her side at a banquet. 'Not yet,' she confessed, 'but I'm still looking.' Meanwhile, news continues to trickle in about the mad maharaja, whose beard now reaches his navel, while the pony-tail has turned grey and scraggly. He still lives in his palace, surrounded by pet bats and a batty lady he calls his wife.

*

I am constantly asked about being featured in *Vogue*, as if it's the ultimate badge of distinction. For the record, the answer is, yes, I made it to *Vogue* clad in an early Yves Saint Laurent gown. So what? Did the earth move? Did anything change? Did the sky fall down? Did I look different, feel different? In other words, did my picture affect me in any significant way? No. I did not benefit financially, professionally or emotionally. But the story of how the assignment happened is rather interesting.

Remember those famous Air India calendars of old? The ones that were visualized and commissioned by a legend called Bobby Kooka? Each one eventually became a collector's item, and I am glad I got to feature in two of them, sometime in

1969. The Air India creative team at the time realized the value of 'imaging' much before image management became a full-time career option as it presently is. Air India in those days was up there, acknowledged as being among the top ten international airlines of the world. It's hard to believe that now, when our national carrier does not rank even in the first hundred and has degenerated into a tacky, downmarket operation run by unmotivated non-professionals who could do with a serious makeover themselves.

The year of the *Vogue* assignment, I was called by the statuesque Uttara (Pakwasa) Parikh from Air India's publicity department. 'There is a *Vogue* team in town . . . they're looking for two Indian models to wear the latest collections they've brought with them. Henry Clarke, the photographer, has seen and liked your photographs from among the ones we'd submitted. He wants to meet you.'

'Okay,' I said without any particular enthusiasm.

I went along to the Air India office . . . no excitement, no sense of anticipation, nothing. It was just another potential assignment, that's all. I saw the luscious Uttara (a former model herself), bent over a sheaf of photographs. Next to her was the ancient mariner himself—a doddery old man who was inspecting the pictures closely.

'Meet Mr Clarke,' Uttara said.

Oh my God. This man was a *Vogue* photographer? In my ignorance, I didn't know he was rated as the number one man in his field, someone who'd stuck to the classical mould of fashion photography and was regarded as a guru by the likes of Richard Avedon, who'd already started making big waves in the fashion world with his new style of lighting and unconventional approach to shooting some of the world's most beautiful women. Henry Clarke had a large black-and-white photograph of mine in his hands. He scrutinized my face, turned to Uttara and nodded. She told me she'd get back to me with the details. Air India had worked out an arrangement with *Vogue*. They'd flown the team in gratis and had agreed to pay for their travel and stay in India, in return for publicity in *Vogue* and a set of pictures for their own calendar. The Indian models were to be paid a nominal fee, but would get to travel to Srinagar and other exotic locations and be photographed by the maestro himself. Frankly, there was nothing very much to gain. It would be an experience worth having, but that was about all. Although I agreed instantly, I was neither thrilled nor flattered. Maybe I was too dumb then to be either.

Our first shoot took place at the magnificent Elephanta Caves, a one-hour boat ride from Mumbai. This was my premier encounter with how the glamour business was conducted internationally. I was told merely to present myself for the assignment—all the other details were to be taken care of by a battery of stylists and their assistants. The French models in the *Vogue* team were predictably aloof, cold and self-absorbed. They didn't make the slightest attempt to be polite or friendly. Their focus remained steadfastly on their own appearance—a wayward curl here, an unstuck eyelash there. Clarke himself looked like he'd drop dead before we finished the first roll. Exhausted by the steep climb up to the caves, and drained by Mumbai's heat, flies and humidity, he seemed awfully cross as he set up his camera and lights.

No extra words were exchanged. Everything was undertaken in an impersonal, businesslike fashion. My hair was teased, sprayed and patted into shape by an effeminate (I didn't know about gays then) hairdresser. Another delicate young man made up my face. The exquisite clothes from the Parisian fall collections were handed to us by female dressers who surveyed our bodies with the detachment of morticians

60

assessing a corpse.

'This one's for you,' said one bitch, handing me a long tunic with a turquoise scarf.

I got into it obediently and presented myself to the flushed and wheezing Clarke. His instructions were minimal. He knew precisely what he wanted. He'd arranged his final frame before a single picture was shot. Nothing was required of me other than to stay still and turn my face a few degrees when requested. 'Perfect,' he pronounced in his clipped British accent. The shoot was over. He'd got his picture. Unaccustomed to this style of working, I waited, expecting to be herded to a fresh location for a few more variations. 'No . . . that's the shot,' he said.

In Srinagar it was the same story. Clarke, however, surprised us with his perfectionism. He wanted to capture a certain pre-dawn light and he decided to test his film. For that, he was up at 4 a.m., ready to move with his assistants while the rest of us slept in our luxury houseboats. We were required slightly later . . . make-up, hair, accessories in order. When we got to the location, there was this old man with rheumy eyes, all set to roll. Once again, he'd visualized his shot down to the last petal in the flower-bedecked shikara; he wanted a model to lie down on this colourful bed of blossoms. The picture, I now realize, required great precision and deft handling since the shikara wouldn't remain still enough as it bobbed around gently on Nagin Lake. Clarke had obviously figured out a technique that took care of the problem. The shot was over in five minutes flat before that all-important soft opal-pink light changed. And the final picture was perfect.

I was certain Clarke was going to die on the shoot. In fact, he died several years later. The calendar was spectacular and so was the *Vogue* spread. But seeing my pictures in that glossiest of glossies did not thrill me in any way—as I said, my world continued to spin as before, no real changes. Which is why when young journalists ask me in awestruck tones these days, 'Is it true you were featured in *Vogue*?' I merely nod and change the subject.

Then came a slimy French photographer who was working on a book on India. Mrs Jagannathan, the dynamic head of the Maharashtra Tourism Board, suggested my name along with a couple of others. We shot the pictures at various locations around Mumbai, finally ending up on the terrace of the NSCI club where the photographer was staying. The man was supercilious and conceited, impatient with India and irritated that India was not France. It wasn't an experience I enjoyed, even though the pictures were wonderful. My antenna was up and I half suspected the man was a bit of a fraud, even if I couldn't put my finger on what exactly it was that gave me that impression. I found out two years later, when one of his portraits of me appeared on the cover of a prestigious international magazine on photography. He hadn't had the courtesy to either seek my permission, obtain a formal release or even mail a complimentary copy. Neither was I given due acknowledgement in the credits which read 'Indian Beauty'. As if his roving lens had accidentally caught the image of some anonymous woman in an obscure by-lane somewhere in India. I was furious. But there wasn't much I could do about it except rave and rant when I ran into Mrs Jagannathan the next time.

Foreign photographers were, and still are, interested in just a single aspect of India—the exotic one. I was invariably asked to pose draped in silk with my head demurely covered. 'Stick on the caste mark,' they'd advise, referring to the bindi. Bejewelled and made up in the style of a bharatanatyam dancer, I was a surefire shot for the western market. I remember resenting this representation and voicing my reservations, only to be told, 'But it sells.' Not much has changed in terms of perceptions more than twenty-five years later. 'It' still sells—nose-rings, bindi, kaajal, silks. Only 'it' has been repackaged and made sexier, with pierced belly buttons and more on parade.

It was years later (in the early Nineties) that I discovered how dramatically relaxing the modelling business could be if the person behind the lens was a woman.

The first time I was shot by one, I realized how very differently I reacted in front of the camera. She was an Italian fashion photographer doing the shoot for a New York-based designer (also a woman). Their approach was rather unique. Rather than shoot the smart, stylish clothes on regular models, they picked personalities who represented the city of their choice. And the city of the year was featured in a plush catalogue that reflected both the social and cultural life of—in this case—Mumbai. When she walked in, cameras slung over her handsome shoulders, I drew in my breath. The woman was an absolute stunner who looked like she'd just stepped out of the pages of a 'Banana Republic' fashion spread. Turned out she was a former model who'd shifted to photography and was doing a brilliant job of it too. Her crew was equally interesting—the stylists, make-up people, hair dressers and lighting assistants. As always, they wanted an over-the-top picture heavy on exotica—which meant loads of jewellery, dramatic smoky eyes and very fat hair.

It was what happened once I was in front of her camera that surprised me. I felt every muscle in my body relax. And it showed. She was also the first photographer who encouraged me to open my mouth during the shoot. 'Talk, laugh. You have great teeth,' she urged. Talk? Laugh? Great teeth? Who, me? For twenty years I had been told by our photographers to keep my lips together, hold still and look a certain way—what was it, sultry? Grim? I would go into that awful routine automatically, instinctively. And here was this gorgeous woman with a great tan, fabulous legs and easy manner who was saying, 'Yes—laugh. Yes, yes . . . more laughter. Yes. Show those teeth . . . ' I began enjoying myself hugely. It didn't matter where the extra lines appeared—under the eyes, around the mouth, on the forehead. This was fun.

Then came another beauty from California, Catherine Karnow—very casual, very laid-back. She was interested in capturing a specific element of the city—street life at its busiest. And I was to provide the contrast—a pool of saree-clad serenity in the midst of all that hectic activity. We went in search of Art Deco buildings—and found them. She wanted balconies with colourful clothes drying from the banisters. We found those too. She was looking for curious people staring at me while the session was on. Well, we had more than we could handle. But we made one major miscalculation—we picked the wrong hour, unknowingly. The location was Bhendi Bazaar, one of the most photogenic Muslim ghettos of Mumbai. A place I'd done innumerable shoots in during my modelling years. It was different then—and I should have known it. After the Mumbai riots of '93, the character of the very same crowded by-lanes had altered to an extent I could not have imagined.

We parked our car (a vintage Jaguar) in a quiet alley, fifty metres or so away from a picturesque mosque. I was clad in a shocking pink saree and had my teenage daughter Avantika with me. The photographer was modestly dressed in working gear—trousers, and a jacket with dozens of pockets to hold her film and lenses. We had a local guide hired by her, plus my driver, accompanying us. The frame looked brilliant. The lighting was perfect and the details, just right. We'd barely shot a roll when we noticed a change in the mood of the large crowd gathered to watch. I sensed trouble.

Suddenly a harsh voice shouted, 'Do you people think this is a film set? If you want to shoot, go hire a studio, get out of our street.' Startled by that, we immediately stopped clicking. Soon a woman with a high-pitched voice shrieked, 'What is all this nonsense? How dare these people come into our locality and cheapen the atmosphere?' Cheapen the atmosphere—how? Every one of us was appropriately dressed. And we were only doing straight portraits against this backdrop. Even so, if the residents were offended, we were ready to clear out, and fast. But it does take some time to fold tripods, pack away reflectors and cameras.

By now five more people had jumped into the ring and started thumping the car aggressively. The signals were unambiguous and frightening. My driver tried to get our monster car to start. Just our luck, its twin petrol tanks refused to fire up. It was the oppressive mid-summer heat. The old engine needed to cool down in the shade as much as these irate people, who by now were spitting contemptuously and hurling abuse. There was menace and danger in the air. We folded our hands to say we didn't mean to bother anybody. The guide, who turned out to be Muslim, finally took the right step by approaching a resident to ask the people to calm down since we were leaving anyway. He in turn, took our appeal to the local maulvi, who reluctantly agreed, then added ominously, 'You have approximately three minutes to get out—the call for prayer is scheduled for 5.15 p.m. When that happens, this road will be blocked by the faithful and your car won't be able to negotiate its way past them.'

We pretended to be calmer than we actually were. The hysterical woman was whipping up crowd frenzy and obviously revelling in the attention. Occupants of flats around the narrow by-lane were hanging out of their windows and balconies, occasionally joining in the fray with their own foul-mouthed comments.

With a jerk and a splutter, the Jag got going. We lumbered out clumsily, too afraid that someone would block our way, drag us from the car and lynch us there and then. One can never say with mob frenzy.

The photographer remained remarkably cool through it all. Looking at her well-scrubbed face, bright blue eyes and blond hair, I could only imagine her sunning herself languidly on one of those picture-postcard beaches of California. And here she was in a hostile mohalla in Central Mumbai, all controlled nerves and relaxed smiles. I understood how and why later when she told me about her experiences in Bosnia and elsewhere.

We got our picture finally. But in a far friendlier locality. So determined was she to get the backdrop right that she placed her camera practically in the middle of a busy street, right across the famous Chowpatty beach. I held my breath each time a double-decker bus whizzed past her shapely form as she bent over the lens, squinting into the tiny viewfinder, fussing over the smallest detail, pushing, pushing, pushing, till she got the frame right. Later, I saw her pictures in a few international glossies and smiled at the recollection of how they nearly didn't happen.

Just before the Bhendi Bazaar fiasco, I'd spent a week with another woman photographer, Dayanita Singh, who'd been commissioned to shoot me for a feature being written by Christopher Thomas of *The Times*. When she arrived at our home, I could sense a barrier. It was like she was studying me . . . observing everything very closely, very critically. I took to her immediately—the petite form, the quiet manner, the discretion, the involvement, and above all, the refinement that a good upbringing bestows. While I liked her enormously, it was easy to tell she didn't exactly reciprocate the feeling. Later, she told me so herself. 'I came to your home with all kinds of mixed emotions. I'd always thought you were the kind of woman I wouldn't like . . . wouldn't wish to photograph unless I had to. I was prepared to dismiss you as a typical Bombay socialite. Everything I'd read about you had made me believe you were nothing more than a superficial, arrogant, conceited person. When I got this assignment, I took it because I always enjoy visiting Mumbai. I have several friends here. I thought I wouldn't waste more than two hours shooting you. Quick pictures—and out. Job done.'

As it turned out, we were together practically night and day for nearly a week. Dayanita would arrive in the morning—an unobtrusive, calm presence, so compact and so contained. She'd set up her frame, wait for the light to change and converse with the kids if they were around, while I finished my own writing or domestic chores. It was so easy and non-invasive. Not once did I resent her presence. On the contrary, it established the base for our current friendship. During those days, while she was working on her assignment, we found ourselves in several funny situations. Since it was understood that she'd accompany us wherever we were committed to go during the week, I'd call up and inform our hosts about the presence of a photographer and check whether it was all right to bring the person with us. Most people gamely agreed. But they probably didn't expect the photographer to be a diminutive, soft-spoken woman.

One of these occasions saw us at the launch of a computer-related event at which Amitabh Bachchan was the chief guest. When we got to the venue, he was already there, surrounded by the usual phalanx of press photographers. We greeted each other and I introduced Dayanita, merely saying she was in Mumbai on behalf of *The Times*, London. Mr Bachchan, stiff and self-conscious as always, bowed slightly in her direction and continued to politely converse with me.

'Is it all right if I shoot a few frames?' Dayanita asked. I guess Mr Bachchan assumed she was seeking his permission to photograph him. He nodded and carried on talking. When he realized her focus was not him but me, he stepped aside lightly. She noticed. I noticed. Later, in the car, coming home, she commented on how uncomfortable he seemed. 'Maybe he just isn't used to someone else being in the spotlight when he's around,' she laughed. Maybe. Those pictures didn't get used, which is just as well. For if they had, they might have caught a particularly uncomfortable looking Bachchan and a very embarrassed me.

What I enjoyed about this experience was Dayanita's technique of blending seamlessly into the picture, of becoming family, of participating in the lives of the people she was going to be seeing in all kinds of situations and moods. Soon enough the children got used to her presence and relaxed sufficiently to fight, cry, argue and generally disgrace themselves without the slightest shame. I was entirely comfortable too. Which would not have happened had the photographer been a man. In fact, it didn't happen when only a few short months later, Pradeep Chandra, a Mumbai-based photographer, was assigned to shoot my pictures for a cover story scheduled by *Asiaweek*. Even though I knew Pradeep reasonably well and respected his work, I was very conscious of his gender during the few days we were together. There was more formality, more of a strain, as we both struggled to get the right picture. The problem had nothing to do with Pradeep or his talent—it was me. I could feel the lines of tension creasing my brows. I couldn't unwind, and it showed. Despite his cheery enthusiasm and all the hard work that went into the assignment, the pictures reflected my own reservations. Eventually, it was one of Dayanita's stock pictures that made the cover.

In direct contrast to my experience with Dayanita was the photo-shoot with *Time* magazine for their September 1991 issue. Once they'd interviewed me for the profile (the interviewer was Anthony Spaeth, a senior writer with the magazine and a novelist himself), the photo-shoot was assigned to a big-name Delhi-based photographer. He called to fix up the session. I'd imagined the picture would be nothing more elaborate than a straightforward, one-column mug-shot and said so, using rather unfortunate terminology.

'Isn't it going to be just a simple snapshot?'

There was a longish silence at the other end of the line. Finally, the photographer snapped, 'If *Time* wanted just a snapshot, they certainly wouldn't have hired me.'

Humbled by the rebuff, I asked what exactly he had in mind. 'Tiger skins, crystal, flowers paintings, candlesticks, extravagance . . . bright pinks, great make-up, bindi, jewellery . . . the whole bit.'

I gulped. This sounded more like a fashion shoot. I stammered apologetically that I could perhaps manage the colour and some of the accessories, but I had no access to tiger skins. 'Be there,' he said firmly and rang off. He found his dream set-up—a prominent Delhi socialite had graciously agreed to let us use her opulent living room. I flew into the capital on the punishing early morning flight, bleary-eyed and a little nervous.

The photographer and his wife met me at the airport and we went over to the bungalow where the charming lady was waiting for us. First shock—she was perfectly made-up and dressed for a cocktail party at that hour. Did she sleep that way? Or had she woken up at the crack of dawn to present her impeccably groomed self to scruffy, indifferent me? I was very impressed. It took me half an hour to get organized. By then the photographer had moved all her stuff around in the incredibly lavish living room, set up his lights, and was ready to roll. The star of the shoot, as you've probably guessed, was the majestic tiger skin spread over a priceless Persian carpet. I was asked to position myself so that I appeared to be reclining languorously, my elbow resting on the snarling head of the stuffed animal. It wasn't a particularly comfortable position to hold, and I blessed my years of previous experience as a model, as I contorted my body into an unnatural stance. Something was wrong. The photographer seemed terribly cross. Was it my bindi? My expression? Was I wearing the wrong shade of pink? None of the above. His camera was acting up. Or was it the lights? The shoot was progressing at an agonizingly slow pace—and I wasn't responsible for the delay.

The photographer switched to a much slower film. Which meant I had to freeze my pose, not blink, nor breathe, for that much longer. He didn't want a single variation either. He'd decided on his ideal frame and he was sticking to it, no matter that I was getting cramps in the bargain. 'Don't move,' he'd command before each click. And I'd promptly blink. I thought I'd develop a tic out of sheer nervous tension. This wasn't fun at all. I tried to swing my body over into an easier position, and he came down on me gruffly. 'I said, "Don't move".' I went back obediently into the earlier stiff pose and tried to maintain a pleasant expression. I was beginning to hate the session. This wasn't fun at all. So what if it was for *Time* magazine?

I lost track of the number of rolls he shot that morning. It was an absurdly large amount. All for a single perfect shot.

I'd grown up economizing so much on film that we'd do an entire photo-feature on a single roll—four exposures per outfit.

By then the hostess looked weary too, even though her teenage son seemed to be enjoying every minute and was eagerly assisting the short-tempered photographer. I wanted to get the hell out. In any case, there was a flight to catch a few hours later. After what must have been the five-hundredth click of an identical nature, the photographer declared the session over. I haven't met him since then. I guess he knew exactly what he was doing since pictures from that shoot have appeared in various publications internationally, indicating that he did his bit brilliantly, he knew the requirements of his editors, and he delivered.

I didn't like the photograph when it appeared. I found it much too vamp-like. Besides, it (and the write-up) slotted me for several years in the rather exasperating 'Jackie Collins of India' mould. It's taken me a long time to shift away from its ludicrous implications. I've tried joking ('I'd love to possess her fat hair and fabulous home'), but that's how it works with foreign correspondents—once an image is set by the leader of the pack, it sticks, and no amount of aggressive denial can get rid of it. I encounter the question 'How does it feel to be the Jackie Collins of India?' at least half a dozen times a year. I can respond to it on auto-cruise. It is a tag I've learned to live with—uneasily, of course. But it no longer gets my back up.

Nothing compares, however, with the over-the-top shoot I did with Karan Kapoor for *The Sunday Times*. Karan was keen on a stylized picture that told a story. For that, several improbable, hard-to-get props were needed at short notice, including a vintage car. A Silver Ghost was his first choice. We settled instead for an ice-cream pink Buick convertible from the Fifties, loaned by that incredible collector of vintage cars, Pranlal Bhogilal. To go with the car, I needed to fix my own look. 'Load it on,' said Karan, 'let's go to town.' Which is what we did with the help of super-stylist Mickey Contractor. I wore an antique Benarasi saree, old jewellery, and Karan's grandmother's cat-eyed, diamante-studded, pale silver Ray Bans. They added just the right period touch.

The pictures were fabulous, shot by Karan precariously hanging out of a Jeep driving alongside the Buick. But the woman in them was not me. She was a fantasy creature invented by the photographer—a totally dishonest representation, a distortion I'd been a party to. I didn't blame Karan. I kicked myself.

*

No matter what they say, modelling was and remains a thinly-disguised cattle show. The attitudes of those involved in it have hardly changed. Very recently, I was on a flight to Calcutta. Seated right behind me was a former beauty contestant, a music director, a top model-couple and a choreographer. I didn't have to turn around to figure out their identities—it was obvious from the snatches of conversation I got to hear.

'Hey . . . what have you done to your eyebrows?'

'I decided to bleach them. Nice, no?'

'Umm, I'm not sure. I liked your old ones better.'

'Have to keep changing. I was so bored with that shape. What about my new hair-cut? Like it? Blunt and black.'

'Suits you. Is that why you changed your eyebrows?'

'Yeah, I was shooting a new portfolio so I thought, let me get a new look. Are you growing out your perm?'

'Have to. Hair is breaking. Remember, I had platinum streaks put in for that show? Huge mistake.'

'But they looked cool. Different, went with your lenses. Which colour will you be wearing in Cal for the show?'

'I'm thinking of grey. But I've also brought the brown-gold ones along—just in case.'

'God, guess what? I think I've forgotten mine. I've had it!'

'Don't worry, you can always borrow.'

'And guess what? I've left my strapless bra behind.'

'So long as you've got a black g-string for the finale.'

'I'm thinking of not wearing it. Just a body stocking, what do you think? Last time the panty-line was showing so badly. Very embarrassing.'

'What time are rehearsals?'

'Evening. Thank God. We can lie by the pool and get a nice tan.'

I smiled to myself. The same nauseating self-indulgence. The same vanities. The same silly banter about hair, clothes and make-up. The only real difference is the serious money today's models pick up. In my time just the thrill of travelling by air to different cities and staying in five-star hotels was deemed compensation enough.

The main reason why modelling never interested me sufficiently was that I wasn't vain enough. A model has to be passionately in love with herself to take the profession seriously. Even while I was a part of it I continued to maintain a self-mocking, cynical attitude towards the business—perhaps that's precisely what saved me from turning into a conceited, narcissistic bore. I never felt or behaved like the typical model—I was far too self-conscious to do that. I went for assignments sans make-up, and so casually dressed, I could have been the carelessly put together college girl next door which, in a way, I was.

Modelling didn't make me feel more attractive or

beautiful either. As a matter of fact, I've never really believed in my so-called 'beauty' and have always suspected the motives of people who've described me as one. During the Pond's shoots (I did the campaign for three years), I'd wonder whether the clients were mad to consider me their 'face of the year'. Each time I looked into the mirror, I'd see a very average person with tawny eyes, a largish mouth, crooked nose, big teeth and too-high cheekbones. It didn't add up to 'beauty'. In any case, my looks were something I didn't think about—others obviously did. I wasn't tall enough for the ramp, nor gorgeous enough for photographic modelling. And yet I managed to make it without really trying. It must have been the attitude. I was punctual, prepared, and easy to work with. No tantrums. No giving anybody a hard time. Unlike some of the other girls who preferred the 'princess' route to the top—royal airs, habitual latecoming, snapping and snarling through the shoot—I liked getting on with the assignment and getting out as fast as possible. I didn't hang out with the ad set (I found them as phoney then as I do now), nor did I find it necessary to flirt with the art directors.

The only time an adman tried his well-rehearsed number on me was when I'd gone to an agency to pick up my cheque. The managing director (a bearded dog with a comical Brit accent) followed me to the elevator and asked for a date. What I really wanted to say was something stupid like 'Seen yourself in the mirror lately?' What I did say was something even more stupid. 'How dare you? Just who the hell do you think you are?' To which the dog growled, 'I happen to own the agency.' I pressed the 'Down' button after saying, 'Do you? Good for you.' I left the premises determined never to accept another assignment from that agency if it ever came. It didn't.

*

74

As a fashion model I was part of a very wealthy set—maharajas, socialites, princesses, young men from a privileged public-school background, young women from prominent business families. All these people owned fancy cars, lived in luxury, wore fabulous clothes, travelled extensively, entertained lavishly, led luscious, pampered, extravagant lives. I was neither awestruck nor envious, merely curious, and fascinated by the unreality of their existence. How did I get to be a part of this set? It's not difficult when you are young, single and considered beautiful. That's how it works the world over.

I wonder what those people made of me way back then? In all probability, I didn't make much of an impression. I didn't belong to their world. I happened to be around more by default than design. But I was pretty enough and innocuous enough. I minded my own business. Didn't argue or contradict the men. I wasn't interested in stealing anybody's boyfriend. Nor was I competing with the other women. I spoke when I was spoken to (which wasn't often), and didn't make a complete ass of myself at parties. I didn't drink. And I didn't bitch. If anything, I was different and decorative, good to have around, like that exotic plant from Jakarta everybody remarked on. This sort of an attitude suited me fine too. They left me alone just as I left them alone. I was not bored in the least. To me, these evenings were like a night at the movies—mostly entertaining and occasionally brilliant.

I observed a great deal. Took in all the details. Watched these people and their antics closely. Absorbed. Learned. Accepted. And rejected. Their magnificent mansions filled with fine *objets d'art*, exquisite paintings and tasteful fittings transported me into a world I'd only read about and seen in Hollywood movies. But these people were not contracted players, they were for real. Their lives, too, were real, no matter how absurd or phantasmagorial they appeared to me. Modelling by day and partying with this set by night, it's a wonder my own perceptions didn't alter or get permanently affected.

Is the world of fashion as glamorous as it's cracked up to be? From the outside, definitely so. But for someone who is merely flirting (as I was), it can be be a bit of a nuisance in the long run.

On a working holiday with my family in Goa this year, every interviewer kicked off the questionnaire with, 'You started your career as a model . . . so how come you didn't stick to the glamour business? Why did you choose writing?'

I tried to disguise my exasperation as best as I could. I was tempted to snap, 'I didn't choose modelling, it chose me. I didn't choose writing, writing chose me.'

But of course I knew I'd be wasting my time, besides antagonizing very young, very impressionable, very idealistic journalists who couldn't possibly go beyond the stereotype.

It happens regularly to me even with non-journalists who weren't born at the time I was modelling. A group of earnest ladies in a small town of Maharashtra waited for a break in my address to their group to ask, ' . . . and modelling? Tell us about that phase. What do you do to keep your hair dandruff-free and glossy? What about skin care? Facials? Mudpacks? How do you maintain yourself?' That's the point at which something goes 'boing' inside my head. I have a mental image of my 'maintenance'—I see a huge garage with an outdated model of a car being serviced by an efficient crew that's busy oiling, cleaning, washing, with a spare-parts mechanic hanging around to replace a malfunctioning carburettor, change a valve or two.

The fact is, modelling did not give me a high. But it did give me a certain level of self-awareness which has been a great help in later years. Today, when I tell my daughters, 'Don't wait till you're forty, start looking after yourselves right now,' what I want to convey to them is the importance of a daily regimen. It's not so much a 'beauty' routine as physical discipline—basic exercises to tone up the muscles and a skin-care programme that includes scrupulous cleansing.

Ever since reports of my turning fifty appeared in the press, people (particularly women) have started treating me like the eighth wonder of the world—a rare museum piece.

'Gosh. Fifty, huh? How do you do it?'

I deadpan, 'Here . . . let me show you. Exactly like this . . . by breathing in, then breathing out at regular intervals. Try it. It's good for you.'

I'm also frequently surrounded by women twenty years my junior who gasp, 'You're incredible. What's the secret?'

I'm seriously considering ticketing the act.

I often wonder whether the course my life has taken would have been significantly different had I looked different and lacked the modelling-glamour angle. A year ago, organizers of an all-India meet for women in business came to see me. 'We would like you to be the chief guest,' said a starry-eyed lady in shiny blue silk. I was flattered. I said I'd check my schedule. 'Could you also suggest two other prominent women who could inspire members of our organization?' I rattled off a few names I thought would be appropriate enough. The women stared at one another sceptically. Finally, the spokesperson said innocently, 'Yes . . . but they aren't glamorous.'

'I thought you were looking for good speakers . . . achievers,' I said.

The women exchanged quick looks. 'That's true. But they must look good too. Our members will be disappointed otherwise.'

I was amused by their lack of artifice.

When I reached the venue, I was devoured by at least three hundred pairs of eager eyes. I could make out they were staring at my appearance, taking it all in critically—every last detail. I spoke for half an hour. I thought it was a good, sensible speech. I doubt those ladies heard any of it—they were too busy forming their own questions which were entirely unrelated to the business at hand. Sure enough, when I accepted queries from the audience, a dozen hands shot up. 'Which shampoo do you use?' was the first question. 'How do you keep your weight down?' And similar enquiries rapidly followed. What was meant to be a serious forum for exchanging views about the changed environment for working women became an informal beauty workshop with detailed, probing discussions on blackhead removal, waxing versus threading, yoga versus aerobics . . . and the inevitable 'Do you miss modelling?'

After thirty years? Heck, no.

'But you are still a model . . . we saw your shampoo ads.'

That led me to explain the difference between celebrity endorsement and straight, anonymous modelling. They didn't quite get it. Not that it mattered.

Not so long ago, coming back on a late evening flight from Delhi, I had a bunch of Mumbai's catwalk queens on the same flight. I knew most of the young girls and we greeted each other warmly. But had I not met them earlier under different circumstances, I would have been prejudiced for life, merely eavesdropping on their long conversation and watching the exhibitionistic manner in which they were behaving. Immediately I thought about my first ever flight to Delhi on an Indian Airlines plane. I'd been about the same age as these girls, say, nineteen. And excited out of my wits at the thought of flying, the show to follow, the idea of modelling itself. I'm sure I behaved equally immaturely and tried to attract attention on board. I do recall making an ass of myself on the flight when the stewardess brought the breakfast tray and it had a runny, sunny-side-up egg on it. Thinking I was in a restaurant, I said in my best worldly manner, 'I'd like it done on both sides.' The stewardess glared at me and said frostily, 'I'm sorry. We don't have a kitchen on board.' That shut me up all right, and brought me down to earth with a thud that I can still reconstruct when I feel I'm about to fly a bit too high and need serious levelling off.

Unprofessional, disorganized and amateurish though modelling was back then, it had a certain warmth about it that was important to me. Today, that aspect of the modelling scene has changed forever.

Recently, my eldest daughter Radhika came home waving a calendar dating back to '68, which featured three exceptionally garish photographs of mine. It had been found by her then boyfriend while spring-cleaning—the textile mill that had commissioned the shoot belonged to his father. We pored over the horrendous pictures which had me clad in ugly, gaudy outfits, my hair teased into an unnaturally large bouffant, the eyes painted peacock blue, the lips outlined in plastic pink. Arundhati turned to me and said, 'Mother, you look so much better now.' She said it with complete sincerity and I hugged her gratefully. No regrets about those five years. No regrets at all. Now, in my new avatar, I often have to be in front of the camera and the entire process is so familiar, I don't feel either self-conscious or uncomfortable. But I definitely feel my age.

The last time I endorsed a product, the crew could have been from another planet; they were focused, serious (definitely no horsing around!) and surrounded me with high-tech equipment that must have cost the earth. But some things don't change. The ad was for a shampoo, and despite the futuristic approach and all those blinking monitors, when it came to getting the hair ready for the cameras, I was ushered into a backyard of the run-down studio, where a makeshift 'salon' had been set up. It consisted of a rickety chair, four plastic buckets filled with hot water, two brand-new bath towels and a plastic mug. The hairdresser was ready with a jar of gooey conditioner which she'd made herself in her own suburban kitchen.

'Your hair will look like silk,' she assured me, 'it takes three hours to prepare.'

'What—the conditioner or my hair?'

'Your hair,' she answered crisply as she went to work massaging the gooey stuff into my scalp. 'Now, we'll steam it,' she announced cheerfully.

'Where? How?'

'I've got a pressure cooker,' she replied.

I couldn't believe my ears. 'You're planning to steam my hair in a pressure cooker?'

'Not exactly, wait, you'll see.'

While steam hissed out of the nozzle of an old pressure cooker balanced over an even older gas stove, the woman affixed a rubber pipe to the nozzle. 'Sit here,' she indicated while I took my place nervously next to the cooker. She picked up the hose and directed the steam gushing out of it into my gooed-up hair. 'Relax,' she instructed, as I froze with fright in my chair. 'It's important to relax or else your scalp muscles will tense up. If that happens, the hair won't fall correctly. I'll give you a massage to loosen up your forehead.' Fifteen minutes of angry steam bubbling through my hair later, I was marched back into the courtyard. She yelled out for a studio hand to assist her. Swathed in towels, I let my gooey, steamed hair hang from the back of the rickety chair while she poured

80

tumblers of hot water over it. 'Relax, relax,' she kept repeating. 'If you don't relax, the hair won't move.'

I didn't know my hair was supposed to be mobile.

'Of course, movement is very important. But that will happen after I've dried and ironed it thoroughly.'

Ironed? My hair?

'Yes, baba. It won't shine otherwise. The shine only comes after ironing.'

This was my first public shampoo, but I seemed to be the only person conscious of this fact. Workers and sundry hangers-on walked past nonchalantly, as if it was perfectly normal for a woman to have her hair washed, steamed, wrung dry and ironed in full view of dozens of strangers. I guessed they'd seen that and worse.

It took three hours to get my hair ready. Another to organize my face. Four hours before a single shot was taken. I wanted to go home. I needed to talk to my children, have a cup of tea with them. What was I doing in this lunatic set-up, taking orders from a bunch of pony-tailed men young enough to be parked across my knee and spanked? Dutifully I twirled, turned, twisted and trilled (the one line that was 'to camera'). The hair moved obediently enough. But I wasn't having fun. I had nothing to say to these intense kids staring bug-eyed at the monitors and going 'Oh shit . . . did you see that strand flying out of the frame? We'll have to clean it up. Rewind . . . rewind. She turned too quickly there, we missed the twist. That one . . . yeah . . . that one . . . let's try the cascade again. Lights . . . LIGHTS . . . where the fuck are the light guys? Come on . . . no extra shift. It has to be a wrap-up. Fix her hair. Up, up, up. Swing it . . . yeah . . . move, move, move. Good. Cut.'

The hair specialist would gather up my tresses like they were so much straw and ask, 'What do you want next?

Trrrrrrrr? or phooooochak?'

It was a terminology only they understood. 'Trrrrrrrr' referred to twisting the hair and releasing it slowly, 'phooooochak' to bunching it up into a top-knot and letting it cascade down when the director called 'Action'. After each take, I'd wait for their verdict. Twelve pairs of male eyes would study the images on the monitors minutely. For all the difference it made, I could have been a store mannequin wearing a nylon wig—so long as my hair moved silkily. On one level it was enjoyable; I couldn't get over the intensity of their involvement in the assignment. Each strand mattered. Equally, I couldn't get over the intensity of their non-involvement in the human being to whose head the strands were attached. Of course, they were all consistently polite, respectful, considerate and all of that. But that was just the point. One is polite, respectful, considerate etc. with distant strangers who occupy a different world . . . who don't belong. I missed the old camaraderie, the easy rapport, the bantering and laughter. For these twenty-somethings, I was a remote figure, an alien from another planet, someone they read about and occasionally maybe read too. They weren't there to get to know me. Hell, no. Time was money. They had a job to do. Deadlines to keep. They weren't being paid to be warm or friendly. That wasn't part of the deal. Their sense of purpose scared me. Their narrow focus scared me. Their fierce self-absorption scared me. Didn't these people ever let up? Relax? Wasn't there any joy left in the business any longer? Was everybody this time-and-money conscious? This driven? This strung-out?

I guess I had the answers. I guess I also knew this wasn't for me . . . if it had ever been. I was relieved. I felt freed. If I have to do it again I know one thing—my attitude will be different this time round. I won't go to the shoot looking for smiles and light-hearted chatter. I'll be as steely as the best of them . . . keep an eye on the ticking studio clock, weigh each second in hard cash. Clean up . . . and clear out. It's a new lingo—worth learning, too. And who knows, I may be able to add to the vocabulary after all. Surely those five years weren't for nothing?

Cutting Loose

It was a wet, gloomy morning in mid-1970 when I climbed the wide wooden stairs leading up to Creative Unit, a modest-sized ad agency at the corner of Mahatma Gandhi Road. Even by Seventies' standards, there was nothing impressive about the place—low ceilings, plywood partitions, coir matting on the floor. I didn't know who owned it or even which accounts the agency serviced. I was there as a model to see the rough layouts of a textile campaign before the actual shoot. I'd been invited over by Shilpa Shah who'd been a few years my senior at St. Xavier's College. She shared her tiny cabin with a short, bald, genial-looking chap whom she introduced as the copy chief, Nicholas Gonsalves. I was in my 'model' get-up, which included ugly platform heels that gave me an additional four inches height-wise. Shilpa was hugely pregnant, I noticed. Dressed in a printed chiffon saree, she looked exactly as I remembered her from college.

We glanced at the layouts, discussed dates and chatted about people we knew. Out of the blue, I heard a voice saying 'Can you write?' That was Shilpa asking me the one question I hadn't ever asked myself. I was ready with the answer: of course. But was I any good? I wasn't in a hurry to find out. It was a question that was thrown at me without a preamble . . . no warning. It caught me off-guard. Why was she asking me that in the first place? What did it have to do with the modelling assignment I was there for? I found out soon enough, after I'd jauntily replied with a 'Yeah. Sure, I mean, I enjoy writing. Always have, you know . . . through school and college. Why do you ask?' Shilpa looked at me indulgently . . . fondly. She still does. She explained she was looking for someone to hold the fort while she went off on maternity leave. And she thought I was that someone? Hey, this sounded like fun.

I volunteered to fill in for her without having the slightest notion of what exactly she did at Creative Unit. She said she and Nicholas *were* the copy department which meant that if she pushed off to have her baby, Nicholas became the copy department all by himself. After six months at Bhawan's College of Mass Communication, I had a vague idea about copywriting but not enough to become one-half of a copy department. Shilpa laughed. So did I. What the hell. Three months. Headlines, stuff like that. No problem. It would be a breeze. Besides, I was bored to death with the modelling scene, even if it did mean good money. Shilpa walked the three short paces to the glass door of her cabin and said, 'Let me check with the bossman. Maybe he'd like to see you . . . give a copy test.'

'Right now?'

'Why not? You're here.'

'Okay. Fine. Who's he? What's his name?'

She looked over her shoulder and said, 'Oh . . . Nari Hira. Nice guy.'

Five minutes later she was back . . . and she was grinning. 'What?'

'He said he needs someone who's willing to work hard. Someone who can write . . . not a glamour doll. He thinks you're one of those dumb models. Go prove him wrong.'

I figured I had nothing to lose.

85

'Did he say he'd see me now?'

Shilpa nodded. I gulped. Gawd! He sounded awful already. Maybe he was a sleazeball, one of those slimy, smooth-talking ad types wearing a Paisley-printed tie over a pink shirt.

'Parsi?'

'No. Sindhi.'

It was getting worse. Sindhi? Then he had to be fat, bald, paunchy. Maybe he wore surma in his eyes, oiled his sparse hair and sported outsized gold rings on both his index fingers. Shilpa gave me a friendly shove. 'Go on . . . go!'

I knocked on his office door. A sharp 'come in'. I walked in. I nearly walked out. Panic-stricken. This was no fat, bald, smelly Sindhi. Nari Hira had movie-star good looks, with large, lustrous eyes that bored holes through one's skull. Maybe he'd splashed on far too much after-shave, but that was better than mustard oil dripping from greasy strands of hair. Or furry arms. All this in a micro-second.

'Can you write?' he asked aggressively. What was going on in this joint? Imagine being asked the same question twice within the space of one hour. Was it part of a plan? Was every person walking up those dusty, rickety stairs asked that as a matter of routine?

'I . . . I think so,' I answered tentatively. Funny. If I hadn't been asked that crucial question on that particular monsoon morning, my life might have taken a completely different course. Even if the full import of those three words didn't strike me then. I thought it was supercilious and silly. What did they mean, 'Can you write?' Of course I could. Everybody could write. Everybody I knew wrote. It was something we didn't ask questions about. You had something to say, you wanted to put it down in words, you went ahead and did it. Naturally. That's how I'd been doing it at any rate. Well, not professionally. Not for money. But ours was a communicative family. Verbal, yes. But also a family that wrote stuff down. I was annoyed by the question. By the tone in which it was asked. There was a built-in assumption that I couldn't. That girls who modelled couldn't. I resented that. I'd been to a good school, a good college. I spoke well enough. What was so tough about writing that I'd been asked whether I 'could', twice already?

The conservatively dressed man behind the enormous desk got up abruptly and consulted his watch. 'I'll give you a copy test,' he said briskly. 'I'm leaving for a lunch appointment. You sit here and do it.' I nodded dumbly, not daring to say what I was in fact thinking. 'The nerve of the man. What makes him think I'm dying to do this? Why don't I just turn around and walk away?' His brief came in a staccato burst. 'If you're good at drawing, sketch the visual. If not, indicate what it should be. I want a headline, body-copy and baseline for these three products—an eyeliner, bedsheets and a lipstick.' With that said, he was gone.

I looked at his retreating figure. Should I just pick up my bag and leave? Walk into Shilpa's office and say, 'What a joke. Listen . . . this isn't for me. Sorry.' Something made me stick on. It wasn't a 'lemme show them' thing. More a 'why not? Looks easy. I'll take a bash at it.' I had food on my mind, not bedsheets or eyeliners. I could hear steel lunch-boxes being opened across the partition. The art department adjoined Nari Hira's office. Spicy aromas were wafting in under the door. Voices speaking in Marathi. Laughter. Jokes. And there I was staring at a writing pad and wondering what on earth I was doing here.

An hour later, the man walked in. Impersonal, businesslike, cold. 'Finished?' I handed over the sheets like a schoolgirl giving in a badly-written test paper for grading.

He looked through my effort. Expressionless. I was beyond caring. My thoughts were on lunch at home. My mother would be waiting. It was pouring outside. Cabs would be difficult to flag down at that busy intersection. 'Do another one,' he commanded. Whaaaat? This was cruel. I hadn't come in here looking for a job in the copy department in the first place. The man was presumptous and rude. I didn't need this. I'd thought Shilpa was my friend and well-wisher.

But something about the way I was ordered to do the second on-the-spot test kept me stuck to the chair. I can't explain it. Did I just not have the courage to challenge Nari Hira's authority? Why didn't I say, 'Sorry. But I am not really interested in writing copy. I just did it for a lark because Shilpa asked me to. Now, goodbye—I'm late for lunch.' He was busy shooting off fresh instructions, and I was meekly taking them in. Another watch consultation. Another crisp 'Fifteen minutes . . . that's it.'

This time he sat across me looking through papers. I scribbled away furiously. I was mad at him. Mad at Shilpa. Mad at myself. Beyond caring what he thought or didn't. I just wanted to get out and go home. I handed him the sheet indifferently. There was nothing to infer from his face—he was as expressionless as before. I didn't have a thing at stake. If he didn't like what I'd written, too bad. I didn't want the job anyway . . . or did I? I was fed up with modelling. I'd put in close to five years, appeared in several major campaigns, participated in countless shows, made a little money—now what? I was twenty-two. Restless. Directionless. Drifting along. The route had been a bit too easy, too predictable. I wanted to move on. But to what? Marriage was the obvious option. I didn't want it. A master's degree from Bombay University? Not stimulating enough. A regular, conventional job in, say, a bank? Hell, no. I didn't fancy sitting at home either. There was stuff happening in my head, but in an unfocused kind of way. I wanted to do something. I wanted someone to tell me exactly what.

I didn't—couldn't—take that decision because I didn't really know. Confused and frustrated, I was waiting to be told. Waiting for a person to come along and say firmly, 'Look here, that's enough. It's time to get on with your life. Modelling was fine then. It isn't so now. Here's what you should do . . . ' I wanted direction. A strong firm guide to lead me through the tunnel and show me the light. Somebody with a definite plan of action who'd take me in hand, sit me down and say, 'Now listen very carefully. This is what I want you to do . . . '

Nari was that person. Even if he didn't know it . . . doesn't know it. Even if he didn't intend playing that role. Even if it happened by default. I've always waited for happy accidents. So far, they've always happened. Almost on cue.

It was that one casually uttered but perfectly-timed question,'Can you write?' that changed the direction of my life for me, gave me my future vocation.

Another identity. A new future.

It's time to say 'thank you' to both Shilpa and Nari. They didn't know then (and maybe still don't) that if they hadn't made me ask that simple question of myself, I would have walked out of Creative Unit the way I'd walked in—yet another model with a campaign under her belt.

But later that afternoon, the girl who pranced out on to the busy road was someone who'd just chucked up a modelling career and got herself a brand-new job as a trainee copywriter. The salary? Three hundred and fifty rupees.

It was a turning point.

I was walking in blind, into a career I knew nothing

about. Nari Hira had attached a precondition—one that I instantly accepted without a single regret or even a single thought. I was instructed to say goodbye to modelling overnight. I was kissing a lucrative hobby goodbye, without any idea of what I was getting into. It had been an easy enough decision to take—but I hadn't thought it through. Nor had I consulted anyone—not even my family.

I was not a careerist. So many years later, I still don't consider myself one. But a little voice inside my head told me I was doing the right thing . . . and even if my stint as a copywriter was to be a short-term fling with the business, there was nothing much at stake, nothing much to lose—except a great deal of pocket money, of course. My considerable earnings from modelling were just that—pocket money. But a casual income of ten to fifteen thousand a month in those days was not to be sneezed at. Yet, I waved it away without a second thought, settling for a petty stipend instead. I lived a reasonably comfortable life with my parents picking up all the bills. What did that money—or money itself—mean to me? Not a great deal in real terms. It took care of my small indulgences, cab fare, clothes, make-up, accessories. Most of it was in a savings account I operated arbitrarily.

Turning my back on modelling was easy—what wasn't was getting used to an 'office' atmosphere, regular hours, muster-signing, getting along with people far older than me without making a complete fool of myself.

I don't know why Nari Hira hired me. I never asked, he never said. I still don't know whether he thought I had it in me—a glimmer of talent, some potential. There was no reaction from him, nothing to indicate what he'd made of my amateurish efforts. Today, we can joke about it, the encounter being at such a safe distance. Today, I can call him a friend even if I never address him by his first name. He was Mr Hira then, he remains Mr Hira even now.

*

So, what was it like working as a trainee copywriter at Creative Unit? I knew I was only filling in for someone, maybe that coloured my attitude. I wanted to learn but wasn't in too much of a hurry. Nicholas was a good teacher even if I did distract him with unending, childish prattle and juvenile jokes. I talked compulsively between proof-checking and brain-storming. It wasn't really a 'hot' agency and the volume of work allowed most of us to goof off, read, chat and take it easy. The assignments that came my way were hardly taxing. It was probably understood that I would only be around briefly. Nobody took me seriously—nobody could for very long. I was the 'Ponds' or 'Bombay Dyeing' or 'Vimal' model who was 'flirting' with copywriting. The new girl who talked too much and had no previous experience other than the slightly dubious one acquired in front of a camera. She won't last. Not here. The place isn't glamorous enough.

I made it to work bang on time, hung around the studio, shared lunch with the Maharashtrian visualizers and paste-up boys and generally waited to be summoned by 'Mr Hira'. These meetings were few and far between, scrupulously formal but vastly entertaining. I liked this man—his abrupt manner, sharp comments and irreverent opinions. He kept his distance from everyone, as did his portly partner Lalu Bajaj. They were the 'bosses' who walked in at precisely 9.30 a.m. after parking their Volkswagen Beetles in the designated slots, left for lunch at the Bombay Gymkhana at 1.15 p.m., got back at 2.00 and then pushed off around 5.30 to attend to their other businesses—hair-removing wax, face packs, real estate, a suburban swimmers' club.

91

I knew within the first month that copywriting wasn't for me—I found the business of creating headlines depressing, mechanical and unrewarding. One spent days pushing semi-colons and commas around a page when all the client wanted was a pretty girl in sexy attire hawking his product provocatively. I recall the months spent on the launch of Johnson & Johnson's Carefree sanitary napkins. Heated debates raged around the merits of highlighting the revolutionary blue plastic shield—a woman's ultimate protection against public embarrassment. Hours were spent huddled over 'roughs' which featured colourful daisies against a white background. It was as if the world would stop spinning if we didn't come up with a slogan for the first sanitary napkin with it. I couldn't get excited about the blue shield. I didn't connect or feel involved. I really and truly gave not a damn for either the client's budget or the product. I found the whole business of creating interest in something I wasn't the least bit interested in, utterly and monumentally tiresome. Besides, Shilpa by then had decided she wasn't coming back in a hurry after the birth of her son. I was stuck in a job I was beginning to detest. By that point, I'd run out of wisecracks. Perhaps run through Nicholas' reserves of patience too, and started experiencing the old antsy feeling—what am I doing here? Why am I wasting everybody's time? Why don't they just fire me?

There was another reason why life at Creative Unit had ceased to be amusing or even tolerable. Mr Hira had decided to let me have a shot at assisting a senior executive handling the agency's top account. This man was obnoxious—or at least, he chose to be obnoxious with me. We didn't make good music together. I hated him and he reciprocated the sentiment with equal passion. He was in a position to give me a hard time—and he made sure he did just that. I tried my damndest to go along with the situation while every bit of me resented his loud, bullying, boorish ways. I told myself, 'This is the real world, baby. If not this SOB, there'll be another SOB, someone even worse, perhaps. Grow up. Learn to deal with it. Cope. It doesn't get better.'

Then one day I wondered why the hell I was putting up with him and the set-up. There was nothing in it for me—not even money. I didn't really need the job. I wasn't learning anything in that hostile environment. And I was miserable. Really and truly miserable. I figured I'd resign and stay home for a while. Take some courses. Maybe enroll for a master's degree. Anything to escape from that smelly dump. My self-worth was at its lowest. I was beginning to feel like a brainless bimbo, because this man made it his mission in life to treat me so. There were countless jibes about my being a former model. And offensive remarks aimed at women who didn't really take their jobs seriously enough. What was it about me that raised this man's blood pressure? I suspect it was my non-deferential attitude which was in stark contrast to that displayed by others. While I was consistently polite even in the face of nauseating rudeness, his intimidatory tactics didn't get to me. I wasn't playing a modern-day Joan of Arc. I was merely being myself. I didn't see any need to bow and scrape in his presence—he was a paid professional and I was trying to do my job, that was all. Besides, I was far too inexperienced and gauche. I didn't know I was supposed to pretend, to act overawed and feign respect for a person I found despicable and low.

If Nari Hira was aware of my discomfiture he didn't indicate it. Nor did I go whining to anyone. I had a busy life outside working hours. The Bombay scene was lively and stimulating, beginning with rows and rows of pavement shops right outside the main entrance of the office building. Rhythm

House was next door, Samovar, Bombay's original arty café, across the street. A line of boutiques selling cheap ready-to-wear clothes and watches; old books sold on the narrow, crowded footpath leading to Flora Fountain half a kilometre away; the magnificent Gothic monstrosity housing the Bombay University down the road; Smart and Hollywood, tailors to the fashion and theatre world in the Army & Navy building opposite; several South Indian restaurants in the by-lanes at the back of the building—and I had enough time on my hands to explore all of this and more. No, there was no real reason other than rage for quitting, not at this stage.

Occasionally, I asked myself whether I was behaving like a brat. A spoilt princess who'd been pampered in the glamour world she'd walked away from. Did I expect preferential treatment? Did I demand concessions? In all honesty, I have to say I didn't. I was far too aware of my vulnerable position. I may be wrong, but I was probably the youngest employee in that office (not counting the telephone operator). I was keen to prove myself, keen on joining the adult world, keen to be seen as part of the team. I knew that I ran the risk of being treated less than seriously, so I went out of my way to prove myself by being 'one of the guys'. Clearly a mistake. I wasn't one of the guys. Never could be. My tormentor knew that only too well and capitalized on my anxiety by treating me like dirt, with unwarranted attacks and acts of such a petty nature, I'm astonished I didn't strike him. Arrogant, overbearing and ugly to boot, he became my daily punishment. A torture I forced myself to endure because I didn't want to be seen as a quitter. There was nobody in that office I could talk to or enjoyed spending time with. Except one person—the remote and distant Nari Hira. But he didn't want to make time for me—he was far too busy becoming Nari Hira. This was the take-off stage in his life. He had half-a-dozen ambitious projects to tackle. Gradually, he distanced himself from the advertising business, leaving it to mediocre executives and a weak general manager. He began spending less and less time at the office. Nobody enjoyed interacting with his partner. Nari Hira's dynamism was hard to duplicate. People began to lose interest in daily operations without him being around to crack the whip. I'm sure it's the same today as he presides over his media empire from an office building at Prabhadevi—a few metres away from the crater created by powerful explosives that blew away most of the passport office close by.

'NMH', as he is reverentially referred to by loyal staffers, is an excellent motivator of people. He's consistently described as 'dynamic', though I believe a better, more apt description is 'magnetic'. Even well after the initial magic has worn off and one has seen through the carefully cultivated exterior, the spell is hard to break. Here's a man who takes his chances and projects fearlessness. But above all, he instils confidence in people he employs, mainly by letting them be. I can't say how it works in other set-ups since his is the only one I have ever worked in, but during my twelve years in that organization, I never encountered anything but encouragement and support from him. Even during his long absences when he was busy acquiring NRI status, I felt confident knowing that I could count on him in a crisis situation. He has that effect on young, impressionable minds which is why he shrewdly employs twenty-somethings, sure in the knowledge that he'll be able to exert absolute authority and control over them without their realizing it. Which is why I'm equally sure I wouldn't have been able to work with him (or anybody else) once I'd seen more of the world. Nari Hira was the right man at the right time in my life. He gave me the opportunity to break loose from a life I had outgrown.

Did I miss the lights? Make-up? Attention? Not for a moment. Maybe if I hadn't walked in and given that copy test, I would have lingered on for another year out of a lack of viable alternatives. The copy test changed it all. Even if it didn't convince me that I could write, it opened another door. I felt better about myself. My family felt better about me. I had a 'proper' job—even if they didn't understand exactly how different this was from modelling. To them an ad agency was an ad agency—part of a world they knew nothing about. A bank job, yes. Now that they would have known how to assess. A job with any government body? Indeed. But as my father would point out, 'How can you expect to get into any of these organizations with your qualifications? Nobody will give you a job unless you study further and appear for a competitive examination.' He was right. But his impatience with my seeming lack of ambition and choice of modelling as a first career option was somewhat assuaged by my job at Creative Unit. And I was comfortable enough, if bored . . . till the tyrant entered the scene and ruined the experience.

I can see him clearly as I write this—blazing, bloodshot eyes, thick lips curled into a nasty sneer, a gravelly voice that hadn't quite broken. But, above all, he had attitude—loads of it. A man who clearly over-estimated himself. An insecure lout who exerted power over juniors who couldn't fight back. He didn't last very long at Creative Unit. As a matter of fact, he disappeared altogether, leaving just the memory of his heady, overpowering, cheap cologne behind. But not before he'd succeeded in reducing me to a state where I dreaded the thought of stepping into that office each morning.

Often, my sister Mandakini would drop me to work, her Standard Herald pulling up alongside Nari Hira's Beetle. He'd pretend he hadn't seen me and bound up the stairs. My sister would comment on his rudeness, but I knew it was part of his act—I bet he still doesn't wish staffers if he meets them on their way up. Unlike other admen of his generation, he chose to stay away from the politics and parties of the business. He didn't chase accounts either. He broke several rules including the one that said 'send the prettiest girls for campaign presentations—if nothing else works, maybe a smile will.'

Most agencies employed lookers in the client servicing department. Their job was to accompany senior male executives and impress the potential client using whatever it took to clinch the deal. The only time I was asked to be present at a presentation was at the SOB's insistence. I probably didn't do a great job of batting my eyelashes for that was the last time I tagged along.

After a while of putting up with my tormentor, I wanted out. It took me a while to reach the decision. The man was a dog. A rabid one. I didn't see myself as a lamp post.

I'm sure Nari Hira was expecting my buzz when I called on the intercom and asked to see him (I rarely took that liberty). I was dressed for a funeral (not deliberately so). White bell-bottom pants, a white lace shirt and white platform shoes. Complexion to match. Once, earlier, I'd hinted I was fed up and Mr Hira had laughed and asked me to hang on. I could hang on no further. There was no point in making myself still more miserable.

I was offered a cup of coffee (uncharacteristic). It meant I'd be compelled to sit across the table for a minimum of ten minutes while Dattaram, the skinny peon, organized the beverages. No preambles. I said flatly that I'd had it. It was time to say goodbye. Mr Hira abruptly asked, 'Have you thought of magazine writing?'

I figured he was trying to be nice, and making it easier for me by suggesting another career. Perhaps he'd put in a word somewhere? I shook my head. Why bullshit? I hadn't thought of magazine writing. I hadn't really thought of anything beyond picking up my handbag and walking out.

'I'm planning to start one,' he continued smoothly. 'Do you want to try your hand at it?'

This was Big Daddy offering a lollipop to a tearful little girl who'd produced a lousy report card. Without waiting for an answer, he went on to outline his project. It was to be a film monthly. Hindi films? Yes. But . . . but . . . I stuttered, I know nothing about them. I'd seen perhaps twenty altogether. It was a world that didn't interest me in the slightest. I barely knew the names of the reigning kings and queens of Bollywood.

'That's all right,' he replied. 'You don't have to know too much about the film industry. I'm looking for someone who can write provocatively, interview the stars, put various columns together. I'm sure you'll be able to do it. Tell you what, why don't you write an imaginary interview with a star—any star. I want to see whether you have the style. Pick anybody—it hardly matters. Ask the sort of questions you'd like to read about. Make up the answers. And then we'll see.'

The coffee was much too hot. A layer of cream covered the surface. I gulped it down anyway. I still had a job. I wouldn't have to walk home forlornly and say, 'I gave up.'

Stardust was conceived as undramatically as that. Nari Hira was absolutely clear about what he wanted—a clone of the popular Hollywood fanzines of the time like *Photoplay* and *Screenplay* (since extinct).

He wanted their format, their gossip, their pictures, their punch—but Indianized. He didn't tell me this before I shot off my fictitious star interview for his assessment. Whom did I pick? Shashi Kapoor. And why? I guess he was the least ridiculous of the stars (I still think the same). I'd seen him in a couple of films, never mind that *The Householder* didn't exactly qualify as a potboiler. I'd read a few pieces in which he'd spoken like a normal person, he was maddeningly good-looking, and 'westernized' enough for idiots like me to feel comfortable.

From what I remember of that attempt, it was pretty dreadful—snide and supercilious, besides being far too long. The tone was all wrong—smug, superior and smart-alecky. A silly, school-girlish stab at one up-manship. I could curl up and die at the memory. But hey, it got me the job . . . so who's complaining? I still think Nari Hira was being kind to a confused young person, nothing more. Nobody is that intuitive or far-sighted. He couldn't possibly have sensed even a glimmer of talent in my half-baked efforts.

Operation *Stardust* was launched soon after, in earnest, with one paste-up artist, the strong, silent Harish, and a very inexperienced but suddenly enthused me.

The two of us, Harish and I, were promised a new office next door—there was no additional space in Creative Unit. In any case, we'd become overnight pariahs in the agency since we were working on a project nobody thought much of. We were in the way. And pretty clueless. It was Nari Hira's never-say-die optimism that charged the otherwise dead atmosphere. We didn't have the slightest notion of what went into a magazine—any magazine. Nari Hira made us believe it would be a cakewalk. That there was nothing to it. All we needed to do was get hold of eight or ten freelance writers, co-ordinate production with the burly guy at the press he'd picked, locate appropriate pictures—beg, borrow, steal, plunder, pillage . . . And bingo! We'd have an issue. That was fine—but what would we fill it with? Articles. Right. What sort of articles? Aha—that's where his instincts came in. He was very clear about the sort of magazine *Stardust* was to be. Racy, gossipy, wicked, chatty and shocking (by Seventies' standards). There was no question in his mind—this would be the breakthrough magazine designed to shake up the sleepy competition and set newsstands on fire. The word 'scandal' was never mentioned. As for the name itself, it reminded one of the famous Nat King Cole number . . . or the Las Vegas casino. Would it work in India, I naïvely asked the man who'd come up with it. 'Of course it will,' he replied jauntily, 'it's different.' But . . . I interjected . . . dust? Stars? Were we planning to make compete kachra out of our beloved sitarey? Nari Hira smiled enigmatically. He resembled the cat who'd swallowed the cream.

Blazing Trails

People often ask me what it was like working for India's number one film magazine. Did we know it would turn out to be such a success? What were the early days all about? The truth is, the whole thing stank. Literally.

Our move to the new premises took a few months. The building was less than a block away and perhaps even more dilapidated than the one Creative Unit was housed in. Since Nari Hira wanted to save on costs the *Stardust* office turned out to be a dank dump of a place located next to a public toilet shared by the entire floor. My little room was above a water tank. Adjoining it was a cramped studio shared by Harish and another junior artiste (we continued to use the old dark room and dispatch facilities). To get to my desk upstairs I had to run up a narrow flight of stairs through a plywood door and into a square, bare room with two desks. Nari Hira's cabin was downstairs—all six feet by four feet of it. That left just enough space for a typist-receptionist and a peon. You could say we started small—really, really small.

One of the first freelancers I was asked to contact was Mohan Bawa (he died a few years ago). He minced into the office, asked for tea and gossiped madly for two straight hours. He knew everything about everybody connected with the film industry. Short, thick-set and very camp, he had a way with words and wasn't entirely illiterate. He wrote like

Hedda Hopper/Louella Parsons and would have loved to dress like them too. He was our best bet—the only person I knew who was on first-name terms with 'Dev', 'Raj', 'Sunil' and 'Dharam'. Bawa was also the only film journalist who wrote decent copy in grammatical English—entire sentences with punctuation marks. This was more than anybody could say about the reigning goddess, Devi, who presided over *Star'n'Style* and was the number one gossip columnist—truly a queen, in manner, deed and thought. Mohan, poor soul, wasn't a patch on her, or maybe he hadn't got a good enough break. Where could he have pedalled his stuff anyway? *Star'n'Style* was off-limits. It couldn't handle two queens. *Filmfare*, the stuffy dowager, would never have touched his stuff and *Screen* was a trade paper restricted to printing box-office collections.

To Bawa was entrusted the task of attempting the first 'Neeta's Natter'—the column that went on to shred more star reputations than a slasher on speed. Bawa did a pretty good job of it too, since he was assured anonymity. Unlike Devi's 'Frankly Speaking' which was a first-person account of her fortnightly rounds in filmdom written in catchy but clumsy Marathi-English, 'Neeta's Natter' was to be a short, snappy item-ised column that invited contributions from all over. Nari Hira had used popular Hollywood columns as prototypes. The column heading had been debated and discussed, but he'd been adamant about retaining it even after somebody had pointed out that the English was incorrect. 'Make it "Neeta's Nattering" or "Neeta Natters",' suggested Gonsalves, the copy chief. Nari Hira stuck to the original and we came up with the famous feline with a cigarette holder who sits smugly on top of each page. The peculiar dome on the cover, combined with the dated typeface, would have been any self-respecting art director's nightmare. Not ours. We thought it was just great—more then twenty-five years later it remains unaltered, untouched and yes, grammatically imperfect too. As do most of the original sections inside—'Court Martial', 'Snippets', 'These are a Few of My Favourite Things', staples all.

The cover story for the premier issue had been pre-written in Nari Hira's mind. It had been given to him by starlet Anju Mahendroo's mother, and concerned Rajesh Khanna, her daughter's boyfriend of seven years. How we were going to play it—straight or gimmicky—that was the only question. Those were the days when Rajesh Khanna was the unchallenged superstar—far bigger than Amitabh Bachchan during his heyday. Known as he was for his childish tantrums, petulance and conceit, nobody wanted to mess with the man, not when he had Devi as a full-time devotee dedicating reams of adulatory copy to him week after week. Devi's obsession with 'The Phenomenon' (a nomenclature coined subsequently by *Stardust*) was well known in film circles. Khanna could do no wrong in her eyes and nobody else could do any right. That was okay. It was a common enough celebrity syndrome. But there was another Rajesh Khanna hiding behind the public mask—a complex, insecure man who needed a strong, opinionated, intelligent woman like Anju to run his house and life for him. So, why wasn't he making it official? Maybe Shanti Mahendroo hoped the material she so helpfully supplied to Nari Hira would jolt the recalcitrant Rajesh into making an honest woman of her daughter.

The inaugural issue of *Stardust* hit the stands in October 1971 with a headline that asked, 'Is Rajesh Khanna secretly married?' This was classic Hollywood—but new to India. The unflattering cover shot (a flashlit, stock picture by Dhirendra Kishen) showed up every pimple, boil and whitehead on Mr Khanna's face in close-up. The issue sold out within a week.

When I see it now, I shudder. The effort looks clumsy, amateurish and shoddy—which it was. It's a good thing nobody noticed. The readers lapped it up. Over the years, slick designing has never been a *Stardust* attribute. If it continues to sell, it's because of its written content. The layouts are as lousy as they were then. And the proofing equally careless.

We, the motley staff, had no idea the magazine—our magazine—was a success. For us, it was just a job that had to be done month after month. We did it enthusiastically enough. I know I did. But the reasons for my complete involvement were different. For the first time since joining an office, I was on my own without anyone breathing down my neck. This is how I functioned best—and still do. The atmosphere was relaxed, casual and free of hierarchy. We were all equals, including the peons. We sat together, ate our *dabbas* together, gossiped together and enjoyed ourselves hugely. What's more, we were actually getting paid for it. Away from the cesspool and intrigue that Creative Unit had become for me, I flowered. But more than anything else, I fell in love. With magazines. Not so much the writing but the production aspect of magazine journalism. I liked going to the press and taking deep breaths—printing ink is the sexiest fragrance in the world. I liked the smell of rubber solution in the studio, I enjoyed being in the dark room scanning potential cover subjects through the enlarger. Layouts were fascinating—the meticulous arrangement of headlines, sub-heads, slugs, breaks, lead-ins, intros, captions. Virgin manuscripts were a turn-on too. I devoured each one of them eagerly, often in the presence of a nervous contributor. Since we depended largely on freelancers, our tiny cabin was a crowded place with visiting journalists, photographers, publicists . . . and soon, starlets and other hopefuls lobbying for write-ups.

Rekha was an unknown when she walked in with Vinod Mehra (dead now). Let me see . . . First impression? Gross. She was overweight, loud, giggly, and ridiculously dressed. Her face still had baby-fat deposits on it, her plucked eyebrows formed artificial arches over small eyes. Dusky—well . . . dark, and dumpy. Nobody could possibly have visualized the Rekha of today—Sultry Siren . . . Seductress Supreme. She chattered incessantly in a distinctly 'vernie' accent, much to everybody's amusement.

There was a tiny landing on the staircase that led up to our cubby hole. Over that we'd hung a rug someone had picked up somewhere. It featured a black cat very like our mascot. We asked Vinod to pose in front of it, with or without his companion. He opted for 'with'. Rekha's permanent love affair with the camera couldn't be missed. The lens transfixed her. She abandoned her silly, childish prattle in a jiffy once the clicking began. She would have happily abandoned Vinod Mehra—but she knew that she was included in the photograph thanks to him. No Vinod (whom she called Vin-Vin), no picture. The picture won.

Six months down the line, we were still around and still selling brilliantly. Nari Hira would gloat about doubling the print-run with each issue—but I don't know. It wasn't circulation figures that interested me. That wasn't my department. He handled all financial matters and still does. I wouldn't be surprised if he runs one of the most cost-effective shows in town. Nari Hira has the special ability to project extravagance at the cheapest possible price. He ran a pretty tight ship without a single wasted paisa. There was no such thing as an expense account—nobody entertained. I paid my own travel bills (that is, cab fares to and from home). And there were no perks. The only freebie the staff could look forward to was two cups of coffee or tea twice a day. We cut costs on everything. If that showed in the final product, no one was complaining. There was no competition, really. Compared to the cheeky, spicy, masala-mix of *Stardust*, *Filmfare* seemed like a widowed aunt. *Star'n'Style* without Devi's column was little better.

Emboldened by our early success, and not knowing any better, we carried on recklessly and, frankly, very irresponsibly at times. The older generation of established stars recoiled at the effrontery of it all—naturally. They'd been used to syrupy write-ups that rarely went beyond chronicling Asha Parekh's poodle giving birth to a new litter of pups or Waheeda Rehman's cute nieces. Photo-features dared not go further than Jitendra Arya's lens took them—which meant ghagra shots stopped at the ankles, and no one had the courage to ask what lay behind Mumtaz's choli. 'Is Rajesh Khanna secretly married?' was a clear cop-out—another one of those teaser stories that led nowhere and didn't come up with answers. But it was still a long way from '"My best friend is my mother," confesses Sharmila', or '"I sleep with my teddy bear," admits Nanda'.

Heady with the galloping circulation figures, we took on additional people—Uma Rao, Ingrid Albuquerque, Vanita Bakshi, and started referring to our office as the Cat House (note: no pun). By then, I'd taken to walking back home. For one thing, that was about the only exercise I got, for another, we worked late and taxis were hard to come by after office hours. It was a spooky street and an even spookier building after office hours, once the pavement vendors had packed up their wares and left for the day and the rest of the offices on our floor had downed their shutters. Rats the size of well-fed puppies scampered around foraging for lunch-time leftovers. The stench ('follow the smell') from the community bathroom wafted up, carried to our 'penthouse' by warm sea breezes.

The studio air was fetid and dank from leaking tanks and broken roof tiles that allowed the rain water to seep in by the bucketful. Our cubby hole was air-conditioned but we didn't spend too much time there once the monthly deadline approached. Over soggy dosas, watery sambar and rancid chutney sandwiches, we slaved. away cheerfully—what the hell, this was new to the lot of us. We enjoyed our work—besides, there wasn't time left over for a life outside it anyway. We entertained each other. We became expert mimics. Each star encounter was re-enacted for the benefit of the others in excruciating detail. An unspoken decision had been made at some point that I didn't have to budge out of the office if I didn't want to. I didn't want to. So I stayed put and held the fort while Uma, Ingrid, Vanita and, later, Prachi and assorted freelancers did the rounds of studios, star homes, parties, muhurats, premieres. Didn't I want to be there myself? Wasn't I curious? Frankly, no. I went into *Stardust* without being even remotely interested in the glamour. And that's how it remained. There was no question of getting sucked into something I wasn't attracted to in the first place.

In all those days spent at *Stardust*, I did not step into a film studio, attend a muhurat, visit a star home or party with the film crowd. I remember two exceptions—the premiere of the Zeenat Aman-Rex Harrison starrer *Shalimar*, and a small dinner party at the home of a compulsive party-giver, the late Shankar B.C.

If the film industry was curious about my self-isolation, I did nothing by way of explanation. It was the right policy and I have no regrets. I did not want to become friends with the movie people. I preferred the enforced distance and it worked in favour of the magazine. Since there were no 'favourites' to shield, everybody became a potential target—no strong biases, no strings attached. *Stardust* spared no one, and that was its real strength. A credible level of objectivity was sustained in the magazine's pages, which contributed to its success.

People ask me whether I was offered film roles myself—after all I was rubbing shoulders with the industry, so what if it was a long-distance affair? Yes, I was. But nothing could have horrified me more. I abhorred the film world. There was no question of my becoming a part of it. I can honestly state that I wasn't remotely interested, nor was I tempted. Not even when the great Satyajit Ray walked up to me at a film festival in Mumbai and asked directly whether I'd like to try out for the lead role in his forthcoming film. I gulped, blinked and shook my head. I would have made a lousy actress. My embarrassment would have shown through.

And that's how it stayed till I moved on and away ten years later. Besides, my eyes and ears were so attuned to reportage that I preferred my colleagues' versions of their meetings with the stars to personal encounters. But occasionally I wasn't left with much of a choice—like the time Shatrughan Sinha strode in with his chamchas.

The stars who dared to show up at the Cat House did so at their own risk, often setting themselves up for future ridicule in the pages of the magazine. Shatrughan Sinha, with his broad Bihari accent and crude manner, could do very little to salvage his image once he'd crossed the threshold and slapped his pack of imported cigarettes on my table. He thought it constituted style—we thought it was a pathetic affectation, especially when he clicked his fingers without turning around and two lackeys rushed up with lighters for the 'boss'. He had obviously rehearsed his dialogues before venturing in. Using his deep voice and bulbous brown eyes to advantage, he went ahead and made a complete fool of himself—even though the man is not a fool at all. It was his lack of exposure, the absence of sophistication and the mistaken belief that this sort of posturing was making us all go weak in the knees. Watching him conducting his current show on television, I feel he hasn't moved too far away from the loudmouth he was way back in the Seventies. Neither has he felt the need to outgrow the bragging and strutting bravado which eventually did him in. Shatrughan was a passable screen villain, sometimes a convincing one. Success (limited as it was) shot to his head, making it balloon to five times its original size. And he thought the audience would accept him as a hero. He overestimated himself then . . . he continues to do so now.

Shatrughan Sinha made several gaffes during the visit, but the one that sticks involved offering me a ride home. Since he showed no sign of being in a hurry to leave, all of us pointedly reached for our handbags and indicated we were ready to shut shop. We walked to the semi-deserted, darkened street below, he blowing smoke rings into the still late-evening air, the rest of us barely able to conceal our boredom and impatience. A dull green Mercedes Benz was parked along the pavement.

He pointed and said, 'That's my car.'

There were no audible gasps. 'How are you going home?'

'Like I do every day—I walk.'

'Why don't you come with me in my Mercedes?'

'No, thank you. I need the exercise.'

He almost wept.

Someone else who overestimated himself was Kabir Bedi who strode into the office like he was auditioning for *Tughlaq-II* (a role he had immortalized on stage by appearing in the opening act clad in a red loincloth). His large frame filled the doorway as he struck a dramatic pose, arms extended, to better show off his magnificent physique.

Urbane, handsome, well spoken and maddeningly sure of himself, he alas, went the Shatrughan way by also slapping down a pack of foreign ciggies (Dunhill, if I recall correctly). Deep eye-contact (a tactic that has served him well over the years, given the number of wives and girlfriends in his fifty-something life) followed by 'meaningful' conversation was meant to set the tone. What he was saying was simply this: Look ladies, I know I'm gorgeous and hard to resist. I'll give you time to get your heartbeat down to normal and then allow you to fall in love with me. He was so entirely sure of himself and his effect on women, he failed to notice our quick exchange of looks and suppressed sniggers.

Kabir Bedi, for all his impressive attributes, is perhaps the most self-absorbed human being I've ever encountered. Nothing matters to Kabir Bedi besides Kabir Bedi. He's incapable of loving anybody—there's nothing left of love since it has all been used up on himself. Despite that, he is likeable because he is so transparent. That was the time in his life when he was playing the intellectual from Delhi who'd wandered into filmdom—more as a favour to filmdom than anything else. He was doing a good turn to movie-goers and being gracious about it. The problem was his lack of talent—Kabir Bedi on screen is hard to separate from a gigantic log of wood. Socially, he was a big hit given his propensity to speak grandly in the third person ('One believes', 'one thinks', 'one feels'), well read, well travelled and smart enough to play humble. ('One is just a learner . . . one travels through life choosing the path of least resistance.')

Kabir was great at recycling Buddhist philosophy, Zen thoughts, Allen Ginsberg verse, and ad-speak. This didn't endear him to the filmi crowd which was more familiar with discussing box-office figures and heroines than J. Krishnamurti's gems. Sensibly, Kabir packed his bags and moved westwards—Italy and Hollywood—where he met with slightly more success. Unfortunately, for an actor from the East who could have been another Omar Sharif, Kabir Bedi ended up as a poor man's version of the Egyptian star. But a man with his appetite for wives needed steady employment to settle bills. He found it. Ignore the narcissism and he isn't a bad chap at all—just tiring.

And then there was Zeenat Aman, the most glamorous of them all. Quintessential sex-symbol. With a cleavage (unenhanced by silicone but attractively pushed up with clever underwiring) that apparently gave Gina Lollobrigida a complex about her own awesome one when they met, Zeenat was someone I'd known as an overweight but very sexy teenager who spoke in a peculiar American accent. Her mother was her world, no matter what illusions the men in her life may have harboured. And 'Babusha' (as mum lovingly called her) was Mrs Heinz's little darling. I met them both for the first time when they walked into the *Eve's Weekly* studio for 'test pictures'. Zeenat was a sixteen- or seventeen-year-old student who had just returned after an exchange programme in America (that explained the strange accent). Teenage fat deposits sat obstinately on her hips and waist but the legs were fabulous, and the face (what one could see of it under the puffiness) had an attractiveness that wasn't beauty but something else—a pouty knowingness of sexual power. Irresistible to anyone, when packaged with brains and a way with words.

I helped her put on make-up while her mother breathed down my neck anxiously. While I was no expert, Zeenat trusted me with her face, only because she knew her own efforts would have been worse. That was Zeenat's forte and continues to be—she's clever enough to know her limitations. She got into the film industry to make money, cash in on her body, enjoy the fame and get out. At no stage did she kid herself about either her intentions or talent. To that extent she met her objectives and plotted her career-moves ruthlessly. The breaks couldn't have been better—Raj Kapoor, Dev Anand, Krishna Shah (opposite Rex Harrison, would you believe it) and for five years the Zeenat magic had India under its spell. By then, *Stardust* was by far the number one film magazine and Zeenat made sure she kept on the right side of the publication's proprietor. She was there at all his parties and she was available for any 'exclusives' we came up with. Which may be why *Stardust* spared her by soft-peddling when it came to covering her off-screen performances with various married men —including Sanjay Khan, who gave her a false sense of respectability and security by designating her 'wife number two'. The turbulent relationship finally ended in the lobby of the Taj Mahal Hotel, where a battered and bruised Zeenat was publicly humiliated by 'Abbas' (Khan's real name) and his socialite friends. It remains one of the most sordid and shocking incidents in the history of Bollywood. Had it occured in today's times, it would have made it to the front pages of our dailies. And Abbas would have been jailed for abuse and assault.

Back then, we were instructed to play it down. I called up Zeenat at home. It was rather late. She suggested a drive. I couldn't wait. She turned up in a chauffeur-driven, russet-coloured Mercedes (a gift from her stepfather) and we headed for Worli Sea Face. One of her eyes was shut, her face swollen, black and blue bruises were visible on her bare arms. But Zeenat was smiling. The car stereo blared 'I will survive', Zeenat threw back her head and laughed. 'Call that my anthem.' Well, Gloria Gaynor had already claimed it as hers, so had half the world's female population. It was apparent Zeenat was flying on something more potent than a pulped

112

psyche; she'd already consumed half a bottle of champagne. The remaining half was in the backseat, chilling in an ice bucket. We clinked flutes . . . the chauffeur headed out towards the Sea Face. We watched monster pre-monsoon waves crashing against the concrete parapet and felt perfectly in sync. This was the closest I'd got to female bonding at that point in my life.

I admired Zeenat for her fortitude under the circumstances. I wasn't sure whether or not she was manipulating me (she used to be pretty adept at that). Were we meeting as 'friends'? Or did she actually want me to write a sentimental, teary, girlie piece about the encounter? It wasn't specified. Like I said earlier, Zeenat's a clever girl—a pity that native intelligence let her down when it came to falling in love. Yet, in her prime, Zeenat's appeal was unmatched—sexy, confident, bright, successful. A trophy girlfriend, sadly, never quite making it to trophy wife. I met her after a gap of several years when we posed for the cover of *Society*—two forty-plus women who weren't embarrassed by the fact. She was polite, warm, correct, amusing—but something vital was missing. Self-worth. I met her again a couple of years ago. Gossip magazines had chronicled the years spent nursing her ailing husband (since divorced), virtually broke but undaunted. That evening, she looked stunning in a short, fitted black lace cocktail dress. One eye was considerably smaller than the other. The rough heel of Sanjay Khan's boot ground into it all those many years ago had left its permanent mark. As I'm sure it had on her soul, too. But the façade was intact. That's class. Or that *was* class. After her mother's death, something has obviously snapped in Zeenat's life. She seems adrift and anchorless as she floats around with an escort half her age, alienated from her peers, unwanted by her juniors.

113

It has been said that it is always the voice that eventually gives a person's background away. No amount of veneer is sufficient once the mouth opens and badly modulated, poorly accented words pour forth. That was Rekha all over—the original one, not the new, improved version. It wasn't her weight but her voice that had got to me, grating, harsh, coarse—the voice of an illiterate washerwoman. Today, the same person articulates her words with the finesse of a Hollywood diva who has taken expensive lessons from the world's most accomplished voice coach (which may be yet another way of describing Amitabh Bachchan). Rekha's transformation goes to show what a determined woman in love is capable of achieving if she puts her mind, heart, soul and body into the endeavour. The person one meets now is unrecognizable from the one who got off a train from Madras and pushed her way up. Stamina, grit, ambition, imagination and high intelligence contributed towards the make-over. Today's Rekha is a soft-spoken, soignée, sophisticated woman—at least when she's in public. Insiders insist the essential persona remains the same once she barricades herself behind the imposing doors of her white marble bungalow.

A few years after I left *Stardust* in 1980, I was asked to do a piece on Rekha. It must have been particularly sharp for I was told that she was miffed and hurt by it. The question of mollifying her didn't arise—our paths never crossed. Till one day, in the mid-Nineties, we were to be at the same place at the same time—Gautam Rajadhyaksha's studio. I could have left after finishing my shoot. I chose to stay on when I heard Rekha was expected post-lunch. Her entourage arrived—the advance party, as it were, carrying an enormous trunk filled with costume changes and accessories. She walked in a little later—simple white salwar kameez, no make-up (only meticulously-pencilled trademark eyebrows). For an instant, she froze at the sight of me, then recovered swiftly enough to whisper a low 'Hello . . . how are you?' I believe it was the presence of Avantika (my young daughter) that did the trick. Rekha turned to her and it was love at first sight for both of them. I saw another side to the ravishing actress as she visibly softened and chatted comfortably with Avantika (who, of course, was over the moon). Rekha gamely posed for several pictures with my daughter, shot a few with me, till she finally grabbed the camera out of Gautam's hands and insisted on clicking the two of us herself. This was another person altogether, girlish, skittish, warm and spontaneous. I haven't seen her since. But Gautam tells me she never fails to enquire after Avantika, who in turn continues to admire the woman regarded as an enduring icon of beauty and style by generations.

Rustic, ill-mannered and uncouth is what I found the late Sanjeev Kumar. This may come as a shock to those who identified him with his screen presence which was that of a polished, sensitive gentleman incapable of anything low or distasteful. Sanjeev Kumar after a few drinks was an animal capable of rowdy showdowns and abusive shenanigans. Uma Rao and I were unfortunately exposed to this awful side of the great actor's personality when we accepted a dinner invitation at his suite during an international film festival in Delhi. We watched in horror as he steadily knocked back one whiskey after another. The others present were obviously accustomed to it and carried on like they hadn't noticed his slurred speech and glazed expression. Uma and I decided to get out of there as quickly as possible. I excused myself to go to the bathroom to wash my hands. I sensed someone right behind me. Looking up in the mirror above the sink I saw our host's face leering stupidly. I turned around calmly, expecting him to step aside and let me pass. He stood there like an obstinate ox blocking my way, his voice that of a grain-seller . . . a shopkeeper . . . his choice of words disgustingly crass. Finally, with one small shove, I pushed him aside and found Uma standing a few feet away waiting for me. We rushed out without saying goodbye to the others. It was not just distasteful but disillusioning as well. A man both of us had greatly admired as an actor had behaved like the worst kind of boor. It was the degenerate nature of his voice that lingered long after I'd forgotten his exact words. If I'd had to hear that same voice from behind a screen, I'd have associated it with a man born on the wrong side of the tracks—an underprivileged, uneducated, frustrated labourer, not a refined, gifted actor whose very presence on screen spelt restraint and respectability. So much for illusions.

There were star bores and star whores—after chronicling their tinsel lives for a few years and moving the office to swankier premises (a converted flat in a residential building at Foreshore Road in South Bombay), the old familiar restlessness was beginning to creep in once more. By then, Nari Hira was spending very little time in India, only the obligatory six months carved up into two-month packages. He spent half a day at *Stardust* mainly going over business matters and financial statements with the accounts people. We knew he read each and every manuscript scrupulously before we sent it off to the press, but there wasn't enough time for face-to-face discussion or comment. When in doubt, we sent telexes (those were pre-fax days) and waited for instructions. Life was difficult without 'daddy' to hold our hand. It was still an amateurish operation despite huge jumps in circulation. There were troublesome lawsuits to deal with—several summons to appear in the police court next to my old college, St. Xavier's, as 'Accused number one'. Yes, Nari Hira had competent lawyers to keep our necks from swinging. And after the first five appearances, there was no embarrassment left. I would present myself in court and stand around with underage prostitutes, seasoned pimps, pickpockets, even shackled men accused of murder. We'd be around long enough to hear our case number being called out and the adjournment date given. It was the old waiting-it-out game. Sooner rather than later, busy stars would lose interest in the case, get fed up of seeking exemption from personal appearances, and withdraw. The lawyers would collect their fees for doing precisely nothing and it would be back to business as usual. If my family felt shamed by any of this, it wasn't articulated. After a point, I stopped informing them altogether, unless the case got high-profile enough to make the tabloids—as it happened when Raj Kapoor sued us for a critique of his ambitious film *Satyam Shivam Sundaram*. After watching a preview, we ran a two-pager titled 'Satyam Shivam Boredom'. Incensed by our prejudgement of his magnum opus (it starred a scar-faced Zeenat Aman in a micro-mini version of a saree, worn without a blouse or any undergarments) and possibly worried about its commercial prospects being adversely affected, he sent *Stardust* a notice claiming an apology along with damages. As was Nari Hira's standard practice, he refused to oblige and the case went to court. Nothing happened. Everybody soon forgot about it. And the film was a modest hit.

*

Initially, I'd find it strange that the same people whose lives we'd ripped apart, whose sentiments we'd often hurt, whose reputations we'd shredded, were ready to extend party invitations and grant interviews to the staffers they were supposed to be at war with. How could anybody forgive so easily? Apparently Dharmendra couldn't, since it was he who decided to break the cosy pact between maligned stars and reporters by almost assaulting Devi at a public rally. There was probably a history to it, but the version that appeared in the press made a martyr out of the columnist and had the sloshed-to-the-gills actor chasing a helpless woman and threatening to kill her. Despite its provocative contents, nobody from *Stardust* was similarly threatened—a fact that amazes me to this day, given the number of rude names we'd coined, including one for Devi's attacker: 'Garam Dharam'. There was 'Asli ghee' for Yogeeta Bali (a dig at her ample proportions), 'Idli' (for Hema Malini, who vastly preferred the studio-approved 'Dream girl'), 'Bengal tigresses' (for Sharmila Tagore and Raakhee), 'Jaani' for the eccentric Raaj Kumar, and so on.

It was the time when Rajesh Khanna ruled, and hardly an issue passed without gossipy stories revolving around his love life. The surprise announcement of his wedding to the sixteen-year-old *Bobby* star, Dimple Kapadia, took the film industry off-guard while The Phenomenon's fans all over India threatened suicide. It was the scoop of the decade which left two devastated women in its trail—Devi and Anju, to say nothing of his heroines like Mumtaz ('Mumu' to *Stardust*) who went into mourning.

It was around this time that we set up a British edition of the magazine to cater to the sizeable Indian population in the UK and America. I was visiting, but it was more a holiday than an official trip. The office informed me that Rajesh Khanna was there with his young bride, staying at the Hilton nearby. We called him up and asked them both over to the mews house that functioned as an office-cum-residence. We didn't expect him to accept so swiftly, given that we'd been running some pretty juicy stories about his past. He surprised us all by showing up on time dressed in an ill-fitting denim suit—without Dimple. It was the first time I was meeting the superstar. I stared at the shortish, fattish, exceedingly pink and pimpled person shivering in the cold outside and thought to myself, 'My god! This is Him? That's it?' He was cute all right, but not impressive, and much smaller than he appeared on screen. He also seemed nervous without his usual retinue of hangers-on. I invited him in and asked Bertram, our man in London, to fix him a Scotch and water. We exchanged quick reactions at the bar. 'He resembles a Gurkha,' I said. Bertram kept his expression impassive as he handed Khanna a drink with a friendly, informal and very Goan, 'Here men . . . have a drink, cheers.'

Four doubles and two hours later, Rajesh showed no sign of leaving. We'd run out of conversation—there hadn't been much to begin with. I stood up and brightly suggested a walk. Bertram glared at me. It was freezing and wet outside. 'Where? At this hour?' I mentioned Hyde Park which was round the corner. Rajesh Khanna got to his feet rapidly after draining his drink in two quick gulps. He wasn't carrying a coat. I didn't possess one (and I was clad in a chiffon saree). Bertram struggled into his coat and said, 'C'mon, men, let's go and all.' Maybe Rajesh was relieved. It couldn't have been much of an evening for him. He hadn't made a single reference to his bride cooling her heels at the hotel. We stepped out into a damp cold night. After walking ten paces I turned to him and said, 'Shall we call for a cab?' That was Bertram's cue to offer to fetch one from outside the Churchill's Hotel. 'Wait here, men, I'll get it,' he said and bounded off. Five awkward minutes later, he turned up triumphantly and bundled Khanna into the cab. Just as well he did, or India's number one star may have frozen to death on that chilly sidewalk alongside a cheeky editor dressed for an Indian summer.

Women continue to fall in love with Rajesh Khanna even though he is no longer the crinkly-eyed god of *Aradhana*. Intelligent women. What is it about the man that fascinates women so? I've had a beautiful, besotted, artistic socialite sitting in my drawing room and weeping over her unrequited love for the ex-phenomenon. I asked her what she saw in him. 'He's complex, paranoid, secretive and sadistic,' she rhapsodized. 'He gives women hell. He makes them feel unloved and insecure. He is mean with money. And entirely selfish.' I stopped her. I got it. In other words, he has all the qualities that make men irresistible.

When I meet Dimple, his ex-wife, nowadays, I search her expressive face for clues. I imagine I can see scars. She is wounded, I tell myself. She escaped. She was lucky. Their break-up was expected. Nobody commented on it when it happened. They're still officially married to each other. They have two lovely daughters and the d-word (divorce) is never mentioned. Maybe neither needs it now.

Amitabh Bachchan is equally complex but far more sophisticated. Rajesh Khanna and he have several traits in common—reticence amongst them. Amitabh is a low-impact guy. You notice his voice, his eyes and then the aura takes over. It's the aura of success that transforms the most ordinary of individuals into larger-than-life beings. Amitabh wears his very well. Or used to, till his career and image hit a downslide. Be that as it may, he's still a cut above Khanna. But then Khanna was never a part of the Nehru-Gandhi coterie. He was only an inner city boy who made good. Amitabh came as a package with all his antecedents clearly marked on it. Well spoken, well read, urbane and suave, he was the sort of man who'd be comfortable in the world's salons. Not Rajesh, with his innumberable hang-ups and self-doubts. Both men flopped in politics—Amitabh got out prematurely, Rajesh hangs in there for want of a better career option. Rajesh is marked by a persecution complex he doesn't bother to disguise, Amitabh by his studied silence. The one thing they do have in common is their aloofness. Rajesh may be 'kakaji' to his hangers-on, and Amitabh may gamely put up with fawning socialites dying to be seen dancing with him in public, but nobody back-slaps these two or acts familiar with them. It's important for even fading superstars to maintain a distance if the mystique is to be preserved.

I've found my few and brief meetings with both of them interesting. The last time I spoke at length to Mr Bachchan was when he was projecting himself as a hounded, helpless, marked man with faceless enemies who were out to get him. After years of 'banning the press' (whatever that silly phrase means), or the press banning him, he had started courting any and every pen-pusher in town. Some were so overwhelmed by his attention, they were honoured to carry his explanations without so much as a counter question. Others just keeled over and died at the sound of his voice asking for them over the phone. Little did they know or care that his press relations exercise was part of a well-planned strategy, given a host of issues that he was grappling with at the time. He'd worked out his appeal to the last detail, shrewdly figuring that minor reporters in small-time papers would be his slaves for life after receiving requests issued in the famous baritone. He was right, of course. They're still around, faithfully standing up for their hero as he battles to save what's left of both his tattered career and battered empire, stupidly referring to themselves (in print) as Amitabh's 'friends'. Little do they know that men like Amitabh and Rajesh don't have friends—only docile devotees, and obsequious hangers-on.

I wasn't expecting a call, but when it did come it was from a veteran film publicist, Gopal Pandey, who paused dramatically after saying, 'Madam . . . Mr Bachchan would like an appointment with you.' I thought that was slightly precious. I mean, here's a guy one has known for as long as he's been in the movies. A man who appears almost 'normal' by moviedom's bizarre standards. Why the hell couldn't he have made that call himself? You know—just picked the phone, said 'hello' and then taken it from there? One strike against him. But a bigger one against myself for assuming he'd be a regular sort of chap given his background. Bollywood leaves its ugly mark on everybody and everything—why should the most successful star of this generation have been spared? Why should Amitabh have been any different? Because he'd studied at a good school? Been to college? Belonged to a 'good' family? It doesn't work that way—not in movie biz at any rate.

The day was fixed. Unfortunately the appointment coincided with the first day of my kids' vacations. I was in the midst of shutting shop, closing down the house for summer, before taking a plane the same night. It was also my daughter Radhika's birthday. All in all, not the most auspicious of times in the Dé household. The man was running late, which I was assured was unusual for him. Not that the assurance helped. I had far too many unfinished jobs to attend to and the tension was getting to me. Gopal called at regular intervals to keep me informed about Amitabh's precise location along the long route from his residence at Juhu to mine in South Bombay.

The big moment arrived nearly two-and-a-half hours behind schedule. He seemed awfully self-conscious, almost awkward, as he tucked in his long legs before settling into one of the stuffed chairs in the living room. Long pause. Throat clearing. Forced smiles. No eye contact. My husband (who had known Amitabh in his pre-moviestar avatar) joined us and the atmosphere lightened up a bit with ha-ha, ho-ho, guy talk about the good old Calcutta days. I could hear a growing buzz right outside our front door. The domestics were in quite a tizzy, giggling and peeking from a safe distance. The children were cross, the birthday girl furious, and I was distinctly worried. One of the two refrigerators had been emptied out and the one that was running had nothing in it except leftovers. I didn't know what I could offer the big star besides swigs from the bottles on the bar. But I already knew he didn't drink—officially, at least. Once we were through with coffee and the conversation was beginning to sound absurdly stilted, I was tempted to yell, 'Come to the point—and fast.' This was no social visit—he knew it, I knew it. There was obviously an agenda but Amitabh was taking far too long to raise it. I don't know who brought up the B-word (Bofors). Perhaps it was my husband, but once that had been uttered, the man found his tongue and launched forth. Nothing I hadn't heard or read before. He had a prepared spiel. He knew his lines. He played the part of a marked man convincingly enough. It was a bloody good performance—but just that, a performance.

By now it was well past lunchtime. The children were hungry and angry. I looked at my watch significantly and turned to Bachchan. 'There's nothing to eat at home except for a packet of frozen samosas. Aren't you famished?' Without missing a beat he replied, 'Frozen samosas are fine by me.' There, I'd done it. Talked myself into a spot. I thought Radhika would burst into tears. The crowd waiting to see Amitabh was getting restless outside. The servants were embarrassed. '*Itney badey hero ko siraf samosa khilaingey?*' they demanded. I snarled, 'Get on with it,' and rejoined the men.

By the time he got up and left (I noticed he hadn't asked to use the bathroom even after drinking three glasses of water and two cups of coffee), my children weren't talking to me.

The gawkers in the landing near the lifts went berserk. He was gracious enough to sign several autographs. He'd been awfully gracious with our domestics too, willingly posing for photographs with them. When the prints arrived, the children's bai, Beena, looked at the picture of her standing an inch away from a man she considered a demi-god and shook her head sadly. 'Nobody in our village will believe me.' 'But you have photographic proof,' I pointed out. She remained sceptical. Sure enough, on our return from the vacation, she told me the villagers had laughed at her claim and scoffed, '*Trick phootu hai yeh.*'

But Mr Bachchan's visit had raised our staff's consciousness and standards. When lesser stars came over in subsequent years, they refused to pose with them saying, '*Bahut chaalu hero-log hain . . . joker log, hamey nahi chahiye.*' I felt bad on behalf of the guys who didn't qualify.

Then came the Urmila Matondkar incident. I still blush at the memory. She and I were on a panel of judges for a prestigious beauty contest. Hema Malini was also present, playing queen (it comes very naturally to her). I was enchanted with young Urmila especially since I had seen *Rangeela*, her big hit, twice over and loved her spontaneous performance in it. Being a fellow-Maharashtrian definitely helped. We must have behaved very rudely, ignoring the other judges on the panel and chattering away in Marathi. 'Where did you buy your contact lenses? I love the colour. It looks so natural,' said the bubbly young actress, innocently looking deep into my eyes. It broke my heart to tell her I wasn't wearing lenses, sorry, she'd have to shop around some more. I asked her if she'd consider coming home after the show. 'My children adore you,' I gushed. Well, that's the impression they'd given me.

She was game. The function ended around 10.30 p.m.

Urmila was to go off to a nightclub with friends after saying 'hello' to my kids en route. I thought I'd warn the family—just in case. I borrowed her cell-phone and called ahead. My husband was indifferent. I thought the kids would be delighted. I knew the maids were delirious. When I rang the doorbell, I could barely recognize the girls who worked for us—they'd hastily donned their gaudiest salwar kameezes, plastered their faces with talcum powder, pushed their feet into plastic heels, fixed their hair into trendy bangs and were out there grinning like crazy.

Urmila is only a little girl—not much older than my daughters. I was treating her as such. Chirpy, cheerful, chatty and natural, I'd liked what I'd seen of her during the show. 'Where are the kids?' she asked enthusiastically. I looked at the maids. I could tell something was slightly amiss from their strained expressions. 'Sleeping,' said one. 'Fine,' declared Ms Matondkar, 'let's go see them in their room. I'll wake them up.' She strode purposefully behind the shuffling maids and walked in. I noticed Radhika had abandoned her own room and had snuggled under the covers with the little ones. Three sleepy faces stared irritably at the ravishing actress smiling at them from the foot of the bed. I heard Anandita moan, 'Mama—we're sleepy. Please switch off the lights.'

Urmila cooed, 'Hel-lo. Yoo-hoo. Hi. I'm here. Do you want my autograph?' Radhika scowled and pulled the covers over her head. Anandita waved us all away but not before mumbling a polite 'good-night, good-night.' Only Arundhati remembered her manners. She struggled out of bed and made a show of being at least interested if not exactly impressed. Urmila looked crestfallen. I was devastated. And angry with my horrible children for snubbing a very charming young lady who'd come home at my urging to meet them. Once again, I found myself in a fix—and turned to the maids to salvage the situation. They obliged by fussing over Urmila and begging to be photographed with her. I vowed never again to expose a star to my celebrity-immune family. It was far too humiliating an experience—not for the movie people, maybe, but for me.

I was often asked during my *Stardust* days whether it was possible for journalists and the movie people to be friends. No. It isn't. I don't know how it works in Hollywood but out here it's pretty clear—the only apt description for a reporter who hangs around heroes/heroines after hours is 'chamcha'. It is a neat little arrangement which involves trade-offs—for every positive bit of publicity, the writer is given further access besides a token gift during Diwali. If the relationship gets any closer, the stakes are raised. Most magazines evolve a list of 'untouchables'—stars on the favoured list. New reporters are subtly told to lay off. No nasty item appears on them, in exchange for 'exclusives'. These 'scoops' are jealously guarded from rivals, with much cloak-and-dagger plotting—all for an idiotic story that asks rhetorical questions like 'Is so-an-so two-timing such-and-such?' The answer is known to all (readers included) but it has to be presented as an earth-shaking revelation.

Movie people are incapable of 'normal' feelings—loyalty, friendship, caring. But they get pretty good at faking them. Wide-eyed young people who walk into magazine offices overwhelmed at the thought of actually meeting their idols, often fail to recognize the in-built manipulation of the system. They learn soon enough, and become equally heartless themselves. And that's the only level at which these wobbly relationships can work. Selfish, self-absorbed stars have no time for those pen-pushers who don't play ball. The same journalist who deludes himself/herself about 'closeness' to an industrywallah then goes into a tailspin of depression when the same 'close friend' snubs the person in public, either because the poor fool is now jobless or has moved out of a mass-circulated magazine to a smaller one.

At *Stardust* such friendships were discouraged. It was one thing to gain the confidence of a reclusive star, another to get cosy enough to actually start liking the person sufficiently to spare the victim during a controversy. If the stars had no scruples about exploiting gullible journalists and planting stories, it was hammered home to staffers that they didn't have to spend sleepless nights over a broken confidence either. 'If it's a secret, don't tell me,' was the rule. 'Nothing is off the record,' was another. Once the ground rules got established, the rest was easy. Stars often screamed 'betrayed', but it was more a token protest than a real grievance. It used to astonish me how rapidly they kissed and made up after a major misunderstanding . . . If the stars were a thick-skinned lot, the writers weren't all that better. Night after night, the stars would hang out at their garish bungalows, drinking made-in-India Scotch at some harassed producer's expense, and bitch about those absent in the hope that the interloper in their midst (the journalist) would pick up the plants and obligingly run them in the next issue.

Since we had a predominantly female staff at *Stardust*—girls from 'good' families—it was understood they they wouldn't have to get into the night-prowlers act. The code of behaviour was equally well-defined. No gifts, no favours, no deals. Star-secretaries (the scum of the earth) were discouraged from soliciting plugs and were rarely entertained in the office. This surprised the industry initially—most of the other publications had 'routinized' the 'packet-system': specified amounts of cash slipped into marked envelopes and passed on to reporters on a regular basis. So it was Rs 250 for a one-paragraph mention of a new film and thousands for a well-timed cover.

Outdoor locations were where the real 'lafdas' took place—between the leading actors, between journalists and stars, between heroes and buxom extras, between director and heroine. The permutations and combinations were endless. It was almost inevitable given the exotic settings—hill-stations where there was nothing to do after the day's pack-up was announced, beach resorts and foreign locales free of prying eyes. Journalists who went along on these junkets came back with enough material to fill three bumper issues. The Seventies were a time when people still got scandalized by stories of married heroes seducing co-stars. Now the question of star morality has been oddly redefined. When an affair is reported these days, the sexual inclinations of the protagonists have to be specified. Gay relationships still remain in a slightly grey zone, but there is enough innuendo to make the preferences perfectly plain.

It is a well-known fact that stars are amongst the stingiest and meanest of people. The more money they make, the faster and tighter their fists close. They quickly get accustomed to other people picking up their bills—even if it's for throwaway amounts like the cost of a cold drink or a packet of cigarettes, the producer has to pay. And it is the spot-boy's job to ensure his star need never reach for his wallet. Those in the big league travel without a paisa on them. Heroines move in packs, with as many as six hangers-on in their entourage—suites, room service, chauffeur-driven cars, travel bills . . . even crates of booze are billed to the producer. If he protests, the leading lady reports sick for days, maybe months. She starts showing up later and later on the sets. She sulks in the make-up room, forgets her lines and insists on countless takes. The producer gets the message soon enough—it's cheaper to give mummyji and her baby whatever they ask for in the long run.

The movie business is freebie territory. Someone somewhere is stuck with the tab. But nobody asks. Nobody wants to know. When *Stardust* brought in the no-freebies culture into the game, it was greeted with suspicion and cynicism. Several attempts were made to woo Uma, Ingrid, Vanita, with goodies—but it has to be stated to their credit that they consistently refused. There was an incident revolving around a soft loan given by Rekha to one of them when she was short on cash while buying a suburban apartment. Rekha was present at the housewarming party which I had attended. I didn't believe that a deal had been struck. If money had in fact changed hands, it must have been on a no-strings-attached 'friendly' basis. I'd like to continue to think that.

Considering these girls were young and attractive, didn't they go the way of other young and attractive pen-pushers, given their proximity to good-looking heroes? I did hear a few whispers now and again—of Dharmendra chasing one of them round the table, of Shatrughan Sinha spreading malicious stories. But nothing really stuck. Such was the credibility of both, the magazine and the staffers. The stars certainly didn't accept the pot-shots with grace. But an uneasy truce was reached after the first two years. They hated us in private but co-operated in public. No attempt was made by either side to get more intimate.

At the only film party I recall attending at Shankar B.C.'s residence (he had one every three days) I remember meeting Devi dressed in trademark white. She took me aside to say (in Marathi) about herself, 'My body is like alabaster—milk white. I have the most beautiful hands in the film industry.' She held them out for inspection—they were beautiful, with manicured nails, several rings. She let on that Dilip Kumar fell in love with Saira Banu because Saira's hands resembled her own. With her paan-stained mouth, fair skin, curly strands of hair and voluptuous figure, Devi was irresistible to some men. It was her practice to hold court at parties, often sabotaging the host's efforts by staging a parallel soirée of her own in one corner of the lawn or bungalow. Devi's durbar attracted all sorts—she was a high-profile star in her own right, unlike our schoolgirlish reporters speaking 'convent' English to all the 'Punjab da putters' who couldn't tell a compliment from a slur.

Stardust photo-sessions established a new tradition of commissioned shoots. Most magazines then were happy enough to publish stock shots. Since we did not have a staff photographer on the premises, special assignments were forked out to freelance photographers. One such involved Jaya Bachchan. It was decided to give the goody-goody 'Guddi' a new look. Risqué gowns with long slits, monstrous wigs, heavy-duty false eyelashes, high heels, the absolute works. She was game. The photographs were shot in Nari Hira's terrace flat, with Jaya contributing ideas enthusiastically. It was a dramatic departure for the actress who had built her image around looking like the submissive behenji next door.

I've always maintained Jaya is a remarkably shrewd woman. In her case, what you see is definitely not what you get. The world stops at the surface—wholesome, non-threatening, plain. Sure, she has acquired a personality but one could still pass her on the street and not look twice. Hers is a carefully cultivated 'image'—the homegrown, sensible, mature woman stuck in a superficial, flaky world. Of the two (Amitabh and Jaya) she is the smarter, more ambitious, fiercely motivated partner. The façade is misleading. Jaya is as tough as they come—Hillary to Amitabh's Bill. Nobody can push this little lady around—not even her husband. She has her priorities worked out and she plans ahead. Jaya would love to replace Nargis as the first lady of cinema. Chances are, she'll succeed too. I enjoy her candour and complete naturalness. Jaya doesn't bother with diplomacy or tact—she doesn't need to. She believes in telling it like it is—take it or leave it. Most people in the film industry take it.

But the photographers' darling remained Zeenat Aman who, with her modelling background, handled shoots with the ease of a professional, her body language communicating effortlessly with the camera. For one of the early Annual issues, she posed with the pigeons outside the Taj Mahal Hotel on a windy, rainy day, the dull light adding an extra dimension to her dusky complexion.

It was around this time, when Zeenat mania was raging, that a Marwari businessman I vaguely knew fell madly in love with her. Every evening he'd call and badger me for an 'intro' (as he put it). I'd tell him the same thing each time: find someone else. Once he got back from London bearing what he imagined was the perfect gift to impress her with—an enormous, signed Lalique vase. 'Will she like it? Accept it?' he asked eagerly. 'Send it across and find out,' I suggested.

He set up an elaborate plan which involved his chauffeur, who had to be given an inducement to keep his mouth from opening in front of 'bhabiji' (the tycoon's overweight wife). The man acquired a heavy silver tray, placed the vase on it, decorated the gift with sprays of imported orchids, enclosed a discreet embossed card and sent it to Zeenat's seaside address. He waited near the phone. Days went by, weeks, months. Nothing. I still don't know what happened to that vase. Did the chauffeur flog it? Did Zeenat's maid receive it and forget to tell 'madam'? Had Zeenat even noticed the arrival of a great big vase in her cluttered home and decided to keep it without bothering about a 'thank-you'? The man was devastated and disillusioned. Years after the incident he found himself on a flight from Calcutta and noticed Zeenat sitting with her then boyfriend, a Canadian lighting technician, a few seats away. Incensed at the sight of the ingrate, he started talking about her in loud tones, cursing her for not saying 'hello' after retaining his swanky gift. Zeenat played deaf and dumb. Convincingly for once. Stupid man. It was an expensive lesson, and he learnt it the hard way. She probably thought she'd done her admirer a favour by accepting something she hadn't asked for in the first place. Besides, where was the question of saying 'hello'? The identity of the sender meant nothing to her. And what was a Lalique vase to an actress who by then had been romanced by a besotted suitor who'd bought her an apartment in London as their love nest?

Most movie stars are uncouth, coarse, small-minded egotists. People deal with them at their own peril. So long as you expect nothing from the association, your sanity is unthreatened. Those who dare to go beyond that invisible barrier end up disillusioned and shattered. It's not as if *Stardust* didn't goof up or carry naughty stories that turned out to be false. There are innumerable examples of the magazine having been completely wrong. So, were apologies printed? Rarely. It was simpler to work out a deal. For every nasty reference that appeared in print, future issues tried to compensate with puff pieces. This mollified most of them. Public memory being astonishingly short, nobody really had the time for corny star scandal once the initial interest had waned. In time, the more intelligent of the stars realized as much and taught themselves to ignore barbs. On our part, we trotted out a rehearsed speech (we were well tutored by Nari Hira). The defusing strategy rarely varied. Before the offending article hit the newsstands, a reporter would phone the star and issue a friendly warning. This was to prepare the person psychologically and to establish trust. 'Look ... I don't have to tell you, but I thought you should know that our next issue carries . . .' Since no deaths-from-shock occurred, it was assumed to be the best route to eventual peace talks. Stars were easy enough to soothe ... even manipulate into talking themselves further into a corner. 'I'm giving you a chance to put the record straight,' generally worked wonders. So did 'If we didn't want your version, would I be calling?' It was a neat trap, and most of them fell for it. For the magazine it meant another scoop, another screaming headline. For the stars, it ensured additional publicity.

After ten years and a hundred and twenty issues (not counting Annuals), I was ready to move on, without really knowing where. I was as uninterested in the movie world as I'd been when I first started. There was just no meeting ground. I didn't see more than four films a year. The stars were nothing more than printed names to me. Their love lives may have been amusing, but after a point it was boring to monitor just who was having it off with whom. The old restlessness had returned. I enjoyed interacting with colleagues, but putting the magazine together month after month no longer involved me. It was a job I was doing to the best of my ability. Often to win additional brownie points from the boss. That was it. I could have been the semi-anonymous editor of an engineering journal for all the difference it made.

Besides, Nari Hira was often away during times of crisis—like the clamping down of the Emergency, for example. And I was beginning to resent the responsibility of having to deal with tricky censorship issues without the authority to do anything in the matter. Editors of film magazines had decided to form an association to fight the new, draconian laws imposed by Sanjay Gandhi. Every single article, column and item had to be submitted to the chief government censor before publication. This was a tedious, nasty process, nothing more than a pathetic power game designed to browbeat and harass those of us who weren't 'co-operating'.

It was widely, perhaps even mistakenly, believed that Amitabh Bachchan was behind this move, given his closeness to Sanjay Gandhi. The editors collectively decided to stop writing about him—it was the only punishment possible under the circumstances. We met regularly in the Natraj Hotel on Marine Drive. Seniors like B.K. Karanjia and Gulshan Ewing presided, while I tried to take some interest in what I thought was a futile exercise (not the banning of Bachchan, but the other more important one of influencing the minister, Vidya Charan Shukla). The association decided to invite him to Bombay for a dialogue. Shukla was staying at the Raj Bhavan. I was nominated (along with Mr Karanjia) to escort him to the venue. I knew their reasons for sending me—as it turned out, the decision backfired horribly. Shukla was seated in the middle, with the two of us flanking him in the backseat. He'd glared at me malevolently after the introductions and snarled something unintelligible. In the car, as we cruised along Marine Drive, he turned to me abruptly and announced, 'We could hang you in a public square for what you are writing in *Stardust*.' It wasn't a joke. I smiled uneasily and asked him to elaborate. He turned his face, looked straight ahead and delivered a stern speech on social responsibility. B.K.'s expression was stiff and frozen. The fixed permanent smile I'd always associated with him had vanished. He looked visibly paler. We drove the rest of the way in stony silence. When we got to the Natraj, Shukla strode

134

out rudely and walked to the dais. He wasn't there to listen. There was no question of a dialogue. He thundered on about our 'irresponsible' writing and warned us of worse strictures to follow. Devoid of charm or even basic good manners, he was the face of the Emergency—autocratic, despotic, despicable. After he'd left, there was complete gloom. The directives were harsh and unrealistic. The chief censor had been instructed accordingly. His red pencil ran through eighty per cent of all submitted copy. Often, almost the entire issue had to be rewritten at the last minute.

Nari Hira closely monitored these developments from abroad and during his visits to India. Besides the toned-down contents of *Stardust* he had something else to worry about—a newsmagazine called *Peninsula* which was to be edited by M.J. Akbar. Everything was in place—the name registered, the staff (handpicked by M.J.) crowded into a single room at 'Advent', articles commissioned, and a dummy copy pasted together as a mock-up for ad agencies. It was to be a hard-hitting challenger to *India Today*. With a fiery, talented editor like M.J. at the helm, Nari Hira was confident of pulling it off as a commercially viable venture.

The atmosphere at 'Advent' had undergone a subtle change with the arrival of the intellectuals—Akbar and his handpicked team of young devotees, bright writers for whom Akbar was god incarnate. They'd look at him with eyes brimming over (Worship? Hate? Fear?) and hang on to his every commandment. If the rest of us felt downgraded, it was understandable—nobody took film journalism or film journalists seriously. We were the fringe people writing frivolous gossip. They were the real journalists who did important stuff like report on world issues, expose political scandals, interview ministers. They spoke in their own lingo and tried being 'nice' to us. The condescension was unmistakable. We'd enter the room and be 'tolerated' like simple people often are. The intellectuals would stop talking, regard the intruders with fixed, polite smiles and wait patiently for the person to get the hell out so they could get on with their serious journalism once more.

Peninsula was hastily aborted given the changed climate in the country. If Nari Hira regretted his decision to shut that particular shop, he didn't come right out and say it. Akbar and his loyal band left as quietly as they'd entered, with businesslike goodbyes and a murmured 'See you'. It was back to stars and bitching, gossip and 'items', movie talk for breakfast, lunch and dinner.

*

The first time I went abroad, it was thanks to Nari Hira. It had been a good year at *Stardust*, I was entitled to an annual bonus, like all the others. He called me into his office and asked, 'What would you rather have—cash or an international airline ticket?' It didn't take me more than a second to make up my mind. A return ticket to New York. I didn't care at that moment to get into details like—who did I know in New York? How would I manage once I got there? I wanted to go. Desperately. It was like a fantasy finally turning into reality and I jumped at the chance. I broke the news to my astonished parents. This one time I didn't seek their permission, I merely informed them of my decision. Perhaps taken aback by my obvious resolve, they didn't ask too many questions either. I didn't possess a passport. I didn't have the slightest notion as to what I'd be packing into my suitcase—why, I didn't even own a proper suitcase at the time. None of this mattered. I was going. And that was that. The ticket I had was a cheap discounted one on Sabena Airways, with a stopover in Brussels. I got the travel agent to throw in London (it didn't cost anybody anything) and I was all set, with just the official foreign exchange in my brand-new travel folder, a few traveller's cheques and boundless enthusiasm. I'd bought a dull green suitcase for myself and packed the most ridiculous clothes. Around the time I was due to leave, I'd met a New York-based Indian couple—academics who lived in Queens and taught there. They'd liked me enough to say they'd look after my initial stay, collect me from the airport and show me around. I'd also managed to locate an old classmate who worked with the Indian mission there. She too was generous enough to assure me I could have a camp bed in her tiny apartment which she shared with a batty Swedish masseuse. That was all the reassurance I required. I was young, inexperienced and had led such an over-protected life till that point, I wouldn't have known how to get from my home in Mumbai to Pune, 120 kilometres away, without a great deal of confusion and plain nerves. And yet, I was ready to embark on this long trip without having thought anything through. I'm surprised my parents let me out of their sight without a fuss. In their place, I would have been a nervous wreck. It does seem scary and reckless now. But back then, nothing could possibly have held me back.

I was clad in a hand-block printed Chamundi silk saree in jewel tones (I still have it) as I embarked on the flight, my eyes shining with excitement, my heart thumping in anticipation. And that's when I heard what still remains a compliment I cherish—it was so spontaneously uttered. Showing me to my seat, the Belgian stewardess whispered, 'You are the most beautiful woman I have seen in my whole life.' For a change, I believed her. And my spirits rose along with the sleek aircraft, as I saw my city, my old life, shrinking away into insignificance . . . nothingness.

I was far too excited to sleep. When I looked around, I spotted several other 'cheapies', mainly students going abroad for 'further studies'. I'd seen one of them at the airport, bidding a tearful farewell to a large gathering of family and friends. He must have been from a village in Saurashtra, going by the traditional way his aunts and uncles whose feet he was diving for were dressed. I'd been very moved by the sight of all the garlanding and feet-touching going on. On the plane, he seemed miserable as he continued to gaze out of the window, refusing all snacks and meals saying, 'Vegetarian, vegetarian'. He'd kept all his garlands on, sniffing the one made from dried sandalwood shavings. My heart went out to him. Temporarily, I forgot all about my own family—every member had been surprisingly calm and cool about the journey. Nobody had given me last-minute instructions. Nor had I left any contact numbers (I didn't have too many to begin with). Before leaving, I'd mailed letters to the professor couple and my classmate, giving them the flight number and arrival time at JFK international airport. Beyond that, I had no assurances nor confirmations.

A few better travelled friends had explained the basics of changing money (always at a bank, never at a money changer's). And I'd been warned about excess baggage—how much it cost. Someone had told me about stopovers—airport shuttles, souvenirs (you paid), meals (you didn't) and phone calls (you paid). With these rather basic instructions, I nearly fell out of my seat as the aircraft began its final descent. What I saw below was everything I expected 'abroad' to be—dull, yellow halogen lights had transformed Brussels into a land straight out of Disney. Summer lighting added to the warm glow by casting a pale golden haze over the city. It was close to 9 p.m. but the sky was still very light with shell-pink streaks across it. I was enchanted. Yes. I was here. I was on foreign soil. My adventure was about to begin.

It nearly didn't. Rather, it started off somewhat disastrously by my not being able to locate a baggage trolley. Dragging my brand-new suitcase to the bus shuttle proved to be awfully unwieldy, what with my saree, worn fashionably low, sweeping the terminal and getting in the way. I was attracting far too much attention—yet nobody offered to help. In those days (early Seventies), Europeans weren't accustomed to the sight of fluttering silk sarees, and my slow progress got far too many stares when what I really needed was assistance. I found the shuttle. Clambered on. So did the Gujarati student in his shiny, ill-fitting suit. Somehow, his presence reassured me. The other Indians were government officers on a junket—loud, aggressive, crude and rude. One of them asked me my name. I had no choice but to give it. He noted it down and passed it along to the others in his delegation. Nobody bothered to ask the Gujarati student, whose eyes looked puffy from all that pre-departure weeping.

We checked into a cheap downtown hotel with scruffy carpets, shabby curtains and nylon bedcovers. Even though I noticed its rundown state, I still loved it. My room overlooked a busy pedestrian plaza. The shuttle had driven through a magnificent square with old stone buildings illuminated by the same yellow lights. They had colourful flags on the roof, flying cheerfully in the breeze, while people sat around in informal cafés along cobbled streets leading from the square. The air was crisp and cool. I shivered more with the excitement of that moment than the slight chill in the air.

I wanted to go downstairs, stroll around and eat the waffles a roadside vendor was selling. But before that, there was dinner to finish, on the house. Part of the package. And the dining hall was about to shut. I went into a dismal, dingy room with mournful-looking waiters in stained uniforms.

There wasn't much of a choice, I guess, for those of us on the cut-rate plan. A large plate of beef with boiled veggies was placed in front of me. I saw the student (sandalwood garland still in place around his neck) staring glumly at his own place with identical slop piled onto it. He was repeating 'vegetarian, vegetarian' almost to himself, but nobody was paying the slightest attention. I decided to intervene by resorting to my broken, schoolgirl French. Two doddering old waiters rolled up and nodded. The student, too shy to look me in the eye, indicated his gratitude with a slight gesture of his hand. Minutes later, a platter of boiled haricot beans was shoved under his nose with the waiter saying firmly, 'Zees . . . vegetarian.' No arguments here. Take it or leave it. The student took it. The beans disappeared. I signed a voucher and ventured out.

Suddenly, I heard someone calling out to me. 'Rajadhyaksha, Rajadhyaksha.' Unaccustomed to being addressed by my surname, I turned around to see the government delegates grinning broadly. 'Rajadhyaksha,' their leader started, 'we are having a mind to go to a hot cinema . . . you are knowing?' It took me a minute to figure out what they were asking me. Another one added, 'Hot film. Hot cinema . . . you understand? Blue film . . .' I shook my head and fled. Minutes later, I saw them heading off determinedly in the general direction of the sleaze district just a few streets away. Going by the bright neon signs advertising 'Topless Girls,' 'SEX SEX SEX', it wasn't the best of areas for a young, unaccompanied girl to be hanging around in. Even I could sense that. After the waffle (I've never tasted a better one), I decided to go back to my room and get some sleep.

While asking for my key, I noticed a small crowd around the Gujarati student. A bunch of American tourists was talking to him, using sign language and basic English. Little old ladies were touching the garland around his neck and asking questions about the red tikka on his forehead. I overheard him saying, 'Holy. Holy mark. Sacred. Very sacred.' He held out the garland for the wonderstruck dowagers to smell. They did so before stepping back respectfully to marvel at this exotic object. 'Parents are giving,' said the student, wiping away a few tears.

'Oh. Isn't that sweet?' the women sighed. 'Don't feel so bad.'

'Parents giving and saying "farewell, farewell", "goodbye". I'm going away—four, maybe five years,' the student continued, holding out four fingers and then adding the thumb.

'Poor you,' the fattest lady in the group consoled him, 'you must feel so bad.'

The student sniffed some more.

Just then, one of the husbands in the crowd decided he'd had a bit too much of all that sniffling. 'How much?' he barked, fingering the garland.

The student snatched it back from his large pink hand and said, 'No. No. No. Parents giving. They're feeling bad. Praying, God's garland, spiritual. Holy.'

The man barked even louder, 'Fine. Just fine. How much? I'll give you ten dollars.'

The student wiped his eyes with the back of his hand and whispered, 'Twenty.'

The man didn't hear.

The boy spoke up, looking sheepishly in my direction, 'Twenty dollars . . . I'm giving for twenty dollars.'

The next minute I saw two crisp notes exchanging hands. The man who'd bought the garland swung it over his wife's head. She cooed with pleasure and attempted to kiss the student. I was stunned by what I'd seen and almost went up

141

to the fickle fellow to yell 'traitor'. Before I could absorb the incident, he'd melted into the crowd. For all I knew, he was joining the government officials at the cinema showing *Pussy Galore*. Anything was possible.

I got to my room feeling sad and disillusioned. I could barely sleep that night. I rechecked the hotel voucher and realized there was breakfast thrown in too. The next morning, as I ate my hard roll, drank lukewarm coffee and signed for the 'continental breakfast', I saw the government guys with the Gujju student, applying generous pats of butter on their rolls. One of them called out, 'Rajadhyaksha . . . you should have come with us last night.' The others waved—a bit too exuberantly. They were on their way to America on another flight. I was going to London. We said goodbye. The student avoided looking at me. I understood. Maybe he really did need those twenty dollars desperately, I told myself.

As I was preparing to check out, the accountant thrust a handful of bills at me.

'What are these?' I asked.

'Your friends. They have not paid. And now they've left. You pay,' he said belligerently.

'What rubbish,' I exclaimed, 'they weren't my friends.'

'Yes. But they are from your country—India. And they've gone away without paying.'

'But . . . but . . . didn't they have airline vouchers like the one I showed you?'

'No, no, no. Their tickets were different. Not the same plane.'

I shrugged. 'Too bad. It's not my responsibility. I don't know them. Never saw them before in my life. Sorry. But I have to leave—the coach is here.'

I dragged my bag across to load it on. I could hear the man at the desk grumbling angrily, 'Bloody Indians. Bastards.

Merde.'

It wasn't pleasant. At that moment, I felt ashamed about being an Indian . . . being associated with those cheapskates, being tarred by the same brush on account of my colour, my clothes. Perhaps it would have been wiser to stick to a more anonymous get-up. Jeans. Skirts. Years and years later, I discovered that the universal uniform had built-in hazards too. For me.

I used to agonize over the fact that I was the one invariably singled out for a body search everytime I travelled to Europe. 'Would you step aside, please?' became such a familiar request that often I found myself anticipating it and stepping aside seconds before being asked. At first, I thought it was the gold bangles I wore. Heck, every Italian in the queue (men included) had far more of the metal gleaming on his or her person. So, if it wasn't the gold, what was it? My husband once said irritably, 'The trouble is, you look like one of those hippies. Why must you travel in jeans?' I pointed out at least three hundred other jean-clad women at the same airport who were strolling through the immigration checkouts without a single 'beep'. We ruled out jeans. And then, just to please him (plus, prove a point), I started wearing salwar-kameezes or sarees. 'You look far too conspicuous, why must you stand out and attract the wrong kind of attention? They'll think you're a Pakistani drug runner.' Okay. Fine. I threw out my ethnic clothes. The next time round I wore a business-like trouser suit. 'Madam . . . would you step to one side, please?' said the burly policewoman. After the systematic search I walked through the metal detectors again. The 'beep beep' continued. My husband said, 'Take off the bangles. Stop wearing clunky jewellery . . . It's the expression on your face.' 'Sorry, mate. Nothing I can do about that. Nothing I want to either,' I sulked. And so it continued, irrespective of the fact that there were times I was tub-like in my pregnancies, clad in shapeless, nondescript tents.

Finally, in Frankfurt, when I was stopped for the zillionth time, I asked the woman conducting the body search, 'What is it? Why me? Why am I always stopped and searched?' She looked at me sympathetically, probably wondering whether or not to open her mouth. Then she said, 'You fit the computer profile of one of the world's most wanted fugitives—the terrorist Leila Khaled, who was responsible for the massacre of Israeli athletes. Remember the bombing of an EL AL jet at Frankfurt airport? Well, Leila Khaled has been on the run ever since. In your case, it all fits, the age, the appearance . . . so long as she's alive and not captured, take it from me, you'll be stopped. If I were you I'd start praying that she's tracked down soon . . . or declared dead.' Well, at least I now had an explanation. It didn't make me feel any better, but I understood why. That was enough. I told the story to my husband, feeling triumphant. As if to say, 'See . . . it had nothing to do with my jeans, my expression, my bangles.' He didn't seem too convinced.

In 1996 when we were travelling extensively through Europe and America, the 'beep beep' became something of a family joke. At a tiny Midwestern airport, when I actually went through a metal detector without incident, my younger children applauded, danced a jig and exulted, 'Yeah! Mama wasn't stopped', which wasn't the smartest thing to do. I half expected the well-muscled black mamas to drag me back for a strip search. Instead, they smiled indulgently and waved us off.

Landing at JFK International airport for the first time on that maiden trip would have been intimidating had somebody prepared me for the mini-township that JFK is. I'd probably have been more careful about not missing my flight from

Brussels and landing in New York without anybody to receive me. What had happened was that I had landed at the right terminal in Brussels at the wrong time to find that my flight had taken off hours ago. I'd sat down and wept, till a Sabena ground stewardess assured me there was another connection leaving six hours later. Never having travelled outside India before, I'd asked with tear-filled eyes, 'Does that mean I'll have to throw away this ticket and buy a new one? Because I don't have any money.' She'd assured me the ticket I was holding in my hand was good enough, she'd endorse it for the next flight. It was as easy as that.

But I hadn't thought of phoning and letting my friends in New York know about the change of plans. But then, they weren't as dumb as I. Naturally they'd phoned and found out. Which was why I was being persistently paged by an announcer who wasn't even tripping over my name. I felt important and very special each time I heard the message. And then, when I saw a beautiful ground staffer holding up my name on a placard, it nearly blew me away. It was a message from my school friend Saroj, telling me to call her for the exact address. 'Just jump into a cab and get here. It's all right. Perfectly safe. I'll be waiting.'

While getting out of the terminal, I spotted the professor couple and ran straight into their open arms. It was just the relief of it all. I hadn't wanted to jump into a cab. I was terrified. And there they were, with kindly smiles, ready to take me to their home. I called my friend from the professor's at Queens and said I'd see her the next morning when they'd offered to drive me into Manhattan. And that's what happened.

I fell in love with New York on sight. And have been in that condition ever since. I don't care what its critics say, there is just no other city in the world quite like New York. I love it unconditionally, including its ugly underbelly (which doesn't appear ugly to me at all—just fascinating). While driving to my friend's mid-town ground-floor apartment, I greedily gobbled up whatever my eyes rested on and couldn't wait to become a part of it, if only for a brief two weeks.

The Swedish masseuse didn't look delighted to see me. It was her apartment and my friend was a 'paying guest' (she shared the rent) with limited access and few facilities. In her cramped bedroom we managed to squeeze in an extra bed, plus my suitcases, watched balefully by the landlady and her ill-tempered tomcat. Not that I cared. I was just so happy to be there. The apartment was wonderfully located and everything seemed to be happening within walking distance. The weather was brilliant. And although I was broke—well, on a measly budget—I was flying, ecstatic.

My friend was warm and welcoming. I was touched by her affection and thoughtfulness. But equally wary of the woman in the next room, who kept the television set on all twenty-four hours because she was scared of silence. And yet, if she overheard us chatting happily, or if my friend received a phone call, she'd show her impatience and displeasure, snapping, 'Too much noise. I am getting a headache.' We crept around the place literally with our fingers on our lips. Whenever the masseuse had a client (not frequently enough) we were instructed to stay put in our room, or go out and return after a couple of hours. This woman resembled my image of the giant in the fairy tale of Jack and the Beanstalk. She was awful to look at and frightening too, with those bulging eyes, severe clothes, short-cropped, wispy blond hair and military walk. It was obvious she resented my presence. I decided to toughen my hide and hang in there regardless.

Strange, or maybe not so strange, I did not miss my home, my family, my job or my friends. Not once. I thought of them my family, my job or my friends. Not once. I thought of them distantly and felt completely remote from the world I'd left behind. During the first few days, I was fully prepared to say a cheery goodbye to it all, tear up my visa and stay on as an illegal immigrant—never mind my uncertain future, my shocked parents, my angry boss. This is life, I felt, as I strode briskly down those incredible avenues confidently, enjoying what I now realize are routine, meaningless compliments from total strangers. Clichés like 'Are you for real?' thrilled me when I first heard them. My ticket included a trip to Los Angeles, San Francisco, Montreal and back to New York. I really didn't want to budge out of Manhattan. I can easily count my stay there as being one of the happiest fortnights of my life.

My school friend had always been something of a depressive all the years I'd know her. Living with a batty Swedish masseuse had worsened her lows. But it was her sincerity and affection I'll never forget. With our limited budget, we still managed to get around quite a bit, including an evening at what was then a phenomenon that had America talking—the world's first singles bar which, contrary to popular opinion, was anything but a pick-up joint. Maxwell Plum was a great place to hang out in—the sort of place two young women could confidently walk into without feeling like hookers. I don't know how we had the nerve to check it out. But I do recall the absurd sense of bravado we affected as we took our places on high bar stools at the counter and tried to look terribly sophisticated, as if we did this kind of thing regularly. We left an hour later after making meaningless conversation with half-a-dozen yuppie types—very white, very WASP, and very indifferent. New Yorkers, I realized at that moment, are interested in other New Yorkers they can network with—not obviously touristy around, but not too many. They were mimicking white behaviour, language and dress, even though Black Power was terribly chic at that point. Afros, beads, clenched fists, one encountered these at streetside demos, but things were still at a stage where people regarded them as conversation pieces. It took over a decade for the aggressive, assertive black consciousness movement to finally come into its own. Back then a great deal of self-consciousness was evident, particularly in fancier clubs where blacks with big bucks flashed their newfound confidence (and affluence) while their less loaded white brothers glared or merely stared morosely. As someone who was neither white nor black, but a vague shade of brown, I belonged in no man's land, often mistaken for a 'real' Indian (read: red) or even a South American.

It was in New York that I was introduced to new flavours, new foods, new everything—from pastrami sandwiches at Jewish delis to submarines at the wharf. From spinach and mushroom quiches at The Brasserie to salad bars opposite the Plaza. Why, I even dared to stroll casually into what is rated as one of the world's finest hotels (the Plaza), disgracefully dressed in shabby Levis, with Bombay-made Hawaii rubber slippers on my feet. Nobody threw me out.

That's when I discovered one more thing about New York—nobody cares a fig about how anybody talks, looks or dresses—New York absorbs all sorts. You can be yourself—and take what comes with it. You can dress up or dress down. Walk into the plushest of theatres for an evening of opera or ballet, wearing jeans—it's your funeral. Some people find this casual attitude revolting. I think it's liberating. Nobody knows you. Nobody even wants to. You walk around like a slob, you get treated like one. That's about as bad as it gets. More often than not, you are completely ignored. There are far too many local weirdos around for anybody to bother with tourists in rubber chappals striding into the grandest of grand hotels. My big buy on this trip was a black T-shirt that cost fourteen dollars. I still remember the price—I'd found it outrageous. I still do.

There was fear on the streets then—and there is fear on the streets now. Only, I was immune to it. My blood didn't run cold even when I got lost in Harlem (of all areas) on that maiden trip, and the only explanation I have to offer is that I was far too naïve, trusting and in love. New York had got me under its spell, and I was too blinded by its amazing energy to think about its ugly (and dangerous) aspects.

That day, I was at least fifty blocks away from the address I had scribbled on a piece of paper. The first person I stopped to ask directions from was a huge black liveried chauffeur leaning against a menacing-looking stretch limo. He glanced at the paper and said, 'Look . . . you are in the wrong place. I mean . . . you shouldn't be here at all. This is Harlem. You know—Harlem?' I nodded dumbly. He tried again. 'The place you want to get to is a twenty-minute ride from here—understand?' I nodded again. He paused. Shut his eyes. He seemed to be in deep thought. Or making some quick calculations. Finally, he said, 'Aw . . . what the hell. C'mon. Hop in. I'll give you a ride.' And hop in I did.

He drove me to the right block, spoke to the doorman, handed back my crumpled piece of paper and before driving off, wagged a fat finger in my face and said sternly, 'Next time you get lost in Harlem, I may not be around to give you a ride. Like I told you—this ain't no place to get lost in. Now . . . you take good care of yourself, girl.' I thanked him profusely. But his message still hadn't sunk in. Nor had the potential consequences of my decision to get into a stranger's limo with its tinted glasses rolled up.

But I'd obviously not learned my lesson. A repeat was to

follow on my return trip via Paris. There I was in a long, flower-printed skirt (they're back in vogue) and T-shirt, wandering vaguely through the charming gardens next to the Louvre (the Tuilleries) when I decided to take a break on an inviting-looking bench. My feet were shod in soft white leather clogs (also in vogue now) which looked trendy enough but were rubbing painfully against my corns. I must have been more tired than I knew, for minutes later I fell fast asleep, right there on that hard stone bench with my handbag as a pillow. Perhaps two hours later, I was woken by raindrops on my upturned face. Disoriented and confused, I blinked a few times wondering where I was. My view of the sky was obscured by a bunch of curious faces staring at me. I was in such deep sleep that I still didn't awaken fully but continued to lie there lazily.

The rain was starting to pelt down. The four faces (one woman and three men) were honey-brown and beautiful. They started to laugh and indicated that I should make a run for it before all of us got wetter than dish rags. Someone held out a hand, I grabbed it, got to my feet and we ran together, making a dash for a parked egg-yolk yellow Beetle at a distance of a hundred yards. Without a word, I got into the car and we started to drive off. Nothing was spoken till this point. One of them asked me something in musical French. I shrugged and said in my own faulty, jerky French that I wasn't fluent enough to conduct a full-scale conversation. Lots of gesticulations and slow speech later, I discovered they were students from Martinique visiting family in a distant Parisian suburb. I had no real schedule . . . besides, I liked their laughter and unusual looks. I decided to go along with them for the two additional days I was going to be there.

It was one of my better decisions. That battered yellow Beetle took us everywhere—not to fancy restaurants or naughty nightclubs, but all over the incredibly beautiful city. Was I crazy to trust a group of absolute strangers in a city I myself was a stranger in? We didn't speak the same language, we had nothing at all in common, besides our youth, enthusiasm and energy. Why did I do it? There's a one-word answer to that—instinct. I knew when I ran towards their car that these people would never harm me. How did I know? It's hard to define. I'm a great believer in instincts and mine haven't let me down too many times so far. Call it a fine-tuned sixth sense or plain stupidity.

In the Seventies the word 'vibes' or 'vibration' was over-used to describe this quality. But it is possible to read signals and tell quite a lot from a person's eyes. I'm wary of those who don't level with me gaze-wise. A shifty-eyed individual becomes an instant suspect. Perhaps wrongly so on occasion. Maybe he or she is plain nervous. But I can't take that chance. I like interacting with people who are transparent—but not entirely. That would make them boring. Just transparent enough to figure out where a person stands, since I don't play games with anybody (what a wasteful exercise). I prefer it if the other person also cuts through the tripe and we can talk straight.

The Paris trip ended on a high note. I was finally ready to go home. I'd made new friends. Stayed in an artistic Parisian home with an old and charming Parsi couple. The only terrifying moment had come one night in their flat when a huge tomcat had decided to spend a couple of hours parked on my chest. He'd landed silently with a heavy thud. In my deep sleep, I thought I was being murdered . . . it was worse when I opened my eyes and looked into shiny, yellow ones glowing in the dark. I tried not to breathe, but how long could I hold my breath—a minute? Two? The furry black cat I'd seen on the window-sill earlier seemed all set to spend the rest of the night on my frozen-with-fright body. I dared not call out, afraid that would startle him and those sharp claws would gouge out my eyes. I lay this way for heaven knows how long—it seemed interminable. At some point during the night, perhaps spotting an inviting-looking mouse, the cat leapt lightly off my torso and disappeared. Whenever we go to Paris now I keep an eagle-eyed look-out for felines. Paris is full of the human kind—those I can handle. It's the real ones I avoid.

When I finally got back from my maiden trip abroad, I didn't reveal my adventures to anybody, least of all to my mother. I felt possessive about my memories. They were only to glad to see me back after several postponements, happy that I was safe. And they weren't being inquisitive. I felt I'd grown up a great deal during those eight weeks. Literally, seen the world—the West Coast, L.A., San Francisco, the mid-West, Aspen, Denver, Montreal, up North. Yes, it was quite a trip.

Since then, I have travelled to most of my dream destinations: Istanbul, Cairo, Berlin, Lisbon, Vienna, Seville, Jerusalem. There are hundreds more I'd like to visit—Buenos Aires, Rio de Janeiro, Stockholm, Beijing, Tokyo, Moscow. On each visit and in each place, I've watched, absorbed, learned. Not from museums or monuments (you can keep them) but markets and street corners. Ruins don't interest me. I have no feel for history. There's nothing romantic about fossils; give me a busy bazaar bursting with activity, a street-side café, a theatre, crowds, people, chaos, noise. And give me new foods to excite the palate. New textures, new smells, new colours.

Shining Through

Although I stayed out of the way of stars for the most part during my *Stardust* days, over the years I've encountered quite a few of them, some of whom I've written about in the previous chapter. There are some other stars I ran into who are worth mentioning for a variety of reasons.

Easily the most beautiful actress I came across during my magazine years was Parveen Babi. I can see her now as clearly as the first time, over twenty years ago, when she floated into my line of vision dressed in a soft white Grecian-style gown in floaty chiffon. Ravishing is an understatement. People compared her sex appeal to Zeenat Aman's, but I don't think it was a fair comparison. Zeenat was dusky, robust, buxom; Parveen, far more ethereal, fine-boned and soft. With her interesting background, lonely childhood and amazing looks, here was a girl who was clearly a misfit in the movies from the word go. She simply didn't belong to this crude, hard, vulgar world. There was a strange vulnerability about her, an uncertainty that added to her appeal. While Zeenat oozed confidence, Parveen seemed slightly lost and bewildered, even as she spouted philosophy, quoted from obscure books and claimed she wrote poetry. She wasn't your average 'filmi'. After her picture appeared on the cover of *Time* magazine (not for being Parveen Babi—she was randomly picked to represent Asian cinema), Parveen got to enjoy big league celebrity status—but not for long. Two men walked into her life and turned it upside down—Mahesh Bhatt and Kabir Bedi. I met her somewhere in between these two phases at her Juhu flat and was struck by the physical change. Though she was still breathtakingly beautiful, she looked ravaged. The expression in those lovely, soft eyes was distinctly crazed. I attributed it to the turbulence in her personal life. Bhatt was present at her flat and the two of them spoke in the then fashionable stream-of-consciousness style. Most of it was boring, derivative, garbled bilge. Recycled, borrowed philosophy which relied heavily on the Zen masters, Rajneesh, U.G. Krishnamurti and Marshal Mcluhan.

Subsequently, I heard Parveen had gone away after suffering a nervous breakdown. For years one didn't get any news of her, till she resurfaced one day in Bombay and began issuing bizarre statements in the press. I ran into her while she was shopping at the Taj sometime during the early Nineties and shrank from what I saw. Initially, I couldn't believe the woman examining fine fabrics two feet away from me was really Parveen Babi. This person resembled a bag lady—the body bloated beyond recognition, the hair wild and uncombed, the skin blotchy and spotted. And those doe-like eyes, two narrow sunken slits surrounded by unhealthy-looking flesh. I'd been told she had flipped to an extent where she now existed in a delusionary world, eating upto forty egg whites and raw lettuce a day, writing reams and reams about Amitabh Bachchan's plan to eliminate her. I'd received some of those 'press releases' which accused the actor of conspiring with the CIA/ Mossad/FBI/M15, any other agency you can think of, to kill her. Wild theories involving radiation, poison darts, killer waves through TV transmission—Parveen had covered them all. Even if the two of them had had an affair and then a falling out, her charges were those of a seriously ill person. She stared at me for a few seconds and seemed to switch off. I met her a year or so later—she seemed slightly more in control. Slimmer, certainly, and slightly more in touch with the real world. She said she was a successful interior designer and was planning to write a book. I confess I didn't take either piece of information terribly seriously.

Raakhee (remember her?) was another strange one—but oh-so-beautiful. Uma Rao had befriended the temperamental actress and was close to her. Close enough to persuade Raakhee to attend a *Stardust* dinner being hosted by Nari Hira at his terrace flat in mid-town Mumbai. She arrived like a coy bride, all downcast eyes and sidelong glances, a vision in pink lace, her face devoid of make-up, silky hair down her back and those incredible light eyes which had bewitched audiences in a string of successful films that very year. I was dying to speak to her and asked Uma to introduce us. Raakhee continued to stare at her toes wordlessly. I told her how beautiful she was. She grunted. I paid extravagant compliments. I thought she'd burst into tears. She was clearly uncomfortable in that setting. She wasn't there to socialize or make small talk even with her contemporaries. Raakhee had attended the party to please her journalist-friend. Having performed her duty, she was ready to leave and did just that. Today, when I see her wasted in meaningless cameos playing mother to men who can't be all that much younger, I feel exasperated. Rakhee, like several other actresses before and after her, threw it all away. She had looks, breaks and talent—yet, she didn't get too far. Some say it was drinking that did her in, others insist it was chronic depression and ongoing insecurity. What a pity.

What a pity, too, that Smita Patil's life ended as tragically as it did. While she wasn't a conventionally good-looking woman, Smita had presence and fragility. People reached out to her and she to people. Even though I wouldn't describe myself as her 'friend', we did have a rapport. And I found her screen persona compelling, completely devoid of any artifice. It was easy to see why so many people (of both sexes) fell in love with Smita—she inspired such emotion in those around her. Vulnerable, insecure and slightly off-the-wall, Smita had remarkably low self-esteem despite her success. She needed constant reassurance, mainly about her dusky looks—yes, the same looks the world admired. I suspect one of the reasons she 'married' Raj Babbar was to get over her own incredulity that a tall, fair, North Indian film star could fall for a dark-complexioned, imperfectly-featured Maharashtrian actress like her. She was flattered and overwhelmed, whereas it really should have been the other way around. While people wondered, 'What did she see in him?' she was still asking herself, 'What did he see in me?'

*

A couple of years ago, I attended an event (as opposed to a dinner). This one was major, with wall-to-wall mega celebrities packed into the Taj Ballroom. Several self-conscious legends were standing around wondering what to do next (it happens to supernovas stuck with a cluster of minor league stars). Right across the room was one such legend. Hema Malini. Regal, composed and radiant. She was still playing screen queen—and very convincingly at that. She'd altered her appearance dramatically, by abandoning the old South Indian amma look. No temple sarees for the 'new' Hema. She was dressed in chic black. It was when she turned around that Hema watchers gasped at the sight of her sexy, backless choli, held together by zig-zag strings. The hair was different too—streaked, treated, stylishly cut. The eyebrows looked a little weird, sort of plum coloured. The bharatanatyam eye make-up had been replaced by a more subtle, smudged 'cover girl' technique. Hema had always known how to do it right—even when she decided to make another woman's husband her own. Unwavering and unabashed, Hema went right ahead and listened to her heart, uncaring about the reactions. Strangely enough, she got away with her farcical 'marriage' to Dharmendra and didn't have to face even a squeak of criticism.

It has to be Hema's formidable personality. She's one lady nobody wanted to mess with, not even the most daring of her many heroes. She managed to create an image of herself as a proud Brahmin girl who was in the dirty business of movies almost by default when actually she should have dedicated her life to God and classical dancing. She wore sexy costumes on screen, danced provocatively and flirted outrageously when the scene demanded it. Yet, her reputation remained untarnished and chaste. She exited the industry with her head held high, even after the birth of her two daughters who had to be legally 'adopted' by their biological father, Dharmendra, since the marriage between him and Hema was not valid in the eyes of the law.

Women admired Hema for her 'courage'. She was seen as a person who refused to buckle under pressure, someone who went on with her life, ignoring convention and flouting society's rules—but quietly. The message she sent out was simple: What I do is my business. My relationship with Dharamji is of no concern to anybody else. I will live life on my own terms and be answerable to no one. Over the years, she has consistently maintained a dignified silence about her arrangement. She lives in her own home with her daughters and picks up all the bills. Her 'husband' lives with his family in a sprawling bungalow that also houses his wife's sons, their wives and his grandchildren. Hema leads a busy, productive life and looks perfectly contented. There hasn't been even a whiff of a scandal about her involvement with any other man in all these decades. She deals with her problems on her own without resorting to cheap tactics like involving the press in her affairs. Her references to 'Dharamji' are always affectionate, respectful and indulgent.

Others who have tried to follow in her footsteps (Sridevi comes to mind) have been far less successful, mainly because they've taken their private conflicts to journalists in the hope that by revealing their side of the sorry mess, they'll be able to mobilize public opinion in their favour and win the first round. It rarely works like that, as Neena Gupta will readily admit. For years, her daughter with Viv Richards was a dark secret, till Richards decided to make an honest woman out of Neena. Masaba, the little girl, who looks alarmingly like her West Indian father, must have to deal with all sorts of intrusive questions. Even though Neena had openly and boldly acknowledged Viv as the father of her child, even she found it necessary to bow to convention and formalize the affair with a marriage announcement.

There is something slightly tragic about these movie kids, forced to lead unreal lives and deal with pressures they can't always handle. When they do crack up, they crack up big, as Sanjay Dutt's life testifies. When I watch his clips on television these days, my heart goes out to this mixed-up, messed-up child-man with his doped-out good looks, sad, hangdog eyes, straggly hair and pumped-up biceps. The product of two high-profile, legendary stars from the Sixties, Sanjay grew up in a large home, surrounded by loving family members. And yet, there was a short circuit somewhere down the line, and the handsome young man nominated for instant stardom shot himself in his own feet, metaphorically speaking, when he got embroiled in the ugly aftermath of the infamous Bombay blasts of '93, a particularly shameful chapter in India's history. Powerful explosions flattened landmarks and devastated a metropolis that had long fancied its cosmopolitan image. Sanjay Dutt spent several months in jail waiting for the courts to grant him bail. It is up to him and the courts to establish his role in the conspiracy, but what it did indicate was the state of his troubled mind, and worse, his inability to cope. All sorts of explanations were put forward by friends of the family but drug abuse is the one that stuck, by Sanjay's own admission.

His erratic, unstable behaviour was rationalized by the press as being the result of parental absence. Sanjay's mother, the legendary Nargis, had died of cancer when he was an adolescent, while his father had dedicated his life to public service. Left to his own devices, this school drop-out fell into a familiar enough pattern starting with alcohol, cigarettes, late nights and drugs, culminating in the acquisition of automatic weapons from underworld kingpins. Despite a failed marriage, several stormy relationships and many shortcomings Sanjay was poised to join the ranks of top-drawer heroes. Dismissed by the critics as a wooden actor with two left feet which he tripped over in the mandatory dance routines required by commercial films, Sanjay still managed to get himself a commercial slot, signing films with the most successful leading ladies and attracting a considerable fan following in the bargain. It wasn't so much Sanjay's inexplicable rise to the top of the charts that surprised me (after all, Amitabh was no Adonis either), it was the reaction of the press that warranted closer examination. Traditionally harsh and unforgiving, in Sanjay's case, journalists *en masse* rallied to his defence and readily overlooked serious charges levelled against the actor by the police and the Central Bureau of Investigation.

Fortune favours the dumb—sometimes—and Sanjay has certainly emerged from his ordeal a very successful, very wealthy young man. Oh, but he's such a 'lovely' person, say those who've known him over the years. He must be. So very many unconditional, all-forgiving admirers can't possibly be wrong after all.

There are at least half a dozen star-kids and their kids running around Bollywood these days—a third generation of people brought up in the glare of studio lights. The sprightly Kajol comes to mind, with her lineage going back to grandmother Shobhana Samarth, who at eighty-plus will still not be caught dead in public without lipstick, high heels and long earrings. Young Kajol has resolutely turned her back on off-screen glamour, often appearing at glittering functions deliberately dressed down in drab clothes, her face devoid of any make-up, her springy hair uncombed, large spectacles sitting on her even larger nose. If this is her way of asserting her identity and defying the system, she sure is in a position to do it—like Julia Roberts in Hollywood. Kajol certainly ranks amongst the top ten actresses today and is regarded as someone who's in it for the long haul. With a string of hits to her credit, she has no reason to worry on the professional front. She probably figures her job is to deliver on screen and if audiences are willing to accept an attractive but far-from-beautiful actress who doesn't bother to tweeze her eyebrows or her upper lip and wears hardly any make-up while her rivals slap on the gook with a vengeance, Kajol is not about to compromise and glam up.

The first time I met her, she was sitting on Gautam Rajadhyaksha's lap in a darkened preview theatre. The film was *Bekhudi* and Kajol was wonderful in it, even if she did look unwashed and scruffy in a few scenes. There was a spontaneity and naturalness about her performance that reminded me of Audrey Hepburn in *Roman Holiday*. It was easy enough to see that a star was born that night even if the film bombed at the box office. Kajol was a complete natural—unaffected and at ease, such a welcome change from her over-made-up, synthetic looking contemporaries. She had neither conventional good looks nor an hour-glass figure. What she did project was an earthy, believable sex appeal. Her conduct off-screen was equally off-beat. Kajol obviously didn't believe in following the film industry's rules—or else she wouldn't have parked herself on Gautam's lap, even if he did treat her indulgently like a fond father.

The next time I ran into her was once again with Gautam, at his residence-studio. She was to be photographed for *Filmfare*, posing as a journalist in Mumbai's red-light district. It was a gloomy, drippy Sunday afternoon . . . and Kajol was clearly nervous about shooting in such a notorious area. If Kajol was edgy, the rest of the team was even edgier . . . and worse, clueless about the location. I was frankly amazed. Mumbai's 'cages' are world famous—a must-see not only for curious visitors but anybody who likes to check out life in the raw, gritty though it is. I offered to lead the way. Kajol looked at me gratefully and then asked whether I'd plait her hair. At that moment, she was an uncertain schoolgirl putting on a brave act. 'Will she be mobbed . . . attacked?' someone asked. Parvez, Gautam's assistant, was instructed not to attract too much attention fixing reflectors, while Gautam himself wondered how he'd be able to swing the grab-shots—something he'd never attempted in his long career as a studio portraitist. It was close to 2 p.m., a time when the kilometre-long strip in central Mumbai just about begins to stir after a long and busy Saturday night. It's the time when the sex-workers can be spotted stretching and yawning at the narrow entrances of their shabby cages which are doorless, with just stained tattered curtains flapping in the low breeze generated by passing buses and cabs. It's also the time street vendors selling 'breakfast snacks' like hard-boiled eggs crowd the narrow road, briskly dealing with madams and pimps while the girls (most of them alarmingly underage) loll around on the unwashed steps of their hovels, dangling babies on their hips, gossiping and giggling before another busy working shift begins.

Kamathipura can turn into a hostile place without warning. One minute you may be surrounded by friendly, curious residents, and the very next someone can start hurling abuse. I warned Kajol about such a possibility while braiding her thick, untamed mane. It was decided we'd drive in, slide out quietly after finding an appropriate spot, and give just enough time to Gautam to focus, shoot and pack up. Kajol was game even if she didn't exactly look the part, granny-glasses notwithstanding. The entire operation was accomplished within minutes—a real hit-and-run job. Kajol did get recognized despite the disguise, but just as word of her presence began to spread, we jumped right back into the cars and fled.

The next time Kajol and I found ourselves at the same function was just after she'd become the star of the moment. *Dilwale Dulhaniya Le Jayenge* was the major box-office hit of '97, and Kajol, the darling of the masses. It was an annual felicitation event organized by a body called Giants International. Kajol and her co-star Shah Rukh Khan were amongst the awardees, along with Dr Manmohan Singh, Leander Paes and Rajat Sharma. The function was being presided over by the governor of Maharashtra, P.C. Alexander. Kajol arrived fashionably late, accompanied by her mother, the actress Tanuja, and grandmother. She flounced on stage, occupied her chair and proceeded to make faces, stick out her tongue and wave to acquaintances in the audience even as the keynote address was on. Half an hour later Shah Rukh Khan strolled in puffing on a cigarette, which he stubbed out on the carpet of the glittering banquet hall before stepping on to the dais. Once there, he switched his nameplate so as to sit next to his co-star Kajol and exchange gossip. Minutes later he lit up again and blew clouds of smoke into another awardee's face. The two of them behaved like delinquent children being punished outside the principal's office. Their acceptance 'speeches' didn't get beyond immature inanities. I don't know about the invited audience, but I was horribly disappointed especially where Kajol was concerned. Here were two successful young stars representing the Nineties generation, the bold new breed, and what were they telling the watching world? That they were ill-mannered, self-absorbed and unsophisticated enough to chatter idiotically through other people's speeches (no matter how long or how boring), that they were arrogant enough to keep several senior citizens waiting, that they didn't have the grace to apologize for coming late and worse, nobody had taught them better or given them lessons in basic etiquette.

This sort of conduct might have been overlooked in the old days when stars like Mumtaz or Meena Kumari literally popped out of nowhere and into movies, skipping school (and children). They were not prepared for public life in any form, were without parental guidance or even a studio system to groom them. To their credit, they learnt on the job and I don't know a single instance when any of them behaved as disgracefully. Shah Rukh Khan is an educated chap with a college degree. Kajol's mother and aunt were sent to Swiss finishing schools to acquire social graces. Why hadn't any of it rubbed off on young Kajol? At the dinner that followed, I met Shah Rukh Khan and Kajol and was once again astonished by their overly casual behaviour.

Star quality is a mysterious thing—either a person has it or doesn't. Often it has nothing to do with the actor's actual standing in the movie world. The aura doesn't always go with success. I have seen minor-league film people who exude it, as also has-beens no longer in the running. But it's perhaps best exemplified in the case of Sushmita Sen and Aishwarya Rai. Both women went on to win the most prestigious titles in the beauty business—Sushmita became Miss Universe while Aishwarya walked off with the Miss World crown. The manner in which the two queens responded to their spectacular success was what separated the really royal one (Aishwarya) from the pretender.

Here were two girls with a similar middle-class background, both raised in a comparable milieu by conservative, low-profile, non-showbiz parents. To all appearances, they came from solid, sensible stock. Once again, it was the Nineties spirit in evidence. Whereas earlier contestants had been from more showy, more needy, non-professional backgrounds—just pretty young girls with neat figures and big ambitions—Sushmita and Aishwarya were seen as forerunners of a different class of contenders: well spoken, well bred, smart, focused and intelligent girls who'd grown up reading something slightly weightier than Archie comics. Beauties who were perfect ambassadors for the new India—upfront, confident, very together. And then what happened? With the coveted titles behind them, they predictably leapt into the next glamour trap—Hindi movies.

The first time I met Sushmita ('Sush' to her friends in the fashion world), it was on Chowpatty beach at sundown. She'd recently been crowned Miss India and was on her way to the

Miss Universe contest in Miami. We were both appearing on a Channel 4 programme anchored by Nikki Bedi (this was a few months before Nikki got the boot from the other, more controversial chat show on Star TV). Sushmita had finished her segment and was standing on the beach holding hands with her boyfriend-of-the-moment, a rather sad-eyed young man who looked honoured just to be seen with his high-profile companion. She looked lovely in a white shirt and blue jeans, with hardly any make-up. Her crinkly hair was off her face and tied into a teenage pony-tail. She appeared and behaved like the eighteen-year-old she then was. Or so I thought till I heard what she'd said in her interview when asked by Nikki what qualities she looked for in a man. 'Oh,' Miss Sen had responded brightly, 'he must be good in bed.'

Next round: India was rejoicing over her spectacular victory at the international contest, and Pradeep Guha, her powerful mentor at the *Times of India*, wasn't wasting a single opportunity to derive mileage from the event. Sushmita was back in Mumbai for the first time after winning the crown and Mr Guha had organized a bang-up party to welcome her home. The ballroom of the Taj Mahal Hotel had never looked prettier, with silver bows, white balloons, banks of flowers and dimmed chandeliers lending a fairy-tale glow to the venue. I watched the Queen from a safe distance. She was being escorted to the dance floor by various celebrities—movie stars like Govinda, co-models, others. I could sense the change—see it. Yes, it was visible. Dressed in a red slinky gown with long slits up her slim thighs, Sushmita's body language had altered almost as much as her spoken one. When she spotted me, she sashayed up, planted the mandatory kisses in the air and drawled in a perfect parody of put-on Americanese, 'So-o-o . . . howyadoin'?' I looked over her shoulder and spotted an apparition. It took me a moment to recognize Sushmita's mother. Mrs Sen had reinvented herself to look closer to her image of a beauty queen's manager-mother. The Vasant Kunj housewife had been transformed into a polyester pant-suit wearing power lady hiding behind large sunglasses in a darkened ballroom. I couldn't stop blinking at the sight of these two in their fancy feathers.

In Aishwarya's case, Mrs Rai wore her daughter's success more discreetly—or rather, more smartly. She still dressed like a suburban housewife (thankfully) but a posher one, with diamonds glittering on her earlobes and a shimmering silk saree outlining her trim figure. If one had to predict then how the two girls would fare by looking at their mothers, Aishwarya's success was guaranteed. Here was a woman (her mother) who was shrewd enough to hang on to her original roots while grooming her beautiful daughter for a well-orchestrated career minus the mistakes made by the Sens. Both girls started with comparable advantages. Both got promising breaks. Both pitched their market worth sky-high. Sushmita's came crashing down with a series of tactical errors, negative publicity, indiscreet interviews, an acknowledged affair with a married man and a falling out with the family. It was rumoured that she was unstable and unreliable, a reputation which for a budding actress can spell instant doom, especially if her debut film crashes. Aishwarya on the other hand maintained her ice princess image and soon convinced her colleagues about her work-ethic and discipline by her impeccable conduct on the sets. All she needed was endorsement at the box-office—a mega hit to justify the one-crore-plus price tag she was demanding from producers. Studying the career graph of these two girls, it's not difficult to see where Aishwarya scored and Sushmita lost out.

Aishwarya has her head well screwed on. She's no flake,

I can tell you, after a long, involved discussion I had with her over a TV series we'd both been sweet-talked into. The man who'd been commissioned to shoot it was a complete ass who fancied himself no end. Since he was Delhi based we couldn't have known that he would show up for the shoot with more wardrobe changes lined up for himself than we'd have bothered with for a month-long assignment. He was offensive in several other ways. It all had to do with the fact that he thought he was the real star of the commissioned programme and therefore deserved to be treated as one—airs and all. It would have been an unbearable experience had it not been so comical—the man was an absolute dolt, unlettered and gauche. It was time to do something about it. I spoke to both Aishwarya and her mother in this regard. I was pleasantly surprised by both. They spoke well—very well. Especially Aishwarya, who seemed so much older and more poised than her scatty contemporaries. Her choice of words was impeccable. So were her manners. Impressive? Definitely so. A secure home environment with the right guidance can often make that significant difference between success and failure.

There are countless such examples in Bollywood—Karishma Kapoor and Manisha Koirala come to mind. As does Madhuri Dixit—the one actress who has held on to her position at the top of the heap without letting 'minor' matters like a personal life get in the way. Her middle-class Maharashtrian family has been her mainstay, with her conservative parents accompanying her on location and looking after her financial dealings. If the seeming contradiction of having their daughter setting the screen on fire with her sizzling, blatantly sexy dance number, while leading a chaste, scandal-free life in private has confused them at all, they've never discussed it or let it interfere with the marketing of Madhuri. Apart from her Sanjay Dutt phase,

Madhuri has stayed out of gossip columns and is rarely seen in public. Those who know the family say the Dixits lead an unstarry, mundane existence in which Madhuri is treated like any other unmarried career girl who has chosen to live in her parental home.

Other young actresses aren't this lucky. In my *Stardust* years I was constantly astonished at the pushiness displayed by hungry mothers peddling their under-age daughters. And peddling is the only word that comes to mind when I recall one particular incident. An overweight woman with dark circles and eyebags hanging down to her chin had come huffing and puffing up the narrow *Stardust* staircase and had sat down heavily in the chair across me. Without much ceremony, she slid some transparencies over the table top. I held them up to the light . . . and blushed. 'My daughter,' the woman explained proudly. 'Fourteen . . . but mature.' You can say that again, I thought to myself as I took another look. The teenager was posed in an apology of a blouse which had no buttons but was knotted tantalizingly below her pumped-up bosom. The girl's face, hideously made-up though it was, clearly belonged to a child. But given the angle, nobody thought of looking at it since the gaze got arrested at the melon-sized breasts pouring out of the tiny blouse. The photographer who'd shot the pin-ups was a tiny, mousy-looking chap one wouldn't associate with anything more lascivious than close-ups of bees sucking honey out of flowers in full bloom. These pictures qualified for a paedophile's personal library. And here was the subject's mother begging to have them published.

'My daughter can dance. She is very talented,' she announced, while the mousy photographer grinned sheepishly (he'd arrived a few minutes after her). As it turned out, the daughter went on to become a reasonably successful star who led a blemish-free life and married well, within the industry. the younger son of a Bollywood legend. With matrimony came respectability. The mother had made enough money off her by then and invested it in business. The cheap publicity pictures are now history and it's only people who were in the magazine business in the Seventies who remember them. But each time I see an alarmingly young girl being nudged into the film industry via the semi-nude route, I think of the gross woman who, twenty-five years earlier, had walked into my office to make money out of her daughter's overblown mammaries. And I recoil at the memory.

I was asked this question way back then, and people continue to ask it even now: Do men in the film industry have it easier? I laugh it off by saying, 'Men anywhere, in any sphere, always have it easier.' Which is partially true. But more so in the case of movie people of the new breed. The chaps most likely to stay on and succeed are those who reflect the driven work-ethic of the Nineties—focused people who don't let the trappings of stardom distract them from their career goals. One such person is Aamir Khan, the diminutive actor who drives directors crazy with his 'commitment' which dictates that he demand countless retakes for key scenes till he feels he's got them right. This drives his co-stars and the rest of the unit crazy, but Aamir the perfectionist plods on, investing each role with special touches that warm the hearts of his admirers even if they cost the producers a great deal of time and money. Aamir in person is devoid of star quality, charisma or charm. He is an intense young man who engages you in equally intense conversation when he chooses to speak—which isn't often.

Aamir and I were guests at a charity event in Bangalore and our flights landed within minutes of each other. A reception committee of eager, sincere, well-dressed ladies was waiting expectantly for the star and his wife to arrive. From a distance we saw two young people dressed alike in jeans, Tommy Hilfiger sweatshirts, running shoes and baseball caps. They could have been American sophomores on tourist visas. The ladies squealed with delight at the sight of Aamir, handed him flowers, looked at the person next to him and gushed, 'So nice of you to bring your brother—but we were expecting bhabiji.' Aamir's face didn't register any emotion as he impassively turned around and said, 'This is my wife, Reema.' Several embarrassed apologies later, we went to the hotel where the confusion was finally cleared up. Aamir's wife could very easily pass off as his brother, with her cropped hair, identical complexion, brown eyes and similar build.

That night, the only way to tell the two apart was by their respective outfits. Aamir was still in jeans, but she had sensibly changed into something less unisex, more feminine. But the embarrassment quota wasn't yet complete. A spectacular fashion show was followed by a short felicitation ceremony, after which members of the audience were invited to pose question to the two stars present—Aamir Khan and Nana Patekar. A mid-thirties woman rushed on stage, grabbed the mike out of Aamir's hand and asked aggressively, 'You were once in love with my best friend, you'd even promised to marry her. I want to know why you ditched this girl and married someone else?' Without displaying any signs of being flustered or outraged by the audacity of such a personal question on an occasion like this (to raise funds for a cancer unit), Aamir took the mike and explained calmly and honestly that, yes, he had been involved with so-and-so, but unfortunately, things hadn't quite worked out between them. But he was lucky that despite all that, his wife Reema had accepted him—after seven rejections. I thought it was brilliantly handled, without any awkwardness and with enormous tact. I swore to myself I'd see every single film of his. I'd loved him in *Rangeela*, and now, after his Bangalore performance, I'd become a complete convert.

Nana Patekar fared equally well that night. I'd known Nana vaguely before he hit the big time, but something about his overpowering, raw-edged personality had scared me off. Nana can (and does) have that effect on people. He is too much to handle with his exuberant, untamed ways and very direct manner of speaking. For a man who has come up the hard way, Nana makes no attempts to disguise his beginnings, and this is certainly his strength, but it can also frighten strangers unused to someone spontaneously getting into a touchy-feely situation at the first meeting, or even the seventeenth. Nana simply does not know better. Not governed by society's rules, he behaves like an untutored child, following his instincts, going after whatever grabs his fancy, unmindful of the correctness or otherwise involved in the act. This must get him into a great deal of trouble. But Nana wouldn't be Nana if he followed all the rules. Being an instinctual person, he goes with the flow, even on screen, using his powerful voice, smouldering eyes and compact physique to full advantage. The masses love him—he is one of them. He looks and behaves like a person who's been raised on the wrong side of the railway track—no apologies. For all that, Nana is a charmer—and he knows it.

He is also one of the few stars who has a great future in politics—if he so chooses. The man has the pulse of the people. He understands crowds, connects with them, becomes one with the masses and plays up his own non-starry personality to the hilt when the situation demands it. Nana's annual Ganapati puja is a well-publicized event, open to the public. On the final day, when the deities are taken to the sea for the immersion ceremony, Nana walks with the multitudes, just another humble worshipper tearfully bidding goodbye to the elephant-headed god. Stripped of movie-star airs Nana is distinctly naff—but that's also his strength. Nobody really cares—Nana in a designer kurta or an Armani tux would look ludicrous, and he knows it.

Today, his brand equity rests on his down-market image. He can be the rough and tough dada riding a suburban train, terrorizing commuters—but he can never be the suave Savile Row-clad tycoon charming the girl with champagne. Nana is street smart—and streets ahead of the competition because of his native intelligence. Today, he was come a long way career-wise but for all his success, he remains a roughly-cut diamond, crude, intense, raw.

The Nana I saw in Bangalore was a different character. When it was his turn to speak, he took the mike and made several self-deprecatory jokes that had the audience lapping up his every utterance. He then decided it was time to settle a couple of old scores—in public, where the embarrassment potential would be at its highest. Spotting his first director, Muzaffer Ali, seated like an indolent nawab in the first row, Nana reminded him of the fact that he owed him (Nana) money. He went on to narrate an amusing story of how he'd accepted Ali's film, been promised ten thousand rupees (a pittance) for the role and only received five eventually. He added sardonically, 'It was a film that won many awards—but I didn't understand my role in it. In fact, I went to see it with my brothers and a neighbour. We bought balcony tickets. When we arrived at the theatre, we discovered we were the only people upstairs. Nobody saw the film—but that's all right, it got lots of good reviews from the critics.'

If Muzaffer Ali felt like squirming, or lynching Nana, he covered up wonderfully. Unable to provoke him, Nana finally announced, 'I'm ready to donate ten lakhs to the Cancer

Patients' Aid Association right now—provided Muzaffer Ali starts the drive by giving those five thousand rupees he still owes me, to the organizers tonight.' His statement was greeted with thunderous applause—but it didn't move or shame Muzaffer sufficiently to reach for his wallet. Not satisfied by the ripples he'd created, Nana leapt off the stage and took over from the tabla player. He spent the rest of the evening in a dark corner, playing the tabla and providing the necessary sound effects.

The film industry girls may not be political firebrands in the Nana Patekar mould, but the newer batch is definitely smarter and a whole lot younger. They have the media savvy to package themselves more slickly and appear brighter than they really are. If in the past, starlet quotes were stuck at the 'me and my soft toys' level, these days they carefully work on 'things that matter'. They develop a social conscience somewhere along the way and lend their names to worthy projects—AIDS, cancer, the National Association of the Blind, environment. When Aishwarya pledged her eyes to the eye bank in a commercial that was more an ad for smudge proof make-up than an appeal for corneas, the nation went into a collective swoon over her 'noble' gesture, little realizing that those incredible cat-eyes that resemble liquid opals would only be fitted into the lucky recipient's sockets after her death—and worse, the donor's eyes wouldn't automatically resemble hers. On such gross ignorance are great campaigns built. But hey, why quibble when super celebrities are lending their names and images for free?

Increasingly these days, star brats seem to be crawling out of the woodwork like so many busy ants, scurrying from studio to studio on the strength of their surnames and little more. I feel a little sorry for most of them. Take Twinkle. Blessed with neither her mother's unusual looks nor her father's romanticism, the poor girl goes from disco to disco asking indifferent teenagers, 'But . . . but . . . don't you know who I am? I'm Twinkle Khanna. My films are super hits.' It must be awful not being able to gain acceptance within your peer group, to lace all introductions with a silly preamble. But the poor kid simply does not have it and she probably knows it. It must be doubly awful for her mother, who, in her mid-forties, has the unbearable burden of her fading beauty to deal with.

Whether or not Dimple is a party to the beauty trap, she (along with Rekha) cannot escape it. Wherever these two go, their appearance is minutely scrutinized—any new lines? Face lifts? Eye tucks? Hair colour jobs? Lipo? What's fixed, what isn't? I've met Dimple off and on for years and I like her direct gaze and abrupt manner. There is no attempt to charm or play up her considerable power (which she's fully aware of) over dumbstruck strangers gawking at a woman routinely hailed as the 'most beautiful' creature on the subcontinent. I believe Dimple does not take such tags all that seriously. In some ways she has yet to grow up and face life as an adult. While she is conscious of the effect she has on people, she also seems slightly impatient with it. Almost as if she's saying, 'Okay guys, can you please put those popping eyeballs back where they belong . . . and get on with other stuff?' She gives the impression of watching people who interest her very, very, closely—not for their reaction to her (which is a more typical star reaction) but as if by studying her subjects she can find a few answers, maybe learn something—a new make-up trick, a new word, a new facial expression.

Dimple is like a sponge absorbing everything eagerly, which is why directors love her. Self-taught, self-groomed and finally, with only herself to fall back on, she shares an interesting relationship with her two daughters, often lapsing into role reversal and having them mother her. She also shares a strange bond with Rajesh Khanna, the man she unsuccessfully played child-bride to before fleeing to her maternal home. Dimple has an appetite for self-punishment—it's evident from the choices she's made, especially the men she has chosen. She appears to have experienced a dysfunctional upbringing, bypassing childhood. Her career graph hasn't conformed to a predictable pattern either, with her dropping out of the movie business after her smash debut-making film *Bobby*. *Sagar* saw her return to the big screen as a separated wife and single parent trying to put the fragmented pieces of her life together, with two young girls to raise. Her parental home was no safe haven, with drug addicted siblings (one of whom reportedly died of an overdose a few years later) and parents who, by all accounts, didn't run a 'normal' domestic set-up.

For all that, Dimple is a tough woman with expensive tastes and a voracious capacity to spend huge sums of money even while her bank account reflects a zero-credit situation. Given to excess (with a tongue and temper to match) Dimple at the card tables makes an awesome sight—her jaws moving incessantly on the perennial gum in her mouth, sips of beer slaking her thirst, a string of friendly (yet graphic) abuse streaming forth, and those hungry, predatory eyes fixing her opponents with their piercing intensity as she deals expertly, with all the practised finesse of a casino croupier at the gaming tables in Monaco. I don't know this Dimple at all, since I'm not a card-player. I meet her in social situations when she greets me warmly with a bone-crunching bear hug, often forcing me to stay in the clinch for far longer than is comfortable or even conventional. Then she holds me at arm's length and examines my face like a surgeon preparing for some deft scalpel work. After an affectionate 'You, bitch you', we lapse into kiddy-talk . . . till the next encounter.

At glittering parties, she prefers to arrive with her favourite companions—one on each arm. Since she is their trophy-client and their most glamorous showpiece, her entries are never less than dramatic. If out-of-towners happen to be around, she treats them disdainfully, not by design, but because that's her manner—brusque, short, devoid of grace. The evening is spent secluded in a corner with her coterie of gay admirers for whom she is a luminous icon—ask any gay fashion-victim whom he'd love to trade places with and you'll get one of two names—Dimple or Rekha. These two women are role models for a generation of gays who admire their beauty, style, attitude, and spend hours trying to clone their appearance and movie roles. Rekha's 'mujra' from *Umrao Jaan* remains number one on the gay charts with enthusiastic groupies mimicking Rekha's every glance and gesture besides striving hard to get the costume and make-up just right. Out on the same fringe, Jackie Shroff's slim-hipped silhouette looms large. He has been adopted by the gay community without a single reservation. They love his style, they claim. But it's more than that. Jackie has an androgynous appeal that straddles the gender divide. Women find him macho . . . and so do men. Behind that rough granite façade there lurks a soft sentimental individual who is unafraid to wear his heart on his sleeve and weep copious tears in public without shame. Is Jackie Shroff the New Age man then? Perhaps he is even if he doesn't know it himself.

For a person who started life on the mean streets of Bombay, Jackie's present penthouse lifestyle is the stuff Hindi movies are made of. I used to see him frequently in the old, pre-star days when he was a well-known and greatly-feared tough heading a gang of local bullies at Nepean Sea road—one of Bombay's more affluent areas. I used to take my kids for an after-dinner ice cream to a parlour (since defunct) called 'Pastry Palace'. And there would be Jackie (or 'Jaggu') strutting his stuff, clad in a pair of dirty jeans, with his trádemark gamcha flung over one shoulder. I've witnessed fights with chains and knuckle dusters, the roughing up of 'soft' rich kids, the heckling of passers-by and general '*mastigiri*' that could have passed for an angry young man's disposal of high energy levels had it not been so menacing.

Jackie Shroff managed to stay on this side of the law most of the time, but for a guy who'd dropped out of school and would have been just another streetside hood, he didn't do too badly . . . especially not after being discovered by an ad person and given his first modelling break in a cigarette commercial. From that to being signed up to play the lead in a film called *Hero* wasn't too hard a transition, what with Subhash Ghai playing godfather. It was the sort of debut any newcomer would gladly break a leg for. The film may not have broken box-office records, but Jackie became a star overnight.

One of the correspondents working at *Celebrity*, the people magazine I'd launched in '81, was a young, pretty girl staying as a paying guest with a well-off family at Nepean Sea road . . . yes, Jackie's hang-out. While waiting for a bus each morning, she'd notice Jackie and, we at the office supposed, he'd notice her. We decided to play Cupid by asking her to accost him for an interview. Not being a brazen Bombay girl, she baulked at the suggestion, but succumbed later. They met a couple of times for the interview and Jackie took to visiting her at her place of residence. This was a cause of enormous embarrassment to the poor girl who rarely entertained male visitors since she didn't know very many people in the city. The people she lived with (old and stuffy) weren't amused either. But we were. It was obvious she had a crush on him

177

by the way she coloured deeply each time his name was mentioned. We pushed her into inviting him over to the office and even provided a convincing excuse—a variation of 'come up and see my etchings'. She asked Jackie to come and see his photographs—the ones we were planning to use with the article.

The man who walked into the office was indecently clad. Jackie chose to show up in a pair of sawed-off denim shorts that were so inadequate, I dared not ask him to sit down for fear that he'd be arrested for exposure. In fact, the lot of us were deeply embarrassed and didn't know where to look. Jackie is physically imposing with more brawn than is legally permissible. Add to that his choice of singlet-and-shorts for an office visit and it became doubly awkward. I decided to tackle the tricky situation head-on by pointing out to him that he was in a magazine office and not on a beach in Phuket, and would he please come back another day more appropriately clad? He shrugged and sauntered out after throwing the girl he knew a knowing smile, a quick wink and a thumbs-up sign. I doubt if Jackie remembers this incident . . . but all of us who were present that morning most certainly do.

The little romance that had never really taken off died as quickly. The blushing maiden went on to a better job, a well-placed husband, a secure life of bourgeois domesticity. And Jackie? He's still around in the movies. Nobody can wear a pair of jeans the way he does. I don't believe his wild days are behind him, even if he does do a pretty good job of playing the tamed rebel, wedded to a busy personal and professional life, with a wife and two wonderful kids completing the picture. We run into each other now and again. He is unfailingly polite, awfully charming and very handsome in a haggard, ravaged way. We communicate in Marathi, and I always look for some signs of his old rakish self—disappointingly, there are none. Today's Jackie is a successful star surrounded by a coterie of suited supplicants, not snarling roughnecks. He still smokes bidis and prefers to hang out with waiters, drivers and doormen rather than fancy socialites at fancy parties, but now it appears more like a tired pose, as if he is obliged to play up a suppressed side of his personality just to remind himself and the world about the man he once was—maybe still is.

Former child-star, the luscious Sarika, is a little like Jackie—a spirited street-fighter in her own way. She grew up with an attractive, alarmingly young mother who had big ambitions for her pretty, light-eyed daughter. The father didn't figure in Sarika's upbringing and she only discovered him years later after a painstaking search. Her adolescence was spent in the studios where her mother assumed total control over her roles and more importantly, the money she made. Without formal education but a great desire to learn and improve her lot, Sarika chose improbable friends. Like Karan Kapoor, the half-British son of Shashi and Jennifer Kapoor. Their backgrounds couldn't have been more different—she didn't know which world she belonged to other than the small film family she'd been raised in. He was a suave, sophisticated rich kid—very much a South Bombay product, well travelled, well spoken, confident. The sort of chap equally at home with Sloane Rangers and Hauz Khas designers. A charming man who at the time he knew Sarika, hadn't made up his mind what he wanted to be—a photographer or an actor. He gave acting the first shot—and flopped spectacularly. With his strange good looks (blue eyes, blond hair), amusing manner and obvious *savoir-faire*, the cluttered, clumsy world of commercial Hindi films wasn't for him—nor he for the roles he was offered. Without money but with the Kapoor name, Karan was viewed as quite a catch.

Sarika's canny mother obviously didn't think so, especially since her daughter was beginning to spend every spare minute away from the studios, in his company, besides subsidizing their dates with the meagre allowance she enjoyed. Constant arguments between the mother and daughter ended predictably enough with Sarika walking out of the flat that had been bought from her earnings and into a pokey little place where she stayed as a paying guest.

Sarika found herself stranded, emotionally and financially. Her career wasn't really going anywhere without her mother to propel it forward. And her mother's own priorities had changed with a brand-new husband to cater to. Sarika found herself embroiled in a relationship with the much married Kamal Hasan, with whom she bravely decided to move in, despite the strong opposition from his then wife, Vani Ganapathy. Kamal and Sarika went ahead with their plan, producing a daughter and then another before formalizing their relationship with a traditional wedding attended by close family members.

As the wife of South India's biggest star Sarika had a brand new role to play—and she obviously revelled in it. Determined to win the title of superwife and supermom, she threw herself into domesticity, turning her back on whatever roles may have come her way. This suited everybody just fine, especially Sarika who'd never known a 'normal' childhood. Gradually, she began to take an active interest in her husband's productions, officiating as his dress designer, studio hand, documentary maker, stills photographer. Together they attended all the major film festivals and devoured all there was to enjoy about world cinema. The uncertain, bruised woman gave way to a more poised, confident wife-mother, who, with her new status, was no longer afraid to be herself, speak her mind and dress as she pleased even in the highly closed, arch conservative film community in Madras. If purists recoiled at the sight of her attending prestigious festivals clad in jeans, others admired her for her individuality and courage. Her defiance was eventually accepted and absorbed, even if it wasn't understood. When she decided to shave her head, not a single question was asked—Sarika had attained a position where anything was expected of her, even a bald pate.

I'd always been curious about her, more so since we had a good friend, Bhawna, in common. Our meeting took place in Hyderabad, and coincidentally enough, the same friend happened to be in the same city, staying at the same hotel, and was walking down the same corridor of the same floor when she spotted Sarika and did a double take. For one, Sarika's shaven head now sported a platinum stubble à la the World Cup football heroes. For another, even by her own standards, Sarika was strangely dressed. I couldn't wait to meet her. After dinner, the common friend and I knocked on Sarika's door (she was two rooms away) and even though I had been sufficiently warned about her altered appearance, for a moment I was stumped for something to say when she opened the door. Sarika was clad in an undergarment, a corset, to be more precise. I was neither prepared for the awesome cleavage on display nor for the excess weight she'd gained. The Sarika I remembered from her old films had been an Aishwarya Rai-like beauty—pale, fragile, light-eyed. This buxom creature was Amazonian and altogether delightful in an earthy, bawdy kind of way. Devoid of any artifice and entirely unselfconscious, she moved around her room with a length of flimsy fabric tied loosely around her hips enthusiastically showing off her latest purchases—priceless, precious antique textiles and sarees she planned to convert into authentic costumes for her husband's new film. It broke my heart to think of the fate of those incredibly beautiful fabrics and I said so.

She laughed and seemed totally unmoved. 'You can't do this,' I nearly wept. 'You can't possibly cut them up. I'll buy them off you.' Sarika laughed some more and ordered a biryani through room service.

I thought to myself, this woman is either completely crazy or madly in love with her husband. It occurred to me that she could also be ignorant—maybe she really didn't have any idea about the rarity and aesthetic value of her purchases. I tried to convince her . . . appeal to her . . . plead with her. It didn't make the slightest difference. After a while, I gave up and concentrated on watching this very attractive former actress with her heavy, milk-white breasts half out of the underwired cups of her corset, as she chattered animatedly about her new project. She also seemed excessively interested in the goings-on of the Bombay film industry. She obviously read every gossip magazine in the market and was aware of all the link-ups and break-ups. I was astonished at her recall—she was quoting from interviews past and present. She knew exactly which actress had said what to whom and in which year. It was amusing and touching to see the extent of her interest and involvement in a world she'd left behind years ago. Did she perhaps miss it just a little? Did she long for the limelight? Was being Kamal Hasan's wife and the mother of his daughters enough? Why the platinum hair, the provocative underwear-as-outer-wear? Why the non-conformism, the deliberate breaking of age-old rules? Was it the attention these received?

She laughed too much, talked too much, smoked too much. There was so much energy in that cramped room, I was beginning to feel the heat as she paced around restlessly, took her husband's call, flicked through a stack of film magazines . . . and kept up a steady stream of frequently disjointed conversation. This was a woman with something to prove—I could sense it. Her present role is not enough. She needs something more, something bigger, something challenging to make her feel good about herself and her identity, given the fact that she is a self-taught, self-created creature who has learnt to land on her feet. I'd say Sarika will be okay the day she follows her own instincts and does what her heart, not mind, tells her—which is, to explore her own talent, exploit her own potential. I think she deserves something more worthwhile than being a full-time nanny to her ambitious husband. Even the world's most loyal secretary-spouses get bored after a time and start longing for a role to call their own.

One woman who has managed to retain her aura (and beauty) years after she gave up making films is Sharmila Tagore. She is looking lovelier today than she ever did in her *Evening in Paris* days. She wears her age and position exceedingly well. Her skin radiates a healthy glow and the salt-and-pepper in her hair only adds to her personality. Here's a woman who speaks well, is highly intelligent, is very well read and is completely down-to-earth. I recall a lunch in Lahore a few years ago. We were all guests at a posh marquee affair on the lawns of a Pakistani businessman's bungalow. A band played in the distance, various lovely local ladies were sprinkled decorously around the pool. And there we were—a motley Indian contingent, outnumbered and out-dressed by the glittering begums of Lahore. Sharmila was very simply clad with just a thin gold chain around her neck. I didn't know then that her husband, the Nawab of Pataudi, was barely on talking terms with their actor-son Saif, and his wife Amrita. I asked about them since the previous evening at the stadium, the match had come to a virtual stop with delirious fans screaming 'ole, ole' at the sight of Saif. The chant was from his dance number in a commercially successful film and he was clearly the darling of the crowd that night. At one stage, he'd had to be rescued by the police and escorted into the press-box where his father and mother were seated. Others present were surprised when Pataudi refused to greet his son and daughter-in-law even after Sharmila urged him to, hissing wifely advice under her breath. Ignoring her, Pataudi had chosen to leave abruptly thereby making the rift very public.

If Sharmila was disturbed by any of this at that lunch, she certainly didn't show it. I was running a high fever and was feeling slightly delirious. She came across and sat with me while Pakistani women crowded around for autographs and photographs. Pataudi walked past a few times, scowling ferociously. But she seemed perfectly relaxed and at peace. She said she loved the idea of being a grandmother—and I thought what a ravishing grandmother she would make. Sexy, flirtatious, full of good humour.

Sharmila's sense of humour is sly and schoolgirlish by turn. She comes across as a woman who knows her mind and priorities and is practical enough to make the necessary shifts. I was told how she grumbles good-naturedly when she comes to Mumbai and finds she has to travel by cab everywhere since she no longer rates VIP treatment by people who invite her to, say, participate in a TV show. Even when the Nawab's fortunes were low and Sharmila had to cut back on her lavish lifestyle, she did so with grace and humour, joking about how the two of them were being forced to model for textile companies in their old age in order to supplement the family kitty. When her son decided to marry an older actress, Sharmila maintained a discreet distance and silence.

The few times I've met her, I've found her great fun to be with, like the way she reacted to an overawed pest at the

Lahore lunch who came up to both of us and gushed away foolishly. To Sharmila, she said, 'Oh I just adore your roles. I'm such an admirer. I've seen all your films. I liked you best in . . . in . . . in . . .' and Sharmila hastily said, '*Aradhana*'. Then the woman turned to me: 'Oh, I love your columns. I love your books. I've read all of them. The one I liked best was . . . was . . . was.' And taking my cue from the more seasoned Sharmila, I prompted, '*Socialite Evenings*'. The woman was ready to keel over with gratitude as she whipped out a camera and clicked a picture of 'the two most gorgeous women in India'. I was tempted to ask, 'And what are our names again?' When she left, Sharmila looked at me tiredly. 'This happens to me all the time. I squirm and cringe with embarrassment for the person who's making such a fool of herself or himself, and promptly supply the answer, out of consideration for the idiot.'

I understood her feelings perfectly. And yet, I thought back to the time she was ruling the film-roost in India—paired with Rajesh Khanna as the number one romantic couple. She was known to be arrogant, spoilt, temperamental and fussy. But was she sexy! And she knew it. Her famous bikini picture on the cover of *Filmfare* is daring even by today's standards. But it isn't cheap. Sharmila knew then, as she does now, exactly where the line has to be drawn. It needs someone of superior intelligence to figure that out.

Others of her generation haven't aged half as wonderfully. Admirers of Waheeda Rahman, who to this day remains the epitome of classic beauty for all those who've seen her in *Chaudavin Ka Chand*, would be shattered to meet the once-lovely actress now. As I was in Bangalore when I found myself next to her at a function and averted my eyes to lessen the shock. It isn't as if she looks awful. Oh no. It's worse. She looks ordinary, like any middle-aged wife with bags under her eyes and paan-stains on her teeth. She is vain enough to dye her hair, wear expensive sarees and well-picked jewellery. But the aura has gone along with the looks. Perhaps she is perfectly happy—fat and happy, as they say. But I'd rather live with the illusion. I tried talking to her. She wasn't particularly interested or interesting. She introduced me to her husband who looked like any other overweight businessman. The two of them seemed completely bored (maybe not with each other) as they chewed some more paan-masala, made desultory conversation and left as unobtrusively as they'd arrived. Waheeda didn't ever have star quality (exactly like Jaya Bachchan) but she did captivate hearts with her on-screen persona.

*

I had zero memory of it, but Govinda obviously hadn't forgotten my printed reference to him as a walking-talking porn machine in *Cine Blitz*, a popular fanzine. I'd said that strictly about his screen persona—the vulgar, pelvis-gyrating dancer-star whose song routines relied heavily on *double entendre* and cheap puns. But I guess a description like that is hard to either forget or forgive. Which was why I was astonished that he agreed to a two-way dialogue for the *Stardust* Annual. The meeting was set up after a great deal of complicated juggling. Govinda is notorious for turning up hours, even days, late for an appointment. It is habitual and the man is unrepentant. Producers who sign him up know better than to expect the actor to show up on the sets on time, which means the entire unit hangs around from 10 a.m. (and gets paid for it) while Govinda finally drives up around 7 p.m. with earnest promises of shooting through the night . . . and never mind the overtime tab that gets run up to accomodate the tardy star. As things work in Bollywood, anything goes so long as there's a hit at the end of the day. Govinda has been delivering at the box-office, not big, but well enough for his producers not to dump him.

When the idea of the interview was first suggested my reaction was, 'Why him?' And then it grew on me—why not him? I'd reacted strongly to his screen self, it was time to find out what the fellow was all about. I called Gautam, my reliable source. His version of Govinda was not merely charming, it was a rave. He told me about Govinda's natural talent for singing, his strong family bonds and his spontaneous sense of humour.

I'd figured out a few things myself. The guy was definitely smart and he obviously knew his audiences far better than the likes of me. Matter of fact, Govinda was so bloody tuned in to what his fans wanted, my kind of a response really wasn't of any consequence to him. What I (and others like me) thought was completely unimportant and irrelevant. His yellow suits, green ties and orange lipstick may have jarred my aesthetics but millions of fans considered them an integral part of his unique 'style'. They didn't want Govinda clad in an Armani jacket—that wasn't their idea of a hero's image. Govinda was smart enough to know as much and shrewd enough to discount my barbs. This wasn't going to be as simple as I'd originally figured. But it was certainly going to be interesting.

I told the editor who was co-ordinating the feature to call me on his cell-phone when they were about a half-hour away from my home. She called instead from Juhu. The Govinda entourage was already running two hours behind schedule. It would be another hour before they showed up. Add a couple more for make-up (his), and the setting up of lights, and the session would overshoot by four hours, provided there

187

weren't other unexpected hiccups to contend with.

The doorbell rang. A police inspector (Govinda in costume) marched in smartly, saluting everybody. He was followed by broadly-grinning minions, plus the giggly editor who was clearly in love with Govinda. We greeted each other in Marathi and decided to get the pictures out of the way. He needed to change out of his uniform. I pointed to my son's room. Govinda walked in and shrugged off his shirt without bothering to shut the door. My two younger daughters promptly ran up to report that they thought he was a 'shameless' man to stand bare-chested in their presence without even apologizing. I didn't bother to explain to them that the movie business is full of 'shameless' people who condition themselves to strip and change in public places. No big deal. When he emerged with a fresh layer of pancake and another layer of lipstick, my youngest turned her back on him and steadfastly ignored all overtures. This man was not likely to impress Anandita—not that evening at any rate.

We got talking. In Marathi. I found him remarkably relaxed. Very curious and genuinely interested in what I was saying. After a few minutes he glanced at a neatly written questionnaire he'd been provided by the adoring editor and said, 'I don't want to ask you these questions. Let's just talk freely.' Since I hadn't prepared a counter questionnaire, I was delighted. Besides, I was beginning to warm to the guy. Even his blush-on and lipstick weren't distracting me now. He himself seemed so easy about it—the eyeshadow, eyeliner, mascara, hair spray—that soon others too disregarded the incongruously made-up man in the room and accepted the apparition for what or who it was—a professional actor still on duty.

Everything Gautam had said about Govinda was true (I didn't get him to sing, so I won't vouch for that particular gift), but he did have a sparkling sense of humour with witticisms rolling off his tongue in several languages. He appeared a happy-in-his-skin guy, who enjoyed his vocation and gave it his all (at absurd hours, to be sure). He successfully dodged trick questions and responded to other 'iffy' ones with humour if not candour. His wiggling out of situations that other heroes might have found difficult was achieved by adopting a mixture of little-boy gullibility, feigned innocence and wide-eyed surprise. A pretty convincing 'who, me?' act. It was obvious he was on top of things—unapologetic and entirely unselfconscious. If he found his screen persona ludicrous at all, he wasn't saying so himself. But one could tell that behind the bonhomie and the 'I'm only an unsophisticated suburban lad, a bumpkin if you will,' there ticked a sharp brain that didn't miss a trick. Govinda is nobody's fool—he knows his onions, and just how he likes them cooked. He also knows what he's best at—broad comedy, suggestive dancing and corny dialogues. He leaves the method school of acting to all those foolish losers who get great roles but no hits. Right now, Govinda has his priority and that is to make money. The only way a Hindi film hero can do that is by playing to the gallery. If Govinda has to climb into a purple monkey suit and swing from trees to achieve that, he isn't likely to refuse. On the contrary, he'll be the one asking the director, 'Where's my tail?'

*

After my meeting with Govinda, I revised and reviewed my low opinion of the filmi crowd. The only way to come to terms with their ways, their lives, their lingo, is to tell yourself they're different. They occupy a different world, an unreal, bizarre one which defies categorization, common sense or logic. You either accept it or you stay away. And then you run into someone like Amitabh Bachchan or Shekhar Kapur or Ramesh Sippy and you wonder what the hell these guys are doing in this business. What attracted them to it in the first place and why do they continue to hang in there?

Money is far too obvious an answer, even if it is a major part of it. The commercial magnet is the aspect easiest to figure out. But how do these men function in an environment that to an outsider appears not just alien but lunatic? Most of the people they interact with are illiterates whose reference points are restricted to industry talk. They know how to light up a complicated scene, overcome location sound problems, improvise their way out of crazy situations, make do with last-minute dialogues hastily written on scraps of paper, and can shots without a regular script to guide them. They can produce props that range from caparisoned elephants to cardboard castles out of seemingly nowhere, cajole a sulking star to emerge from the make-up room and give that vital shot, get an unwieldy unit to work in harmony on a difficult location, go without food, water or proper bathrooms, deal with obstinate extras, drunk fight masters, menopausal choreographers, temperamental star mothers—all this and more. But what about normal conversation? What about dealing with the real world? Real people? Real problems? How does their life in the studio prepare them for the outside world when they don't really belong to either?

These men (Amitabh and gang) are urbane, educated, well-travelled chaps. They read voraciously, listen to music other than tracks recorded for their next blockbuster, they enjoy going to the theatre, dressing well, drinking fine wines, eating gourmet food. And yet years and years of their lives are spent in filthy, ill-equipped studios in the company of talented but uneducated people. Amitabh protects himself with silence. He withdraws into his make-up van and stays there till he's required for his shot. Given his eminence, nobody dares intrude. He's left alone to enjoy his music while the unit sets up.

Ramesh Sippy is very much a film man, being a part of the larger film fraternity. But even he must find it difficult to hobnob with men who often resemble pick-pockets, cut-throats or petty thieves, and behave likewise. Shekhar Kapur with his chartered accountant's background is the maverick who uses arrogance to advantage. Given his peculiar career graph (precisely two hits—one commercial, the other critical) spanning twenty-five years, he isn't really in a position to call the shots or throw his weight around. Yet, he does just that—and gets away with it too.

Shekhar fancies himself as Asia's answer to Steven Spielberg and has no problems stating as much in interviews. Not one to be bogged down by boring qualities like modesty, Shekhar brazenly declares his genius to anybody who's interested. After the international acclaim of *Bandit Queen*, he became even more vocal about his brilliant self.

Amazingly enough, women seem to find Kapur maddeningly attractive and he's routinely voted as being amongst the ten most attractive men in India. He has had a succession of good-looking, high-profile women in his life, but by all accounts he makes an inconsiderate love-partner, being so full of himself there's little space for someone else. Despite that, women go for him in droves, perhaps drawn to the aura he has successfully created of a mercurial, intense, passionate director capable of making world-class films on his own terms. *Bandit Queen* certainly opened up a new market for him—a discriminating international one. Following its release world-wide, Shekhar declared rather grandly that he was through with India. Hollywood was not merely beckoning, it was all but dragging him westwards. So, what happened? Five years later, he's very much around, with one major project in England keeping him busy. He claims he is choosy and exacting. Others say he's just a pain in the rear and awfully difficult. There is no doubt that he's intelligent, suave and sophisticated—the sort of man who can easily blend into the select international film community and hold his own amongst peers like Quentin Tarantino or John Woo. It is in India that he's a misfit and he realizes it.

Miffed by my opinion of *Bandit Queen*, he chose to retaliate with a childish, abusive piece whose main thrust was aimed at my husband's Mercedes. It was Shekhar's contention that a woman who glides through life in such a car cannot know about the ground realities of caste and oppression. There were references to porcelain potties as well. The article made me laugh. It also made me wonder whether Shekhar dug a hole in the ground each morning to perform his ablutions in. And whether he shunned imported cars and only rode around in humble Marutis. If he could depict Phoolan Devi's life so graphically without having been a Chambal resident himself, how could he presume that others leading lives similar to his were less qualified to comment on his magnum opus?

I met him a couple of years after the *Bandit Queen* brouhaha had subsided. It was at a celebrity-packed party on the lawns of a prominent industrialist's plush home. Shekhar seemed relaxed enough as he strolled over with a glass of wine and drawled a lazy greeting (it's common knowledge that it's his trademark). The conversation that followed was slightly bizarre. I attributed it to the casual mood that night, the live band, the denim-clad glam-crowd and just the fact that he was playing the man-about-town mingling with the monied natives. He asked me a rather strange question. 'Isn't it lonely at 25,000 ft? I feel so cold up there. There's nobody to talk to. Very few people understand you, approach you when you're up there at that height. You must experience that yourself. I don't know your solution, but I've decided to climb down. I'm more comfortable at 10,000. What about you?' I was too astonished to reply. Speechless. Stupefied. Especially when I realized he was serious. I excused myself and rushed towards a bhel stall. I had had enough food for thought for a decade. What I needed right then was food for my tum-tum.

Sitting Pretty

I'd reached a point where it didn't matter one way or the other whether Garam Dharam was warming Idli Malini's bed each night or not. In short I was bored out of my skull. Again. It was curtains for *Stardust*. Time to move on. This time I actually had a plan. An idea. A good one, too. I was afraid my indifference and boredom with what I was doing would start getting reflected in the magazine. And that wouldn't be fair. If there was one thing that I held sacred it was a strong work-ethic. I'd hate to have been paid for doing nothing, or worse—doing my job badly. No short-changing the employers. Uma, Ingrid, Vanita, Binoy, Prochi—there was quite a gang in there, working independently and enthusiastically. Besides, 'daddy' held the remote control firmly in his hand, no matter which part of the world he was in.

There was an air of unmistakable *déjà vu* when I finally set up my little chat with Nari Hira. I had been squawking about my non-involvement for a while. I also knew that I wouldn't get the same freedom anywhere else. Nari Hira may not have paid the top buck, but he was a non-interfering, distant boss-man who was pretty fair with his employees—annual bonuses, increments that happened as per schedule. I had a company car and driver—but more than any of this, I had flexitime. So long as the magazine appeared on the scheduled date, without glitches and with sizzling contents, Nari Hira didn't really care whether I spent four, six, two or ten hours in the office. I did receive a couple of job offers during this period, which I dutifully discussed with him. If he found my consulting him somewhat strange, he was sporting enough to advise me objectively without showing his irritation or bias. There is the other possibility—he probably knew I'd be a misfit in another set-up. The work environment he fostered ensured a womb-to-tomb level of loyalty. Once you got into the Cat House you didn't leave. Or if you did stray, it was only to check out new territory and come back home to 'Daddy' with your tail between your legs.

I didn't really want to go anywhere, or test my wings. But I did want a change of pace. I was sick to death of dealing with narcissistic, neurotic movie people and their juvenile flings.

The idea for *Society* had already taken root in my mind—I enjoyed *People*, the immensely popular (in the Eighties) weekly American magazine. I sensed there was a market for a similar publication in India. We now had an impressive roster of celebrities, socialites, sports people, designers, dancers, painters, and no journal to showcase their lives. Celebrity feeds on itself. It's generally other celebs who read these sort of magazines just to monitor the competition and place themselves in the appropriate slot. Personality profiles till then had been restricted to wives of prominent politicians or cricketers. Even *The Illustrated Weekly* under Khushwant Singh preferred hard news ('religion, sex, politics') and crime stories to what falls under the broad category of 'society writing'. Years earlier, an attempt had been made via *Onlooker*, while *Eve's Weekly* and *Femina* predictably ran flattering little pieces about the good work being done by a Rotaract President in Agartala, or a charity sale organized by the generous ladies at the Cheshire Home. Air Force officers' wives got their micro-seconds of fame while collecting funds for war widows. Outside this framework, very little coverage was given to the glittering, glamorous trophy wives of industrialists—flashy, sexy women who travelled the world, dressed flamboyantly, had affairs brazenly, entertained stylishly and spent their husbands' money on things that mattered—designer wardrobes, face lifts, gigolos. What fantastic photo-ops. What entertaining copy. Finally, India was readying itself for real-life *Dynasty*-like sagas featuring gorgeous women, cuckolded husbands, amazing homes. Lust and lifestyle coming together in one glossy frame.

I ran it past Nari Hira at an informal meeting. He bit instantly—a man who knew his business all right—and *Society* was born. He gave me the go-ahead to create a dummy, design the masthead and work out the various sections. I felt enthused and excited about a project after a long time. I felt this was it—a magazine right up my street. It was a world I'd crashlanded into and knew at first-hand. Earlier, during my modelling days, and later, as the wife of a businessman. If as Shobha Rajadhyaksha, the model, I had access to the same world—but as an outsider—as Shobha Khilachand I was willy-nilly privy to a ringside view of the action.

Nari Hira did caution me to go easy on the subjects. These were not showbiz hussies with nothing to lose—women who'd be willing to strip, gossip, carry tales, accuse, expose, reveal etc. etc. We had to get the tone just right—fair without being adulatory, amusing without being insulting. Access was important. After all, movie people were thick-skinned and desperate for publicity—even if they did feel deeply offended, they needed us more than we needed them. It was different with these vibrant-winged butterflies and the dolts who financed them—their doting husbands. They were the early subjects—easy on the eye, good copy and not all that hard to get. Socialites and performing artistes made up the initial stable. While these people welcomed the chance to be projected, it was on condition that the write-up was an ego-boosting puff piece designed to project their beauty and their husbands' wealth in the best possible light. 'Don't make mincemeat out of them,' warned Nari Hira. He should have saved his breath. The idea behind *Society* was slightly more sophisticated. It wasn't designed as a slash-and-slander sheet. It was more ambitious, more *Vanity Fair*, more *Interview*, more hip, more classy, more clever. Well—that was the aspiration. I wanted a mix of witty and bitchy, naughty and notorious, with a few social issues thrown in for good measure, arbitrary style rules, event coverage and off-beat photographs.

The first thing to get right was the cover story, always the bane of editors in search of the right (read: saleable) subject. International research on the matter had shown that women sold better than men, photographs better than illustrations and babies best of all. Bimbos in bikinis did not always guarantee great returns. Neither did religious heads or disaster stories. People were interested in people—that was the simple premise behind *Society*. To get readers involved in the lives of those we featured in our pages. And who better than one of the most controversial women in India for the first issue?

From our carefully culled shortlist, one name jumped out—Rukhsana Sultan, the Emergency Bombshell who was rumoured to be Sanjay Gandhi's henchwoman. And what a woman. She had all the elements we were looking for—good looks, French chiffons, diamonds and pearls, a belligerent personality, a gift of the gab, a monumental ego and a dubious but passable pedigree. Poor woman died at age fifty in 1996 and I am not going to speak ill of the dead—but Rukhsana's world was fascinating by any definition.

I met her in Delhi over two or three days and in Bombay at her 'permanent' suite (as she referred to it) at the Taj Mahal Hotel. She was amusing and amazing. An attractive divorcee with a young horsey looking daughter (who later blossomed into the well-muscled actress, Amrita Singh), Rukhsana lived in a sprawling bungalow in New Delhi, near the Jantar Mantar. She billed herself as a jewellery designer but she had her own gang of hoods working for her—mainly brawny pehelwans (professional wrestlers) who were not permitted to stage bouts without her say-so. She was their patron and I suspect they gave her a cut from the gate money besides providing protection. On her insistence, I did the rounds of various akhadas with her and was suitably impressed when she played the visiting empress, accepting garlands with imperious grace, while burly young men fell at her feet and sought her blessings. 'My boys,' she said indulgently, waving her long, well-cared-for hands in their direction. Her narrow cunning eyes, shielded by enormous wrap-around sunglasses at all times, gave her a slightly sinister appearance. With her drawled 'Dah-lings' and unceasing conversation, she was almost caricatural. An inveterate name-dropper, Rukhsana threw so many around ('Yunus, dah-ling . . . he is nothing but a Gandhi-servant') one stopped counting and kept listening.

She was the only person I interviewed who attempted a clumsy bribe. Very clumsy indeed. While in Delhi, she invited me into her 'boudoir' (women like Rukhsana never have bedrooms, always 'boudoirs'). It was surprisingly ordinary—no star frills, just tacky, painted neo-baroque style furniture and Janpath tapestries. 'Dahling,' she said, sweeping past me and heading for an ugly cupboard, 'this is what I do for a living.' She threw open the doors of the almirah and stood back to see the effect her performance had had on me. The cupboard was filled with assorted necklaces, strings of Basra pearls, rubies, emeralds, most of them pretty awful. The kind of things a Karol Bagh kitty party wife would wear on her big night on the town. I was expressionless and silent. With a grand sweep of her arm she declared dramatically, 'Take whatever you like, dahling. It's yours, go on—just tell me . . . I think pearls would look fabulous on you. Here . . . wear these.' I stepped back, smiled and shook my head. She didn't understand. So I spelt it out for her. She feigned shock and hurt. 'Dahling—I love you. You are like my sister. This is a small gift. Just a token of our friendship. You are insulting me.' I shrugged and smiled some more. She pretended to wipe a few tears. I left her alone in the boudoir to recover. When she re-emerged, she was fine and tried a weak joke. 'Dahling—I'm sure you think I was trying to bribe you. Listen, I'd never do that. I really, really like you. Somehow I can't think of you as a journalist. We must have known each other in our previous lives.' I assured her I loved her equally and left.

When we next met, it was in the company of Haji Mastan, Bombay's notorious smuggler and underworld don (transformed into a messiah by his followers after his death a few years ago). He and his henchmen were comfortably settled in 'her' suite at the Taj. 'Dahling, he and I are social workers,' Rukhsana said, offering me a silver salver filled with almond rock chocolates. 'I want you to come with us to our area and see for yourself what we're doing for the poor.' The phone was ringing constantly. Mastan-mia's voice changed according to who the caller was—from a low growl to a firm command. There was no mistaking the menace behind those soft-spoken words. The two of them seemed well matched and perfectly in tune. I could picture them and their 'field workers' terrorizing cowering slum dwellers. 'Nobody from Pakistan can perform in India unless Hajibhai or I clear the visit,' she bragged. 'Crawford Market falls at his feet, dahling. Every shopkeeper there garlands us when we go. We've done so much for them,' Rukhsana continued. Crawford Market was infested with smugglers and unofficial money changers. The funny thing about her boasts was that every word was probably true. And to think the enormous, covered market was located right opposite one of Bombay's largest police stations.

I set up a meeting for the next day since I hadn't been able to arrange for a photographer that evening. As I was leaving, Rukhsana asked one of the goons to accompany me to the car. 'Dahling, I'm worried about your safety,' she said. Precisely. I was worried about it myself. She thrust a gift-wrapped packet in my hand. 'Almond Rocks. For the babies. You insulted me in Delhi. This isn't for you. It's for the kids. Don't insult me again.' I took the chocolates.

The cover story appeared. It wasn't flattering. It wasn't a complete hatchet job either. That Diwali, a large parcel from Rukhsana arrived at my home. I thought it was a bomb. On opening it, I found a heavy, rather gaudy Benarasi saree—the kind Haryanvi brides wear to their devar's wedding. I re-wrapped it. On my next visit to Delhi, I sent it back to Rukhsana with a small note. I never saw her again.

Society took off well enough. We covered a lot of fascinating people—dancers, writers, painters, industrialists. I interviewed several myself—often catching them off-guard. Like poor George Fernandes whose house in Delhi I barged into fairly late in the night with a common friend. There was George relaxing in the ante-room, lungi pulled up way above his knees, when we trooped in. Down came the lungi, up went the eyebrows. Flustered and visibly embarrassed, George attempted a fast recovery but didn't succeed. When my piece appeared, the common friend went into hiding—he was the son of an MP, and the politician-father wasn't amused by what I'd written about his friend George, the giant killer.

From my *Society* days onward, I have always been amused (and alarmed) by the notion that people seem to have that I'm supposed to 'know' what makes Bombay society tick. It used to be money. Just money. Preferably, old and titled. Today, it is balls. You have them, you go for the main chance. You don't, you die. I like to think of Nelson Wang, the celebrated restaurateur, as the person who most represents the spirit of the city. Here was a man who started his career as a fire-eating cabaret dancer and is today, the *numero uno* of his tribe. China Garden, the eatery he launched, continues to win awards year after year. Wang parties with the *haut monde*, a charming man-about-town who works twenty-six hours a day and revels in his success—as he deserves to. Nobody wants to know his antecedents. Nobody asks Nelson, 'Who are your parents? Where did you study? What's your wife's grandfather's name? Are you related to . . .?' Nobody cares. He has made it. Nothing else counts. Nelson's story is the story of Bombay. Excess is all.

I monitor these changes. Chronicle them in my columns. This is all a part of the city's social history. It matters. Tomorrow's Nelsons will be different. I'll be looking out for them when they arrive . . . balls clanging. That's the music Bombaywallahs recognize and understand the best—even if they're tone-deaf.

While I was enjoying editing *Society* enormously, one side of me was acting up: 'Listen. You can do this on your own. Why work for somebody else? Go on. Float your own magazine. Do it now.' It was time to troop into Nari Hira's room once more. This was getting predictable and silly. He talked me out of my decision the first time I brought up the resignation. And I stayed. But he knew and I knew my time was running out in his organization. I was being 'advised' by the wrong people. And I was foolish enough to listen to them. 'Start something you can call your own. There is big money to be made. How long are you going to make somebody else rich? Look at Nari Hira—look at the money he has raked in from *Stardust* and *Society*. Don't be a fool. This is exploitation. You have to shed your middle-class attitudes. Take risks.'

Take risks. That convinced me. I'd always taken risks. And won. I liked risks. Risks liked me. Not this time. Not when the 'risk' involved money, other people's money.

Nari Hira gave me a wonderful send-off party, complete with champagne and heavy with sentiment. It was hard saying goodbye to people I'd seen more of over ten years than I had of my immediate family. But I was charged up with the idea of turning entrepreneur. I'd be a businesswoman. And I'd make big bucks for myself—not someone else. Prodded on and encouraged to go ahead with the project, I left my old office and moved into a hired cubby hole opposite Churchgate station. Yet another phase was beginning. I was impressed with my own daring. I could not lose—would not. How wrong I was. And how foolish.

Flying Solo

The next couple of years were difficult, very difficult. I had never been in such a situation before. Nothing, but nothing, was going right—financially or emotionally. My marriage was breaking up. The magazine I had started, *Celebrity*, was facing all sorts of problems. For the first time in my adult life I felt alone, alienated and isolated. My meagre savings had dwindled to almost nothing. I didn't have money for two square meals a day and often made do with coffee and biscuits, or an egg sandwich. Even with everything collapsing around me, I managed not to let it daunt me to the point of powerlessness. I soldiered on cheerfully, never letting the staff sense my feelings of utter wretchedness and despair. If they were aware of what I was going through, they didn't let on. I was deeply touched by their loyalty and faith even during those desperate months when salaries were withheld indefinitely and there was no petty cash in the box.

Perhaps for the first time ever, I was dealing with failure on several levels. After eight years of being Mrs so-and-so, I was being forced to deal with an identity crisis. Who was I now? What was my standing within the community? My own family? How did my peers view me? How did I view myself? What had happened? Where had I gone wrong? Would I be forgiven—ever? I'd made mistakes—big ones. I'd misjudged. Miscalculated. I was thirty-four years old, and ready to begin again—but would I be given the chance? My self-esteem was in tatters. It was only within the protective haven of the makeshift office walls that I felt relatively safe, relatively in control, relatively understood. I didn't have to apologize or explain to anybody there. I just had to keep the show on the road. Keep working. But it was tough. There was no place to call 'home'. None of the support systems I had got accustomed to. Wracked with guilt and shame, I hid behind a nonchalance I didn't really possess. But about one thing I was very sure—I couldn't have carried on living life on the old terms. No price was big enough for getting out of a situation that I felt an imposter in. Most other women I knew wouldn't have carried on had the circumstances been similar. I couldn't. Friends called me foolish—'You've got a good thing going. Why do you want to give it up?' I didn't think I was being foolish. Selfish, perhaps, but not foolish. This wasn't the way I wished to lead the rest of my life. I wanted out. I wanted out so badly my heart dictated my actions. I clutched desperately at the first available escape route—a relationship that wouldn't take me far but which I valued at the time—and I called it quits.

Since circumstances had spiralled out of my control, I didn't blame myself entirely for the mess that my life had become. And I didn't give up on myself—even when my parents did. It was tough being so completely alone and not knowing where I was headed. Though my father didn't ostracize me completely, he made his disappointment and disapproval perfectly obvious. I wasn't welcome in his home except as an occasional visitor. He wasn't going to condone my 'conduct' or endorse any of my decisions even indirectly by making their home my home. This hurt. There was no other home left for me to go to. I was marooned—literally and metaphorically. My mother must have been caught between her loyalty to him and love for me. She was the only person (besides Kunda) who did not withdraw, was not judgemental, refused to preach, and even in her silence, let me know there was always room in her heart (if not in their home) for a 'sinner'—me.

I lost weight. My appearance changed drastically. I looked gaunt and hollow-eyed. My energy levels fell. I lived in the cheapest khadi kurta-pajamas. It was a testing time for me and those who claimed to be my 'friends'. My self-worth was at its lowest. I couldn't have felt more wretched. It was my cousin Gautam who came through shining like burnished gold. I can't think of anybody I know who would have taken me and the staff of *Celebrity* into his home—no questions asked. We had nowhere else to go, nobody to turn to at one point. In sheer desperation I phoned Gautam (he's single and lives in a sprawling flat in central Mumbai). 'Just come right now,' he said without hesitation. And that's exactly what we did—trooped into his neat, well-ordered apartment and turned it upside down. We stayed on for months. I managed to find paying guest accomodation. The cloud lifted, if only temporarily. And we survived. Not once did Gautam complain or even hint that we might have overstayed. His gesture went beyond generosity. It was nothing short of noble.

Celebrity was jinxed from the word go. There was far too much upheaval in my personal life at that stage. I didn't really need additional difficulties on the professional front. Besides, I discovered for all time to come that I was no good at handling money. It simply did not speak to me. For the first time in my career I was having to deal with financial issues and understand terms like 'cash flow.' Each day added to my debts to paper merchants, printing press owners, freelance journalists . . . and finally banks demanding an early settlement of all dues. My energies were diverted from what I really liked and was reasonably good at—putting a magazine together—to keeping my head above water. The books were a complete mess. I tried hard to take an intelligent interest in the manner in which the accounts were being handled, but I was totally at sea with figures. Frustrated at each level, unable to devote myself to the magazine's creative inputs, I spent a large part of my day juggling numbers and pretending I knew what was going on.

It's a wonder I didn't crack under pressure. Or develop a thick skin for that matter. There were several shameless people surrounding me—people with no scruples, people who took a little fiddle here, a little fiddle there, in their stride, people who tried to convince me that all this was an inevitable part of 'business'—that lofty male preserve in which a naïve woman like me had no part to play. 'You stick to your work,' I'd be advised. And it would have suited me fine too, except that in the very next instant a sheaf of papers would be stuck under my nose with crisp instructions to 'sign here', 'sign there'. I still don't know what I affixed my signatures to and shudder at the memory of those humiliating days when I hated to pick up a phone, knowing it would be a creditor on the line.

Despite these behind-the-scenes problems the magazine managed to maintain its upbeat, cheeky, irreverent tone. It was fun to write, fun to read, featuring racy profiles, catty celeb comments, provocative quotes and tongue-in-cheek send-ups that succeeded in pricking many mighty egos. It surprised me that our comments got under people's skin, given our measly circulation. Our views ought not to have mattered. We were nobodies. Small fry. Tiny frogs croaking away in a huge pond infested with publishing barracudas. I like to think of us as the proverbial ant biting an elephant and driving the enormous pachyderm mad.

Celebrity packed quite a stylish punch between its

pages . . . but the biggest one was reserved for my nose. And when it was delivered, it sent me reeling. I was informed that we were broke, broke, broke. And the debts were huge, huge, huge. My back was to the wall. I looked around desperately for a way out. All I wanted was to offload the magazine and break free. But I was caught in a peculiar cul-de-sac and found myself well and truly trapped. If the magazine suspended publication abruptly we wouldn't be in a position to recover our paltry outstandings. If we carried on bringing out the issue month after month, we'd need to continue borrowing. By now our debt-trap had grown still bigger. To me it seemed like a bottomless pit into which I'd disappear eventually. I was scared out of my wits. And not the least because of a new problem that had cropped up—I was named Accused number two in a case of treason against the State of India. Imagine. Treason. That was all I needed. Accused number one was Simranjit Singh Mann—a former police officer who had been charged with being a part of the conspiracy behind Indira Gandhi's brutal murder in 1984.

Where did I fit? The sequence of events leading up to the absurd charge sheet was comical, to say the least. I had met Simranjit Singh Mann for an interview while he was still with the IPS. It had been set up by a journalist friend who had been most impressed by Mann's views. We met at an arty café attached to a gallery and talked for a couple of hours. It was hard to see the expression in Mann's eyes since he wore thick glasses. There was nothing impressive about him, not even his voice which was a semi-squeak. He looked and talked like any ordinary sardarji, except when you listened closely to his words—which were deadly. He gave me reams and reams of cyclostyled papers—all the letters he had been shooting off to various VIPs, the President of India among them. There was a manic, fanatical energy about him which was unmistakable.

I dismissed him as yet another crank—a 'causewallah' beating his turban against a stone wall and getting nowhere. He was just another interviewee with a militant point of view, that was all. We were to meet again the following day for a few clarifications. That meeting never took place. Instead, his wife contacted me and had some relevant papers delivered. I had no idea at the time that Mann had gone underground, perhaps a few hours after our meeting. I didn't know that he was on the 'Most Wanted' list as the main person accused of plotting against the government, the master-mind behind Mrs Gandhi's assassination. A man on the run. A fugitive from the law.

We ran his interview in a question-and-answer format. *Celebrity*, after all, was not a political magazine. We had no agenda. We didn't want to change the world. I wouldn't even have heard of Mann had my friend not insisted on the meeting. Once the issue hit the stands, I threw away all the notes I'd taken and the bundles of papers he'd given me. We were running such a tight ship, there was physically no room to store files . . . even tapes. We recycled everything. The minute we were through with transcribing an interview, we promptly taped the next one over it. Yes, it was that bad. We couldn't afford new tapes and monitored each phone call, worried to death about mounting bills. I wonder how many of our readers bothered to read Mann's interview. The photograph his wife had supplied was hazy, grainy and as unattractive as the subject. Hardly *Celebrity* stuff. I'd carried the piece for two reasons: to oblige Olga, my journalist friend, and because I enjoyed meeting controversial, kinky people. They provided better copy than the holier-than-thous.

When I saw the summons I was confused and a little shaken. Surely there was some mistake? I passed them on to a lawyer, and wondered what to do next. I didn't have to wait too long to find out. Two burly chaps from the intelligence wing showed up at home for an 'informal' chat. They questioned me closely about my meeting with Mann and demanded the tapes. I said I no longer had them in my possession. They asked for the notes, for Mann's cyclostyled sheets. I explained I'd gotten rid of them, as most publications get rid of old papers once the interview is published. They went to the printing press, the old office, the new office and back again to my residence. The lawyer told me to sit back and wait it out—nothing was likely to come of this case, just as nothing had come of the others. I wasn't so sure. This wasn't an ordinary matter. Mann had surfaced in Nepal and had been brought back to India. He was locked up in the high security prison in Bhagalpur. The situation in Punjab was violent and volatile. He'd formed his own political party. He was being viewed as a martyr to the Sikh cause. His family was being harassed. And I was being dragged into the mess only because of bad timing—the *Celebrity* interview with Mann was his sole interview in print besides being the last one published before his dramatic disappearance. The cops wanted to establish some sort of a link.

A hearing was fixed in Mumbai. My lawyer looked grim as he briefed me. Trouble was expected, major trouble, despite the tight security. The lawyer warned me that there were chances of a shoot-out in court—anything was possible in those days, with extremists hitting unlikely targets across India. He told me not to make eye contact with Mann who was to be brought all the way from Bhagalpur, or speak to his wife who'd also be present in court. I was told exactly where to sit in the courtroom—out of the direct line of fire, in case some terrorists tried to spring their hero and make a dash for it. Strangely enough, I found myself unusually calm and pretty certain Mann would not turn up. Moving him from

Bhagalpur to Mumbai would have required an enormous amount of planning, man-power, strategy and risk. Simply not worth the effort. Sure enough, the much-feared moment came and went without incident. And I did spend a few minutes talking to Mann's brave and good-looking wife. The next date was fixed in Bhagalpur and I was asked to present myself there. I instructed my lawyer to appeal for an adjournment or at least exempt me from personal appearance. The magistrate would have none of it. When my lawyer gestured in my direction and pleaded that some consideration ought to be shown (I was pregnant at the time), the magistrate coolly turned down the request saying, 'No concessions can be made. She should have thought about the possible consequences when she took the interview.' My heart sank. I dreaded the train ride more than anything else. Bhagalpur was pretty inaccessible and from the looks of it, I didn't have much time left to pack my bags and go.

Fortunately, just then the government fell. And Chandra Shekhar became India's new prime minister. One of the first things he did on assuming office was to release all political prisoners, Mann being his most high-profile dischargee. I delivered Arundhati on schedule at the Breach Candy Hospital, while Mann went back as a hero to Punjab and contested the next election successfully.

The few people who were aware of what I'd been through in the preceding months joked that I should head for Punjab myself and stand as a candidate on Mann's party ticket. 'You'll win hands down,' they assured me. I would have, too. With Mann's blessings. But my priorities had shifted. Yes. Again. I was that much older. I wanted to do everything right every inch of the way. After years of restlessness I was experiencing a sense of calm and peace. I'd heard my friends out when they'd cautioned, 'You'll get bored. Don't be crazy.

You can't sit at home doing nothing.' I knew they meant well. But I also knew my own priorities. I'd been swimming against the tide for far too long. I was getting slightly tired. I wanted to slow down. Since the age of seventeen I had chosen to be my own person, flying solo, even when I was within a secure family environment. The life I was enjoying right now was the one I'd dreamed about and I wasn't about to surrender even an inch of it for some dubious 'ambition'.

Celebrity was history by now. Almost. After struggling to keep it afloat for three years I had finally managed to offload it. But instead of a knight in shining armour, it was a knave in white khadi who'd shown up with promises of instant blood (and more importantly, money) transfusions. In my hurry to get rid of the limping magazine and get on with the rest of my life, I didn't want to look beyond the knave's smooth talk and fake smile. So long as he was ready to pay back the creditors and free me of the financial burden, I was only too happy to sign everything over and escape. But that's not how things work in the real world. The knave had well-trained bulldogs (chartered accountants and wannabe publishers) who were let loose from time to time to bare their teeth and indulge in some old-fashioned bullying. This uncouth bunch represented all that I loathe about small-time North Indian businessmen—their oily, unscrupulous ways, crude mannerisms, lack of basic etiquette, bombastic words, annoying swagger and the worst sin of all—lack of scruples. Behind all the sweet talk, these guys were slimy opportunists. God knows why the knave stepped in to 'buy' *Celebrity* (not a paisa was eventually paid). He must have had his reasons. It's possible he wished to buy the editor's name, but I had made it clear that my future agenda did not involve the magazine.

I was relieved, though, that *Celebrity* was no longer my

financial problem. Money matters have always embarrassed me. Perhaps 'stumped' is a better word. I hate discussing money, though I enjoy making it. How can I forget two of the longest hours in my professional life spent across the impressive antique desk of a pompous publisher, tongue-tied when asked by him, 'What sort of money are you looking for?' The only experience I had had in the job market till that point had been my solo interview with Nari Hira where I'd cheerfully settled for Rs 350 a month. I had no idea where to begin with this gentleman who was so obviously relishing my discomfiture. Finally, I stammered a figure. He readily agreed. I knew I had undersold myself. It was too late. That one experience taught me a valuable lesson—it's best to talk turkey. And it's best to do it fast. The longer you hedge, the worse it gets. Train yourself to say 'How much?' Let the other guy squirm. Today I can cut the meanest deals. But I learnt my lesson the hard way. I belonged to that self-conscious generation of woman who thought it 'unfeminine' to discuss money. Bullshit. Money is sexless, only suckers are stupid enough to bring gender into it.

While running *Celebrity*, a major portion of my time was spent on money-talk. While discussing overdraft facilities with a nationalized bank, I would assume an appropriate expression while understanding zilch. The accountant would bring the monthly statement to me and I'd feign comprehension. It was hopeless and the people around me knew it too. Fortunately, the editorial staff was more accomodating, even putting up with delayed salaries, maintaining a discreet silence when things were down, working overtime without any expectations of getting paid for it, and cheerfully keeping my spirits up. At this point we were working out of a cramped room at the Ritz Hotel in downtown Mumbai. It's a great place to be in. Well located,

212

not too expensive, and close to the main local station, the Ritz has a unique reputation for being the favourite hangout of outstation politicians. The management handles its VIPs with admirable tact, making sure to keep warring camps in different wings. The Eighties saw an influx of down-market Arab tourists visiting Mumbai with their harems and a large entourage of kids, especially during the monsoons. The Ritz coffee shop suited them well with its jukebox and friendly service. Often, our female journalists would get propositioned as they went in and out of the hotel. But one visitor who caused the maximum excitement was Farah Rustom, the gifted pianist who had once been Farouk Rustom, a pale, effeminate man with delicate fingers and an ego to match. Farah was one of the first Indians to go public with her sex-change operation. And go public she did with a vengeance. She breezed into our office soon after she'd acquired an impressive silicon bosom. Desperate to show off her new assets, she literally bounced from table to table, urging startled paste-up artists to touch, feel, admire her perfect breasts. I decided to take her to the coffee shop downstairs instead of having something brought up. Besides, I wanted to spare her the furtive glances and inevitable giggles from staffers who'd never encountered anything or anyone quite like this.

Farah was provocatively clad in a low-slung chiffon saree. Her saree blouse was not fitted at the waist like conventional cholis, but hung like a bolero, barely covering her bosom (it was possible to see the lower half of her breasts if she lifted her arms even slightly). Two dozen glass bangles jingled on her forearms. She wore far too much make-up: heavy lipstick, eyeliner, plus an enormous bindi on her forehead. Her childlike enthusiasm was touching as she whispered sweetly, 'You know how it is for pretty ladies like us—we have to put up with stares.' I looked away and gulped. Then she asked one of the Maharashtrian artists, her baritone booming, 'I wish to powder my nose, where is the girls' room?' He nearly fell off his chair.

As Farah sashayed into the coffee shop minutes after powdering her nose (and adding another ten layers of bright red sticky lipstick) the Arabs present stopped twirling their amber beads and seemed transfixed by the sight. Several 'Mashallahs' followed. If Farah noticed any of them, she didn't show it. Instead, she took my hand and placed it gently on her firm bosom. 'Feel. Go ahead. Touch. My breasts make me believe I'm one hundred per cent a woman.' There was nothing vulgar or even remotely suggestive about the gesture, and I was very moved. But the Arabs were affected differently. We became aware of several pairs of eyes staring interestedly at us. One of the men at an adjoining table summoned a waiter and asked him to request 'the lady in the saree' (not me) to join him at his table. Farah giggled and preened, delighted by the attention.

Back in the office I gently suggested to Farah that she go easy with her new-found femininity, tone down the make-up, hitch up the low-slung saree, reduce the number of bangles around her wrists . . . just take the transition one step at a time or risk attracting the wrong kind of attention. She was silent and pensive. When she looked up, it was to throw her head back dramatically and growl testily, 'You know dear . . . had those words come from a lesser woman, I'd have said she was jealous of my beauty. We women are so competitive . . .' I was speechless. But I had tried.

My encounter at the Ritz with the painter M.F. Husain was less dramatic but equally interesting. I ran into him hobbling past the lobby, his leg in a cast. 'Why don't you come on up for a coffee and a chat?' I suggested. When he limped into our one-room office, the atmosphere changed instantly. In those days (a little less now) Husain cut a sensational figure with his flowing beard (since trimmed) and stylish clothes (they remain). He was also a more relaxed individual with a quirky sense of humour. The cast was covered with doodles. He sat across me and doodled some more, chatting over chai about the art world, making light fun of his contemporaries and lots more of himself. This was the Husain I admired and liked—a man in touch with his times, cued in, switched on, informal, caustic and charming by turns. Something happened somewhere along the way: Maybe he reached a personal turning point in the Nineties the world will never know about. But back then, he was accessible, likeable and quotable. Always a media-savvy painter, he knew exactly how to pitch his spiel. Arrogant, even imperious while dealing with lesser mortals, he understood perfectly the far-reaching value of positive publicity and made sure he flirted with hand-picked members of the press, taking the trouble to cultivate relationships with the chosen few while keeping up the mystique of elusiveness with the others.

What I've always enjoyed about Husain is his impeccable sense of timing. The man knows his moments—and plays them well. In the past, he always managed to be the right guy at the right place and with the right people. For a person who is eighty-plus, it is nothing short of a feat that his energy levels don't seem to flag nor does his enthusiasm when it comes to self-promotion. He is one painter who understands the importance of shrewd marketing and misses no opportunity to cash in on waves or trends. He may go hoarse defending (or explaining) his Madhuri fixation in obsessive phrases, but I suspect he picked Madhuri because she was the national obsession at the time. And she was the best. Husain goes for winners. And he can teach marketing gurus a trick or two about product positioning. I also suspect what developed later (love, admiration) grew naturally out of his initial association with the smart, beautiful star. Today the story is different. His involvement is one hundred per cent genuine and unconditional. There is nothing he will not do for Madhuri and he has no reservations about going public with his feelings.

At a dinner in a politician-businessman's home, late in 1997, over succulent kebabs and coconut water, we discussed his Madhuri fixation. He didn't bother to couch his words or camouflage his feelings. He spoke about her incomparable body language. 'Even when I watch her in her own home, doing something simple—serving tea, moving from room to room—I'm fascinated by her movements. The angle of her neck, the way her arms are crooked when she places a cup down on the table—there is perfect co-ordination and harmony in simple gestures. This is instinctive. It cannot be taught. Madhuri can easily rule for another ten years but she doesn't care about her success. She has scaled the top. What more is left now?'

And how does his family feel now that his priorities have been defined? 'They don't understand or accept it. I have made it clear to all. It's my life. I'm free to lead it the way I choose. If they don't like it . . . well . . . it's their problem. It has been my lifelong dream to make a movie—which is what I'm doing now with Madhuri. Nothing and nobody can stop me.' Husain's present schedule revolves around Madhuri's priorities—rumour goes he spontaneously bought three cars, one for himself, one for her and one for her accountant. If his family resents the time and money invested in the actress, he is unmindful and nonchalant. I asked him what he admired most about her and he said simply, 'Everything.' Personally, I consider Madhuri to be one of the three smartest

Maharashtrians I know. Smart as in sávvy and on-the-ball. The other two? Sunil Gavaskar and Sharad Pawar.

About Husain's genius, I have no reservations in saying I believe in it. He is mercurial and brilliant, an exceptional man with a mind that's capable of several creative leaps. A mind that is rarely still. He reads more than nearly anybody else I know—everything from film rags to philosophical tomes. Since he requires very little rest or sleep, his waking hours are crammed with frenetic activity as he moves compulsively from city to city, continent to continent. Agile, curious, perennially in search of fresh stimuli, he wanders the earth untiringly, seeking new highs and finding them.

My encounters with him have always been exciting, even if he has infuriated me on occasion with his notorious no-shows. The thing about Husain is, even the so-called unpredictability-factor is well calculated. He turns up all right when he knows he is likely to be the star, and the occasion is prestigious. But don't expect him to be present at a down-market, low-key affair, no matter how worthy the cause. Husain is his own man, someone who understands priorities. Like most busy VIPs he probably asks himself, 'What's in it for me?' If the answer to that is 'zilch', well, organizers can forget about Husain's presence even if he has accepted the invitation.

Husain has never let me down. Nor has he spurned special requests. When I asked him to design the jacket for my second novel, *Starry Nights*, he agreed enthusiastically . . . and delivered on schedule. He was kind enough to give me a painting for yet another book jacket—*Uncertain Liaisons*, the anthology I co-edited with Khushwant Singh. Fortunately, I've never been at the receiving end of his temperamental outbursts either. We share a good rapport and an easy relationship that includes light-hearted banter and

Husain-style jokes. A week after my marriage to Dilip, I ran into Husain near our home (he lives close by). He teased me about a gossipy item that had appeared in a news magazine. It had stated that Dilip had wooed me with a priceless painting a week (not true). Husain told me in all seriousness, 'Had I known, I would have wooed you with one Husain a day.' A few years later he did produce a gift on my birthday—a portrait sketched on lined paper. It bears a startling resemblance to Indira Gandhi, but I take the master's word for it—that's me. Twenty years hence.

I don't know whether Husain has any 'friends'. There are enough people who claim they know him well. Husain lives for himself—not even for his large family. Yes, he is a generous provider, though 'careless' might be a more accurate word. While he may sanction lakhs for airline tickets and five-star hotel stays world-wide for his children and grandchildren, it's equally possible that he forgets to leave basic house-money to pay for provisions. I used to be a frequent visitor to his flat as I was very fond of his wife—a dear, warm, good-hearted woman who loved her husband till the day she died, despite knowing all about his other women. Husain was invariably respectful and affectionate towards her, but it was obvious she did not engage him intellectually or emotionally. She was the mother of his six children, the gracious lady who made a home out of his house, the one person who waited up for him—and she had one hell of a lot of waiting to do during her lifetime. Husain would frequently leave the house saying he'd be back for lunch. The next thing she'd know he'd be in Delhi. No explanations. No apologies. These sudden decisions would be taken impulsively, spontaneously. For example, he'd set off to go to the Jehangir Art Gallery. Somewhere along the way he'd remember something or someone in Delhi/ Madras/ Calcutta/

Ahmedabad. He'd hail a passing cab, go to the airport, buy himself a ticket and be gone. Just like that.

Often, I'd find his wife depressed and weeping. Ill-health, financial uncertainty and loneliness had begun to gnaw into her. Few people know that she maintained her own sketchbooks filled with drawings. She'd shown them to me shyly one afternoon, explaining the strange figures and forms that dominated the pale yellow pages.

Husain's contempt for the glittering socialites he is always surrounded by, is well disguised at most times. But I've been there during his low periods when he'd spit out angry words and dismiss them in one or two harsh but accurate sentences. That very evening he'd be there at their ritzy homes, flirting, laughing, his eyes cold and distant, his words soft and appealing. 'They understand nothing about art,' he'd hiss while accepting a nariyal-pani with one hand and a cheque with the other. Not that these ladies always paid up. I remember one afternoon when a socialite's driver came panting up the stairs and asked for a particular canvas his 'madam' wanted. Husain pretended to be busy, but he instructed his son to say, 'Tell him to come back with the money and then take the painting.'

So, why does he part with his best work in that case? Partly because it hangs on the right walls and attracts attention. And also because through these ladies he gets to flog his canvases to monied buyers overseas. It's a neat arrangement that suits everyone. Though he claims he is as comfortable at a roadside dhaba as he is in a billionaire's summer home, Husain likes his creature comforts and loves glamour. His longest-standing association with any woman has been with a buxom, raven-haired, much-married lady from Delhi. To her belong some of his largest and most impressive works—some of them featuring her.

I was very keen to interview his muse and asked him whether he'd fix up a meeting. He seemed delighted, almost thrilled.

The moment I met Rashda I immediately understood why the painter was so taken with her. Here was a woman who was all woman— the sort of woman who can keep a man in a permanent state of insecurity by knowing when, what and how much to withhold. When I met her to discuss the interview and photographs she seemed awfully flattered and was far from nervous at the prospect of the whole world discovering what was in any case an open secret—the mutual adoration between Husain and Rashda. I didn't see any visual evidence of a husband in her bungalow and wondered whether she was a divorcee. Rashda laughed and mentioned that her husband, an army man, was posted at a non-family station in the foothills of the Himalayas. Well, from the looks of it, it was a semi-permanent posting since the man was rarely around.

Rashda, like Rukhsana, had a boudoir, not a bedroom. She sat herself on a stool in front of a large mirror. I was distracted by the frequent dropping and gathering up of her trailing saree pallu. It was a gesture she repeated compulsively while gazing at her image in the mirror. Why couldn't she keep it from falling off her shoulder by pinning it up, I wondered. I found out years later. Rashda worked hard on perfecting her little pallu-dropping act and her efforts definitely paid off, going by the reaction it had on men. Once I met her while I was checking into a hotel in Delhi and she was leaving to go home after a classical music concert. The hour was late. She was relaxed and informal. We were chatting lightly, when I saw her eyes had shifted from mine and her expression had changed. She'd also sucked in her tummy and stuck her chest out while performing that

220

Flying Solo

beautifully timed pallu-dropping gesture that had so
fascinated me. I followed her gaze and saw a media baron
walking in. He spotted her and came up for a chat. Rashda
had switched to her courtesan-mode, simpering, preening,
tossing back the long black hair Husain had immortalized on
so many canvases—and, more significantly (she was at it
furiously), the well-synchronized pallu-dropping. Bravo.

The interview itself was remarkably clever. Rashda gave
nothing away. Her quotes were discreet and shrewdly
worded. She spoke about her relationship with Husain in
poetic, flowery terms that didn't suggest anything besides a
respectful, respectable 'friendship'. She agreed to pose for
pictures with Husain the next morning—and did. We used
one of his countless canvases of her as a backdrop. The tone
of the piece was formal and correct without a single
insinuation or wisecrack. It was that kind of a piece—if you
knew the score, you put two and two together. If you
didn't—well, it was a charming story about loyalty and
goodwill. Husain seemed pleased.

A few days after the issue came out, I received a call from
Rashda to say her husband was looking for me. When last
seen, he'd had a shotgun in his hand. I reminded her that the
interview had been voluntary and without any coercion
involved. 'I know, I know. But my husband has hit the roof.
He is very angry with you,' she whispered. Why was he angry
with me? He should have been angry with Husain, or his wife,
or both of them, why me? She added, 'I haven't given him
your address. He thinks you live in Delhi. I called to warn you
. . . in case he contacts you.' She made out like she was doing
me a favour. I waited for the poor man to show up, knowing
he wouldn't. Next thing I heard he'd been posted to Ladakh
or some such remote station.

I lost touch with Rashda completely. On Husain's

seventy-fifth birthday, his admirers and business managers decided to stage a grand 'event' in an old film studio to celebrate the occasion. It was the hottest ticket in town. The place was crawling with 'names'—movie stars, socialites, media people, tycoons, the usual suspects, in other words. Husain's family had been rounded up and roped in. Around midnight I heard a little commotion. I'd been told Rashda had flown into the city and was holding court in one corner of the cavernous studio. Husain's wife was sitting quietly in the shadows and weeping bitterly, and one of Husain's daughters had decided to confront Rashda and ask her to leave. Some of the other family members were against creating a scene. By then, the tempo of the music was up and Husain had been dragged to the dance floor by one of the drunken invitees. Someone sensible decided to escort the old lady home and spare her further humiliation. Rashda, I guess, stayed on.

Naming Names

Some months ago, a well-meaning compère at a function in Pune introduced me as a 'celebrity' and a 'doll'. I found both descriptions equally comic . . . and said so in my short speech. I'd been accused of being a celebrity often enough. But nobody had ever dared call me a 'doll'. A doll? The compère blushed and apologized. The audience simpered. The function carried on.

Everybody and anybody is loosely described as a 'celebrity' these days especially if that person has no known profession, talent or gift. The fact that a face appears more than five times in a publication or on television is sufficient qualification to dub him or her a celebrity. I cringe when people address me as one and feel worse about the fact that several more think of me as one.

So many years after closing down the magazine of that name which I had started in 1981, I continue to believe it was the timing that was off. The national pastime of creating and fêting overnight 'names' hadn't reached present-day proportions. Now there are celebrities at every street corner. However, the rather depressing fact is that one important qualifying criterion was (and continues to be) good looks. In the case of showbiz people, good looks go with the job. But in other fields where the emphasis ought to be on achievement rather than appearance, attractiveness is still a prime consideration. Take sports—Ashwini Nachappa is the glam-girl of the track even if her best timing is nowhere close to P.T. Usha's. The media favoured her over Usha only because Ashwini projected the sort of undisguised sex appeal rarely seen on Indian sports fields. She looked a winner—particularly off the track. And she hogged the headlines even if she wasn't breaking any records. Ditto for Ajay Jadeja. Even Leander Paes. How many column inches does Vishwanathan Anand get in India? And he's the one making serious moves and money.

If I bristled at the Pune function (but good-naturedly), I felt like the guru of celebrity when I found myself explaining the phenomenon of current celebrityhood to a disbelieving columnist at a well-attended media event. The occasion? A book launch with a difference. Since it was a volume (*India—The Making of a Nation*) related to fifty years of India's independence, the publishers, writers and promoters had decided to get maximum mileage by pegging the function around the defining decades leading up to the Big Moment—15 August 1947. Each decade was given a visual and a speaker. Each speaker was allotted approximately two to three minutes to wrap up ten years of history. Sounds absurd? Nothing sounds absurd in these days of soundbyte-living. If you can't condense an event-filled decade into a viewer-friendly two minutes, you're in the wrong business. I was assigned the Nineties. My visual was a blow-up of Miss World Aishwarya Rai's ecstatic face—the wire photograph that was flashed worldwide after her triumph in Sun City.

A venerable, kurta-pajama clad columnist asked me why the Nineties were being represented by as vacuous a symbol as a beauty queen. I explained it was not an accident—nor was it an excuse to use a gorgeous portrait in an otherwise drab gallery featuring half-clad leaders and toothy cricketers. Aishwarya, Sushmita and the other lovelies in the forefront of the beauty business are the undisputed icons for countless young Indians who look up to them as role models. The columnist looked stricken as he said, 'You can't be serious.' I can and I was. I told him to conduct a random survey, check with school kids and young collegians, ask them whom they admire the most. Cricketers? Not any more. Movie stars? Not even them. Music channel VJs? Yes. Radio DJs? Oh yes. Models? Yes, yes, yes. Beauty queens? Swoon.

What is it? Just the glamour? I suspect it's something bigger. Glamour and publicity, yes. But what else? Could it be filthy lucre? That's exactly what it is. Kids' fantasies go into overdrive at the thought of the megabucks they imagine their idols are making for doing very little besides looking great. No special effort is required. No real attribute or ability. Well, fine, a gift of the gab helps while chatting inanely through half-hour slots punctuated with the latest hits. And judges at beauty contests at least pretend to mark contestants on something other than their vital statistics during the 'serious' interview rounds. But everybody is aware that the questions and answers have about as much relevance or depth as the beauty queen's pancake. But in these times of political correctness it has become obligatory to ask and make a show of assessing the response . . . never mind the foolishness of the exercise which rarely goes beyond trite exchanges that invariably drag in Mother Teresa and Nelson Mandela whose names are invoked by the Breathless Babes like a mantra that guarantees them a place in the final round, if not the crown itself.

Youngsters can identify with the hypocrisy of it all, even sympathize with the poor creatures on the lavish sets who are compelled to declare their interest in eradicating the world's

225

problems when all they really want is the prize money and the baubles that go with the titles. In such an undisguisedly materialistic environment where hedonism rules, who needs sports stars or social workers?

The columnist thought I was being overly cynical. The sad truth is, I wasn't. I have children of that age. I know just how disconnected their generation is with the sort of ideals we grew up on—old-fashioned ones that celebrated old-fashioned virtues. Our heroes were not hirsute hunks with pony-tails. Our heroines did not parade in underwear disguised as outerwear. But I have no quarrel with changing mores, changing definitions. Every generation feels morally obliged to register its horror at falling standards. Every generation suffers (and I mean that literally) from an unbearable superiority complex vis-à-vis the next. It is so tempting to assume the 'we know better' stance. And how easily we fall into the trap. If kids today chase nineteen-year-old, spaced-out veejays at airports, if besotted fans tear off their clothes during public appearances, if the veejays feel the need to hire the services of top-grade security guards with sniffer dogs just to keep over-enthusiastic admirers at bay, it is because they, the pop icons, have achieved this desired status. They are the ruling celebrities, no matter how ridiculous this fact may appear to others. And it is astonishing how many otherwise serious and talented individuals covet the sort of fame these individuals have had 'thrust' upon them.

Take for example the ambition of a young, attractive film-maker who's doing brilliantly for herself. One afternoon, she sat cross-legged from me at home munching on a salami sandwich. She was back from an exhausting shoot in South India at which she'd had to humour a male model with more attitude than Mick Jagger and Madonna put together. Tired of his tantrums, irritated by his petulance and exasperated by his demands, she was in an introspective mode, wondering where her career would take her next. Just then, my mail arrived. A sweet and obliging person from Pune had sent me a set of clippings after my brief visit there. It included a front-page story which was an embarrassing gush. I glanced through the lot and kept it aside. The young woman had been watching me closely. Finally, she hugged her knees and declared, 'I know what it is I want to be.' I waited. And I swear I could not have anticipated the answer that followed. She looked me straight in the eye and said flatly, 'I want to be famous. That's it.' It was very honest of her. Everybody wants to be famous in these celebrity-driven times. It's both scary and amusing, especially when one knows the lengths some people will go to in order to get their five minutes of fame, their little twirl under the spotlight.

One only has to see some of the chat shows on the air to understand what an enormous leap has been taken in the direction of 'let it all hang out' TV confessions. I've watched well-known women candidly discussing menopause, toy boys, mis-matched sexual cycles, breast size, with the active participation of invited studio audiences. I've also watched men talking frankly about penile lengths, premature ejaculation, low sex drive and bald pates. Going public with one's insecurities and anxieties would have been an unthinkable thing to do even ten years ago, given the closed nature of our society. It would be easy to dismiss it as the Oprah-Winfreyization of the masses, but the reality is different—it's that four-letter word: fame. We are rapidly becoming a nation of fame-junkies. Point a video camera into a crowd and chances are no fewer than fifty people will jostle to get into the frame. *Vox populi* has become the latest sport in town with opinions flying around arbitrarily, often

227

irresponsibly.

My mail over the years has given me a pretty good indication of changing aspirations. These days I receive at least five letters a week that basically echo the young film-maker's plea. I want to be famous. Make me famous. Write about me in your column. I don't care what you say. Call me names. Abuse me. Criticize my work, but mention me. I find it scary. A few months ago, a lady came to see me with a book she'd written and published herself. It was a painstakingly detailed autobiography, the kind that begins with 'place of birth', 'year of birth', and goes on to boringly narrate family histories in agonizing detail. I was amazed by her confidence, enthusiasm and presumptuousness in thinking anybody outside her little circle would be even remotely interested in the events and thoughts that had shaped her. I didn't say so to her as I flipped through the pages while she watched for reactions. She'd tried it all—writing articles, modelling, running a PR agency, running a magazine, teaching, consulting, television, films . . . playing godmother. She was obviously intelligent, motivated and frighteningly ambitious. Her self-worth was sky-high and I ended up envying her undiluted delight in her own genius.

She told me her husband found her ravishing and that a legendary film-maker she'd once interviewed had talked about her 'inner beauty' at length. It hadn't occurred to her that the husband might have been prejudiced or that the film-maker, polite. Unable to pay her sincere compliments, he'd resorted to talking about a quality that at best is subjective, at worst, debatable.

After half an hour of aggressive hard-sell, she came to the point: 'I've been told that if you take notice of my book, I'll be made. So, will you write about me . . . it? I want to be known. I want TV crews to interview me. I want to make it

to the covers of magazines. I want people to recognize me.'
Well, so much for candour. And so much more for
undisguised PR.

Coming from a small-town person like this pushy lady it
was one thing, but when the late Indrani Aikath-Gyaltsen
took the same route, I must admit I was taken aback. She was
far more a woman of the world, or so I'd thought. Talented,
productive and acknowledged as a writer-to-watch-out-for
by someone like Khushwant Singh, I expected Indrani to be
far more confident than her letters to me revealed. It began
with short notes introducing herself, and grew into a
full-fledged correspondence.

Her first book had received raves. She was the toast of
the literary set—if only briefly. It was then that she wrote a
longish letter informing me that she'd been asked to write a
weekly column for a Calcutta paper. She wanted to know how
I did it. How did I write my columns? What was the key to
my success (her words) as a columnist? Was there a method?
A formula? What should she put into her own? I wrote back
with suggestions. That encouraged her to phone and shoot
off more letters. There was something touching and plaintive
about her enquiries. 'I want my books to be best-sellers. I want
your kind of success. How do I go about it? Why doesn't the
press write more about me? Why do journalists write so much
about you?'

Frankly, I didn't know how to deal with her insecurities
and gradually backed off. Months later she was dead. I've
kept most of her letters and have re-read the last few which
were full of despair and frustration. I don't know how exactly
she died, I can only hope her death had nothing to do with
her disappointnent as a writer.

In my career as a social commentator, I have dealt with
all types. There are those who believe in the direct approach

and come right out and ask for publicity. Others prefer a more sophisticated route, a subtle one. But the goal is the same. It can start with a charming phone call, a dinner invitation, flowers, champagne, and a request to attend an event. The message is clear: coverage. One is hardened enough to deal with these types. But it becomes embarrassing, even painful, when the person doing the lobbying is a friend or a family member. I have experienced feelings of deep resentment and exploitation when people I've grown close to and trusted have turned around and blatantly demanded a plug. It's not a pleasant feeling. But confronted with the request, one has to weigh the options—oblige the favour-seeker, or risk jeopardizing the relationship. If that happens to me as often as it does, I cannot begin to imagine the levels to which the really important people in media are hounded, people who wield far more power and influence than I. I'm only a newspaper hack. My printed opinions are hardly likely to change the world, topple governments, make heads roll. A mention or two in my column may help some society lady sell a few more salwar-kameezes. It may let a few readers of the paper know that such-and-such person exists and is doing interesting stuff or that I feel strongly about certain issues. And that's where it stops. Yet, the hunger for publicity is so overwhelming it's hard to escape the outstretched hand begging for it.

I am often asked how comfortable I am with my image, my public identity, my own 'celebrityhood.' It's not an easy question to respond to. There is an upside and a downside. I have not as yet taught myself to enjoy the 'up' and completely ignore the 'down'. While I rarely respond to hostile mail, criticism or reviews, I'd be lying if I said I am completely immune to the hurt they cause—at least temporarily. What I have managed to achieve over the years is a perspective of sorts that helps me cope with the barbs and darts along with the compliments and high praise—and shrug both off. I have taught myself to shrink the sulk-period. If in the past I'd brood over a bitchy remark for weeks, I now deal with it in hours. One reason is that I am much more preoccupied and busy now than at any previous stage in my life. I guess I am slightly more confident too. I don't instantly sink into a pit or lapse into depression, as I once used to. I don't feel retaliatory or vindictive either. I attribute this to training rather than a real change of attitude—there's too little time to exhaust in settling scores. Besides, through long experience I have also discovered that people change, attitudes change, I change. I'm far more flexible, far more open to correction, than I was, say, twenty years ago.

With confidence comes a layer of toughness and invincibility. While I have never been naïve enough to think I'm above or beyond anybody's aim, I have mellowed sufficiently to make allowances for attacks, telling myself nothing is permanent. Today's foe can (and sometimes does) become tomorrow's friend. I'm also acutely aware of how easy it is to slot and judge, considering how often I've experienced that kind of branding myself.

If I can laugh at the 'fame thing' and not let it get to me, it's because I've never taken it (or myself) seriously in the first place. But I do know how important it can be to some people. And I genuinely admire TV man Rajat Sharma for acknowledging as much in the wake of his hugely successful series *Aap ki Adaalat* (since renamed *Janata ki Adaalat*).

This quote appeared in an interview when he was asked what he enjoyed most about his new-found status as a celebrity. He said: 'I enjoy being recognized at airports and restaurants. I enjoy being asked for autographs. I enjoy people wanting to pose for photographs with me. I just enjoy being famous. So why should I deny it or pretend it annoys me?'

Some people are just far more comfortable with attention than others. Sunil Gavaskar for one insists he doesn't welcome it and has never come to terms with unwarranted, intrusive interruptions. I remember his telling me how he hasn't quite figured out what a public figure is supposed to do at, say, a traffic light, when he's recognized and strangers call out his name. Should he acknowledge the greeting? Wave briefly? Smile? Scowl? Sink his chin into his chest and pretend he hasn't heard? Then again, suppose he's at an airport and a few people surround him. They want to make the most of the opportunity and start badgering him with cricket talk ('Will so-and-so be included in the team? Why was that bowler dropped? How did it feel when you scored your first century?'). There is no real escape in these circumstances. He can't run. He is cornered. He will soon be on the plane without a mid-air exit route. What does he do? Tolerate the intrusions even though he may be tired and not in the mood to chat idly with total strangers? Be rude and rebuff them—which is what he really wants to do? Kill himself, and them, with exaggerated politeness? Answer shortly and excuse himself? Tough. I've seen him squirm at parties while dozens of people have come up and picked his brains for cricket trivia. I've felt like intervening and saying, 'The man's off-duty. He's entitled to relax and have a good time. Leave him alone.' It is insensitive but unavoidable and inevitable, the price one pays for success and fame. But does it have to be this way?

Celebrities abroad travel with a human fortress around them. It's going to happen here as well. I've seen Sachin Tendulkar at Sharjah and other venues. And observed how very standoffish he can be, to the extent of coming across as a conceited, far-from-likeable chap. No eye contact. No smile. No conversation. And frankly, no grace even in victory.

Maybe he has learned the hard way. Maybe he found out early enough in the game that you can't possibly win them all, so why not conserve your energy and concentrate on pleasing yourself? Maybe he has it right. But I do believe public figures have at least a small debt they owe to their supporters. A smile does not cost very much nor does a friendly wave. But then, I'm not India's former cricket captain. How would I know what the pressures are like out there?

I asked Gavaskar if he missed those heady days. I suspect he was dodging a little when he said he didn't. I saw him respond with a cynical smile once when very young autograph-seekers stopped him in the corridor of the club he goes to each afternoon. He signed on the proffered paper serviette and said, 'How come you want my autograph and not Sachin Tendulkar's or Rahul Dravid's?'

It reminded me of another incident in Sharjah when we'd all been seated at one table, along with former Pakistani cricket captain Zaheer Abbas. Sunil was in a relaxed enough mood when a fan walked up to Abbas with a small cricket bat and asked for his autograph. He waited for his turn and smiled a little wryly while signing the souvenir. Sachin at another table was surrounded by autograph hunters. Sunil sent him several feelers to join us at our table. There was no response. Then a cricketing official explained that the team was not encouraged to fraternize with anybody outside their own circle. It was a surprise to me to realize that India's legendary captain was now seen as an outsider, perhaps due to his position as a television commentator. If Sunil felt slighted, he didn't show it. He is an incredibly shrewd man who does not tolerate fools. Yet, I've always felt he suffers from a slight chip on the shoulder despite his admirable career graph and all those impressive records.

Gavaskar is an excellent mimic with a keen sense of

observation. He can do a take-off on all his colleagues, but he really gives an inspired performance when Ajit Wadekar, his neighbour and one-time captain, is the subject. Behind the good-natured jibing is a sharply observant, highly critical mind. If he appears stiff, even arrogant, to strangers, it is his natural reserve combined with training in public conduct. It's difficult to catch him off-guard. For one, he doesn't drink, except on special occasions and even then, it's the odd glass of wine or champagne. I've never seen him behaving in a boisterous manner. At all times he is distant and formal, except in the company of people he trusts and is comfortable with, and those number a handful.

I enjoy being with Sunil and invariably learn something from him. About five years ago when our skies had just opened up, I was flooded with offers to host various television shows. It was a good feeling. I have to confess I was tempted once or twice. And yet, I knew I didn't want to take the plunge without being clear as to what precisely my reservations were. My family has always been dead set against my getting into that particular medium—and I've accepted their resistance. It was my own mind that needed better definition. I have to thank Sunil for providing it, even if he himself may have forgotten the advice he gave me in an overcrowded, noisy, smoky bar where we were perhaps the only two individuals without a drink.

He was very clear about a career in television. For him it was a job and he'd decided to do it to the best of his ability. Life after cricket does not hold too many options, unless one wishes to get involved in the politics of the game. Sunil chose a far better alternative—and he grew into his new role one step at a time, teaching himself the mechanics of television presentation, voice projection, body language and an easy viewer-friendly manner that's authoritative without being boring. This is one of Sunil's great strengths—when he decides to get into something, there are no half measures. When one sees his early TV appearances, it's easy to be critical about his style of delivery, his hesitancy, lack of fluency and overall awkwardness. All that has gone today. He's a polished, in-command anchor who provides expert analyses and superb sound bytes with finesse and a style that is now being imitated by more recent entrants like Ravi Shastri.

In that crowded bar, what Sunil told me was simply this: television is an intimate, intrusive medium which allows no space for privacy. There are no concessions once you take the plunge. He mentioned how he often shrank and cringed in a crowd when complete strangers thought it perfectly all right to come up, thump him on the back familiarly and start a conversation. It's the medium that's to blame and not the viewers, he pointed out. When you see somebody frequently enough in the family atmosphere of a bedroom or living room, that person becomes a part of your life. People start believing they know him or her. They think nothing of yelling out an anchor's name like they were greeting a long-lost cousin, before initiating a dialogue. He underlined the obvious—he was a man, and he found it difficult to handle it when people refused to maintain a distance. Would I be able to deal with chummy strangers? Would my family? The answer was an obvious and vehement 'no'. I could visualize the scenario most clearly—and it didn't appeal to me. It meant kissing my privacy goodbye. It meant becoming public property. It meant aggressive invasion. I didn't want it. Sunil placed it in the right perspective and made it that much easier for me to say no. I have consistently refused all offers to anchor shows since then. But television is getting harder and harder to ignore. Even I can't predict how long I can hold out.

At various such turning points involving contracts and

decisions, I have called him up and sought his advice. It has always been forthcoming and constructive besides being practical and down-to-earth. Sunil does not live with his head in the clouds. Neither does he delude himself on any level. He has moved on from being the little master to his present status—senior citizen of cricket.

I often wonder where another super celebrity, supercop Kiran Bedi's trajectory will take her. Here's an extraordinary woman with a compelling presence who has the charisma and media savvy to be in perfect control of her public image. She is aware of the hold she has on the public imagination and uses it to the hilt. Bedi is a smart woman who has understood the changing needs of our confused times. She knows she represents this change and capitalizes on it. As a symbol of the New Woman she, more than anyone else, is in a unique position to establish herself as a role model for a generation of Indian women who look up to her as someone who has made it in a male dominated profession. It's true Bedi has demonstrated exemplary courage, but it's equally true that it hasn't been without some amount of compromise in her personal and professional life. Today, she is in a position where nobody would like to touch her in case someone somewhere yells 'victimization' or 'discrimination'. She is well insulated against criticism—who will dare? That makes a large section of men not just uncomfortable but resentful too. I've had several senior police officers coming up to me quietly to pass on nuggets documenting her 'wrong-doings' in the hope that their sneaky revelations will eventually make their way into print. Bedi herself is fully aware of her current invincible position as a Magsaysay award winning supercop who is loved by the media. She is frequently featured in 'The Most Admired Women in India' magazine polls. She clearly loves the attention even as her vulnerable past occasionally haunts her.

I was very curious to meet this woman, especially because she and I have often been featured together in foreign publications writing about unconventional Indian women who've broken through rigid barriers to make a life for themselves on their own terms. I've read her quotes with interest and watched her in countless television interviews. My feeling is that Bedi's ultimate destination lies in politics. She'd be the perfect candidate—intelligent, confident, aware and ambitious. She doesn't just know the system, she knows how to use it to her advantage. She has also mastered the art of media manipulation—even if 'manipulation' is a hard, ugly word. She is always accessible and inordinately co-operative with presswallahs, instinctively knowing that having them on her side is her most potent weapon while settling scores with in-house detractors.

Yet, at least a couple of book editors I know couldn't stand the pressure of being in her company for extended hours and finally gave up their projects. One of them complained about Bedi's lack of consideration in summoning her over on Sundays. Bedi would also keep her waiting for hours without so much as a glass of water. The editor saw different sides to the policewoman's personality, particularly in the way she interacted with her only child—a daughter—her old mother, and her frequently out-of-town husband. Autocratic, impatient and dismissive, the private Bedi was a far cry from the in-control, calm and self-assured public figure. But that's okay. Every individual has secret demons that sometimes emerge at awkward moments. Too bad for Bedi that hers popped out at entirely inopportune times when she had a potential ghost-writer/biographer waiting miserably in the ante-room for her to emerge and talk into a tape-recorder.

I was surprised by these revelations and have no reason

to question them. But I'd have expected Bedi to be smarter, particularly with someone who'd been lined up to document her life and present a flattering portrait to the world.

When we finally did meet, the circumstances were unusual. Bedi was in Mumbai to receive yet another award for 'outstanding service'. My husband and I arrived slightly late since we'd been held up by the annual Ganapati procession. She spotted me from the dais as I walked in gingerly. Our eyes met and she gave me a jaunty thumbs-up signal. I was flattered even though I did find it a little strange that she'd done something like that while a speech was underway. I smiled and gave her a small wave. We took our seats, the function continued and Kiran surprised me by constantly exchanging smiles, making eye contact and mouthing instructions like 'Don't go away', 'We'll meet after the event', 'See you later'. She looked wonderful, if a little masculine, in her no-nonsense Pathani suit and jacket.

Minuter later, it was her turn to address the gathering. I got the feeling she'd worked out a basic spiel which she trotted out at regular intervals, varying it just that little bit to maintain some topicality. That night, her favourite words were 'empowerment' and 'systemic changes'. She delivered her speech forcefully and convincingly, even if I did have the sneaking feeling it was recycled several times over. The crowd, which consisted of small-time merchants, shopkeepers and sundry do-gooders, roared its approval and clapped at all the right moments. Bedi had obviously mastered the art of playing to the gallery and scored several brownie points over co-recipients.

The dinner was at a rooftop venue. It took me a while to get there since my father was with us that night. Bedi sent a messenger to find out what was holding us up. When I was finally face-to-face with her, I was completely dazzled by her dynamism and radiance. It was obvious she enjoyed playing the star, posing for photographs, signing autographs. She had positioned herself brilliantly as a 'People's Heroine' and had become pretty adept at flashing smiles and bussing bábies (a training programme that will serve her well as and when she takes the plunge into politics).

It was a very warm encounter, made warmer by my father's undisguised admiration. She was consistently polite and well bred, addressing him as 'sir' throughout. Very few people in modern India respect age naturally, and restrict their 'sirs' exclusively to people in power. Here was a man close to ninety, an ex-government officer, a retired senior citizen. It was only appropriate that Bedi recognized that and behaved accordingly.

Never one to be daunted by position, fame, money or status, my father, the supreme charmer of comely ladies, leaned forward and asked Bedi mischievously, 'Do you mind answering a slightly personal question?' She answered spontaneously, 'Not at all, sir.' 'Why do you wear such masculine clothes which are more Pakistani than Indian? I find your outfit unsuitable and unflattering. Have you ever worn a saree? I think you'd look more womanly in it.' I could have died that instant. To start with, it really wasn't any of his business. And Bedi was certainly not obliged to answer his questions. But she did . . . and with a disarming laugh at that. 'I find these clothes very comfortable. Yes, I have tried wearing a saree, but somehow, it doesn't really suit me.' I fled the scene. Ten minutes later, my father and Bedi were still deep in conversation. I guessed she'd taken that and other equally intrusive questions in her stride, which was good of her.

We caught up with each other over dinner. I congratulated her on winning the Magsaysay Award. 'You must face a great deal of professional envy,' I said.

'Oh yes. It's terrible. You can't imagine what I've been through . . . the resistance . . . the jealousy . . . the insecurity. So many people expressed their resentment over my getting the award.'

A mean streak in me compelled me to say something I feel a little ashamed of now. It was my way of gauging the size of her ego, though I must admit her response surprised me by its transparent naïveté. A smarter person would have neatly side-stepped and not tumbled into the inviting trap. I asked Bedi with a completely straight face, 'Have you ever considered how much worse it will be when you win the Nobel? And you do know you'll definitely win it some day. The hostility from jealous rivals will be even stronger then.'

'Precisely. Exactly,' Bedi exclaimed in all innocence. I'd got the key I'd been looking for. I felt a little wretched about my silly trick later. But at that moment, I was childishly kicked that I'd confirmed just how highly she pegged herself.

*

It's always interesting to note how celebrities, mega-celebs at that, deal with their celebrityhood. One of my early encounters with an international 'name' took place sometime in the early Seventies. I was flying on a cheap ticket—a late-night shuttle from Paris to London. I'd noticed the shapely, silk-stockinged legs of the little old lady snoozing across the aisle. The hour was late. It was a no-frills, no-service flight. Her hair was wispy, her mouth a brightly painted gash. I paid her no attention at all. My thoughts were on getting to central London at the lowest possible price. There would be no buses at that hour and taxi fares would be unaffordable . . .

After we landed, I was rushing out of the terminal still thinking these thoughts, when I was almost run over by a flashbulb-popping, stampeding mob. I turned around to see who it was they were chasing—and voilà, there she was, the little old lady herself, hiding behind enormous celebrity-shades which scream 'please recognize me', even as the wearer does a pretty good job of faking shock at being identified.

She walked languorously towards the exit while waving the photographers away in a studiedly languid manner. 'Go away, boys,' she purred in that distinctive, low, smokey voice. 'It's the same old face . . . the same me.' The 'boys' whistled, clapped and shouted. 'Look here, luv,' 'One more, sweetie,' 'This side, duckie'. I asked one of them, red haired, freckled and wearing a hideous checked jacket, 'Who is that lady?' He looked at me with complete astonishment. 'Don't chyoo know—that's Marlene. Marlene Dietrich.'

She was on the front page of most of the tabloids the next day with a sell-out two weeks' show at Grosvenor House. The woman who had insured those amazing legs for a million dollars in the Fifties, was still at it—drawing full houses at seventy. But what intrigued me about her was her switchover—the sudden, almost instinctive transformation at the sight of cameras. It was a learned response, a reflex. The rather shabby old lady from the airplane changed in an instant into an ageing but still-in-demand movie star. And the transformation was visible. Once she'd thrown back her shoulders, cocked her head at a coquettish angle, straightened up and altered her shuffling, she·was a different person—growling indulgently at the pesky 'boys' while in her heart she must have been oh-so-glad to see them there.

Like the stunningly beautiful Indian actress I once saw being wheeled out of an operation theatre in Mumbai's prestigious Breach Candy Hospital. It was a short ride from the OT to the elevator which would take the actress to her room. She was heavily sedated, her eyes squeezed shut. Yet, the face visible above the white hospital sheets covering her body on the stretcher was perfectly made-up, particularly the mouth which was carefully outlined with her favourite shade of lipstick. There must have been twenty-odd people in the public area—but she cared enough about her image not to let any of them see her sans make-up.

Years later, I asked her about the incident. She replied truthfully, 'I owe that much to the public. I never let my fans down. I refuse to go out dressed like the woman-next-door. I am not her. That would destroy the whole mystique.' She's right. Movies are about magic. Nobody wants reality—especially when it takes the form of a fiftyish actress lying wan and pale on a stretcher, stripped of allure. Exposed. Naked. Like anybody else. Just another patient.

That's when it occurred to me that it can't be easy dealing with fading beauty and tarnished trophies. An old woman is an old woman, no matter who she was in her youth or how gifted. A new generation has no memory or awareness of her glory days. In any case, young people are so preoccupied with their own 'youngness' that anybody who's more than ten years their senior is irrelevant to their lives. I remember my own daughter Avantika, at nineteen, describing a besotted suitor as a 'fossil'. 'How old is he?' someone asked and she shrugged, 'Who knows? Twenty-six or twenty-seven.'

Women, especially actresses, are the most vulnerable since the public wants to fix them in time, remember them in their prime and discard them once they've crossed the magic figure—thirty, or increasingly these days, forty, which is the absolute cut-off point. Only a Liz Taylor, fat, blowsy, bloated and grey, manages to escape universal rejection. Other women have to live with the crime of growing old. Some come to terms with it, others go down fighting.

Surprisingly, it's often the people who surround them and feed off their celebrity who try and delay the natural ageing process, prolonging the bloom for as long as it's possible. But inevitably the inner circle of admirers also abandons the celebrity and that's when things get really hard. I have heard film star Rekha being derisively referred to as that 'buddhi' by young actresses. Her nickname in the film industry is 'Aunty'. If Rekha is at the receiving end of such cruel jibes, one wonders what is said about even older, still beautiful actresses like Mumtaz or Sharmila Tagore. There is, of course, the 'Curse of Beauty', and actresses have to live with it, though not everyone can handle its loss gracefully. When yesteryear's vamp, Nadira, made a complete fool of herself at sixty-five by claiming on a chat show that despite a string of male admirers, it was she who was finding it difficult to make up her mind, public sympathy for the former screen seductress turned instantly to derision and scorn.

Asha Bhonsle, on the other hand, carries her age very lightly. On the eve of her sixtieth birthday, her well-wishers had decided to go on a publicity blitz for a woman they obviously were very fond of. I was asked to write a profile for the now defunct *Illustrated Weekly of India*, and I needed to spend some time with her for that. Even though I'd been prepared for her girlishness, the woman I met had the natural mannerisms of a coquettish teenager. When she arrived at my home, she was all coy giggles and sidelong glances. Her voice, which is terrifyingly youthful, only added to the confusion. My children took to her instantly. As I did too.

Ashatai is an incomparable mimic (as is Rekha). She can 'do' anybody down to the last tic and twitch. But best of all she can do her sister Lata ('Didi') in an imitation that cuts so close to the bone, it's almost cruel. She regaled us that night with several telling incidents from their childhood. And finally topped off the lovely evening by actually singing for her supper—in Bengali, at that.

Dinner was a relaxed experience for the others, but I was on tenterhooks. Ashatai is a gourmet and a superb cook to boot. She makes the best shammi kebabs I've tasted anywhere—velvety, delicious and perfectly spiced. I was worried about her verdict on our preparations, but our kitchen passed the test. And so did my children who surprised me with their rapt attention that night. After all, Asha wasn't an MTV award winner then. She was a faceless (to their generation) playback singer who resembled a friendly aunt next door. It was her warmth and tinkling laughter they responded to, just as I did, even though I sensed that behind that carefree façade was a clever, shrewd lady who'd mastered the art of disarming her audience even if that audience was limited to a journalist's curious family.

I'd seen her brand of crowd management earlier at a concert on the grounds of a suburban school. She'd adopted the same tactics to charm the crowds and win them over—good-natured ribbing, well-timed jokes, shared intimacies and seemingly careless revelations about the famous 'Mangeshkar' rivalry. This was no spontaneous exchange, every bit of it was probably rehearsed and honed down to the last titter and aside. Asha has got her act down pat—a compelling mixture of little-girl vulnerability, womanly insecurity and injured pride. She skilfully draws you into her world, exposing just enough of her life to add to the intrigue.

Asha knows exactly which buttons to press, how hard and for how long. That is her strength. She is chameleon-like, ready to adapt, change, innovate, keep up, strive. Behind the throwaway lines and casual, breezy approach is an ambitious professional, focused and in control. She has an agenda, and she will work towards it singlemindedly. She also knows her slot—the new one she has carefully carved out for herself by reaching out to the pre-teen, music-channel generation. She knows exactly how to pitch it to them as she demonstrated during the first Channel V awards. Nominated for her remix single '*Chura liya*', she turned out to be the surprise winner in a field crowded with singers young enough to be her grandchildren. It wasn't just youth she was challenging but an entire lifestyle. Her rivals were half her size, quarter her age and dressed in nothing more adequate than sequined underwear. As she simpered on stage while clutching her award, she 'blurted' out mock-innocently that she was stumped for words since the place was full of 'little, little kids in little, little clothes'. The reference wasn't missed on the crowd (high on hash and maybe other stronger substances). It roared its approval and she knew she'd won over a brand-new constituency with that one, well thought-out remark.

Visitors like Ashatai are always welcome in our home. It's the occasional pushy publicity seeker I will not tolerate, no matter where the grand references come from. Zerbanoo Gifford, the Parsi lady hell-bent on carving out a niche for herself in British politics, caught me completely off-guard a few years ago, while I was sitting with the office accountant trying to get my papers in order. I didn't look up when the doorbell rang since I wasn't expecting anybody. It was only the smart clack-clack created by Mrs Gifford's pumps on the flooring that made me look up. I was in a foul mood to begin with. I hate tearing my hair out over piddly amounts of money, and there I was, engaged in a biannual ritual I detest—filing tax-returns—when this attractive, very prim and proper lady barged in on me. Not her mistake at all. She'd been pushed into the (non) appointment by an even pushier person—a Parsi busybody who has made it her business to mind everybody else's.

Grasping, greedy and overbearing, the local Parsi woman had appointed herself as Mrs Gifford's publicist. She'd tried hard to sell her 'client' to me, and I guess at some point, out of sheer exhaustion, I'd probably said, 'Fine, I'll see her on Monday . . . Tuesday . . . whenever,' and promptly forgotten all about it. There had been no phone call to confirm the meeting. No indication of any kind that Mrs Gifford would come a-calling. So . . . there I was, all frazzled and confused, looking stupidly at the stubs of my old cheque books and wondering where all my hard-earned money had gone, when Zerbanoo presented herself. A clear case of unfortunate timing. I asked the accountant to wait while I dealt with this stranger in our midst.

'I'm sorry . . . I don't think I know you,' I started off, my irritation clearly showing. Mrs Gifford introduced herself after which I requested her to sit down while I completed the forms on hand. She must have thought me an awfully rude person. I admit I wasn't on my best behaviour. After the accountant had left and we'd had a cup of tea together, I waited for the social call to be over and Mrs Gifford to leave. At this awkward stage she stated brightly, 'Well then, shall we get on with the interview?'

Wait a minute, I said to myself, what interview? Did she want to interview me for something? I decided to let her provide the cue. It came soon enough when she handed over a thick file of press clippings with a crisp suggestion, 'Why don't you run through these as quickly as possible before you tape me?' Oh-oh. How was I going to get out of this one? 'Look,' I said politely, 'I think there has been some sort of a mix-up here.' She wasn't amused. But being a smart, on-the-ball lady, she wasn't about to let me know just how pissed off she was. 'I was clearly told by . . . that you were to interview me this morning. And that I'd feature in your columns next week.' Right. Everything fell into place now. But I wasn't about to be bullied—not that morning at any rate. I told the alarmingly self-assured lady I had no such intentions nor had I discussed the possibility with the other person. However, since she was at my home and armed with her clippings, I'd be happy to glance through them, which is precisely what I did. This woman was a toughie, ambitious and hard as steel. Well . . . why not?

Her clippings showed her in assorted party situations back home, clad in glamorous outfits, hair carefully coiffured, make-up subtly applied. Here was a clever woman who quite fancied herself but didn't want the other person to know it. She had a programme which basically read: 'Aren't I wonderful?' even while she spoke about all the various social service programmes she was involved in. Frankly, I didn't give a damn. It was one of those cross-connections. A case of lousy timing and over-pushing. I'd seen what I wanted to see. Heard what I wanted to hear. Normally, I take such a shine to good-looking, intelligent women, I lose all pretence of maintaining perspective. But this one bugged me with her one-stop shop crammed with self-promotional material.

She featured in my column all right. I thought it was a fair if not gushy piece. I made a mention of the mix-up. But I did call her 'one hell of a broad', which to my modern mind, is a compliment. Mrs Gifford was not convinced. Having consulted her pocket Oxford about the exact dictionary meaning of the word 'broad', she decided it was derogatory. The middlewoman must have had a great deal of explaining to do. But sorry, it wasn't my problem. And I have no regrets.

Regrets come into the picture only when a helpless person

Selective Memory: Stories From My Life

gets hurt . . . unwittingly, at that. If that person also happens to be someone I admire for exceptional talent, then I'm prepared to take whatever is doled out by way of punishment. I rarely run away from performing a penance when I know I've been a bad girl. In Kishori Amonkar's case, I wasn't exactly bad, just slightly wicked. Perhaps not even that. My sin was that I'd passed a profile in *Celebrity* that was less than reverential. It was written by a woman whose viewpoint I respected. Besides, it wasn't as if she'd said anything terrible about Kishori in the piece. She'd just been a little naughty in the introductory remarks, that was all. She'd written something to the effect that when she met the great singer at her residence the sky didn't fall down, neither did the earth rise up. There were one or two other digs that had more to do with Kishoritai's monumental ego than her music (who can dare to criticize that?).

When the interview appeared I received a furious call from the singer, summoning me to her residence. She was incoherent, obviously out of control and terribly upset. I tried to calm her down. She would have none of it. 'You come here. I have to talk to you,' she cried. 'But what are you objecting to—give me some idea? Is it factually incorrect? Have you been misquoted?' Kishori wasn't listening, just hollering into the instrument. Finally, she spluttered, 'The cheek of that girl. Can you imagine—she has actually mentioned my age. Nobody will believe her, because I don't look it at all. But how dare she write about such a thing?' Kishori was fifty-plus then. And it was true, she didn't look anywhere close to it. I found her outburst most touching. So that was it—her vanity had been pricked. I decided to go over and assure her she looked no more than thirty.

When I walked into her suburban home, clad in my standard khadi kurta-pajama, she was nowhere in sight.

Instead, in a largish room sat what looked like a bunch of mourners—her pupils, I later discovered. They glared at me in complete silence while we waited for the diva to arrive. She flounced in minutes later and stared at me, arms akimbo. I was sure she was going to curse or attack me physically—the expression in her eyes was manic. After looking me over with great deliberation she announced mockingly, 'I had heard you were a very beautiful woman . . . but look at you . . . you resemble a TB patient.' I knew I'd lost weight at that stage—but TB patient? I'd walked into that one, now there was nothing to do but take it with a smile.

Maybe she didn't expect such a response. She tried again, 'My God. I am shocked by your appearance. Are you sick? Unwell? Have you just got out of bed after a long illness?' Her pupils tittered nervously while the great singer waited for me to respond to her taunts. I merely smiled and told her how wonderful she was looking. 'Then?' Her eyes flashed. 'Now you can see for yourself. Will anybody call me over fifty? Do I look it? People say I couldn't be more than thirty-five,' she thundered.

'You are so right, obviously my writer was mistaken,' I said quietly. 'But how old are you really?'

Kishori paused. 'Fifty-seven.'

'So why are you upset if she mentioned that?'

'Because I don't look it,' she all but roared.

Once she'd gotten that out of her system, she seemed to calm down. We got along rather well, even if she did subject me to a ridiculous 'trial' at which her cowering pupils and a timid-looking husband were the 'judges'. 'Ask them,' she declared dramatically, 'let them tell you what they think of me . . .' She pointed an imperious finger at one of the browbeaten admirers who nervously stuttered a paean of praise certifying the guru's impeccable credentials (which had not been questioned in the first place). After we'd finished with this round and Kishori had emerged triumphant in her own eyes, she thought my humiliation complete and offered tea, which I accepted. Suddenly, she rose to her feet. 'I will personally make a pure ghee sheera for you—that's what TB patients in recovery are fed. You need to gain weight. Taste my sheera and then tell somebody at your home to make it for you everyday.' By then she'd obviously convinced herself I was consumptive. I didn't have the heart to correct her. She was so childlike, in both her hurt and enthusiasm.

I chatted with her husband whose existence I was discovering for the first time. He seemed a fine man, mortally afraid of his fiery wife. She returned minutes later with a bowl full of hot sheera and stood over my head watching closely as I gingerly took a spoon of the rich, greasy sweet to my mouth. I hadn't dared tell her about my aversion to anything that rich or that sweet. I was tempted to narrate a little story about how I'd consistently refused to eat slices of my own birthday cake over the years since my tastebuds revolted against the assault. The sheera was delicious all right—how could it be anything else, given the amazing ingredients and the dollops of homemade ghee it was swimming in? I pleaded with her mutely. I thought I'd gag after each additional helping. She'd have none of it. 'It's good for you,' she clucked like a mother hen, 'go on, eat it up and I'll give you some more.' Believe me, V.C. Shukla's threat seemed kinder at that moment. I'd have preferred a public hanging at Flora Fountain to this. Kishori had had her revenge after all—and it couldn't have been sweeter.

*

Brand names come with a price-tag. There have been

occasions when I haven't enjoyed being Shobha Dé, the public persona, and remembered Gavaskar's words. I wonder if it's a gender thing or if it happens to men equally? Say I'm eating a pizza at an informal restaurant with my kids. Someone comes up (my antenna picks up a determined pest immediately) and asks, 'Shobha Dé?' I have no choice but to nod miserably, sometimes with a mouthful of pizza preventing a verbal exchange. The instinct is to look away swiftly and engage the kids' attention. The pest, of course, refuses to get it. He stays put and launches into a highly personal, one-way speech. 'I thought it must be you . . . but I wasn't sure. Your photographs don't resemble you. I always thought you'd be a much taller lady. Are these all your children? All of them? Madam . . . what are your views on family planning?'

Annoying, right? But what does one do in the circumstances? Frankly, I don't know. Like Gavaskar, I'm caught between smiling vaguely, snarling, ignoring the intruders, moving away pizza half-eaten, or saying a polite 'excuse me'. None of these work, unfortunately, if the person is thick-skinned.

On the other hand, there can be completely charming moments triggered off spontaneously in, say, a second-class train compartment. I was travelling in one from Pune to Mumbai recently. It was one of those freak mornings when nothing had gone right. I'd lost my ticket, bought another one at the last minute and been seen off ceremoniously by my embarrassed hosts in Pune who'd been unable to get me a reserved seat. I was carrying an armful of long-stemmed roses presented to me at a function the night before. I was perhaps the only woman in the overcrowded compartment. My co-passengers were educated professionals, some of whom made the trip to Mumbai and back daily, spending seven hours commuting. I could sense their eyes on me as I placed my overnight case on the overhead rack and settled down to read the papers.

Oops—the first one I opened had a front-page picture of the book-related function I'd been invited to. I hastily folded it and picked up another. The men next to me exchanged looks and continued to stare though the corners of their eyes. Once the train pulled out of the station, the person to my right edged away, as if I was carrying a contagious virus. The chap across me started a conversation in a friendly but formal way. He said he'd only just started reading my columns since he'd been away for eighteen years in San Diego. We chatted for a bit. He was keen to know what I thought of various people—Arun Shourie and Khushwant Singh, in particular. We discussed Shourie's Ambedkar book—the controversy surrounding it—and gradually other passengers joined in as well. Just then a young couple jostled past those standing in the aisle and stretched out their hands holding autograph books. This wasn't as simple as it appears. I was trying to keep a piping hot styrofoam container of coffee from spilling on my neighbour's trousers. The compartment was so crammed, it was virtually impossible to manoeuvre past knees, arms and feet. And yet, the young couple had done just that and were beaming as much at meeting me as at their feat in having successfully negotiated their way past so many obstacles.

I took their books and signed. They pushed their way back to their own compartment. Minutes later, a note was delivered. It said some very flattering things about me and had their names and telephone numbers on it. 'Please honour us by visiting our home the next time you are in Pune,' they'd signed off. I was touched. It was a simple, innocent gesture full of genuine warmth. Finally, the man next to me broke his silence. He said stiffly, 'I saw you at the station. I knew who you were. Then I watched you come into the compartment. But I didn't want to show that I'd recognized you. Tell me—how does all this feel?' And he waved his hand indicating the note. By then the coffee-vendor was doing the rounds collecting his money. Three young men offered to pay for mine. My neighbour sniffed his disapproval.

'Isn't this irritating? Don't you want to be left in peace?' Yes and no. If only one could choose.

The truth is rather convoluted. I'd be lying if I said it wouldn't have bothered me at all had my presence gone completely unnoticed that morning. Then again, I could have done with a catnap. There was also the feeling of being trapped in a situation which didn't offer an easy way out. Several questions later, I felt exhausted, even though I was touched by the simple, undisguised curiosity of my co-passengers. Two weeks later, I received affectionate letters from four of them, expressing their feelings about the encounter. I know if I run into them again, I may not be able to remember their faces or their names. And at that moment they'll feel hurt and let down, recalling our three-hour train journey with its lively informal interaction. Disillusionment will also set in as they'll conclude, 'These people are all the same—stuck-up egotists.' That's the downside.

It isn't really the attention, the autographs and photographs that touch me. These days every sixteen-year-old veejay on a music countdown show receives that and more. The moments of public recognition I value are those when at least a few people who've come to a function with preconceived ideas about me go home leaving their prejudices behind. I'd like to believe that's what happened late one evening when I attended the annual get-together of a Marathi literary organization. This particular event is considered to be not just prestigious but a trial-by-fire, as it were, since the audience consists of highly informed, intellectually judgemental, exceedingly critical Maharashtrians who arrive at the suburban school grounds where it is held, armed with a no-nonsense matter-of-factness that does not tolerate even a trace of bullshit—no matter who the special invitee may be. They've been known to walk out *en masse* when the speaker has disappointed or annoyed them. They do not hesitate to heckle or make their irritation known if the proceedings are boring. Since it is open to the public and the demarcated area is large, the organizers arrange for mikes, an unpretentious stage with floor mattresses, limited chairs for the elderly, and mats on the ground for the others.

There's also a book fair attached to the week-long diary of events, which attracts a sizeable crowd interested in discounted books. Even though I'd been briefed by the organizers, I wasn't at all prepared for the significance attached to the function by those who look forward to it year after year. There was also the question of its 'Maharashtrianness' and my own, which I felt was inadequate on this occasion. How was I going to deal with long-winded cerebral debates on my writing and life in a language which, though very much my mother tongue, is no longer the primary one I use for self-expression? I'd spoken about my anxieties to one of the organizers, who'd assured me it wouldn't be held against me if I made mistakes, so long as the crowd felt I was making a sincere attempt.

The question of how to dress for the evening bothered me as well. Unfortunately, that rather annoying label called 'glamour' has been stuck on me for far too long. If I dressed down, the organizers themselves would feel slightly cheated. If I dressed like I would for an evening out, it might look somewhat flashy in that setting. A deliberate attempt at going 'ghati' would be phoney. Trousers, inappropriate. I settled for a chamois silk saree worn with a full-sleeved velvet blouse. If, on the train journey to Pune, I'd been conscious of my canary yellow cotton shirt and scarf, this evening I felt uncertain about my sea-green saree. I gulped when the car pulled up outside the school gates and I saw early arrivals briskly walking in to get good seats. Given a choice I would have asked the driver to turn around and drive me back home.

The school ground was flood-lit. I could see the welcome party at the entrance. It was much too late now. I'd have to wing it one way or the other. I walked into the staff room where a tea party had been arranged. My nervousness only increased when I was introduced to stalwarts of Marathi journalism and literature. My god. If these people were going to witness my demolition, my public humiliation, so be it. Minutes later, I was escorted to the low dais and I mentally prepared to commit harakiri—or at the very least, be booed off stage.

After the elaborate and exaggeratedly flattering introduction, I was asked the first question. By now the place was packed, with people hanging out of adjoining balconies. Retired people had come armed with walking-sticks and mufflers, while in the front row sat the very young, their eyes shining expectantly. To my left was a contingent from the Marathi press, pens poised over shorthand pads. I was afraid I wouldn't find my voice and that the few words of Marathi I knew would desert me.

Why was I responding in this manner? It wasn't an election speech. This wasn't even my constituency of readers. And yet, it was very important for me to make a good impression on these people—my people—that night. People who'd judge me for the person I had become, not the one I started out as—one of them. The woman on the low stage resembled an alien creature, and probably was one too.

They'd see that in an instant and hate me. Somehow it was not just another public function in my mind, it was a test. Would my people accept or reject me? I was feeling self-conscious and nervous about everything, starting with my appearance—too glam? Maybe I shouldn't have worn my rings? Maybe there was far too much hair? And the heels—I knew flats would have been better. Was my posture all right? It was ages since I'd sat cross-legged on a fat mattress.

My voice was barely audible when I began to speak. It cracked as well. The mike was readjusted and I started again. I could sense the apprehension on the part of the organizers. My Marathi sounded shaky and stilted. Even the simplest of phrases refused to roll off my tongue. I stumbled over basic, everyday words. This was going to be a disaster. Some more questions followed. And suddenly something clicked inside my head. This was ridiculous. I was behaving like an absolute chump. What was all this business of 'impressing' these people? Screw it, I told myself. Just be who you are—speak in English if you feel more comfortable that way. Be truthful. Be honest. Be yourself. Tell the crowd your Marathi sucks. And take what comes with the territory—boos, jeers, sneers.

It was one of my smarter decisions as it turned out. One and a half hours later, I may have been sweating with the strain of it all but I was happy. I'd spoken strongly and from my heart. You can't go too wrong if you follow that simple principle. It worked for me that cool night. And it has continued to work ever since. In other words, nobody booed. Everybody stayed.

*

The 'celebrity syndrome' ballooned into a national mania with the advent of the TV satellite channels. Andy Warhol's immortal prophecy was about to come true with everybody getting their fifteen minutes of fame. Till fairly recently there were only three celebrity categories in India—filmstars, cricketers and politicians. By the late Eighties, beauty queens and supermodels had joined their ranks. By the time the Nineties came around, it was pop stars, veejays and chat-show anchors who were being celebrated in weekend colour sections of the press and on countless cable channels. Every little so-and-so staked his or her claim to fame. If the old order resented it, they could do little as teenyboppers in even teenier clothes stampeded past the self-styled icons and onto the covers of plush new international publications fat with ads for priceless Swiss watches, French perfumes, American cosmetics, British lingerie, German cars.

Cashing in on this were kids just out of high school, bright, brash, aggressive and talented. It wasn't always this way. In the past, one actually dealt with adults—hard as it is to believe now. I recall my shock while shooting a commercial recently. The art director on the shoot was a twenty-one-year-old Maharashtrian who was so frighteningly self-assured he left me breathless. He obviously knew his job, knew his client's requirements and was competent enough to call the shots during the three days we were in the studio. Others in the unit were under thirty too—a pony-tailed, award-winning director, a stylist who'd worked in Paris, a hair treatment expert who was self-taught, and any number of clever kids who knew their jobs and didn't waste time, money or energy on the set. They were cool customers, businesslike, professional, and in a hurry to wrap up and go disco.

I liked their energy but above all I liked their efficiency and confidence. It was something of an education for me as I watched them work. Especially amusing was the sight of twenty pairs of male eyes staring at a TV monitor after each take. They weren't looking at a woman—all they saw was the application of their product. I wanted to whimper, 'But what about me? Don't I count?' I saved my breath. I knew the answer. I was the just the name around which their precious campaign was pegged. They were consistently respectful but totally impersonal. When the unit broke for lunch, each person grabbed a plate, queued up for food, ate in silence, washed up, and went back to work.

Such a change from the old days when we sat around between shots, chatting and laughing. Relationships got formed, long-term friendships that still mean something. I remember two shoots—one in Aurangabad with Zeenat Aman and Asha Puthlie, another in Agra with Zeenat again. These were for the newly launched Taj Tea (yes, the same one which now has Ustad Zakir Hussain going 'Wah' or 'Aah'). Asha Puthlie was the original free spirit, a true child of the Sixties. Wild, uninhibited and adventurous, with a body like an Ellora sculpture, dusky skin, mischievous eyes and a bohemian wardrobe, Asha could so easily have been the biggest popstar of them all, if she hadn't thrown it away foolishly. She had the talent. She got her breaks. What she lacked was discipline. When we flew into Aurangabad, she was a known jazz singer with a certain reputation. We were sharing a room—a prospect I approached with some trepidation after a few meetings. Asha's energy levels are exhausting to those of us not similarly blessed. She can talk, laugh, sing, dance, weep, rejoice, all with such force, it can be overwhelming. I suppose the agency wanted two distinct images for their premium tea—very Indian and very western. Asha and I were photographed for the former.

Since there were no make-up or hair people in those days we had to fix ourselves up as best as we could. I had my little routine all worked out, using whatever materials were readily available—and those included poster paints, chalk powder, industrial gold dust, talcs, glue and a range of poorly made hair pieces and wigs for variation. Asha, who used to fly for BOAC (as British Airways was known then) came with a vanity case filled with imported make-up. Zeenat had an impressive collection too. While getting dressed for the shoot Asha was helpful, warm and generous. She urged me to slap on whatever I wanted from her case (I declined) and we set off for the location. The executive on the shoot was a pompous Bengali with intellectual pretensions. Ugly as an overfed toad, he tried to make up for his awful appearance by showing off his vocabulary. He found a challenging opponent in Zeenat, who was not just awesomely articulate but could win at competitive scrabble or Spelling Bee. The executive seemed as impressed with her cleavage as with her competence in other areas. This was Zeenat at her luscious best. It goes without saying, her shoot was lovingly supervised by the toad and she hogged the campaign.

It didn't bother either Asha or me. The modelling scene itself was so amateurish and awkward. All of us were playing at being professionals, earning peanuts for our efforts. Fat-cat ad executives haven't changed all that much. They're still as conceited, supercilious and insufferable. The way that toad was one evening when he asked Asha to perform a striptease . . . and she readily agreed. Minutes later, she dashed into the room to change (she said) and emerged hiding behind sheets of newspaper which she proceeded to tear into tiny strips while crooning breathlessly. When she'd shredded the paper to well above her knees and the toad was all but drooling, she waved the ribbons in his face and said sweetly, 'There . . . you've got your striptease. Here are the strips and I am the tease.' He pretended to catch the joke and smiled uneasily while she walked back into the room and collapsed on the bed with laughter.

For each round a 'celebrity' wins, there are ten that are absolute bummers. I have seen yesterday's 'names' humbled by newer, flashier challenges. And I have seen the hurt and hunger in those eyes. The 'fame-fix' is worse than a drug one. There are no de-tox, rehab centres for fallen angels. You have to deal with the fact that a low follows a high. And you should never get into the sort of situation that is exclusively reserved for minor league nobodies who throw their weight around and constantly ask the one question a true-blue Famous Person never needs to—'Do you know who I am?' Darling, if you need to ask, you can't possibly be anybody important. Cringe-making. Puke-creating. But it happens. Sometimes, it even works.

The best way to deal with so-called celebrityhood is to ignore it. With luck, it goes away. Everybody doesn't get lucky. If it sticks—run with it. And stay easy. Don't get needy for the fix. And don't look back. For if you do, over your shoulder you'll spot the next wannabe heading a long queue of fame-freaks. You don't want to be spooked by this lot. It's terribly smelly with all that nervous sweat.

*

When Sudip Mazumdar of *Newsweek* came to Mumbai to interview me, he arrived with the standard impression. The woman he encountered, alas, was far removed from his version or vision of her. After a couple of hours, when he felt free enough to voice it, he said, 'I expected to meet someone who wakes up at noon, bathes in rose water and has six maids standing by with a dozen sets of clothes to choose from.' Ah well, that's the life, I laughed, but unfortunately it isn't mine. Was he disappointed to find a regular, normal working mother in place of a dream woman leading an over-the-top existence of lush extravagance and enviable decadence? No. Relieved. We've been friends since.

Sudip was perceptive enough to cut to the chase quickly and get on with the interview. I'd worn my daughter Radhika's shirt that day—more accurately, a shirt given to my husband by her then boyfriend. Drab, brown, vegetable dye-printed. No make-up. Wooden accessories. No-nonsense air. He'd conducted the interview at the executive centre of a luxury hotel. And I had gone through it with one eye on the clock nearby, businesslike, impersonal, his tone matching mine. Yes, I knew it was *Newsweek*. I had prepared for it. But I was determined not to fall into the same old 'Jackie Collins of India' trap again. And I didn't.

These sort of connections are getting increasingly rare. In March '98, a music channel television crew marched in for an impromptu interview. I could have thrown the three men out and rescheduled it—but that would have involved fresh effort. I decided to wing it instead.

'Do something wacky. Something nobody associates with you,' suggested the young producer, his clean-shaven pate gleaming in the evening sun.

'Like what?'

It didn't take him a minute to come up with a visual. 'Pick up a mop and clean the floors . . . or . . . or . . . sweep the drawing room with a jhadoo . . . or . . . or . . . jump out of a clothes bin . . . just be different from the image . . . just . . . just . . . don't look spectacularly sexy, that's all.' I didn't go along with any of his absurd suggestions. I did it my way.

When it came to persuading Arundhati and Anandita to participate in one shot they were most reluctant. 'My kids always play pricey,' I joked. His eyebrows shot up as he asked archly, 'Now . . . I wonder where they get *that* from?'

*

My husband and I attend evenings at which we switch to cruise control even before leaving home. We know what we have to endure. We are there for a variety of reasons. We are clear about why we are putting ourselves through the ordeal. We rarely expect to meet anybody we would want to know better. And the feelings, I'm certain, are reciprocated.

Conversation rarely goes beyond inanities. It helps that we maintain a steady eye contact through the evening and reassure ourselves that we'll soon be home, away from the interminable tedium of being with a set of people we don't particularly like and who don't like us. If this seems absurd and unnecessary to those of you lucky enough not to have to subject yourself to similar self-inflicted torture, consider yourself blessed. We aren't that fortunate. Given the nature of his business and my vocation, a life of isolation is not an option.

My sole defence these days is to go glacial and withdraw physically if I'm being harassed or feeling ill at ease. If that doesn't work—well, I'm stuck. Nothing to do but suffer in silence and remind myself it would soon be over. A journalist friend watching me deal with irritating strangers commented cynically, 'You sure have mastered the art of enduring undesirables and making the whole thing look so easy and effortless.' If I've taught myself to do so without giving unnecessary offence, it has been a lesson learnt the hard way.

At least thrice a year I have self-styled 'scholars' and 'intellectuals' from out of town turning up for extended interviews that are meant to help them with some vague thesis or the other. Most times they are there out of a sense of intense, almost obsessive curiosity. Rarely do they allow me

The Rajadhyaksha family in the districts:(L to R) Kunda, Mother, Mandakini, Father, Ashok and I (1953).

My parents, a year after their marriage (1936).

Victory in an inter-school athletics
championship (1963).

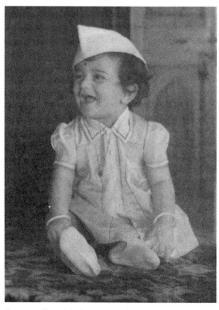

On my first birthday (1949).

With Kunda (1965).

With Mandakini (1965).

Seeing Father off at the Mumbai airport (1961): (L to R) Kunda, Ashok, Father, Mother, Mandakini and I.

Above: Early test shots by Ashvin Gatha in the early Sixties. Below (left): My first modelling assignment.Photo by R.R. Prabhu. Below (right): At a fashion show (1979).

'Panic' haircut at age thirty-nine.

Shot by Gautam Rajadhyaksha in the
early Eighties.

As the 'Gala girl' at the age of eighteen. Photo: Wilas Bhendé.

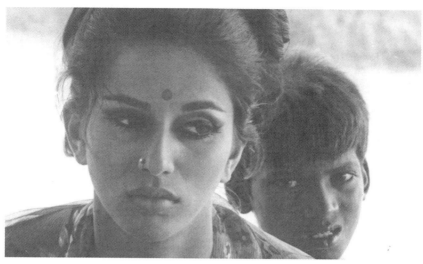

Modelling for Tata tea in Aurangabad (1968).

From Jitendra Arya's feature in *Femina* with Zeenat Aman and me (1969).

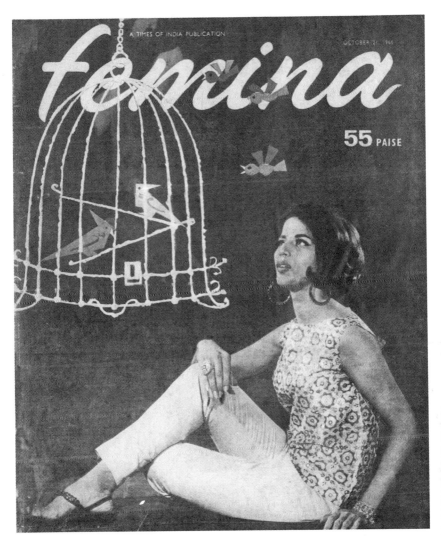

My first cover for *Femina*, at age eighteen.

With the *Stardust* gang: (L to R) Binoy Thomas, Prochi Badshah, Vanita Bakshi, Uma Rao, Ingrid Albuquerque and Nari Hira.

At the Taj Mahal hotel, Mumbai, with (L to R) Maneka Gandhi, Sanjay Gandhi and Khushwant Singh.

Ad for Bombay Dyeing, shot by legendary photographer Jehangir Gazdar.

Above: The children—(L to R) Avantika, Arundhati, Aditya, Radhika and Ranadip—with Sunil Gavaskar (August 1987). Photo by Gautam Rajadhyaksha.

Right: With M.F. Husain at an art gallery in Mumbai. Photo by Rahul.

Below: Interviewing Dilip Kumar at his home in the early Seventies. Photo by Rahul.

With Jaya Bachchan at a *Stardust* party in the early Seventies.

With Rekha (January 1997). Photo by Gautam Rajadhyaksha.

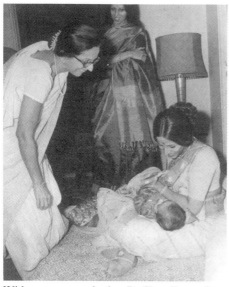

With my gynaecologist, Dr Tara Rama Rao, and Aditya (November 1975). Photo by Rahul.

With Aditya at his mundan (1976). Photo by Rahul.

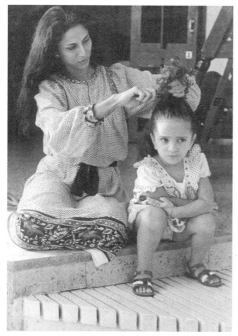

With Avantika in Baroda (August 1980). Photo by Rahul.

Dilip and I on our wedding day. Photo by Gautam Rajadhyaksha.

On my forty-ninth birthday with (L to R) Aditya, Anandita, Radhika, Arundhati, Ranadip and Avantika.

With Aditya in Pune (January 1980). Photo by Rahul.

With Aditya on his graduation at
Boston College (May 1997).

With Ranadip, Radhika and King Tuts
(1998).

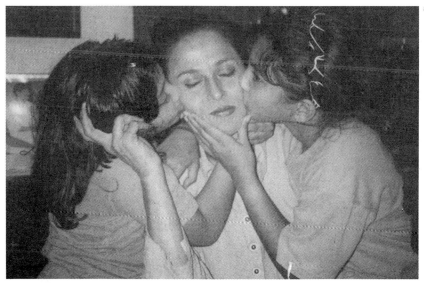

With Arundhati and Anandita (1996).

With Dilip on my fiftieth birthday.
Photo by Farzana Contractor.

At the Satyanarayan puja at my father's home on the eve of my fiftieth birthday.
Photo by Arundhati Dé.

to speak about my own work—they prefer to use the time to tell me about themselves and their motivation for undertaking the trip.

These are well-meaning people—academics who pride themselves on their learning. It is their transparent earnestness that finally gets me. I cannot and will not be impatient with them. Nor will I reveal my amusement at their naïve, probing questions. These are people who occupy a different, far simpler world. I envy them their ideals, their lofty goals. They still believe in old-fashioned virtues like commitment to their profession. They've come from long distances—obscure universities in Madhya Pradesh, for example. And they are genuine in their desire to complete their project. I respect this kind of sincerity and do make time—as much as is asked for—to accomodate them, even when I know that whatever finally emerges from these extended meetings has in all probability already been pre-written in their minds. The meeting is a mere formality. They don't want to find out anything new. All they're looking for is a confirmation of their theories, lopsided as they are.

I remember a professor from Calcutta who spent hours with me over a week. The meetings were mainly monologues where I was made to sit silently in front of the tiny, bird-like gentleman while he held forth in a quaint, sing-song style of delivery. His choice of words was archaic. He himself belonged to another world, another century. Most of the things he said didn't make the slightest sense to me. But I didn't have the heart to say so. Each day, he'd pull out notes from his rexine briefcase and read them aloud. He'd written reams and reams on my novels, seeing into them aspects that weren't intended. It was a deeply moving, even humbling experience. I kept asking myself why somebody like him would spend so much time, effort and energy on researching my books. How could he possibly be interested in my reality? Did I deserve this kind of dedication and attention? The answer to that one was a clear 'no'. And I told him as much.

He looked pained, and genuinely shocked. He was silent for a few minutes, while I glanced nervously at my toes. I realized the folly of my words immediately. No matter what I thought of his interest in my work, I should not have voiced my feelings and hurt his. I tried covering my tracks, but found it impossible to do so convincingly. I wanted to kick myself. That was when I resolved not to let my characteristic cynicism creep in at times like this. I had no right to ruin something for somebody else. The good professor's sensibility had been wounded, perhaps beyond my limited powers to heal it. From that point onward, I meekly went along with his (and those that followed) theories clarifying only that which I felt was too absurd even for my reformed self to let pass.

I routinely receive requests from distant, unheard of universities to either travel there and deliver a lecture, or agree to co-operate on projects based on my work. Both are difficult to comply with. I try and write back to each and every individual seeking this kind of assistance, but most times, this simple act of courtesy is misinterpreted, even when I'm politely declining the offers. I suppose it's a little difficult for somebody in say, Bhatinda, to understand the stressful demands of life in Mumbai. It's perhaps even more difficult for them to believe that I work off my dining table without secretarial help. Or that I have no filing system worth the name—just heaps of plastic bags holding my manuscripts, papers, clippings and correspondence. There is just no easy retrieval system in place. I wouldn't know how to access old articles, for example. An editor called up to ask me for an interview I'd conducted with Sunil Gavaskar many years ago. The only way I could put a date to it was by recalling the ages of my children the day Sunil had come home for the piece. Having worked that much out, I established the year and the likely publication it had appeared in. Beyond that, the actual task of locating it was impossible. I rang up Marshneil (Gavaskar's efficient wife). I knew she maintained Sunil's press clippings diligently enough. But, as she told me, over time they'd grown into a mountainous mass and even she, with all her dedication, had had to give up. 'Old clippings are lying in various cupboards,' she said despairingly. 'I'll try and get my nieces to sort through them, but I'm not promising anything.'

It's an even worse scenario for me. Sunil's stuff is probably safe if scattered—mine is all over the place, in unmarked cartons and handybags. For all I know, it could be damp and pulpy, or may have been chucked away as raddi by a careless domestic. Helpful friends wonder why I don't employ somebody on a part-time basis. They point out archly, 'You can afford to, you know.' Sure I can. But do I want to have a stranger hanging around waiting for instructions on days when I'd rather be a total slob in a faded caftan, with oil in my hair and no particular agenda? I would find the person's presence highly intrusive and find myself creating work out of a sense of consideration for him or her. This is the big downside for those of us who are self-employed and have chosen to work from home. Since our domestic environment is anything but businesslike, it's hard to establish pucca rules and maintain them. It's harder still to stick to an impassive let's-get-on-with-it expression while mayhem swirls around. My children think nothing at all of interrupting me mid-sentence or demanding I play arbitrator in their minor fights, even as I strain to maintain an impersonal, brisk, work-like atmosphere. And our dog only adds to the confusion.

First-time visitors are taken aback when our boxer bounds in to greet them exuberantly. He's a friendly fellow, but that's for me to know. A journalist who I later learned was mortally afraid of dogs, having been bitten by a particularly vicious one in his childhood, nearly suffered a cardiac arrest when King Tuts decided to show his affection by parking himself on the poor man's lap. When I came out of my room to greet the visitor, I found an ashen-faced young man, frozen with fright. He'd obviously stopped breathing and was rapidly turning blue. Had I delayed my entry by even a few seconds, I might have found him in a dead faint outside. He remained in a semi-catatonic state for close to half an hour, even as Tuts went around happily sniffing his person, entirely oblivious to what he'd subjected the chap to. German writers and TV crews take to the dog in a big way because they believe all boxers are German under the skin. They talk to Tuts in German and express great delight when he wags his stub of a tail. 'See—he understands every word,' they exclaim triumphantly. I don't have the heart to tell them he is far too stupid a dog to do anything other than grin and bark. Being as photogenic as he is, he effortlessly steals the show in any joint TV appearance. In fact, he's developing such airs, he assumes the cameras and lights are for him, often jumping up and licking the lens in his enthusiasm. I'm certain a time will come when all these TVwallahs will walk into our home, shoot their Tuts footage and leave with a polite nod in my general direction.

My younger children actively resent these visits and articulate their impatience, often to my utter embarrassment. I don't enjoy them either, but I recognize their relevance in the context of what I do. And am reasonably good-humoured about co-operation. Not so my kids. They see no reason to tolerate strangers in our house even if I do try and keep all interviewers away on holidays and restrict my interaction to school hours. When one of my daughters (Arundhati) was younger, she thought nothing of assuming the role of an art director. When Clive James set up his shoot in our living room for his series *Postcard from Mumbai*, my daughter informed the crew that their angle and location had been done a dozen times over by other foreign TV companies. She pointed to another corner of the room and said, 'Why don't you set up your lights here? This area has not been done in a while.' Thank God for people with a sense of humour, for she went on to tell them about the sort of questions I'm generally asked, adding helpfully, 'My mother gets really bored answering them. I hope you'll be asking her something different.' Mr James' research assistants, who are tops at their jobs, assured her they'd make sure to do just that.

It was an interview I enjoyed. I liked Clive James (a lot of interviewees don't). I liked his wicked sense of humour and the energy he brings to the show. Initially, I'd been asked to go along with him for the entire Mumbai segment and maintain a running commentary through the documentary. A jokey-jokey, conspiratorial chat. I was reluctant on two counts—a daunting schedule that would require me to accompany Mr James to distant suburban locations, and more importantly, being a party to the sort of take-off he's notorious for. It's all right for him to make fun of our people and their foibles. It's all right for me to do so on my own. But it didn't feel all right to team up with a Briton (even though he was born in Australia), be seen as being on 'his side', and send the natives up. I believe it was the right decision.

When I met Clive James, I confess I wasn't aware of his very special position in the world of television. I just thought he was a jolly sort of chap who was finding it hard to beat the Mumbai heat. I'd enjoyed meeting his recce assistants, and had found them delightful. While the lights were being set up, Mr James and I got talking. He narrated his misadventures in the city including a hilarious day spent as a film extra on the sets of an extravagant Hindi film. He'd taken the long and real route by presenting himself at the office of the contractor who 'supplied' junior artistes to producers. And he'd waited it out along with the hungry desperados whose daily wages depend on whether or not their services are required. Since the film Mr James eventually got hired for was a costume drama and his 'role' consisted of dying within the first three minutes, it wasn't too tough an assignment for him to handle even if he did have to get into a bizarre costume and have a gigantic handle-bar moustache stuck over his upper lip. Considering he'd been doing this sort of stuff all over the world for twenty years, wasn't he kind of sick of it? How did he crank up the system on cue? I found out just how.

His questions to me, which rolled off his tongue so smoothly and so 'spontaneously', had been fed to him by his efficient assistants. He arrived at my home minutes before the cameras were due to roll, mopped his profusely sweating brow and got into his professional mode without ceremony. His look on camera was one of amusement and interest. This was a technique he'd mastered. At the sound of the words, 'we are rolling', his expression would alter as if by magic and he'd engage me in a seemingly intense dialogue which was in fact nothing more than a few sentences he'd scanned on a cue-board seconds earlier. This was true professionalism, I marvelled, as I watched the on-off-on-off act taking place. Most impressive. While conversing between shots, I discovered he'd been at college with Germaine Greer. I mentioned how much I admired her as a woman and how privileged I felt that I'd had the opportunity to get to know her just a little during a workshop she'd conducted in

Mumbai. Mr James wiggled his eyebrows and stared at me with a look that said, 'To each his own. But I'm no fan of hers.'

In a small way I understood why when, in London, a few years later, I happened to see a particularly cruel TV show on which Greer was interviewed by Andrew Neil. It was a programme called *This Is Your life*, if I recall correctly. And I was determined to catch it. What I wasn't prepared for was the content. Here is a show that strips you naked and exposes every wart and pimple through a simple yet lethal device. Researchers fan out to all corners of the world and track down the interviewee's family, friends, former spouses, lovers, enemies, rivals and assorted ghosts. They are video-taped discussing the personality in a candid, conversational way. The person is not told who has been located or what has been said. Neil asks a specific question like, 'Did you have a good relationship with your junior school teacher?' And Greer beams, 'Great. Those were truly wonderful years.' The camera cuts to the teacher shot earlier in some corner of Australia—and she narrates a nasty story about Greer's years in the school. It gets worse. 'Did you ever attend orgies?' Neil throws at Greer who replies, 'No, never. Well . . . maybe once in Amsterdam with a friend who thought I should check out the scene.' Neil cuts to Xaviera Hollander, the infamous madame and *Penthouse* columnist, who says authoritatively, 'Germaine was a serial orgyist. I remember her dragging countless young men into dark rooms.' At the end of the hour, Greer was crushed, pulped and pulverized by every single individual who chose to go public with his or her views on the writer. Not a single person had anything positive to say about her, not even a niece who Greer had claimed she was very fond of. 'My aunt doesn't even remember us during X'mas,' the young girl cribbed.

I was shattered. Not by the viciousness of the attacks, but by Greer's defensiveness. This wasn't the woman I'd behaved like a groupie with. This person was over-lipsticked, carefully styled—and worse, lying through her teeth and getting caught with each fib. It was humiliating and horrible. I cringed and suffered through the programme and hated Andrew Neil for demolishing my heroine and reducing her to rubble. Why did she have to lie? She, of all people? She, the great role model for a generation of women the world over? The one person who could afford to be herself, face the truth, brazen it out, care a damn about presenting a 'good' face to anyone? Be honest, warts and all? I'd thought Greer was too big to descend to such a pathetic level where she'd be exposed so rapaciously by a man whose own credentials were sleazy and dubious. She didn't need the publicity. She didn't need to justify herself. She didn't need to explain or defend any area of her life. Or so I'd believed.

I still wonder why she put herself though it. But such is my admiration for Greer, I prefer to think of her as I knew her during her brief stay in Mumbai, when she was either bored enough or kind enough to spare time for a wide-eyed fan who hung on to her every word and eagerly accompanied her through crowded bazaars with the strong Indian sun streaming through her thin cotton skirt, thereby effortlessly establishing the absence of knickers underneath.

I wondered, too, what Stevan Seagal was wearing under his voluminous yellow ochre Buddhist robes when I met him at the premiere of his film *Under Seige* sometime in 1995. This was before he'd been declared a lama, or an incarnation of one. At that stage, he was merely a wannabe Buddhist who happened to break spines over his knee on screen for a living. The premiere was sponsored by an evening paper, and I'd been asked to be there as a chief guest whose sole job would be to make sure the guest of honour (Seagal) wouldn't feel terribly out of it. There were hundreds of fans waiting for the star to arrive at the Sterling theatre in south Mumbai. The security arrangements were impressive as well, with crackling walkie-talkies monitoring Seagal's progress from his hotel to the cinema hall. The foyer was packed to capacity and there I was clutching my daughter Avantika's hand and waiting for the pony-tailed man-mountain to show up.

The motorcade was awesome, with outriders, a bulletproof car, personal bodyguards and an even more personal blonde on Seagal's arm. He got out of the limo and folded his hands in a namaste. Despite the cops, the cordons and several heavy flower pots cluttering the path, suddenly a wall of screaming humanity descended on us even as the introductions were being made. I found a strong arm around my waist, another one shielding my face, my feet by then a few inches off the ground as we were swept along for a good ten feet down the carpeted foyer. I was too worried about losing my grip on my daughter's hand, and concerned she'd be hurt in the mêlée to realize that the person who'd acted with such lightning speed . . . so instinctively . . . could only have been a trained martial arts expert, accustomed to reflex actions in emergencies—Steven Seagal himself. He put me down lightly and asked, 'Are you all right?' I was, give or take a couple of scratches. I looked around frantically for my daughter. She'd been similarly rescued by one of his commandos.

We went up to the balcony for the screening, still shaking from the experience. The blonde took her seat dutifully at Seagal's left, I was on the right. The movie was completely absurd, worse than anything I'd seen on the Hindi screen. We watched it in silence. I tried making polite conversation with the enormous star in the next seat. It was obvious he wasn't interested. He mumbled in monosyllables . . . and meditated. When the lights came on during the interval, he was called on stage to say a few words. He blessed the assembled fans, drawing his silken robes around his monumental person, came back to his seat and meditated some more. The blonde chewed gum and watched him worshipfully. I gave up on conversation and tried to pay attention to the godawful film I'd been talked into sitting through. Seconds before the screening ended, Seagal and his companion got up and pushed past me without so much as an apology for the inconvenience, nor a goodbye. I was appalled by his lack of good manners. He may have been the biggest Hollywood honcho, or a great spiritual master, but courtesy demanded that he and the blonde have etiquette enough to say at least a simple 'bye bye'. A rude, ill-mannered lama? It will be interesting to see just how far this one gets.

When I met V.S. Naipaul during one of his trips to India, I discovered that he too travelled with an organizer-companion. We were having a dinner party at home and he came along with a journalist friend. They were accompanied by his companion at that stage, a largish, proprietorial South American woman called Margaret, who functioned as his look-out, guide, bodyguard, antenna and butler. He walked in with his standard preoccupied scowl and looked around at some of our guests with an expression that clearly indicated his impatience and contempt. The awestruck gathering parted to let him pass, not daring to start a conversation. Margaret, who appeared fierce but communicative, surveyed the room and decided there were one or two people there, after all, who were worthy enough to breathe the same air as the genius. At some point, a plate of mini-idlis (really too tiny to be eaten as anything other than finger-food) was brought around. Naipaul stared at the idlis with horror and asked, 'What are these?' 'Idlis,' I replied without bothering to elaborate. 'How does one eat them?' he demanded. I picked one up, popped it in my mouth and said, 'Like this.' He seemed aghast at the unsaid suggestion that he should try one and dirty his fingers. He looked around desperately for Margaret. She rushed over within seconds, fluttering anxiously while assuring him that it was okay to try one, the snack was edible—and that she'd arrange for a plate and fork in a jiffy. Naipaul scowled some more and seemed most distraught. I was told later that he was a very fastidious eater who picked at his food like a bird and abhorred the idea of physically touching anything that was meant to go into the mouth.

During his visit, a dinner was structured around him by a socially ambitious person who called up all the 'right' people and said, 'Oh, I've invited V.S. Naipaul over. Not too many people. Don't be late.' It came to be known as 'Naipaul's dinner' and became a hot ticket in certain circles. 'Are you going to——? You know it's in honour of Naipaul. He's getting the Nobel this year. About time too.' Forty-odd people waited expectantly in an over-decorated, arty living room for the genius to show up. They'd taken the trouble to flip through his latest book, carefully memorized the names of his earlier ones, and dressed down for the occasion. This was, after all, a literary event, not another cocktail party. Naipaul turned up all right—with great reluctance, it was later whispered. But he didn't bother to show up at the flat itself. Instead, he sent Margaret for a recce while he waited in the car downstairs. She didn't make it past the ante-room herself. After sticking her head into the party zone next door, she shuddered and beat a hasty retreat to the scowler in the car. He took her word for it when she said it wasn't worth his while to even put in a token appearance. They left without so much as an apology, while the host kept calling the hotel to find out Naipaul's whereabouts. Mumbai being Mumbai, after enough Scotch was consumed, it really didn't matter at all that Naipaul had done a no-show. The party swung on regardless. But it said something about the man's intolerance, inconsideration and lack of grace. Conceded, geniuses do not live by the rules that matter to ordinary mortals. But basic etiquette applies to one and all.

A lot has happened to Naipaul since then—he is now Sir Vidiadhar. And his new wife insists on being addressed as 'Lady Naipaul' by everybody, according to an interviewer I met in Delhi who was amused, to say the least, by the pretentiousness of it all. But Naipaul looks happy—he seems to have replaced one control freak with another, and that's obviously how he likes it. The burden of being one of the world's greatest living writers must be unbearable, indeed a bit too 'profound', to use the writer's favourite word. He seems to be dealing with it far more stylishly these days, going by his new moviestar-like wardrobe and publicity pictures (blood-red turtle-neck sweater under a well-cut, dove grey jacket, I tell you) shot by a 'name' in the glamour photography business. Maybe I would have liked him more had he liked me more.

Some seem to carry the load of fame more easily than others—Ryszard Kapuscinski, the Polish writer, for one. When I was invited to attend the Writer's Festival in Melbourne, I was curious, flattered and delighted to know the company I was in. For example, one of the invitees was John Berendt, whose book on Savannah, Georgia, *Midnight in the Garden of Good and Evil* had hit best-seller lists around the world. Another invitee was Kapuscinski, widely regarded as the world's greatest living corespondent and the author of critically acclaimed books like *The Emperor*. When I first saw him in the lobby of the hotel, I passed him by without a second glance. Naipaul is hard to ignore even if one hasn't heard of him or his work. He has the personality and demeanour of one who knows his importance in the world. Kapuscinski was shuffling around almost apologetically, like he was the hotel plumber looking for a leaking cistern. His manner was so meek and unobtrusive that had he not been on the front pages of the dailies, nobody would have noticed him. Whether it was at the festival venue, or at crowded press conferences, he was clearly the star of the event, shabbily dressed and stooped as he was. But when he spoke, it was his genuine humility and humanity that shone forth.

It made one think how genius sits on different individuals. Some wear it like a grand robe and strut around declaring their hallowed position to the world. Others treat it like a favourite tweed jacket—a garment that's become like a second skin over the years and is to be ignored.

Modesty isn't a trait one would associate with Dr Christian Barnard, and yet, he seemed the very epitome of modesty, initially at any rate, when he arrived in India for a lecture series. The one I attended in Mumbai was for a capacity crowd of doctors, mainly prominent cardiac surgeons and the heads of various hospitals. The setting was appropriately opulent: a grand chandeliered ballroom in a luxury hotel with a deep pile carpet and fancy drapes. Dr Barnard is now a permanent fixture on the lecture circuit and there are enough sponsors willing to fly him around the world for a fat fee. Why not? What is the point of being a celebrity if one can't encash a cheque as and when required? For countless people of my generation the South African surgeon was more than just an inspiring figure who'd shot to international fame after performing what was then considered a near impossible feat—that of replacing the human heart with one taken from a donor. More than his surgical skill, it was his colourful life, movie-star looks and undeniable flamboyance that had captured the imagination of the world—an affair with Gina Lollobrigida among other famous beauties; diplomas in karate, bull-fighting and wine-making; awards and accolades from just about every prestigious body; and more interestingly, a certain notoriety which added to his charisma. I wasn't going to miss this lecture for anything.

My husband and I went early, like eager schoolchildren wishing to grab front-row seats. I knew the doctor was now in his seventies, had lost most of his hair, wore dentures and suffered from rheumatoid arthritis. That was fine by me. He was a hero . . . even a heart-throb, during my growing years, and I wanted to be there.

He walked in half an hour late, his gait an awkward shuffle. But once he took the podium, he was brilliant. And it occurred to me as he recounted anecdotes and stories he had flogged to death on the lecture circuit a million times, that here was a highly intelligent professional who'd had the good sense to market his life's work as an attractive (and highly profitable) package. No longer able to wield the scalpel he once did with such dexterity, Dr Barnard had decided to cash in on his own legend by turning into a pro on the big-time lecture circuit world-wide. In order to stay there and capitalize on his past glories, he'd come up with an audience-friendly programme that combined humour, human interest stories, a bit of scientific jargon, some old slides and enough emotional nostalgia to tug at the most cynical heart-strings. He'd worked on the format shrewdly and as it stands today, its effects are dazzling.

There was a particularly grisly moment during the lecture when he clinically described exactly which blood vessels had been severed in Princess Diana's heart, using an enormous close-up of the organ with a laser beam directed at the precise points of severance. Gruesome, highly dramatic, superbly timed (the tragic accident was only a few weeks old then), Dr Barnard's spiel was designed to press all the right buttons.

He was clever enough to play down his individual role in the historic heart transplant, attributing it to great teamwork. At the same time, he was canny enough to let on that no matter how humbly he regarded his achievement, the world obviously thought otherwise, and who was he to contradict universal opinion?

While I listened to his hour-long address, I was mesmerized, even moved. But at the end of it, after he'd deftly handled a few awestruck questions from the audience, I didn't feel the slightest desire to go up to him and shake his hand. At some point I'd seen him for who he was—a wealthy, retired super celebrity cashing in somewhat cold-bloodedly on his very impressive track record, travelling the world with his perfectly-pitched sixty-minute act that didn't fail to bring the expected tears to his admirers' eyes. Nothing wrong with that. There was no real moral issue involved. And yet, it took away a little from his glory, and tarnished my teenage image of a man who I'd once said was the only person I'd care to be marooned on a desert island with.

I'm not so sure about that any more. Not if I'd have to endure a tape-recording of his 'spontaneous' speech, delivered with the flair and flourish of a trained actor who knows his lines and their effect on the man in row three, seat twenty-one. It was an impressive performance. Lawrence Olivier might have approved. But I felt let down. I had gone to hear a living legend sharing scenes from his extraordinary life. I'd come away after watching a polished one-act play complete with impeccably-timed pauses, laughter, even tears. I didn't rise to my feet when Dr Barnard was given a standing ovation. I was too busy coming to terms with my own disillusionment.

It's a terrible thing, really. Especially for someone who has grown up without a pantheon of heroes. Even as a child, I remained largely unimpressed by people in high places. That hasn't changed. If anything, I look for the flaws first—not because I am nasty, but perhaps as a clumsy way of seeking self-protection. During the *Society* years and later, with *Celebrity*, I met several Extremely Important People—not one left a strong enough impression. Not even old man Ramnath Goenka.

The first time he invited me to lunch I was curious. The next, suspicious. The wily fox wasn't known for his social graces or generosity. I went along, antenna up. The *Express* elevator reserved for the penthouse residence took me straight into his spartan living room. The place resembled a neglected government guest house even though it was run by a buxom, well-dressed lady whose job it was to make sure VIP visitors to the place were well looked after. The old man surveyed me shrewdly and figured whatever it was he wanted to figure. We talked over a lavish vegetarian lunch served out of silver thalis. He took calls. He abused various people. He hollered at a few more. He scratched himself unselfconsciously. And he certainly didn't mind his tongue or manners. His utter contempt for the world at large and his editors in particular came through clearly.

This was at the time he was having trouble with one particular person—Arun Shourie. And he was doing a Beckett on him—remember that wonderful line, 'Will no one rid me of this troublesome priest?' I guess he figured (correctly as it turned out) that I'd bite. The story was far too good to pass up. My struggling magazine certainly needed a 'hot' scoop. He was sharp enough to recognize my hunger. He gave me all the dope, stressing it was 'off-the-record' even though my tape recorder was prominently displayed on the centre table and had been switched on very deliberately. It was a great story full of brilliant quotes. It was obvious Shourie's days at the *Express* were numbered . . . Goenka was merely waiting for the best moment to fire him. I went back after the lunch and phoned Shourie in Delhi. I told him I was planning to run the piece and asked for his version.

Over the next two days I spoke to Ramnathji a few times, making it perfectly clear I'd be writing about our meeting and quoting him. He protested mildly and suggested I use his quotes without attributing them to him. 'Write it in your own words,' he laughed. I told him once again I'd do no such thing. The deadline was a few hours away as I frantically put the piece together with a box interview featuring Shourie. A few days after it appeared, Shourie left the *Express*, as colleagues had anticipated he would. Other journalists who contacted Goenka for comments were fobbed off with *'woh ladki kuch bhi likhti hai'*. I objected strongly to the *'ladki'*. I believe the old boy was delighted with what followed—Shourie quit, and Goenka regained full control of his paper. I never saw him again.

It was years before I ran into Shourie. I'd met him at his neat, modest residence in Delhi before the article appeared. And then for more than fifteen years, our paths didn't cross. When we finally caught up with each other, he was soft-spoken charm itself. Someone ignorant asked politely, 'Do you know each other?' And Shourie smiled his trademark smile before replying, 'Yes, of course. She's the one who got me fired from the *Express*.' I was hoping to hear a few words of choice abuse—not necessarily directed at me—but Shourie was awfully restrained that afternoon. Maybe he picked up the habit from his old boss. Otherwise, strangers are often startled to hear explicit Hindi expletives emerging from

Shourie's mouth. It is unexpected coming from a man who has the visage of a latter-day saint, though he can also resemble Groucho Marx and Charlie Chaplin.

I'd discovered what a great mimic Shourie was during that one visit to his Delhi residence. With a fine ear for eccentric speech and a talent for catching the odd gesture, Shourie can be a highly entertaining companion once he gets going. Poor man, he's probably obliged to carry around the rather overwhelming load of eventual sainthood. He has his devoted followers and he cannot afford to disappoint them by appearing anything than thinker, philosopher and intellectual—well, we know he is all of those. But how many of us have been lucky enough to witness his witty take-offs on politicians, colleagues and his former employer?

Another person whom I greatly enjoyed meeting was the grand old man of Indian politics: Morarji Desai. I'd heard that he was impossibly eccentric, rude and autocratic. When I first met him, he appeared to be all that and worse—a Mumbai Gujju (a breed by itself) who even while living in this city seemed to detest everything about it, starting with Mumbai women. Somebody like me. The meeting was set up by his burly, smooth-talking son Kanti. I was rather looking forward to it. I like crusty old men with sharp tongues, and I was prepared to be snubbed by the former prime minister. With me was a young colleague, Salil Tripathi, another Mumbai Gujarati, bright, aggressive and ambitious, who spoke with an endearing lisp. He was the kind of journalist who did his homework thoroughly and went after his interviewee with a doggedness that occasionally led to strong words. He didn't mean to offend, it was his inexperience and unbridled enthusiasm that made him venture into territory more seasoned journalists would have stayed away from.

The moment we were escorted into Morarjibhai's room

I knew we weren't going to get too far—well, nobody could with someone who responded to every question with a counter question. But my charged up colleague wasn't about to let the opportunity go by default. He had a questionnaire and he was damned if he wasn't going to run through it in its entirety. I had a questionnaire too, but how on earth was I going to get even a single question in when the main man refused to acknowledge my existence? Morarjibhai's aversion to females was well known. I hadn't realized just how strong it was till we came face to face and he averted his gaze, like some truly awful creature had walked in and polluted the pristine atmosphere of his neat room. He continued to ignore me, my greetings, even the sound of my voice (I kept trying to butt in, with zero success).

I was rather surprised by his surroundings. I'd expected a Gandhian, spartan ambience—not animal skins, air-conditioners and an overall air of luxury. He looked irritable and impatient—but that was his trademark expression when dealing with the press. I found his determination to obliterate my existence most amusing. I reacted by being equally determined to get him to look in my direction. It became a game—but I was the only one playing. It was time for his lunch (mid-morning), and we were keen to photograph him. Surprisingly he didn't seem to mind that at all. The photographer was also a Mumbai Gujju and that may have helped. We watched the great moralist eat his 'frugal' repast. It was impressive by any standards, served in a gleaming silver thali, with several silver katoris filled with pure vegetarian dishes. Soaked almonds, sliced fruits, yoghurt, honey—this was a meal fit for a very wealthy, very healthy person. Which he was, no matter what he proclaimed publicly.

It wasn't much of an interview. The famous Morarji temper flashed every few minutes. We got very little out of him. But it was an experience I wouldn't have wanted to miss. Strangely enough, all his attempts to pretend I wasn't there made him appear vulnerable and defenceless, like a child keeping the bogey man at bay. I didn't feel snubbed. I didn't feel annoyed. I wanted to lean over and hug him. I felt entirely comfortable with his attitude—understood it even. Better an ill-mannered Morarji than someone arrogant and icky like . . . like . . . Imran Khan.

Imran is a lot like Morarji Desai, come to think of it. I'm convinced he doesn't like women at all (poor Jemima). He certainly doesn't respect them. That's obvious enough from his attitude. He must have his reasons. During those heady days when he was the dashing, impossibly handsome captain of the Pakistani cricket team, Imran must have seen the worst side of females—all those painted society ladies who threw themselves at him and were willing to take whatever came their way, even a well-aimed kick, so long as the foot in the boot was Imran's. With that kind of female adulation, and given his upbringing, it was but natural that Imran grew up with a certain level of contempt for easily available partners who were ready to abandon the stability of marriage for a one-night fling with the cricketing hero. Indian women, in particular, brought out the beast in him. Whether or not the awful, sneering comments about Indian women attributed to him are true, he succeeded in conveying precisely that sentiment whenever he came to town and had his pick of the city's most desirable ladies.

By the time I met him, Imran had rediscovered Allah and was fancying his newly minted role as the moral saviour of Pakistan. We met at a sit-down, post-premiere dinner. My husband and I were at the table that also had Goldie Hawn. Imran took his place stiffly and self-consciously to my right. By now his original looks had begun to fade and he looked a tired, dissipated, middle-aged playboy with bags under his eyes and a huge chip on his shoulder. He carried on like there was a heavy burden he had to bear—Pakistan had to be saved at all costs. It was his special destiny to lead his people out of the degradation they'd allowed themselves to fall into, and make them see the light. This was the future prime-ministerial-hopeful talking, combining a naïve mixture of mullah-speak and politics. I felt rather sorry for him. It must have been such a strain trying to appear well informed, concerned and intelligent. He stuck to freshly-squeezed sweet lime juice while sneering at the crystal flutes of Dom Perignon floating past our table. His expression was fixed and studied. Actually he looked like he needed to use the toilet badly, like he'd be that much more comfortable after passing a particularly hard stool that was clogging his gut.

It was impossible to make polite party conversation with him. He'd gone into his preacher mode and was lecturing all those at the table about the evils of satellite television. 'I do not allow my nephews and nieces to watch music channels,' he thundered. Then he delivered a long speech on the depraved West. We Asians, he said, must stick together and protect our identity, our heritage. I wasn't enjoying my meal at all. I desperately wanted to switch places with my husband and giggle with Goldie Hawn. Imran barely ate his dinner. He was busy concentrating on a distant spot as if that helped him to focus on his own pearls of wisdom. Studying his haggard profile, with wispy strands of hair flopping limply over his forehead, I remembered the old Imran—the graceful, devastatingly handsome cricketer who moved across the television screen like a lithe panther, each muscle of his well-toned body perfectly co-ordinated, his lips twisted in a snarl, his eyes narrowed in complete concentration. That was the man his fans would remember. That was the man our magazine had chased for an interview—and got.

The interview itself may not have been much (it was about the time there were rumours that he'd be marrying Zeenat Aman), but his pin-up pictures were something else. The same talented photographer, Rahul, who'd managed to click Morarji Desai munching on a bowlful of pistachios, had persuaded Imran to remove his shirt and pose bare-chested for the cover of *Society*. It was an issue that sold in the black market on both sides of the border. Smuggled copies in Pakistan had been snapped up for two hundred rupees apiece. It had also led to strong denials from Imran about his impending marriage to the Indian sex symbol. What he had not been able to deny quite as vehemently was the presence of Ms Aman in an adjoining suite at the five-star hotel in South Mumbai where he'd been staying. We'd tracked her down and spoken to her and she'd claimed (rather lamely) that the only reason she was in the hotel was because her flat was being renovated. That's what celebrity confessions are all about—coincidences, coincidences.

I've always enjoyed playing voyeur . . . watching people who interest me. Trying to figure out what makes them say what they say, act the way they act. It was only very recently that the key was provided by my husband when he observed sleepily about a well-known person we know rather well: 'She is acting two hundred per cent of the time. Discount whatever she says. Not a single utterance is genuine.' While I was absorbing that (and feeling a little let-down) he added, 'The strain of performing non-stop often catches up with her . . . which is when she collapses physically and develops all those peculiar allergies.'

He was right. I 'perform' too (I guess at different moments we all have to). But I'm always aware that I am doing just that—performing. I don't kid myself or my family.

Often, we exchange sly glances, even winks. I can hear my children whispering, 'Oh-oh . . . there goes Mom. God, she's really hamming it up . . . stop her, someone.' It's a game that I play when I'm either terribly tired or terribly bored. It's also a useful technique to master when a certain expectation exists and one doesn't have the energy to re-educate strangers. A couple of my friends ask me often enough why I don't bother to correct the notion that I am whatever people believe I am. Fatigue is one fairly honest response. Indifference, another. I feel I have reached an age when I'm beyond caring what the prejudiced think, how they judge me.

But it still irks me to be constantly 'on parade'. I was complaining to a friend that one of the aspects of being what is loosely described as a 'celebrity' (how I detest that label) is to have people walk up and make unsolicited remarks, which in my case are primarily concerned with my appearance. Celebrating my son Aditya's birthday at a newly-opened Mexican restaurant recently, I was taken aback when a middle-aged man from the next table intercepted me as I was going to the exit, saying, 'Hello, Shobha Dé. I didn't expect you to be this thin. I always thought you were a very tall, very large-boned woman. Have you lost a lot of weight recently?'

What does one do in these circumstances? Ignore the comment? I tried doing just that. But the chap was persistent. 'Your photographs make you look much larger,' he carried on, surveying me insolently from head to toe. My children were annoyed. Fortunately my husband missed the little pantomime . . . or else, the indiscreet, ill-mannered man may have discovered the true meaning of the real enchilada.

My friend told me it was a common problem with the people she knew best—movie stars. Dimple Kapadia, in particular, hates being 'surveyed' and she finds herself in that unenviable situation all the time. Women, in particular, seem obsessive about other women's looks. At an art exhibition opening in Bangalore, another friend of mine hung around with the crowd and was amused to pick up a few unguarded comments about me. 'She must have had a face-lift,' said one lady to a group. They looked me over critically and chorused, 'Definitely. It's not possible otherwise. Maybe she went to the same surgeon in New York . . . you know the one Rekha goes to?' That was said with such an air of authority, nobody bothered to ask, 'Which surgeon?' or even, 'How do you know Rekha has subjected her face to a scalpel?'

At the same event complete strangers came up to me and made remarks that ranged from 'Your photographs don't do you any justice' and 'You don't look like your pictures' to 'Do you really have six children?' 'What do you use to keep your skin clean?' 'Where did you buy this saree from?' 'How do you keep your weight down?' 'When do you find the time to write?' 'What is the secret of your appearance?' Flattering? Up to a point. But mainly exasperating.

During an online chat after the launch of *Surviving Men* an Indian woman from Cincinnati asked me, 'How do you preserve yourself?' I answered, 'In vinegar.' She keyed back frantically, 'Wow. Tell me more about it.' I responded, 'I soak myself overnight in a tubful.' She logged in again, 'I got that. But tell me, do you also splash some on your face?' I should have felt alarmed at this stage and clarified that I was merely joking. But then I thought sadistically to myself, let her go ahead and do it. Let her resemble a shrivelled-up prune. What do I care?

My husband and I often dine out together. It's something that seems to surprise people we know—which surprises me. Is it unnatural to go out for an evening—just the two of you? It would appear that way going by the general disbelief and exclamations like 'How come?' 'Is it your anniversary?' 'My, my, how romantic.' 'Anybody else joining you?' We are rarely left alone. If nobody else, eager waiters and restaurant managers decide to liven up what we'd hoped would be a quiet, relaxed evening. Again, nearly all of the time is taken on commenting on the way I'm looking.

'I was your waiter in Hyderabad,' a young assistant manager informed me a few months ago. 'When we were told you were going to be present, all of us wanted to see how you looked.' Had it ended there, it would have been all right. But he was in no hurry to conclude this. 'You were wearing a very beautiful ethnic outfit.' It was over four years ago, and I couldn't remember. He was determined to recreate the entire scenario, down to what my husband and I had eaten . . . or even, not eaten. 'Ma'am . . . you've lost far too much weight since then,' he said regretfully, shaking his head from side to side. My neck was straining after being forced to look up at him while he towered over the table. The thread of a serious conversation my husband and I had been having was broken . . . there was no way we'd be able to pick it up now. I was feeling miserable. I couldn't eat any more. Some more weight was going to be lost that night.

Age. Weight. Appearance. So much seems to depend on them. There I was at a coffee shop in a five-star shopping arcade, being interviewed by some foreign correspondent, when a middle-aged man with a young daughter called out to me in a familiar, friendly fashion to ask, 'Exactly how old are you? My daughter and I have taken a bet on it.' My age has been published in every single one of my books. It is not something I want to either hide or deny. To me, it's just another biological detail that's boring. But obviously not to everyone. I'm still at a loss as to how one is supposed to deal with this—my approach has been an upfront one. Answer briskly and get on with it.

One day, a woman came home to interview me. From the thrust of her highly probing, searching questions I figured she wasn't the garden variety journalist. Everything about her made me curious, even disoriented. When she'd called to set up the appointment I'd been intrigued by her sing-song accent, cultured voice and impeccable manners. The person who turned up punctually was wearing a printed lace-edged burqa that took me completely off-guard. Once she'd settled down to the interview I continued to be fascinated since her choice of words didn't quite go with her appearance. I was familiar with her byline, but I'd expected another kind of woman. Maybe 'modern' is the word I'm looking for. Here she was, modern enough in her speech and thoughts, but why the medieval garment? I didn't think it was any of my business to ask. She watched as I took half a dozen calls and dealt with the usual domestic trivia of my life. She overheard a domestic telling someone I was in the middle of an interview. Earlier, when she'd come in, the same man had cheerfully informed her that I was in the bath and would be out in five minutes.

She looked at me with a mixture of shock and sympathy. 'Why should any stranger know such intimate aspects of your life?' she demanded. 'Why do you talk about yourself at all? Why do you give interviews? Why do you reveal anything about yourself?'

I asked her one simple question. 'Why are you here? Why are you interviewing me? Why don't you respect my need for privacy and leave me alone?'

She paused before saying, 'I was assigned to do the story.'

'You could have refused,' I replied.

'I feel it's very unfair to you—the media interest. The voyeurism. It's an assault. It's an intrusion. You must not be a party to it.'

'Will you then go back and refuse to write this piece? If

you believe so strongly in what you're saying, if you think all interviews are ugly and unnecessary, you shouldn't be in this business yourself.'

She looked into my eyes deeply and asked, 'Why are they watering?'

I said, 'Only the right one is . . . I have a mild allergy.'

She shook her head. 'That's not an allergy at all. It's a sign of stress.'

'That too, maybe,' I agreed.

'You need to get away from all this. There are too many demands on you. It isn't possible for any one individual to cope.'

I listened.

'You've allowed yourself to become a commodity for others to exploit. Everybody around you is a part of this exploitation—time exploitation, emotional exploitation or monetary exploitation—your family, friends, publishers, the press.'

'Aren't you exploiting me, too, by being here and subjecting me to this?'

She looked down. Perhaps I'm fooling myself, but I thought her eyes clouded over. She picked up her notes and walked to the door. I escorted her to the elevator. Both of us were silent. It's been over six months. She hasn't published the interview. I'd like to meet her some day and thank her. At least for a week after her unsettling visit I didn't do anything I didn't have to. I thought about her assessments, agreed with some of them, discarded a few. And I am writing this, so many months later. The conversation did leave an impact. If it is this stressful for me, how much more for a legitimate, bonafide celebrity in the big league? For a showbiz person, a politician, a sports star. What I have to deal with is insignificant—having my name called out by a bus full of tourists at Apollo Bunder, a few unwanted letters and phone calls, a modest amount of attention and curiosity from the public at large. Nothing that is out of control.

Am I a party to some of it—most of it? Yes and no.

After the death of Diana, Princess of Wales, nearly everybody who happens to deal with unsolicited publicity anywhere in the world has asked this question of himself or herself.

When I think about it, I suppose I am guilty of participating in the celebrity trip. I don't always adore the people whose homes I visit. I do talk about them behind their backs. I know they don't like me just as I don't like them. That's life in any competitive city. I've reached a stage when I'm so switched off, whether it's a woman who consistently trashes me in print or another who discusses every aspect of my life obsessively, I really don't give a damn. My sisters are surprised by this when they visit. Their lives have been so much simpler. They see people at our home sometimes whom they know I loathe. They look at me questioningly . . . and then very sweetly, I can see their sisterly loyalty taking over as they shoot dirty looks at the person. I assure them that none of this really matters in the jungle I inhabit, where it's each one for himself or herself. I tell them I'm a big girl now, capable of handling these types—all types. They don't seem sufficiently convinced as they watch me glide from one hostile group to the next, my smile intact, my eyes shining. It comes with training, I inform them in my best worldly-wise voice. They continue to look sceptical. I would too. What a waste. What a strain. But then again . . . what to do?

Writing On

It was in the early Seventies that I was asked by the editor of
Onlooker, S. Venkat Narayan, to write my first regular
column. I took it on without really thinking it through.
Onlooker had gone through several avatars and under
Venkat, it was striving to be a serious, focused political
magazine with teeth. My column was intended to provide
light relief. It turned out to be anything but 'light', in that I
started writing it in the same tone as 'Neeta's Natter', bite and
all. What I hadn't reckoned with was that unlike 'NN', this
column came with a name and a photograph. I wrote on
regardless—a cheeky, insolent, cynical take on the social
scene, often featuring identifiable people. The observations
were spot-on but cruel.

There was one particular piece that led to an on-going
war for decades, involving a society queen and her rather
unusual relationship with a struggling young fellow. I viewed
it as a comment on a prevalent trend. She, as an attack. I can
see it from her perspective now, but back then, I wondered
why she was popping arteries over something that wasn't even
private—she'd gone public with it herself. For years she
stewed, cursing me whenever my name cropped up. Now, of
course, it's all in the past and neatly resolved, even if her
husband can't resist the occasional crack when we are at
dinner in their magnificent home. The young fellow is no

longer a teenager, but he's still around. I can sit across a table from him without either of us wincing.

After Venkat got me going, along came Fatma Zakaria, her face like a luminous full moon. She was then the editor of *The Sunday Review* (a *Times of India* publication). She asked me to write a fortnightly column for her prestigious paper—and I promptly said 'yes'. What she didn't tell me was the amount of resistance she faced within her office. Innocent of that knowledge, I cheerfully wrote my pieces, which were very different from the *Onlooker* columns. These had a more serious, reflective tone and dealt with everyday concerns. I enjoyed writing them and given the reactions from ordinary readers who phoned, I think they worked rather well. It's rewarding that I still get people commenting on something I wrote nearly twenty years ago.

It was the writing of this column which led to all the others that followed. I felt I'd found my forte. Compressing a week's or a fortnight's events into a readable capsule, with my own take on the subject, was something I enjoyed doing and was getting progressively better at. If a writer needs to bring discipline into his or her schedule, columns are the answer. Today, I restrict mine to three a week. There was a time when I was writing six—and not complaining. Even at that stage, I didn't feel I was either repeating myself or just hammering them out mechanically. I chose my publications and topics with care to avoid overlap while keeping myself on red alert constantly.

I wrote on television, food, movies, people, events, fashion, trends, developments and political happenings. These were comments (often sharp ones) that reflected my own outlook. Readers frequently disagreed, or hated what I'd said about a particular situation, but I strongly believed that the column, any column, was meant to generate debate, and a strong point of view was essential. Since I don't fancy fence-sitting in real life, my columns too were feisty and spirited. If some of the editors used the controversies to push sales and generate more heat—why not? That's what opinion pieces are for. Some of my hatchet jobs may have gone a bit far, but I don't regret having stuck my neck out.

I remember a plump lady coming up to me at a grand reception and saying sweetly, 'You've set the cat amongst the pigeons once again, haven't you?' I was flummoxed. I didn't know what she was talking about. 'What do you mean?' I asked. She explained in syrupy tones, 'Your last column has really upset a lot of powerful ladies from my community. My phones haven't stopped ringing.' I still didn't know what she was going on about. She took me aside, where those same powerful ladies couldn't see us. From the relative safety of an enormous pillar which blocked her from view, she mentioned a column in which I'd made fun of ambitious socialites with rich husbands who didn't mind subsidizing their wives' hobbies, so long as the women kept out of their hair. She pointed to one such woman. 'She has taken it most personally.' Oh well, I said, if the cap fits . . . And that was that. I hadn't had that woman in mind at all while writing the piece, but if she saw herself in it, who was I to contradict her?

It's true that when you turn columnist, everything becomes a possible 'item'. You live in a state of perpetual hunger—there are so many column-inches to feed. This has an upside—it keeps you alert and tuned in. The downside, of course, is that one can't relax completely, ever. You are never off the job, mentally filing notes whether you're conscious of it or not. Combine that with novel-writing and there's no real let-up—even in a semi-awake state. I don't even notice it any longer. It has become an intrinsic part of my life. Each day when I awake, my first thought is of the column. I have to finish it by noon. I must remember to include this, check that, corroborate something else. It has become such a pattern, I feel disoriented on days when I'm not committed to writing. I really don't know what to do with my time when the children are away and I'm home waiting for them to return. I have no desire to pick up the phone for a chat, no desire to jump out and go shopping, or do lunch; my entire being is programmed by deadlines of one sort or another. I need that fix. Sometimes this addiction (for it is precisely that) scares me. I know I'll probably go into withdrawal briefly—but I also know I'll be okay after the first few spasms. This is a comparatively new realization. In the past, such a thought would have paralysed me. No longer. I do enjoy writing the columns and getting instant feedback, but I also know that I'm making tracks in a new direction that may have nothing whatsoever to do with writing. This declaration is based on intuition and little else. At this point, I don't have alternative plans. Nor has anybody presented me with the keys to a new kingdom. It's one of those 'girl feelings' which cannot be explained. Call it a strong hunch. But I feel I'm ready for the trip, wherever it may take me.

This is my eighteenth year with *Sunday Midday*. I have been writing columns for the paper since its inception. So much has changed, even the city itself, but the column has gone on, reinventing its original format several times over. Editors have come and gone, so has a generation of readers. It's one column that has given me enormous pleasure since, through it, I have been able to sense the altered rhythms of the city. Glamour is no longer an obsession with the *Sunday Midday* reader—it has been replaced by issues that concern him or her directly. Glamour itself has lost its earlier sheen; there's far too much of it spread generously in all the other papers.

The buzzwords in the newspaper business during the late Eighties and early Nineties were 'up-market' and 'down-market'. Editors were prepared to sacrifice valuable column-inches of hard news and information to accomodate fluff and frippery. I believe that wave is history. There is just so much belly-button gossip that works. My own column in the paper has reflected these changes. At different times, I've tried it all—from television reviews, movies, parties, fashion and people, to what I'm currently doing—a free-wheeling opinion column that takes in the week's happenings without too much emphasis on glitz.

The column has adapted itself to the times almost unconsciously. I've moved on, and so has the writing. I'm not the same person I was eighteen years ago (mercifully) and neither is the column. A much younger generation of readers in the city is getting to know me for the first time, and I'm learning through that feedback. This audience is not interested in nostalgia and neither am I. I don't wish to bore them with tales of past glories, mainly because those stories are of no relevance to me either. Who cares whether I met some incredibly famous fossil at a bar in London during the Sixties? Or what an Irish poet drunkenly confessed during a pub-break in Belfast? Writing a daily column is all about the 'now' of life. If there are reference points from the past worth embroidering the column with, fine, but it's best to use them with caution and economy. Readers, even those who are twenty years older, want to know what's going on, what the current buzz is. Flashbacks do not interest even geriatrics. The world, alas, is desperately youth-oriented. A writer has to keep up or get out.

It's different if one is an academic, in which case there is a specific reader-profile that includes those in search of a learned comment. My columns have always provided a fast-paced, racy overview of trends, attitudes and social changes. It is these attributes readers are accustomed to and look for.

*

As a media person for several decades now, I've always enjoyed observing my fellow media people and what makes them tick. It's always amusing to be present at a media function and watch whose knives are out and for whom. If more than one superstar editor / proprietor / columnist is around, the party breaks up into individual courts, with free-floating groupies dividing their time equally between them. Heaven help the first hack who leaves the party. He or she is shredded into nothingness before the elevator reaches ground level. Since heavy-duty boozing is considered obligatory, words and fists often fly, adding to the excitement of evenings that would otherwise be devoted to nothing more stimulating than boring shop-talk. But just one boozy outburst is enough to break the monotony of dull gossip about who is changing jobs and for how big a pay hike. A lot of journalists consider it a perk of the vocation to give offence. And do so in spades. Abrasive, argumentative and opinionated, it is mandatory for them to tear into someone or something between pegs and pakoras. Often, the victim of a particularly vicious attack by colleagues is standing a few feet away and holding forth on the state of the nation in strident, confident, cocksure tones. There is always an audience, so what if it consists of bosomy socialites or moneybags in satin shirts? Or even that the level of conversation rarely extends beyond 'So . . . what is your opinion about Chidambaram's new policy? When are the next elections? Is it true this government is going to fall in three months' time?' The more inane the question, the greater the scope to hold forth.

Certain 'opinion-makers' stake out their specific territories and call themselves specialists on the subject. It could be the Babri Masjid, the Hindu diaspora, cow-belt politics or the Dravidian mind-set. They've mastered the art of manipulating the conversation in such a way that they can keep it on track and dominate the evening with their 'well-considered' take on the subjects. Some of them are semi-professionals who jet around from one seminar to the next peddling the same tired, recycled spiel to new audiences. Others rely on personality and a gift of the gab to bludgeon their listeners into submission with their partisan opinions. No matter. It's a chance to observe absurd power play at work, lobbyists working furiously towards their next target—these days, the target being an eponymous talk show on television.

Once I watched with amusement a motley group of hungry aspirants who had surrounded a satellite TV honcho and were all but grovelling at his feet. This was one honcho who didn't need grovelling at cocktail parties. He had already mastered the art of neutralizing all opposition by buying it over. At that moment, he was clearly a king getting his kicks out of observing a group of grasping morons boot-licking in public. They weren't getting a thing out of this man, that was for sure. But that certainly didn't prevent him from playing with them that night. I liked his style. It must have been quite a high seeing those fools crawling pathetically at his feet hoping to impress him sufficiently, hoping to cut a deal, get a proposal through, announce a show, become stars. There we are: back to the fame game again. Back to the desperate lengths some people are willing to go to for that orgasmic high of being recognized, of being known, of being somebodies.

Fame exerts its own awful pressures and prejudices. People—even those one has grown up with, expect a famous person to change, to behave in a 'famous' way. A few feel cheated, almost disappointed, if a celebrity turns out to be perfectly normal, perfectly accessible, perfectly sane. Even though I don't count myself in that hallowed league, I'm always a little impatient and exasperated when someone expects me to behave in a certain way, or be a certain kind of person. Apart from anything else, this sort of an attitude wastes far too much time. First, you have to reassure the stranger that you aren't like that at all. Then you start from square one and state what you are. This is boring and wasteful. Tiresome too.

I remember being pursued over months to appear for a TV interview on a channel nobody watches, anchored by a particularly irritating pony-tailed man suffering from a serious case of egotitis. Perhaps because he's witheringly referred to as a 'down-market' Prannoy Roy, I knew the moment I entered the studio that we were not going to make music together. Here was a chap who'd already formed some pretty strong opinions about me. Which was fine. He wasn't interested in discovering that maybe he was way off or that I wasn't the person he thought I was.

While we did a light and sound check, he crammed in as much information about himself as he could in ten minutes. I feigned an interest I didn't possess. His bragging was juvenile and annoying. I didn't really care about his previous lot of high-profile interviewees. He insisted on listing them regardless, adding triumphantly that one or two of them had stomped off the show in a rage. I kept my expression as neutral as possible. He announced he'd sworn never to read my books after he'd read the first one. I looked blankly in his general direction. Then he produced his own credentials—college degrees, jobs held, articles published. By now I was going glacial and wondering what I was doing in that crummy studio on his crummy show. I didn't care that the channel's 'footprint' covered Asia. I wanted to get on with the interview and get out.

Seconds before the cameras rolled, he scratched his untidy beard and confessed, 'I am nervous. I've never interviewed anybody like you. I've talked to chief ministers, cabinet ministers, captains of industry . . . oh, just about everybody.' Well, I suggested mildly, there's always a first time. In two seconds we were on. His questions were poorly researched and unnecessarily aggressive. Besides, he wasn't even listening to the answers or picking up on what I was saying. He was far too busy thinking of his next smart question. In his mind, he was 'fixing me'. In reality, he was making a complete idiot of himself. At the end of the programme he looked at me expectantly. Perhaps he expected an outburst, an explosion. I wasn't about to give it to him. I picked up my things.

'Well?' he enquired.

'Thank you,' I said breezily.

'I hope . . . you didn't think I was being rude.' His eyes were shining in anticipation.

I smiled sweetly. 'You were doing your job.'

He jumped for joy. 'That's exactly what I told Deve Gowda when he accused me of being nasty.'

As I was leaving, his producer, a smart woman, came running behind me. She was apologizing profusely. And there I was patting her hand and soothing her feelings. 'Please don't take offence,' she kept repeating. 'None taken,' I assured her tiredly. In the car, I asked myself why I'd bothered with this particular show when in the past I'd always refused similar ones that required me to leave the house. It was the lady's persistence that had worn me down finally. I thought about Mr Pony-tail and why he'd felt obliged to go ballistic. To prove something to me? 'Who's afraid of Shobha Dé?' Hell, he needn't have bothered. I don't bite. Look ma—no fangs.

It's amusing at the best of times, but irritating too, when a Smarty Pants decides it's time to 'show' me. What these guys end up showing most often is their own insecurity and low self-worth. I feel exactly the same way about columnists and writers who feel they have to 'fix' me with childish sniping that rarely goes beyond obvious puns—something my surname lends itself to so wonderfully. They go to great lengths to construct entire paragraphs around their brilliant word-play ('The Dawn of Another Dé', 'The Déification of Shobha', 'Porn-again Dé') even when they've nothing really to say, no point to make. I guess it's irresistible—the desire to invest such a catchy sounding name with double-meanings. It used to be clever in the first few years. Now, it's merely repetitive and tiresome.

I was once asked by a foreign correspondent whether I'd invented the name. 'It sounds far too much like a brand.' He was right in that it does sound like a label, but no, it wasn't an invention. That's the way my husband's family has spelt it over generations. When I explained this to him, he said thoughtfully, 'It works very well . . . rolls off the tongue smoothly . . . is easy to remember . . . and it suits you.' I guess it does. I'm happy with it. But it also creates comical situations, particularly when we are travelling in Europe and have to identify ourselves over the phone. 'Dé what?' we are asked. To which we say, 'Dé nothing.' So the person at the other end scrupulously writes down 'Shobha de Nothing. Dilip de Nothing.'

*

Writing for a living is something very few people take seriously. When George Bernard Shaw was asked, 'What do you do, sir?' he'd replied, 'I'm a writer.' To which the questioner countered, 'That's fine. What I meant was, what do you do for a living?' At a creative writing workshop where I recounted this, a lot of the earnest participants (aspiring hacks) took it so literally, they came up to me after class to say, 'Is it really so bad? Shall we do something else instead?' No, no, dear hearts, I assured the class, keep writing. It does have its rewards.

In the complex where I live, I'm often visited by school kids who need a quick essay, points for a debate, headlines for a project, missing words from a crossword, even ad copy for their mothers' leaflets for 'short cookery summer courses'. I write all that I'm asked to obediently and think nothing of it. Not even when the young shopkeeper in the arcade next door does not approve of the many names I've submitted to him for his to-be-opened men's boutique. 'Madam—it has to be catchy,' he tells me regretfully as I stare glumly at my brilliant suggestions. Finally, he invites me for the opening. And what has he decided to call his glass-and-chrome marvel that sells cheap Versace knock-offs made in Taiwan? 'Macho's Man'. Okay, I can handle it. My ego can handle it too. But when my daughter's sixth-grade teacher rejects 'her' assignment—a poster for a blood donation campaign, saying 'It doesn't make sense', I feel crushed. And terribly hurt. Not because the teacher has told her it isn't good enough but because my daughter has started to think so too. So I smile a small smile and say, 'It's okay, darling. We'll try harder the next time.' And I really do. I love these requests, especially when they come from someone like my tailor Suresh.

Suresh is very special. When he asks me to drop everything and write a leaflet for his 'bhabi' back in the village who has taken an agency to sell cut-pieces for a cloth merchant, I drop whatever it is I'm writing to do it for him. Suresh doesn't read or write English. And yet, he stares critically at my effort and says, '*Chalega*'. Thanks, thanks a lot, I gush gratefully.

Writing is about reaction. I don't always get a positive one. But I'm willing to settle for any, so long as it's honest. Unfortunately, people expect a writer to be an expert on all matters. Even though I've gone blue in the face explaining that *Surviving Men* is a very subjective take on a touchy topic and not a sociological treatise, I am constantly asked about the 'research' that went into the writing of the book. What research? There was observation, for sure. A great deal of it. The rest was experience (limited) and generalization (unlimited). It was a tongue-in-cheek attempt at decoding male behaviour. No academic judgements were being passed. And certainly, no erudite conclusions were reached. Yet, I was badgered to 'justify' the comments, substantiate opinions. Silly. Such books are common in the West. People are used to reading a writer's individualistic view on different aspects of life. You laugh, chuckle, dismiss, pull faces, disagree, shrug off or take note. You don't convert it into a personal assault. Not if you have even an iota of humour. I discovered that very few people (men in particular) were ready to laugh at their own absurdities. They behaved like wounded pets, all martyrdom and sulks. Some got churlish and rude. But what the hell, a provocative point of view is meant to provoke. I'm not cribbing.

While the fun part of writing columns is the mixed reactions they generate, the downside is when you don't remember your own wonderful words and someone comes up to you at a crowded venue to say, 'By the way—what exactly do you mean by . . .?' only to be met by a blank stare.

My poor memory is notorious within the family. Outsiders think I'm either pretending or being dismissive when I confess to zero recall. The problem is one of sheer volume—three columns a week, written to beat a deadline, are pretty impossible to commit to memory. Even the very day they appear in print finds me at a loss to recall the exact contents since by then three more have already been written and despatched. This does create some amount of embarrassment, but I've learned to deal with it.

People also expect a columnist to be an authority on unrelated subjects. 'After all, you write . . . you should know,' someone might say accusingly. Right. But I'm not a social scientist, anthropologist or political analyst. My columns are always written from 'Every person's' point of view. I don't claim to be an expert, merely a very interested observer with a comment or two (valid, I hope) to make.

When I re-read some of my early columns I'm taken aback at their in-your-face tone. My only excuse or explanation now is that it was easy to be brash and outrageous at twenty. How hated I must have been—nobody and nothing was spared. In fact, I often wonder how I would have ripped *me* up had I not been me. I would have made a pretty good target (as I subsequently became). If the curiosity in those days was about the veracity of what I wrote and the thinly disguised identity of the subjects (mainly society *grande dames* and pompous asses parading as intellectuals), identical curiosity later surrounded the characters in my books—was this . . .? Could it be . . .? It must be . . . So much speculation when in fact, there were only shades of known personalities in the pages. The columns were more direct with names named. If someone asks me whether my opinions about those people I mocked have changed, I'd say an emphatic 'no'. They still hold true. Today, they don't seem worth the space, that's all. Nothing I wrote was made up—somewhat exaggerated perhaps, but not fabricated. In one's mid-twenties, pretence is harder to stomach. It's easier to delude oneself that the power of strong words can change the world. Hogwash. People who aren't directly affected by what appears in print read the columns, agree in private, get a cheap thrill at the subject's expense, and publicly sympathize with the person. Nothing changes. Twenty-five years later, all those characters who inspired the early columns are still around, still talking big, still full of excreta, still insufferable. Still angry. But when we meet anywhere, the familiar pantomime continues. Kiss, kiss. 'How are you? Looking great. Hmmm . . . new book? Loved your last column. So true what you said about Sonia.' I can laugh at the phoniness of it all. None of this matters. Maybe it never did.

*

Nobody trusts journalists. Nobody can afford to. Not entirely at any rate. Even within the family, there is an element of just-under-the-surface paranoia. 'Are you going to write about this? Don't you dare,' my children often warn.

A seasoned publisher once asked me, 'Is every word of conversation exchanged with you filed away for future use? Does every phrase have to be a "quote"? Is anything off the record in your life?'

He thought he was being smart. I think he was asking a rhetorical question. And he, of all people, ought to have known better.

'Speak to me at your own risk and peril,' I tell people who look to me for reassurance. It's so much a part of my life, I don't even think about it. And yet, there are a few rules that even I don't break—except when I'm foolish enough to think nobody will notice or care. People who are affected, even slightly, do notice and do care. And they rarely forgive. I remember saying so to a journalist myself, a couple of years after he'd turned his knives into me in print. We ran into each other on a holiday. At first I didn't recognize the man (he has no personality) in this setting. Assuming he was someone else, I was friendly (it happens on holidays, my guard is lowered). Hours later, it struck me—he was the same SOB who'd gone for me pretty viciously in a widely circulated magazine. When we met with our families at the dinner-buffet, I looked right through him. The next morning he came up sheepishly and said, 'Don't tell me you are still angry?' I smiled, exchanged a few inanities and walked away. Yes, I was angry. I was furious. And I wasn't about to forget.

At that point I thought about the countless people who must have felt the same way about something I'd written. I had been on both sides of the fence by then. But that still didn't make it any better.

Often strangers confide the most amazing things to me at the oddest of venues and I half suspect they secretly want to see it all in print. With movie people this occurs routinely. But the same syndrome has now crossed the big divide. There has been a persistent and rather annoying caller hounding me for five years. Her only 'connection'—we share a first name. This, in her mind, is enough of a link to provide instant access as and when she's low, has had a rotten day, fought with her husband, beaten one of the kids, been cursed by her mother-in-law. I know nearly everything she wants me to know about her life, including sexual details (her husband's celibacy has forced her to abstain herself). I have never met this woman and have no desire to either. Yet, I continue to take her calls, unless I'm frightfully caught up in something. She's obviously lonely, frustrated at the thought that family pressures forced her to give up a career in travel that she enjoyed, and dying to talk to someone who, in her mind, represents something. Articulate, aggressive and forthright, she talks freely about her frequent fights with her husband, how she disapproves of his beer-drinking buddies and refuses to let them party in the house, thereby embarrassing her spouse into hosting his sessions in a parked car downstairs.

'Doesn't he mind?' I asked her.

'Why should he? I send down snacks—hot snacks—with the servant.'

What happens when the boozing binge ends? Does he stagger upstairs sheepishly, apologetically, and beg for forgiveness?

'Not at all. He goes to the loo, changes his clothes and falls asleep. No conversation. No sex.'

'And the next day?'

'No reference.'

*

There have been journalists who've come for interviews and stayed on to become friends. Even those who've arrived at home with the standard pre-conditioning and pre-conceived ideas. These have primarily been women whose lives have interested me sufficiently to build those bridges in the first place. I value their friendship and make the effort to nourish it. We do belong to some sort of a loosely-knit fraternity after all—we have several reference points in common. We can gossip about colleagues, career shifts, changing patterns in relationships, the 'what's on' buzz—but more than any of this, we can connect as women and share our lives.

Often these friends are one generation removed. It hasn't mattered. We've managed to make that vital leap and create an environment that fulfills us mutually. Sometimes, I'm the big sister they've never had (and I cannot be in real life, being the youngest in my family), at others, the experienced worldly-wise woman who can advise them on men problems, the idealized mother-figure who 'understands'. I enjoy these relationships. Cherish them. Invest in them.

Trusting a stranger has always been something of a problem. Either I do so instinctively, completely and unknowingly, or for years he or she is kept on a 'still testing' mode . . . at some point fatigue and boredom set in and we drift away with no hard feelings. Getting close to people within one's profession is hard to do given the nature of the profession. While I can't think of a really 'b-a-a-a-d' experience and do not harbour any grudges, I know it hasn't been easy to confide in or get near enough to anybody I even vaguely suspect. And this I say from my own experience and training.

One of the most off-putting phrases all journos encounter is: 'I hope you aren't going to quote me.' Often this is uttered by a complete non-entity one is merely tolerating for the sake of politeness. It's tempting to say, 'Why would I do you such a favour?' But again, out of politeness, one says nothing at all.

It's worse when a so-called friend chooses to unload a sob-sister story at a vulnerable moment only to call the next day and request, 'Don't put this into your column or book, okay? If my husband finds out, he'll kill me.' I remember a prominent jeweller's wife sidling up to me at a party to say something juicy about a brassy socialite who was present. She stopped halfway through to plead, 'Please . . . please . . . forget what I just said. Don't repeat it in print.' I don't blame her. She was gauche enough to articulate something the others harboured in their minds. Or . . . I'm the fool in this story. Maybe she was hoping I'd say something in print about the other woman—without quoting the source. The hunger for publicity and recognition takes so many different forms, it's both confusing and exasperating.

A crazy dilettante's even crazier wife was determined that I attend one of her kitty parties when she heard I'd gone through nearly half my life without having done so.

'You must come,' she cooed.

'What goes on there?' I asked amusedly.

'Find out for yourself. We meet and exchange ideas.'

'What sort?'

'You ask too many questions. Why don't you just come on over?'

What I didn't realize was that she'd told all the other women about the invitation, and they'd gone overboard with the cuisine and ambience, believing I was there to cover the function and make the hostess famous. I rather enjoyed myself, ignorant as I was. It was a luxury apartment with a great view. The food was catered (vegetarian), the bar tender fixed the sexiest margaritas in Mumbai, and the thirty-odd women present were there to have a good time. The laughter seemed spontaneous enough—after a few shots, everything does appear awfully funny. I was given a guided tour of the apartment and even told how much it was valued at in the real estate market. The hostess took me to the bedroom and showed off her wardrobe. A few other women displayed their latest jewellery, their buys. Everybody raved about the designer-food and complimented the hostess on her choice of caterer. I wondered what was going on in his mind—or the bartender's. Or in the minds of all those well-trained waiters who managed to maintain such impassive expressions while watching a group of extremely wealthy, extremely buzzed ladies giggling uncontrollably, dancing with one another and talking intimately about their husband's sex drives.

The lunch went on to nearly 5 p.m. at which point a woman consulted her jewelled watch and announced, 'We'd better go home now . . . before the men get there.' They left in clumps of twos and threes, punch drunk and entirely happy with themselves. I went down the elevator with four of them. I was cold sober (unfortunately, that's how I always am). I wasn't at all surprised to hear them tear into the hostess, rip the party apart, criticize the food, the booze, her clothes, her make-up, her kids, just about every aspect of her life, including her morality.

'She sleeps around like crazy,' said one.

'Yes. It started with the brother-in-law. Now, her life is like a railway station, men just climb in and climb on.'

They were savage about her husband—the man who'd financed the party—saying he was a weak good-for-nothing. Suddenly, they remembered that I, a total stranger, was present. 'Please . . . please . . . don't tell her we said it . . . don't write about it.' One woman stopped mid-sentence. 'What do you mean, don't write about it? Our hostess will be so disappointed. She has already told half the world her kitty party is going to be covered in your column next week. When does she ever serve such food? Or offer champagne? Don't be stupid. She wants it to be written about.'

Another woman corrected her. 'Maybe, but not this part.'

I got into the car wearily. Before I did that I noticed how the other women were keen on my noticing their fancy, imported cars. They kept hollering for their drivers to bring them to the porch so I could watch them glide away. I felt sorry for these women—I'm sure they felt equally sorry for me.

I did write about the party, mustering up all my discretion

and self-control. It would have been horrible to abuse the hospitality of a person who in her eagerness to promote herself had persuaded a complete outsider to attend what she considered a major event in her life. It wasn't a terribly flattering write-up. I thought the kitty group would cut me dead. Guess what? One month later, I was invited back.

It's true that most journalists are always on the job, whether they're aware of it or not. The mind never stops ticking, taking mental notes and filing them away for future use—while eating, driving, chatting, bathing, cooking, even sleeping. Here I am writing about a kitty party after so many years. I remember it vividly despite my otherwise poor memory. Every detail. I can even recall the pricey outfits worn by the women there—ask me what the label read, I could tell you that too, one woman had forgotten to take it off. Or so I thought. Another one corrected me, 'She hasn't forgotten at all. She wants all of us to know where she's bought her clothes and how much she paid for them.'

It's impossible to go anywhere without incidents, expressions, people, crawling into the invisible file in the mind. It would be strenuous if it weren't so natural. When somebody asked me to 'relax and forget you're a writer', I thought it was a pretty dumb remark. There's no way I can forget it. No way I can shut out even a single image that interests me. It's all there.

*

Perhaps the maximum gossip is exchanged at parties and functions attended by journalists. But while it's fine to party together periodically, I can't get myself to actually like any of my colleagues and I have absolutely no doubt that they reciprocate the feeling passionately. We share a workable, professional rapport. And that's where it stays.

It's not as if our public bonhomie is fake—it's always very entertaining to swap notes, hear awful stories about someone we've all known, express irresponsible opinions on everything and everyone, and know that all of it will be reported to the very person it was directed against, or worse, appear in print as an 'item'. It's an occupational hazard we live with. Talk at your own risk. Even so, and even with a generous coating of cynicism, I still recoil at some of my experiences with the tribe. Like the woman who in the name of 'friendship' wrote at least two spiteful pieces for her highly circulated paper and then called up to say, 'But look . . . I think I was being very fair.' She was so off the mark, I was amazed at her lack of perception more than anything else. Yet, each time someone referred to her as a 'menopausal bitch', I rushed to defend her. It's so easy to damn a woman of a certain age by staging a hormone attack against her. It just isn't cricket. And for every menopausal bitch in the media there are a dozen impotent men using their pens in place of penises to screw the world.

At the end of the day, ours is as incestuous a business as any other. It works in exactly the same way as the notorious old boys' network—you know someone who knows someone and so on. Often, newcomers show up with their written efforts and blatantly ask for recommendations. If their writing skills are any good, why not? It's only a matter of a few phone calls. After that initial access, it's entirely upto them. I still can't resist a well-written manuscript. I devoured them as an editor, and I continue to do so even now. I've always found words very seductive. If they're arranged in a startlingly original way, I want to see them in print instantly, and make every effort to ensure that it happens.

But newcomers or veterans, I've learnt the hard way that journalists are not nice people to know. Fascinating, fun, stimulating, gossipy, yes. But also devious, malicious, vindictive and petty. Most journalists are conceited, despicable jerks with dandruff and pyorrhea to boot. Conduct your own survey and tell me if I'm wrong. Most lead fairly wretched personal lives (they make perfectly insufferable spouses). Most lack a healthy sense of humour—the only time they laugh is at someone else. Most walk around with intellectual hernia, weighed down by the world's problems. I prefer to stay away . . . remain on the fringes.

Getting Ahead

One telephone call. That's it. Just one, single telephone call it was that led to the journey I'm still on. I'm a great one for forming strong and lasting impressions based on nothing more than a voice over the phone. When you think of it, a bodiless, faceless call does convey a great deal about the caller. For starters, the greeting is pretty significant. A friendly tone to the first 'hello' suggests a person who wishes to start the conversation on an easy, chatty footing. A crisp, I-mean-business 'hello' means let's not waste time here. An uncertain one conveys anxiety or nervousness, an assertive, bellowing 'hello' generally comes from an aggressive, opinionated, impatient individual. Enough already. The 'hello' that provided me with a new vocation fell in between two categories—it was businesslike all right, friendly enough, but not familiar.

I liked the approach. But was puzzled by the name. David Davidar. What did that make him? I hadn't heard the surname before and wasn't sure whether it was foreign or not. The hard-to-fix accent added to the confusion. Mr Davidar got to the point swiftly (I didn't know then that the editor-publisher and, more recently, CEO of Penguin Books India, is not a phone person). Very briefly, he mentioned he'd just set up the Indian arm of the international publishing giant in India, and was on the lookout for new writers. He said he'd read my columns over the years and strongly believed there was a book in there somewhere. There was? Oh well. It was his belief, not mine. I listened. But not too carefully, I have to admit. The call was about his forthcoming visit to Mumbai. Would I spare some time to meet him? He had a proposal in mind, the sort of project he felt was right up my street. He didn't define what it was. I didn't ask. I'd find out soon enough.

The reason why I wasn't at all focused or particularly interested was because I was distracted and dreamy—I was expecting Anandita, my youngest child, and feeling dopey, literally and figuratively. This was no age to get pregnant, some of my contemporaries had admonished. Are you crazy? they'd asked. Maybe I was—just a little bit. But I knew and my husband knew that we wanted another baby, and I was going ahead and having one—with my gynaecologist's clearance of course. So, when the fateful meeting finally took place, I found myself waddling towards the door to let in a very large individual who filled the frame almost entirely. For once, my phone-picture hadn't been all that accurate. The voice I'd heard ought to have belonged to a much older man. Maybe not the voice itself but the approach, which had sounded very mature in a taciturn way. This person seemed alarmingly young to be heading a publishing company. It turned out that he was. And far too informally dressed, too—a blue striped shirt casually tucked into dark trousers, sensible, laced-up black shoes. Conservative, yes. But also slightly boring. The conversation that followed didn't turn out to be that much better. David isn't the world's most persuasive salesman and his pitch was far from inspiring. 'I believe you could do a book on Bombay. Reading your columns, I get the impression that you have the pulse of the city. There aren't any good books that capture that aspect. You could be the right person.'

He told me briefly about himself, his background as a journalist and editor, his stint at Harvard and his lucky meeting with Peter Mayer, who at the time was widely regarded as one of the three gods of international publishing. I listened in a vague sort of way, my mind elsewhere. 'But I've never written a book before,' I started lamely, hoping to end the meeting, crawl out of any commitment and go back to eating pakori chaat and paani-puri (the two snacks I couldn't get enough of). In any case, a book about Bombay didn't excite me at all. I said as much. David had another immediate option—make it fiction. Do a novel using Bombay as the locale. Oh dear. This was getting tedious. I had a three-year-old to feed lunch to and I was beginning to feel groggy myself. 'Fine, I'll think about it,' I said cheerfully. David picked up his brown paper envelope (he always carries mysterious-looking envelopes) and loped off, saying he'd be back in a month.

I promptly forgot all about him and my assurance that I'd work on something. After he left, I shook my head in disbelief. Book? Me? A novel? He couldn't have been serious. I'd never written fiction before. Not even the sort of stuff young people submit to college magazines. Maybe he didn't know how to leave, maybe he hadn't worked on his exit lines. Maybe he was being as insincere about his offer as I'd been about my tentative acceptance.

A month passed. I was even larger and more dopey. I had no doubt in my mind that the pregnancy was a good idea, but now I was beginning to worry about how safely I'd carry the baby. By any standards it was a late pregnancy. Yes, I was fit enough, agile enough . . . and . . . and brave enough. My gynae, who'd delivered the other babies, was full of confidence and encouragement. It was really my so-called 'friends', women I'd grown up with and known through school and college, who had sowed the seeds of doubt in my mind. 'You'll be in your sixties by the time the child is a major. Is it fair to the baby? All the other children are so much older. Will you be able to give the same kind of time and attention to this one?' These were some of the more innocuous questions. The scary ones were reserved for later, when I was filled with apprehension myself. 'What if the baby isn't . . . you know . . . normal?' a woman asked, feigning deep concern. The last thing on my mind was a book I'd sort of promised a young publisher I'd write, or at least think about writing.

The call came. It was exactly a month later. 'Have you got the outline?' David asked in his peculiarly clipped accent. I panicked. His attitude was making me feel like a penitent schoolgirl who hadn't worked on her vacation assignment. I feared punishment. Five thousand lines, maybe. I stammered. And then I fibbed. 'Yes. I've got it.' Help. Now what? 'Fine, I'll be over in an hour to take a look.' Oh my God. I clutched my stomach. I swear I felt the baby giving me a hard kick. There, I'd done it again. Now I'd be exposed for the cheap little fibber I never thought I'd grow up to be. David would turn up, ask imperiously for the papers, and I'd have nothing to show him, except my dumb, guilty face. No. That was just too humiliating. I had to produce something—anything. I waddled to the table, pulled out a writing pad and started scribbling.

So many years later, I can still recall the rush I experienced during those few minutes, as the outline for *Socialite Evenings* took shape on the lined pages of a cheap pad. I cannot explain even now where the story emerged from, but as I began to write it down, I felt a sense of urgency to record it all before it went away . . . disappeared altogether.

It was very rough. Perhaps four or five pages, written in

a tearing hurry. There was no continuity involved—just a series of points marked by asterisks that indicated a plot development. I didn't have time to re-read it—the doorbell was already ringing. It was David, the headmaster. And the disobedient student had finally managed to complete the junked assignment.

David is not one for polite small talk or ceremony. 'Where is it?' he asked, his voice terse and stiff. 'Here,' I said, submitting it to him in the manner of a whipped schoolgirl, which I had voluntarily reduced myself to. He was perfectly expressionless as he took the sheets from my hand and read silently. This was eerie—a throwback to my first meeting with Nari Hira in the Creative Unit office. I was equally nervous, even though I didn't really have anything to worry about. At that stage, I was far too preoccupied with impending motherhood and full-time domesticity to bother about the possibility of a brand-new career option. And yet, my stomach was rumbling as David read on, impassive and infuriating in his coolness. A verdict was about to be passed. And I was quaking. More than anything else, I was feeling horribly self-conscious at the prospect of being 'judged' by a much younger man whose credentials at that stage were unknown. Why was I even submitting to such a test? I still don't know.

He finished reading through the outline in less than five minutes. I waited. I half hoped he'd say, 'Well . . . it was a good try. But maybe this isn't for you. Anyway, if in the future you think you can come up with something more workable, give me a call. Nice meeting you.'

It didn't happen that way. David pushed his glasses further up the bridge of his nose and said, 'Right.' What did that mean? I dared not ask him to clarify. Now I know that David's 'Rights' said in a firm, no-nonsense way, indicate uncharacteristic enthusiasm for a future project. At that time, all I could think was, 'Here it comes, get ready. He's going to tell you it's no good.'

Instead he said the words that in a way altered the direction of my professional life—the very one I thought I'd left behind me while opting for the role of full-time wife and motherhood. 'I think you should go for it,' David pronounced somberly. I still didn't understand. What was that supposed to signify—'Go for it'? Go for what? My expression asked the question my voice failed to articulate. 'I think it will make a good book, go ahead and write it.'

Huh? He'd liked the outline? Was he telling me that? He wanted me to write a book—a whole book? Based on those carelessly scribbled notes? That's what it sounded like. But it was best to be certain.

'How should I go about it?' I asked, looking equally sombre, as if it was a significant moment between publisher and author, and I should treat it with due respect. This had to be sacred and sacrosant. I was determined not to trivialize it or laugh out loud (which is really what I wanted most to do). David stared at me as though I was a complete dolt. 'Well,' he said with some deliberation, 'I shall go back to Delhi and send you a contract to sign. And then you sit down and write your book. Simple.' I nodded as if I'd understood. 'Okay. Fine. Thanks.' That was it. He picked up his brown envelope and loped off once more. We hadn't even shaken hands.

Once David went back to Delhi, I was stumped. I didn't have the slightest notion of how to go about writing a book. I thought it would be best to ask. But whom could I ask? I didn't know too many authors I could phone and say something like, 'Hey, guess what? Penguin has told me to write a book. I know you've written books. I was wondering . . . how did you do it?' Were there courses on how to write a book? Or was a real writer supposed to know instinctively how it's done? Maybe I wasn't a real writer. That was it. Had I been one, I too would have known. But the truth is, I hadn't a clue. And now I'd put my foot into it and there was no going back. Oh hell. I didn't need this. I was pregnant, and bloating by the second. I needed to concentrate on the little life growing inside me. Instead, I was agonizing over some stupid book I'd rashly agreed to write for an arrogant stranger who behaved like he was bestowing some kind of an honour on me by asking.

I spent a week feeling hostile and resentful, hoping the book would go away. I argued with myself. I didn't have to write it. I wouldn't be prosecuted if I didn't. What was the worst thing that would happen if I backed out? David would think poorly of me—that's all? Well, who cared? Let him. He wasn't my friend or brother. I wasn't looking for a job in his company. I didn't have to impress or please him in any way.

But the book still wouldn't disappear from my mental radar. It had become something of a nuisance—a persistent earache. I behaved in a manner so distracted, my husband asked whether I needed to see the doctor. 'It's the book,' I grumbled, but in a voice so low he didn't hear it, or in his usual direct and practical manner he might have said, 'Well then . . . write it.'

That was the problem. I wanted very much to write it and get rid of the earache. But I didn't know how. I needed a guide, a guru, someone to hold my hand and take me through the paces . . . just show the way. I decided to make a call to Delhi. What the hell, the man wanted me to write a book. The least he could do was to tell me how it was done. I risked sounding like a complete imbecile. Only one thought protected me—he'd asked. I hadn't gone begging.

'David Davidar? Yes? Hi. Shobha Dé. Look . . . I very

much want to write this book. The thing is, I don't know how to go about it. What I mean is . . . how do authors write books? Where do they begin? Or end? What about chapters and things? How do I know when a chapter needs to be wrapped up?'

There. I'd said it.

Long pause.

'Shobha . . . there's nothing to it. You have a good story—just tell it. And don't worry about the format. You write it as it emerges. The chapters will fall into place as you go along. And you'll know the book has ended when your story is finished. Good luck. Happy writing.'

And that was basically it. I was flying solo. I didn't relish the idea of crashing. I got down to work that very morning after saying a short prayer and very optimistically drawing an OM on the first page. It is a practice I've continued to maintain till today.

Once the process got under way, I couldn't stop. My life was less frazzled at the time. Arundhati was almost three years old, and happy enough to be around me playing with her dolls. The older children were away at school. My 'study' which doubled as a spare room when the kids and their friends were present, was a well-lit, airy room, with large windows that opened out to a spectacular view of the sea. I'd find myself gazing at the changing light on the waves a bit too often. So I moved my desk to face a wall. Right above my head hung a large canvas by Bikash Bhattacharya. It was a stunning portrait of a beautiful woman, the wife of a prominent Delhi industrialist. What was it doing in our home? Good question. The industrialist who'd commissioned it didn't like the artist's interpretation of his wife's looks. Rejected, the painting found its way into an exhibition where my husband bought it. We both loved the work. And I rather enjoyed being watched over by a bejewelled, exquisitely groomed socialite with sad eyes and a melancholic twist to her carefully painted mouth. In a way, she represented all that the book I was writing was about—she could have been Anjali, the main protagonist, with her wealthy husband and empty life. I'd often look up from my writing and stare into the woman's eyes. I could understand why her husband disliked the work—there was far too much truth in it.

Nothing was conducive to writing, starting with my chair with its peculiarly angled back, my desk which was far too cluttered, and the location of the study, which was across the kitchen and a bit too close to the main door. The placement of the phones didn't help either. I could hear varied noises throughout the day, often at decibel levels that were highly disturbing—servants gossiping in the kitchen, pots and pans being noisily cleaned, the doorbell ringing constantly along with the phones, and Arundhati's incessant prattle as she climbed all over me while I tried not to let the other one inside my womb break my focus with frequent, sharply-delivered kicks as she manounevred her body around in her warm, comforting amniotic sac. Sitting for extended periods of time was getting to be distinctly uncomfortable. And yet, as I frantically filled one pad after another, all I really wanted to do was to keep on writing. It was a strangely overwhelming experience, a very new one too. Till that point I hadn't realized just how much pleasure the physical process of putting words on paper gave me. I'd often heard authors saying glibly, 'Oh . . . the story just wrote itself.' Well, that was precisely what was happening to me too. It was out of my control. I wrote for hours at a stretch, only breaking off for meals and sleep. There was nothing, absolutely nothing that I wanted to do more than to get to my desk and keep going. I didn't want conversation, there was no time for friends. I hated the thought of going out, even if it involved running errands. I spoke to no one about the book. Not even former colleagues who·dropped by for a chat. It was a very private act and I wanted to keep it that way.

I noticed I was becoming superstitious as well. I'd devised a set of rituals that made the writing that much easier. 'The book' became my biggest secret. I revelled in the power this gave me. Nobody was allowed entry into the pact I'd made with myself. I was possessive about my own words. Fortunately, nobody was that interested either. Actually, nobody knew what was going on in that study. I'd told myself I wouldn't let the writing cut into my time with the family. Which meant my husband rarely saw me at the desk and even if he did, he assumed I was wrapping up one of my columns. The older children were far too preoccupied with their own school schedules to be curious about my activities. Shut off from the social whirl to the extent that was possible, I didn't feel the need to interact with anyone—not even David. He did come to Mumbai once during this period. Eager for some feedback, I took the manuscript over for his appraisal. His response? A laconic 'Right. Keep writing.'

It became something of a race—which would it be, the baby first or the book? Anandita was due in March. I wanted to put the book to bed well before that. And I did. When it was finished, I knew it was done. A feeling of enormous relief swept over me as I wrote the final sentence. 'Send it across,' said David. I did that. There was no title other than a working one. And there were no chapters either. I'd written the book in one big chunk, reams and reams of handwritten notes that covered eighteen or twenty pads. That made it well over the stipulated hundred thousand words that David had helpfully told me constituted a medium-sized novel. It had taken me four-and-a-half months to put them down. Which meant I'd written approximately fifteen hundred words a day. Today, I realize that is my natural rhythm. I can't do it any other way. I wasn't out to break any speedwriting records, but I must have been in a frenzy to finish it, to write at such a feverish pace.

Was I satisfied at the end of the exercise? I don't know. I was far too close to it. Besides, the newness of the experience still hadn't worn off. It was like being on some kind of a high. I'd done it. I'd actually done it. Written a bloody book. Whether that bloody book was any good was another matter. The fact that I had succeeded in telling a pretty long story was to my mind accomplishment enough. I also knew then that if I could do it once I'd do it again. Nothing else counted. Not even David's verdict. Truthfully speaking, it hadn't so much as occurred to me that he might reject the manuscript. Not once did I think it would be turned down by him. I believe it was my ignorance rather than self-confidence at work here. I didn't know how the book publishing industry worked. I wasn't aware that even commissioned books could be trashed or that the publisher could demand major rewrites. Had that happened to me, I might have written off the experience as an exercise I'd enjoyed but which was clearly not for me.

David, who is never lavish with his praise, didn't help much either when he called to say he'd liked the book but that it needed some more inputs. He mentioned he'd assigned an editor to it and that I'd be working with the two of them on the final product.

What I'd wanted to hear was a detailed critique of my effort. Instead, I was sent a list of 'gaps' that needed to be filled. Since I'd barely re-read the book, I'd obviously left a few of the secondary characters hanging midway without explanation. Some disappeared altogether, others popped in and out of the narrative without logic or reason. This was called 'cleaning up' the manuscript. Only a meticulous editor can catch even the smallest discrepancies in continuity—dates, places, events and people—that need fixing. David also thought I should write a prologue and epilogue (I didn't agree, but wrote them anyway). It was at this stage that I discovered something funny about myself—once the book was over and done with, I felt completely disconnected from its fate. The book was then on its own—free falling or scaling heights, all by itself. There was no emotional attachment left. No desire to cling on. No reason to perpetuate the association. The words weren't cast in stone either. I didn't care whether they went or stayed. I didn't fight with the editor to 'save' anything she found redundant. The book was finished, so was the experience. It had purged itself from my system so thoroughly that the thought of going back to it again and again during the proofing stages became something of a punishment. I wanted to get on with other aspects of my life—I was at an advanced stage of pregnancy. The book no longer interested me. It was irrevocably over, like a relationship that ceases to matter once the decision to end it has been taken.

But that's not how it works in publishing, I discovered. Reading the first proofs was an excruciating experience. I couldn't bear to go over my own words without hating them. I cringed and curled up with embarrassment even as I corrected errors, deleted sentences and added paragraphs. My god, it was awful. And we still didn't have a title. *Socialite Evenings*, declared David flatly on one visit. 'That's it. I like the title. It has a nice ring to it. Try it—*Socialite Evenings*.'

I didn't have an opinion. Actually, I didn't care. The book was out of my hands. I'd given it away. It wasn't my responsibility any longer. These guys seemed to know their business. I assumed David knew what he was doing. This was his area of expertise. Anyway, his suggestion was far better than any of the titles I'd come up with. I do recall most of them sounded like the names of down-market boutiques. I left the cover design to David as well, merely supplying the transparencies shot by my cousin Gautam Rajadhyaksha. The inset carried a portrait of actress Neena Gupta, while the main visual was a sweeping vista of Bombay's famous 'Queen's Necklace'.

When I look at it now it seems cluttered and clumsy. But the sight of that first cover proof was so thrilling when I received it in the mail, I recall dancing a jig with glee. Funny thing is, while going through the proofs minutely, I couldn't connect with my own words. Perhaps it was my long experience as an editor, but I read through the pages with a complete sense of detachment, my trained eye picking out proofing errors and spelling mistakes. There was no sense of involvement at that moment and I found it strange. I'd always thought authors, first-time authors at that, fell madly in love with their own words. I'd heard they couldn't bear to cut a single line, chop a single paragraph. And here I was performing surgery in the most clinical manner, without regretting a single deleted word, paragraph or page. It was a good learning experience. David suggested I write a fresh opening (I still prefer the original) and he asked me to rearrange the sequence of a few loose chapters. Other than that, there was no major work involved.

When the first copy was couriered to me, I was alone at home. I didn't tear the parcel open. My hands weren't shaking when I held the book in my hands for the first time. Nor did I experience any elation. I examined *Socialite Evenings* critically and objectively, and promptly found half-a-dozen faults. Then I called my husband at the office to say I'd received the advance copy. 'We must celebrate,' he said with excitement in his voice.

A small launch party had been planned in the distributor's swanky apartment. And I had persuaded M.F. Husain to be present and do the honours. But before that, I wanted to hand over the book to my parents and seek their blessings. This, above all, was vital to me. When I reached their home, they were a little confused by the whole thing—video cameras whirring, flashbulbs popping. Nothing like this had ever taken place in our family and nobody was very sure about what was expected. We embraced somewhat awkwardly as I rose after touching their feet. I knew I was supposed to be overwhelmed with emotion at this point, but I wasn't. There was only a vague feeling of something different happening to my life, without knowing what that something was or even how different. We went on to the party, which was like any other Mumbai cocktail party—the same known faces sipping champagne and looking expectant. Husain turned up in an interestingly designed silk shirt which had cuffs and collar made out of a contrasting material. I didn't know I'd be called upon to make a speech, but I suppose that formed a part of the ritual. I hadn't prepared anything so I said what was uppermost in my mind—something to the effect that I was thankful for the presence of the assembled guests since without people like them for inspiration, the book would not have been possible. It was true enough even if it did sound slightly cutting.

Nothing changed. I hadn't expected it to, either. There was no real difference in my life, pre-book and post-book. I still had to deal with the dhobi's accounts. I still ate two main meals a day, I still bathed my younger children. I didn't feel like an 'author', or what I'd always imagined authors must feel like. I tried saying it to myself a few times: 'Hey, I'm an author. I've written a book. Hear that? I have written a book. A book. A book. Wow.' I felt foolish and gave up.

I remember my cousin Gautam's excitement when the first copy of his plush coffee-table book of star portraits, *Faces* was hand-delivered at his home. He'd booked a flight to Goa where our family deity is enshrined in the tiny village of Mangeshi at Ponda. He phoned me, his voice choking, to say, 'I am taking the book for Shanta Durga's blessings. I'll place the first copy at her feet, perform a puja, and only then will I feel ready to share the book with the public.' He made the trip reverentially, placing a wrapped-in-silk copy of *Faces* inside the sanctum sanctorum while praying fervently for its success. He'd also told me how spontaneously the tears had poured out of his eyes at the sight of a roughly-bound volume a few weeks earlier.

I recall, too, a book launch I attended in the middle of '97. Ayaz Memon and Ronjona Bannerjee had written *India: The Making of a Nation*, to coincide with fifty years of our independence. The glittering function was held in the chandeliered ballroom of a five-star hotel. And there, in that distinguished gathering, were three over-the-moon people—Ronjana's mother, father and sister, pride and happiness for their dear one's achievement all but pouring out of their taut-with-tension bodies. When the first copy was unwrapped with a flourish by a VIP as is the practice these days, and the room exploded into applause, four overwrought people clung together, tears dampening their cheeks—Ronjana and her family members. At that moment, I did wish I'd demanded and made a bigger deal of at least my first book.

I didn't re-read *Socialite Evenings*. Just as I have not re-read any of my other books. It had happened. It was over. Besides, I was hard at work on the next one. One thing did change however—I had discovered the joy of writing fiction. And I couldn't get enough. Which was good, since the first reviews had started to come in and they were terrible. Really,

really terrible. Had I not been so completely immersed in my second book, I'm certain I would have been deeply affected by them . . . and never dared to attempt a novel again. But there I was, more than halfway through the next project, and I'd be damned if I was going to abandon it at this stage because of the mauling I was receiving in the media. It wasn't a pleasant experience, but it didn't paralyse me either. There was just one way of looking at it, with a sense of humour and as much detachment as I could muster up. It was only a book, dammit. Besides, I reasoned, had I not been me, Shobha Dé, but a contemporary of hers who'd been asked to review *Socialite Evenings*, what would I have said in print? Would I not have taken her apart? I'm certain I would have. Not only because of the book, but for all that she represented to the outside world. I was also lucky in that my husband took the whole brouhaha entirely in his stride and advised me to do the same. 'You go ahead and write. Let the critics do their jobs,' he said soothingly. And I guess that really was my best option—maybe the only one I had.

There were some reviews that hurt more than the others—the sly, subversive ones that tried to demolish me, my personal life and my career, in the strongest possible terms. One suggested *Socialite Evenings* had been ghost-written by David himself, another that the editor had rewritten so much of it, it was no longer my work. Cynically, I added, 'Sure. And I have well-trained goblins and elves to write my columns and features too.'

These attacks were often from unexpected quarters and therefore harder to tolerate. I admit I was slightly astonished by the vehemence of the reaction, but then I also reminded myself of my own early writing which wasn't always fair or objective. It took a while to come to terms with the onslaught. It took even longer not to hit back in the petty, vindictive spirit of tit-for-tat. I was tempted several times. I probably succumbed twice or thrice. But something pulled me back from retaliating when what I wanted to do more than anything else was to throttle those awful people who were trashing my book as if it was the only lousy book ever written.

By the way, it isn't lousy at all. In fact, when I do readings from it now, I rather like its rough edges, its unpolished prose and its unselfconscious narrative style. I find those qualities rather charming, even if they aren't sterling examples of impeccable craftsmanship.

Socialite Evenings wasn't a *roman-à-clef*, but that was the popular perception perpetuated by the media. An endless round of 'Are you in it?' followed its publication, with guessing games galore about the thinly-disguised identity of some of the secondary characters. After a point, I got plain bored issuing disclaimers. Of course, there were several people who closely resembled real-life individuals—but these were broad 'types'. Their lives were not reflected in the book, only their characteristics were. Apart from a particularly obnoxious writer (who has since disappeared without a trace), the others were mere skeletons around whom I created a structure.

There was just one character in the book who was real . . . and she recognized herself straightaway. She'd been a mentor and a friend during my formative years—a lonely lady with a beautiful body and an even more beautiful brain she'd kept a secret from the high-society world she belonged to. She read *Socialite Evenings* while waiting for a delayed flight at a snowed-in airport in Canada. And she wrote me her reactions to it on airline stationery . . . a long poignant letter which conveyed her deep hurt. 'I didn't realize this was how you saw me,' she stated. 'It wasn't how I saw myself. Not in your eyes. I thought you admired me. But reading the book, I now realize how clearly you saw through everything . . . the hollowness of my life. The hypocrisies and compromises. I appear like such a pathetic figure in the pages. I've never felt so wretched about my life. But I also know that what you've written is the truth.'

I cried when I received her letter. I didn't know how I'd be able to look her in the eye when we next met. She solved the dilemma for me on her next visit to India when she came home. She hugged me warmly and held me for a long time. When we separated, tears were streaming from our eyes. I knew the ordeal was behind us. She was dignified enough not to make a reference to her letter or the book. It was my turn to feel naked and exposed.

Why did *Socialite Evenings* generate so much heat, I now wonder. It was innocuously written—no explicit sex scenes. No foul language. Could it have been the theme itself? That a woman could walk out of a perfectly secure marriage out of boredom? Karuna, the main protagonist, is not a bitch, if anything she is far too sensible and controlled. But she's the one who recognizes her marriage for what it is—empty. Her husband isn't a wife-beater, a drunkard or a gambler. There isn't any reason to leave him, yet that's what she does. Lack of communication is a valid enough explanation for her. She doesn't justify her decision, point fingers or attribute blame. That upset middle India no end.

The reactions were swift and merciless. People unfamiliar with Mumbai's social scene refused to believe my descriptions of life in this metropolis. She must have converted Beverly Hills into Malabar Hill, they sniffed.

Anybody who has had even a brief fling with this city's *haut monde* will readily identify with every bit of the book's content—none of it is even slightly exaggerated. Did I feel comfortable in this society? Entirely so. I never lost sight of

330

where I'd come from. I didn't pretend to be anybody other than who I was—or at least the way I saw myself: a middle-class Maharashtrian girl from a family of proud professionals, instilled with a strong work-ethic. We were taught early in life that nothing comes easy, nothing is delivered on a platter. That saved me.

But the controversy over who was who in the book carried on, and got to be quite enjoyable once I'd learnt how to deal with it. This was the crucial stage of 'image-promotion', even though I was not consciously aware of the process then. Specific typecasting was taking place and I had very little control over it. Several tags were stuck on to me and the book. I didn't bother to contradict or fight them. It would have been a waste of time, anyway. A few lingered on, most faded away. I still encounter some, but even those trying to flog a dead label realize there's no story left in that any longer. Curiosity gave way to confusion and finally to acceptance but that took an entire decade.

Most of the books that followed have a little story attached to them. *Starry Nights* is the one exception. It was an accumulation of countless images and memories gathered during my *Stardust* period. I had watched the film industry closely for a decade, and even if my direct association with it was minimal, I had a ringside view of the goings-on, thanks to the vivid, detailed descriptions provided by our team of talented writers. I'd heard it all even if I hadn't actually seen it. While writing a fictitious account of Bollywood, I was able to harness all those inputs to create the characters. People still ask me whether the book was based on the Rekha-Amitabh romance. I can truthfully say that their relationship did provide a take-off point for the novel but was by no means a faithful retelling of their off-screen lives. There are undoubtedly a few shades of Rekha in Aasha Rani, while

Akshay is only a pale reflection of Amitabh Bachchan. The events in the book are not real but are based on reality. Having had a close view of the action (albeit vicariously), I attempted to tell it like it is in our movie world, without putting a nice face to the business.

Most of the characters in the book are based on actual individuals I've encountered or whose existence I was aware of, but the key word is 'based'. The dirty 'seths', slimy underworld 'dons' and nubile starlets of the book exist all right as subsequent film industry events only confirmed, but at the time it was written, Divya Bharti, the young actress who committed suicide was still alive, and the nexus between Bollywood and D-company was in the realm of speculation and not the established fact it is today. The grime and grit of the movie world was represented in all its squalor, but so was my own contempt, which came through clearly in the narrative. I made no attempt to hide it. Every bit of the revulsion I'd always harboured against the film industry poured out on the pages—it was a dirty business I was dealing with and I had no desire to sanitize it. The language employed was harsh, crude and explicit. It was the only way I knew to capture the underlying tragedy of Aasha Rani, to underline the depth of degradation she is subjected to, to better define the extent of exploitation that dominates this world of sham and make-believe.

Abusive, raw, and employing the filthy idiom of the gutters, *Starry Nights* caused major shock waves when it was published. My deliberate use of choice Hindi epithets and the descriptive sex scenes got everybody worked up, which was rather precious. There was nothing in the book that was not known to the public, nothing the fanzines hadn't already written about. Nothing that wasn't being proclaimed on prominent hoardings dotting the city. Everybody knew just how sordid this life was, but my retelling of it was found obscene and objectionable.

Other books followed—*Sisters* and *Strange Obsession*, in particular, caused similar ripples. Interestingly, *Sisters* was inspired by a single, riveting visual. As I waited in the foyer of the Taj Mahal Hotel one afternoon, I noticed a sleek sports car roll up. The person who emerged so elegantly from it (one silk-stockinged leg emerging delicately before the other followed), was someone who'd make traffic stop anywhere in the world. Young, beautiful and chic, the woman walked with supreme confidence, her eyes hidden behind designer shades. Who was she? A model? An actress? A designer? I discovered soon enough when I was introduced to her. She was the daughter of a successful businessman, just back after acquiring a degree in business management from a prestigious school in America. She'd joined the family firm as senior vice-president and was already making her presence felt in the boardroom.

To me, this woman represented the new face, the changing face of India—glamorous, capable, on top of her life, career oriented, ambitious and successful. As with any book, I needed a mental image of the central character to fix on—and she was it. I knew nothing more about her life—still don't, even though I do run into her frequently. That didn't matter. I'd found my character, the book followed.

Strange Obsession was different. For the past twenty-five years I have been at the receiving end of a woman's obsessive attention. While this person is not the psychotic Minx of the book (or not that I know of), she is equally cunning and complex. I tried to get under the skin of such an individual, whose each breath revolves around the existence of another in a manner so compulsive, it's terrifying. The book developed into a thriller at some point, with Minx meeting a fiery end.

In real life, the woman who inspired Minx is still around. Still stalking, still obsessed. Her life continues, as does mine. She no longer affects me, the old anger has disappeared. I receive her daily blank calls with far more equanimity than I used to ten years ago. I've even started feeling somewhat sorry for her. When *Strange Obsession* was announced, she wrote me a long letter, fearing exposure and threatening suicide. She needn't have agonized. Nobody outside my family and a few others (the *Stardust* gang who'd become so used to her lurking in the shadows, they treated her like Caspar the Friendly Ghost) is aware of her existence or nuisance value. The secret is safe. And will remain so till one of us dies . . . and even after.

Snapshots had an unexpected start. I was invited to an old girls' lunch by a former classmate. It was in honour of a London-based lady who'd been in school with us. She was coming back to Mumbai after an absence of many years during which she'd accomplished various wonderful things. Since I'd been fairly cut off from this particular group, I decided to go, more out of curiosity than sentiment. It turned out to be an extraordinary afternoon. We were meeting after a decade and a half, perhaps longer. Some of us were unrecognizable, others, pretty much the same, down to teenage giggles and schoolgirl mannerisms. We'd all been urged to bring photo albums along so that we could catch up on who had how many children, what the husbands looked like, where we lived and holidayed. It soon became a game of one-upmanship. Triumphs of various kinds ('My daughter is an accomplished dancer / pianist / tennis player.' 'My son stood first.' 'My husband works with the largest multinational company.' 'I run my own furniture business.' 'My mother-in-law is dead.'). One of the 'girls' had brought a video cassette with her. There was no escape. She sat us down in front of the television set and persuaded us to watch her perform. The cassette had her in different costumes, displaying varied skills. There was no doubting her abilities, but did she have to force them on us?

When I got home, my head was reeling even though I hadn't participated in the booze-up. I was feeling ill and uncomfortable. I hadn't enjoyed the afternoon at all. I'd actively resented the scrutiny, the inquisitive, probing, insensitive questions, the underlying cruelty, the ill-disguised envy. I realized I felt nothing at all for any of these women—never had. We had nothing in common. We no longer spoke the same language, if we ever did. The whole thing had been a revolting exercise with everybody hell-bent on impressing the others. The smug woman from London, dressed in a dreadful, synthetic 'suit' and speaking in an affected accent, had been the most obnoxious of the lot with her blatant boasting and even more blatant show of certificates and citations—yes, she'd brought them along in neat plastic folders. I lay down on my bed, glad to be back in my own home. In my half-awake state I thought of the book. The characters fell into place. The story revolved around the pictures a group of old school friends bring to a similar lunch. Only, the protagonist of *Snapshots* was not the fat lady in an ill-fitting blue suit, but a gorgeous London-based operator, more on the lines of Pamella Bordes. None of the other characters resembled the women at the lunch party. But the book was born in that ghastly, *nouveau riche* drawing room crammed with over-dressed, competitive women. At least something positive came out of that unpleasant afternoon—a best-seller.

Sultry Days was a bow to my summers at St. Xavier's College. St. Xavier's in the Sixties. 'God', the male protagonist, was like nobody I knew then, but a composite made up of several types. The female protagonist, Nishi (or

'Nasha' as he, Deb, dubs her), was not me by a long shot. Yet, I enjoyed inhabiting her skin for the duration of the writing of the novel. I rather liked doing this book with its simple tale of doomed love, simply because it took me back to my college days and to the edges of the pseudo-arty intellectual world I flirted with briefly before beating a hasty retreat. The novel is littered with types from that mixed-up decade—the self-styled bohemians out to change the world but not their smelly underwear; the dirty old men of Mumbai, all gas and small turds; the corporate ladies with their 'good life' hang-ups; the pseudo-intellectuals, pariahs and parasites who feed off the rich while spitting on their 'capitalist values'. It was a fun book to do. And for those of us who grew up in that era in Mumbai, there were a lot of familiar echoes and reference points that provided loads of amusement during the recounting. I consider 'God' one of my better-etched characters . . . I can only regret he wasn't for real.

Second Thoughts was a much quieter book, devoid of a single raunchy line. The book didn't warrant it—or so I believed. The critics, of course, thought otherwise—'What? No sex?' They were convinced I'd copped out. Finally thrown in the towel. And maybe they were disappointed. From 'too much sex' to 'zero sex'. Something was wrong. Either way, I got trashed. I made a joke out of my 'vegetarian' novel, but it was lost on the reviewers who'd forgotten their original grouse against my writing—the overdose of 'masala'. Well, here was a sober, spice-free look at a modern-day marriage. It also happened to be a sexless one. 'Why didn't Dé write about the woman's fantasies in that case? Why wasn't the wedding night described in more detail—what exactly did Ranjan do in bed with his wife Maya? And if they didn't consummate their relationship that night, what about other attempted couplings?' Made me wonder who had more sex on the mind—me or them?

If I were to single out two or three occasions when I felt great about being an author, I'd pick my visit to the Calcutta Book Fair in 1994, and my trip to Sri Lanka in 1996. When I published two books with UBSPD, a Delhi-based publishing house, I did so because I appreciated the publisher's approach. Ashok Chopra is a low-key individual whose publishing list is middle-brow and sensible. I get the feeling he doesn't really care what his contemporaries think of him—he knows his business and he's obviously good at it. Not for him the five large Scotches at a plush five-star bar and self-conscious pseudo-literary talk over roasted almonds. Chopra recognizes the unromantic fact that publishing is a business like any other—books must sell. And if they have to move from the shelves, the publisher in India has to know his marketing. The two books I did for his company (he has since left UBSPD) were different in that one was a collection of my columns over the years. And the other, a volume of short stories.

Shooting from the Hip was a triumph of persistence over resistance and nothing else. It was Chopra's idea to put a few representative columns together. But how? I hadn't followed a filing system. My clippings were scattered all over the place. I didn't have the time and energy to sift through twenty years of printed material. I wouldn't have known where to begin. I thought this fact alone would put him off. It didn't.

'Leave it to me,' he said, 'just stuff what you can easily access into a suitcase and I'll have my man pick it up.'

This is exactly what I did. I didn't have the slightest idea what that black-and-grey suitcase contained. I was certain that Chopra would find the task of sifting through it far too daunting, and give up. A month or so later he called to say he had managed to go through everything and give it some kind of order. He'd divided the material into segments: People,

Politics, Travel and Social Issues. It was hanging together quite well. Before we knew it, we had a book. All it needed was ·a catchy title. *Spice* was too obvious. I came up with *Shooting from the Hip*. My superstition about the letter 'S' was also taken care of. Plus it had a zingy ring to it. We were in business. As always, Gautam 'donated' the cover transparency and the book was ready. As I went through the advance copy it came to me that I'd forgotten I'd even written some of those columns. Seeing them like this, neatly titled and efficiently tabulated, I felt the effort (Ashok's) had been well worth it. They provide a healthy chuckle when I reread them now.

Small Betrayals was my idea. David didn't have much faith in the short stories genre, mainly because, as he pointed out when I floated the idea of doing a volume, there is no market for it—not in India, not anywhere in the world. I wasn't convinced. Besides, I was keen to write it, regardless. I did. For Ashok, instead of David.

There was nothing controversial about either of the books, and Ashok didn't really have a strong peg to hang his marketing on. When he suggested I launch *Small Betrayals* at what is the largest book fair in India (in terms of visitors), I was keen to do so for two reasons. One, I regard Calcutta as my second home; two, Calcutta has a large and very interested book-buying public. But nothing at all could have prepared me for what Chopra had lined up. He'd wanted it to be a complete surprise—and so it was. When we landed at Dum Dum we were greeted by huge bouquets, which is a standard and accepted practice. But it was an enormous blue-and-silver satin banner right outside the arrival lounge that caught my attention. It said 'Calcutta welcomes SHOBHA DÉ—the Queen of Indian Fiction.' It was eye-catching and impressive, even if I did feel immodest, staring at it with undisguised glee.

Such was his planning, when we got to the hotel the same banner-carrying men were present in the lobby, with more flowers and garlands. Chopra whispered, 'This is only the beginning.'

I was to get to the venue—the UBSPD stall—at a certain time that afternoon. I discovered that special permission was required for the car to be driven into the fair grounds. Chopra had got the requisite clearance and hired six security guards who were very enthusiastic about their job. When the car stopped at a particular point, I wondered why we weren't taking it right up to the stall entrance. I found out soon enough. As I emerged from the vehicle, a red carpet was rolled out, leading up to the stall. And right there, under a bright sun, were six dancers from Santiniketan attired in all their traditional finery. Two of them held a beautifully decorated ceremonial umbrella over my head while the others sang a specially composed song of welcome. Rose petals were strewn in my path as musicians and dancers escorted me up the carpet and into the stall, which had been cleverly done up with large posters announcing my presence and an eye-catching display of my two books. In a specially cordoned-off area, I was asked to sit on a throne-like chair with the guards standing around, ready to leap into instant action.

Cameras whirred as the crowds surged forward to have a look at what was going on. We sold and signed a record number of books in just an hour. And believe me, the sales had more to do with the manner in which Chopra had planned the signing session than just the public's eagerness to buy my books. He pulled off a major coup that afternoon and demonstrated that with enough thought and planning it was possible to organize an event that generated excitement and interest in a business that for the average person is not all that riveting.

I was presented a memento in the shape of an open book. I thought that was a great touch—it is one memento I'm very sentimental about since it reminds me of the high I experienced for that one weekend when I felt all the effort that had gone into establishing my identity as a writer had been well rewarded after all. I felt appreciated and respected in the best way imaginable. All the barbs and taunts that had preceded this moment melted away as I took time off to revel in the heady sweetness of this well-orchestrated treat. Writing is an extraordinarily lonely experience. It is only at times like this that one realizes how it is really perceived by those very people for whom you've been toiling away for years. It's a good feeling, I can tell you. Even now, when I recall the sight of those graceful dancers, my hair stands on end. Yes, I know they'd been hired by Chopra and were only doing their job—but I did feel deeply honoured and nothing can take away the pleasure of that emotion from me.

Something similar happened when I was invited to Sri Lanka right after the launch of *Surviving Men*. The event manager was an eager, enthusiastic young man called Bandula. I only knew him as a voice over the phone. Given the frequency of his calls, I wondered who picked up his telephone bills. What I liked about his pitch was his transparent patriotism and his keenness to establish better ties with India. He wasn't at all embarrassed about expressing these sentiments, and as I got to know him better, I realized his candour was very much a part of his charm. My husband had been to Sri Lanka several times. I was curious (as I am about any new destination). Bandula had tied up with the largest publishing group in Sri Lanka and arranged a tight schedule spread over four days. This included a press conference, book signings, interviews and a visit to our High Commissioner's residence, besides a round of fancy teas, lunches and dinners. Air Lanka had offered first-class tickets and the trip sounded very promising.

When we landed at the air strip at Colombo, we found that Bandula had charmed his way past security personnel and was waiting to receive us with orchid garlands and enormous bouquets. Swarthy, well built and with a disarming smile, Bandula turned out to be quite a character. During his brief visit to our house in Mumbai to formalize details of the trip, he'd told me his life's story—an edited version. In Colombo, he was determined to fill in all the details. Obviously, he pictured himself as a rebel with several causes—better ties with India being one of them. He talked incessantly on the way to our hotel, which again he'd picked with care to reflect the best traditions of Sri Lankan hospitality. 'I did not want you to stay at an Indian hotel—you must have stayed at various Oberoi properties. There's nothing new in that. The Mount Lavinia is over a hundred years old. You'll see what I mean. I think both of you will love it.'

So we did, starting with the welcome by a group of Kandyan dancers and drummers. As I lit the ceremonial lamp in the lobby, I caught sight of several foreign tourists gaping at this spectacle: there I was in my casual travelling outfit—trousers, silk shirt and scarf—with elaborately costumed 'natives' performing a welcome ritual. If it struck them as being exotic and odd, I was touched by the gesture, particularly since I knew it was all a part of Bandula's strategy to expose us to aspects of the Sri Lankan culture he was so very proud of.

The first interview was scheduled for later the same afternoon. It was with a leading local columnist for the most important newspaper in the country. The locale was the pool-side coffee shop of the hotel, with an incredibly beautiful vista of the ocean. I was in a very mellow mood when the journalist showed up, bristling with hostility. Initially I thought the man was trying to establish his own credentials by being extra smart and asking deliberately provocative questions. It happens all the time. I dealt with him as I do with the others, in a mild and good-humoured fashion. But the guy was looking to annoy me. I could sense his frustration that I wasn't biting. He was one of those individuals who obviously have a problem levelling gazes. He refused to look me in the eye, preferring to address his rude questions to the seagulls on an adjoining balustrade. At one stage I wanted to tell him to calm down, sip a beer and relax. It was all right to hate my books, but why hate me? I could almost see the smoke coming out of his ears. Twenty minutes of persistent hectoring later, I told him it was a mutual waste of time and declared the interview over. He stormed off in a huff.

He fell into a particular type—I encounter his kind frequently. Often these people are failed writers whose manuscripts have been turned down by the very publishers who represent the person they've been assigned to interview. In their own eyes, they are vastly superior (some of them indeed are). They believe they've been wronged and unfairly rejected. If they happen to look like dogs, their anger is even more intense. They resent the published writer on several levels—professional and personal.

Later in the evening, the journalist turned up for the press conference and stood sneering in the background while I fielded some pretty tough questions. About the funniest one came from a woman who asked aggressively, 'Don't you think a woman who commits sati is showing her deepest love for her husband? Why is sati banned in your country?' I was aghast and said so. She continued to argue, accusing me of being anti-romance for not endorsing a barbaric practice. I was a little taken aback by the general line of questioning, which displayed a deep-seated resentment of India and Indians, under the guise of polite hospitality. I ought not to have been surprised by such an attitude, given the history of our troubled relations. But I'd naïvely assumed the average person would recognize the old suspicions for what they were—politically dishonest manoeuvrings by a series of corrupt governments. I'd hoped to find more understanding and wisdom. It was disappointing to find hurt and stubborn resistance instead.

At the end of the hour-long meet, several women journalists came up to me for private chats. They were entirely different individuals now, having discarded their official roles. Most of them wanted to know how my husband 'took it'. 'Ask him,' I said, 'he's right here.' After that, I lost Dilip for the next hour. He was surrounded by a bevy of females asking him what he felt about my books and 'image'. The surly fellow who'd interviewed me earlier also joined the group at some point and attempted to grill my husband. Unfortunately, he didn't get too far with Dilip who disarmed him completely by smiling, not scowling. Maybe the journalist had hoped to provoke him enough to get into a scrap. Now that would have made a good news story.

Bandula, meanwhile, was working the room like a Las Vegas impresario. He wanted me to carry away the best possible impression of his beloved country. He didn't want even the slightest unpleasantness to mar our visit. I assured him I was used to tough questions and considered them a valid part of my programme. I wasn't particularly hurt or disturbed. Maybe a little exasperated. 'I want you both to meet the best people of our country. Not these ignorant journalists.' We told him to relax and not go overboard with his 'imaging'. Bandula, not one to let it go quite so easily, packed our remaining days with lunches, teas and dinners with some exceptional individuals—painters, writers, publishers. We visited them in their gracious homes, ate the most amazing local delicacies, chatted in an informal atmosphere and got the opportunity to discover a few things for ourselves about the Sri Lankans and their feelings about their neighbours—us.

There were other trips, other book fairs, but my experience at the one in New Delhi must rate as one of the funniest as well as the silliest. I still haven't quite assessed the profile of the person who visits this bi-annual fair held at the sprawling Pragati Maidan. I suspect a lot of people idly wandering around from stall to stall are there because it seems like an inexpensive evening on the town (the entrance ticket costs next to nothing). For some it's probably a family outing, more like a picnic, where the kids rush around collecting free pamphlets, pencils, erasers, and stickers on offer at some of the stalls, while the parents wait outside at the nearest food stall.

My visit to the Penguin pavilion was timed for late evening when the crowds are at their thickest. By the time I managed to push my way past the hordes, find the place, and position myself behind the desk next to the cash counter, there were hundreds of curious people milling around wondering who the hell I was, since a couple of camera crews covering the fair were present looking for spot interviews. Once I'd finished with them, I went back to my designated desk and started signing copies, only to be interrupted several times by visitors asking, 'Excuse pliss . . . where there are management books?' Or 'Madam, madam, reference books?' Which section?' 'Madam . . . how much is this encyclopaedia?' or 'Please tell me the total for all these . . .' Some of these queries were phrased in Punjabi or rustic Hindi. And yet, the people asking were ready to put down five hundred rupees and more for books they couldn't possibly read.

That went for the autograph hunters too, who, while they hadn't the slightest notion about my identity, still thought it a good idea to queue for a signature—it was free, after all. They'd present shabby pieces of paper, torn currency notes, pocket diaries, backs of leaflets . . . only to be shooed away by the security chaps. Others would stand a couple of feet away, staring in a transfixed manner for minutes on end. Or buy the cheapest possible book from another stall and bring it over for my signature. It was no use 'educating' them. I thought it was simpler and quicker to sign and get rid of the lot.

I found particularly amusing the man who picked up one of my books, read for ten minutes, summoned a couple of buddies, read some more, and then decided to buy the lot—all the titles on display—hoping to come across plenty of 'hot' passages. I could have told them it was far cheaper to go buy a girlie magazine from pavement hawkers if that's what they were looking for—but we were there to sell books, my books. And to hell with what motivated a potential customer. At the end of the day, it was numbers we were looking for. And fortunately, we didn't do too badly.

I saw the sorry plight of first-time authors who came to the book fair expecting instant recognition, long queues for autographed copies, flashbulbs popping and eager readers waiting to mob them—only to discover that in India, book signing can be a humbling, even humiliating, experience. Two or three excellent writers waited for over an hour for even one single interested buyer to show up. Finally, to save them embarrassment, Penguin employees decided to pose as readers and pick up a couple of copies. This can be a painful experience, considering most writers do have a sensitive ego.

They construe the lack of reader interest as a rejection of their precious work. It's not that at all. One has to see it in the right perspective—the book-buying public is exceedingly limited. Books themselves are seen as something of a luxury. Most families can think of dozens of priorities that would take natural precedence over purchasing a novel. In such an environment, it is difficult for a writer to get noticed and for books to move off the shelves.

Besides, the book-buying tradition itself barely exists in the metros. Here again, it isn't fiction that sells so much as self-help books from overseas. People who visit book fairs are shopping around for bargain prices for expensive journals on technical subjects. They aren't there to pick up best-sellers—those are bought at stations, airports and traffic lights. Writers with a thin skin should stay away from book fairs till they are sufficiently established. I have seen the defeated look in the eyes of several very gifted authors who've come away from a flop signing session without a single copy sold.

I believe there is a method to all this. A tried and tested one that works. We lack both the will and the experience to exploit a book's commercial potential by providing the right infrastructure to the author. If the individual lacks that ambiguous factor called 'charisma', if he or she does not interest the media, if he or she is idealistic enough to believe that at the end of the day a good book will succeed in finding its own audience—that's a major misconception, especially in India. Hundreds of excellent books get pulped by the publishers each year on account of poor sales. Authors complain that the poor sales are because of low public awareness—why would someone think of buying a book nobody even knows is available? Which is why no amount of publicity is too much publicity for this underrated, largely misrepresented vocation.

If nubile, numb-skulled veejays can hog headlines and covers, surely nobody should grudge writers the same? The problem here is one of perception. Authors are expected to look, behave and write in a certain way. There is a tendency to slot, categorize, label. Endless and arbitary debates on high-brow, low-brow, literary, non-literary, popular and populist pulp, distract from the main purpose of a writer—any writer—which is to find a reader. Without readers, there are no books. Only self-indulgence and vanity. It's crowded and competitive out there. A writer is reduced to becoming a performing flea willy-nilly. Not a pleasant option. But there it is. Even a former prime minister—Narasimha Rao—isn't spared the chat-show circuit. Call it a horse race. Call it commercialization. At the end of the day, even this lofty game called publishing is all about numbers.

In the period immediately after independence, it was as though people were waiting for 'voices' to inspire and guide them, chronicle the mood of a newly independent people, record their relief, frustration and anxiety, and reflect their concerns. If in the bargain a good story was also told, terrific. But the person telling it had to be from a socially backward region, preferably economically disadvantaged and ideally, awful looking. This worked very well for the first thirty years. Books that dealt with deprivation, caste, class and poverty were deemed classics, even masterpieces, as they fitted neatly into the pseudo-socialistic model that was *au courant*.

Briefly then, writers had to have a conscience—or else. It was the era of the 'small person' speaking on behalf of a nation. Fine. Then what happened? The nation's writers felt emboldened enough to strike out and write a different kind of book that reflected a new, emerging reality that was as confused as the nation itself. A new chord was being struck but the ears were still accustomed to the old tunes. Anything else was suspect.

I was caught between the two—not quite here and not quite there. Perhaps because of the publicity I received, my books were regarded with suspicion and scepticism for being commercially successful. We were still clinging to the virtue of low-key, underplayed, quiet conformist writing in English that didn't shake the status quo. Writers who preceded me, particularly women, were either erudite elderly ladies or fierce single women with a strong message to deliver. I didn't fit in. There was no clear slot for me. It was far easier to dismiss my books and concentrate on the publicity—which, when I think back, was phenomenal by those days' standards, but modest by today's.

A decade after I began publishing, I believe I have changed a great deal from the impetuous person I then was; from someone who spoke her mind freely in countless interviews to a more seasoned cynic who knows when to keep her mouth shut. Publicity has been a vital tool, an important part of the whole package. But publicity is a double-edged sword that can often slice through the very person it has promoted. Besides, the higher the profile gets, the heavier the burden one is compelled to carry. Publicity operates on its own logic. Nobody can claim to have total control over it. However, if one is aware of its pitfalls and treads cautiously, it's possible to take stock, step out for a breather and then make the next move. Yes, it sounds like a dreadful strategic game—and that's precisely how I view it.

There is no point being stuck with an image over which one has absolutely no control. It's important to remain on top of it, to manipulate the image rather than have it manipulate you. But like I said, there are times when that's not entirely upto the individual. When things backfire, you have to be ready with a fire-fighting operation of your own. The downside cannot be avoided, no matter how clever the positioning. It happens to the best of them—Mikhail Gorbachev being an excellent example, from 'Master of the Universe' to 'Peddler of Pizza Hut'. In India, all it took was a bad business decision to topple Amitabh Bachchan from his supreme position in the film industry. When a poll was conducted by a city paper in late '97 asking readers to name the 'Ten Most Hated Indians', Bachchan's name figured on the list.

We do live in media-driven times. I have books to write and to promote—this has become an inescapable, integral part of the publishing game these days. The two go hand in hand. Not even a Gorbachev or a Maggie Thatcher is spared the drill. You write a book, you go flog it. Or don't cry if it dies on the shelves, unnoticed, unread, unsung. That overused, irritating word of the Nineties—hype—is often chucked around carelessly to describe the promotional aspect of having authored a work. Often 'hype' is not understood in its appropriate context. I'm frequently asked about the irrelevance of well-publicized book launches. While I agree they are a bloody nuisance most of the time, they have by now become a part and parcel of the writing process. Nobody, but nobody, is so well known or so successful that he or she can refuse to participate in a structured programme.

I remember meeting Dominique Lapierre right after I'd written *Socialite Evenings*. I was reeling from the terrible reviews. I was talking petulantly about book-signing sessions and how tension-filled they are. What if nobody turns up? What if not a single copy is bought? What if nobody at the store or venue even knows about the author's presence, or cares?

He told me cheerfully that he had adopted a simple

strategy when he began his career as a writer. 'I'd be in the assigned bookshop waiting for readers to mob me. In the early years that didn't happen. I used to feel defeated and small at being completely ignored even by browsers. That's when I decided to do something about it. I'd stand with my book in hand and attract as much attention as possible. I'd go up to unsuspecting people and say, "Excuse me, this is my book. I've written it. See—that's my name. That's me, Dominique Lapierre. Please buy a copy. I'll sign it for you." It worked sometimes. It didn't at others. I was willing to sing, dance, do a jig, entertain people . . . anything to make them aware of me and my book.'

I was told how total his involvement was with the marketing of his titles. Between the two of them, Dominique and his wife, also named Dominic, had a say in every single aspect of sales world-wide. They participated in all decisions, from the wording of the ads and the design of the posters to the tone of the general publicity. Lapierre believed he knew and understood his product best and he had every right to monitor exactly how it was to be imaged.

Many other authors work closely with their agents in this regard. It is one hell of a time-consuming exercise, but there doesn't seem to be much of an option in a very crowded, very competitive market. If one can do it in a calm and professional manner, it's an experience worth undertaking. Through trial and error, I've discovered there's a right way and a wrong way. In my self-deprecatory, self-protective infant years, I'd got it entirely wrong. I used to think it was smart to tear myself apart before someone else could. That it was better to anticipate criticism and provide a gun with enough rounds of ammunition for potential critics to shoot me down with. Pre-empt a strike. In my self-consciousness and embarrassment, I became a bit too defensive. Some of the

people who wrote me off and penned the harshest reviews for
Socialite Evenings were contemporaries I was on informal,
easy, friendly terms with. When they met me for interviews,
I was jokey-jokey and dismissive about the book, afraid that
if I conveyed the impression I took myself and the book too
seriously, they'd scoff at my earnestness. It was a mistake. My
access and casual attitude were used against me. My uneasy
laughter and the unsure edge to my remarks were seen as
weaknesses to be manipulated. I'd walked right into it. The
fault lay with me. It is not possible for critics and writers to
be friends. It does not work, no matter how it goes. Every
writer in the world longs for words of praise and
encouragement. Those are the real rewards. Critics feel
obliged to do what they perceive is their job—criticize.

No writer 'likes' criticism, even if it is 'fair'. It has to be
a rave or nothing. Since a herd mentality does exist in every
business, why should it be any different for literary criticism?
The tone for all the reviews to follow is set by the first one off
the block—especially if it's written by a critic whose opinions
are worth something. Others take their cue from him or her,
rarely sticking their necks out to say, 'I'm sorry—but I liked
the book enormously, and I do not agree with so-and-so's
assessment.'

Cliques exist in all professions and the world of literary
criticism is essentially a small, closed one. Not that a positive
review necessarily leads to great sales. It's just that the author
feels less persecuted. And then, if the book bombs regardless,
there is no one really to pin the blame on.

It took me years and years to call myself a writer. The
moment of realization came at a chance meeting with the
British novelist Julian Barnes. It was at a small, very stylish
dinner given in his honour by a high-powered corporate lady
in Mumbai. I was invited because at that stage I was being

projected as the most controversial person in the profession, and it's always good to have at least one such individual to spice up an otherwise drab gathering of self-important individuals. I hadn't heard of Barnes. I didn't know his work. I found myself seated next to him; he balanced his heavy ceramic dinner plate on his knees just as I did.

It's hard enough to eat traditional Indian food off fine crockery, with silver knives and forks. Harder still when one is forced to load the plate, with different curries floating around and merging into an unappetizing brown, muddy mess, walk back to a stuffed sofa much too low for comfortable eating, spread the lace-edged napkin carefully with one hand, and balance the heavy plate in another. Then to have to sit yourself down next to a stranger, try and make polite party conversation without too much eye contact while keeping one eye on the runny river on the flat dinner plate to prevent it from spilling over and staining a favourite saree . . . well, that was my precise predicament.

Barnes was accompanied by a woman (girlfriend, wife, agent, I forget) who didn't look overjoyed at the thought of the celebrated author engaging in small talk with an unknown Indian lady whose attention was focused on food. To his credit, he initiated the standard conversation . . . but gently. 'What do you do?' he asked, and I avoided replying. 'What do you do?' I asked him back. The woman glared at me. With charm and extreme modesty he told me he wrote books. One of the titles rang a bell since it had been greeted with ecstatic reviews in the British press. Somehow I didn't feel at all embarrassed by my ignorance. And I didn't feel like fibbing. We talked easily despite the woman's withering looks and obvious impatience. I thought Barnes was an exceedingly kind, responsive person. Maybe he found it a relief meeting someone at a studiedly orchestrated high-brow soirée who'd actually not heard of him and wasn't ashamed of admitting it.

After twenty minutes, I confessed I'd written too. Three books. He stopped eating. 'Why didn't you tell me that earlier?' he asked, looking at me seriously. I muttered and stammered and tripped over my words hopelessly. He seemed to understand my discomfort and awkwardness. He asked about my life and career. I told him whatever was simple enough to convey in that short period. And then he narrated a small incident from his own life that touched me greatly. He said he'd found it difficult to think of himself as a writer during the initial years. It was much later when he was filling in his passport form and he came across the word 'Profession', that he caught himself wondering what to write. After a great deal of hesitation, he printed the word he'd not had the courage to use before—writer. 'With that, my life changed. I started taking myself far more seriously. Once I'd accepted my vocation, I no longer felt the need to run away from it.'

This incident affected me a lot. I got the strength I was looking for. From then on I refused to turn my back on a very vital area of my life. I felt so much more positive about myself and what I was doing. For better or worse, a writer I was, no matter what came with the territory. My attitude changed gradually . . . but change it did. I could handle it all from that point onwards, take the nastiest criticism in my stride, laugh off hostile reviews, stay on top of the ridiculous image I was stuck with. When an interviewer asked me a few years later whether I 'chewed men for breakfast', I looked her straight in the eye and replied, 'I have far better options. Frankly, I prefer whole wheat cereal.'

I watched Vikram Seth doing his reading from *A Suitable Boy* at the British Council auditorium in Mumbai, and marvelled at his brisk, businesslike professionalism. Here was a writer the world had acknowledged as a genius—India's first literary success story (Rushdie doesn't count. It's difficult to think of him as an Indian). Surprise number one: Vikram's sparrow-like frame. He is really, really tiny. One can't tell that from photographs, most of which are head shots that distort his face and make it seem so much larger (proportionately his head is noticeably bigger than his body).

The auditorium was packed to capacity. Vikram surveyed the crowd in a cursory fashion, opened a shabby, battered briefcase, carefully removed his book and began reading without ceremony. He read very well, adapting his voice to suit the passage, dramatizing conversations and modulating his tone. We met right after the reading during the high tea that followed. He came up to me, introduced himself and sat down, while dozens of eager acolytes hung around not daring to interrupt as he engaged me in charming, light, flirtatious talk. I invited him home to dinner. He accepted without any fuss, adding, 'I'd love to meet your family—but no outsiders. I'm exhausted.'

So he was when he walked in a couple of hours later. I was tempted to offer him a comfortable bed and fluffy pillows in place of a drink and a meal.

We had an early dinner during which he spoke easily and warmly to my children. The only indication of overwhelming fatigue occurred when my boxer puppy (Tuts was a couple of months old then) waddled up sleepily after a huge meal of baby food. Vikram's eyes dilated with disgust and horror as Tuts wiped his mouth on his trouser leg and waddled off to pee close by. 'I'm leaving for Calcutta in the morning. I don't have another pair of trousers.' Oh dear! Vikram was led to the bathroom where he tried to get the obstinate stain off. I felt embarrassed by my pet's bad behaviour. There was little I could do to help. I'd so liked Vikram. And now I'd never be able to invite him back.

I liked Pico Iyer, too, when we met for a story he was commissioned to write on Mumbai for a glossy travel magazine. Like Vikram, Pico is a tiny, intense man with great big glowing eyes. Like Vikram, his speech is elegant, polite, old-fashioned and refined. Like Vikram, he writes divinely. Like Vikram, when we met he was single but clearly not ready to mingle. I was ready to adopt both instantly. They obviously weren't looking for a mother figure—my loss entirely. The reason I got along with these two men was because they weren't judgemental. Men who were comfortable in their own skins. Comfortable with success. Comfortable being who they were. Especially, good human beings. Blindingly brilliant too—but that was a bonus. And they were complete naturals who saw beyond the 'image', and I was grateful.

Another famous writer I met and was enchanted by was none other than the author of the sensational *My Feudal Lord.* My husband and I were in Pakistan on a visit that had started badly (I was running a high temperature and had to be pumped up with pills). On our last night, we were invited to what was billed as the party of the season. It was going to be held in the pride (or monstrosity) of Lahore—a particularly ostentatious residence witheringly referred to as the Lahore Hilton by the snobs. We were told the legendary singer Noorjehan's daughter would be performing that night and that the *creme de la creme* of society would be present. We arrived there well past midnight (early by Lahore standards).

It was a scene straight out of a kitsch movie—Fellini in a Pakistani setting. The grand residence was everything I'd been told it was (complete with numbered suites) and more—Italian marble period statues, indoor pools, indoor fountains, hideous paintings, tapestries, gilt, chandeliers, chrome, plate glass, silver . . . and a bar that rivalled the

Hilton's. Frightfully overdressed people moved from floor to floor, one room to another, clutching their cocktails and puffing incessantly. Exquisitely dressed women stared vacantly around them, not daring to shake their heads lest their hair got mussed up. The singer was installed in the living room and seemingly held the audience spellbound with her high-pitched film songs and quawwalis. I wondered how much her obvious popularity had to do with talent and how much with the generous glimpses of deep, milk-white cleavage. She resembled an alabaster statue in sequined chiffon—and seemed just as lifeless.

It was difficult to make any sort of conversation under the circumstances. In any case, I wouldn't have known where to begin with that boozed-up lot. Just as we were discussing a discreet departure plan, a woman in black came upto me and thrust a piece of paper into my palm. 'Phone her,' she hissed. 'She's waiting for your call.' I looked at the paper. It had Tehmina Durrani's number scribbled on it. Within seconds, the woman reappeared with a cellular phone. 'There's a car waiting downstairs. She wants to meet you—but not here,' the woman said. I called. A wonderful voice answered. I didn't have to introduce myself. Tehmina, the woman whose book had shocked Pakistan with its brutally frank account of her abusive marriage with a demon-like politician, spoke in seductive, dulcet tones, urging me to come on over. By then it was 1.30 in the morning. And I was nervous about getting into strange cars, being taken to a strange address, at a strange hour, in a strange country. I persuaded her to come over to the Lahore Hilton instead. Surprisingly, she agreed.

The woman in black was astonished. 'Tehmina is such a recluse. She doesn't go out at all. But . . . she was very keen to meet you.' I was flattered. And very curious. I had not read

My Feudal Lord. Only about it.

I now had a sense of how it must be for women in Pakistan, women who refused to conform, play ball and were lunatic enough to speak out. Tehmina, her friends said, was fully aware of the price she'd have to pay for baring her perceptions of a medieval marriage (her own), and had paid it. With interest. Ostracized and shunned by a certain powerful section of Pakistani society (one of the kingpins we met dismissed her as a 'mad woman'). Tehmina dug in her heels and refused to go away. 'The Feudal Lord' of the book remarried for the seventh time, fathered two more children and became a minister in Benazir Bhutto's cabinet. Lahore was neatly divided into the Tehmina-baiters and Tehmina-followers. I didn't meet a single neutral person. I couldn't wait to meet her.

She arrived like a queen in exile—luminous, beautiful and completely unadorned. She didn't require jewellery or fine clothes. Her presence and beauty were sufficient. When we entered the main party zone together, a hush fell over the gathering as guests stopped talking or drinking to stare. I'm sure she was accustomed to this reaction. She pretended not to notice as she took my hand and we started to walk through the crowd. The interesting thing was that nobody made eye contact with Tehmina. The men stared glumly into their drinks while the bejewelled begums with sprayed blonde coiffures stared skywards. The silence was another thing.

Tehmina obviously knew her way around this monstrous house. She summoned a waiter, ordered a bottle of red wine and asked for it to be sent to one of the numbered suites. 'We can talk in peace there,' she smiled. I was bewitched. Her voice was smoky and musical—a little like Meena Kumari's. Her large, lustrous eyes were carelessly kohl-lined. She wore a crumpled white kurta-pajama with a dupatta thrown over her shoulders like an afterthought. Silver . . . I remember flashes of dull, antique silver. Could have been bracelets, or earrings. I took to her instantly. And she to me (I think, I hope). We settled down in an impersonal room which resembled a business centre, only a fax machine was missing. She seemed unperturbed and entirely calm. I'd been told she had a band of devotees who hung around her every evening and generally protected her from the real world. Tehmina's salon. How appropriate. The Collette of Lahore. The Anais Nin of the subcontinent. Others had sneered, 'She can't write. She is no intellectual. Her book was written by someone else.' What did it matter? The voice was unmistakably hers. That was easy enough to tell after the first few minutes. The story was hers. The experiences were hers. The nightmares too. And that was all that counted—at least for me.

She knew the hosts. The wife was her friend and admirer. But she avoided parties like this one. I could see why. We talked all too briefly. It was nearly 3 a.m. Dilip and I had a flight to catch the next day. And yet, even that abbreviated encounter was enough. I felt enormous warmth for this fragile figure curled up on a settee sipping wine and talking in soft, melodious tones. Here was a woman who could so easily have projected herself as a tragedy queen, a martyr. Instead, she was putting her life together rather bravely, perhaps defiantly. It couldn't possibly have been a cakewalk for a woman like her to speak out and in so doing, open a can of worms—no, not just a can, an entire worm factory. Double standards aren't new to our society, or any society, but in Pakistan, they are impossible to ignore. Even the most refined, educated and wealthy families continue to function in a manner so feudalistic, it makes one squirm. But on the surface, everything appears sophisticated and smooth—the gorgeous trophy wives, the urbane husbands in Armani suits, the luxurious living. But beneath the surface, everything is as sour as the special achchar served with the biryani. It was all rather too decadent and depressing. Yet, Tehmina had managed to bloom in that murky, incestuous environment. And raise a family. I don't really care who writes her books. I read *My Feudal Lord* practically in one go. An autographed copy had been delivered to our host's home minutes before we were to leave for the airport. I'd read the affectionate message inscribed in it and knew it was meant.

*

Publicity is far more cruel to women than men. Many women who generate a great deal of it (beauty contestants, models, actresses, pop singers) do so because of the way they look. Aishwarya Rai is no less beautiful today than she was when she won the Miss World title in '96. And yet, once she moved over to the movies, the very press that had prostrated itself at her feet, turned around to trash her. Ditto for Sushmita Sen. Which is why my case is unique, since I didn't belong to showbiz but was constantly judged by showbiz standards. I found it funny most of the time, and still do. Some of my contemporaries didn't. I remember an intense doctor who aspired to write commercially successful novels, expressing her anger at the lack of press interest in her because she wasn't sufficiently 'glamorous'. At the time, I empathized with her frustration (she'd come to show me her manuscript) and even found a publisher for her. A few years later, she came out with a new book and a new look. Gone were her reservations about not playing to the gallery. At the launch party she pulled out all the stops. She dealt with the new attention like a pro, posing for the cameras and issuing what seemed like well-rehearsed sound bytes. Gone were the reservations about publicity, gone the inhibitions she claimed had kept her back. There she was, aggressively hard-selling her paperback. Good for her, too. She'll find it far easier to get another book deal with the kind of press file she now possesses.

There are countless others—a bearded poet who sat across me asking for a plug in a column when his first volume of verse appeared ('I'm very sensitive. Very shy. I don't know how to go about approaching people.'). He'd had no problems approaching me, though. By the time he'd finished his second book, he'd become a veteran. Everything well organized, quotes and pictures ready. Some would call it self-promotion. I call it professionalism.

Foreign correspondents often wrote that I was the first writer in India to use the services of a glamour photographer. I was lucky I had one in my family and that for Gautam it was a labour of love and a matter of pride. 'Don't you dare get yourself photographed by anybody else,' he'd told me. I've never felt the need to. He is the best. We share an excellent rapport. One hour in his home-cum-studio, and we are through. I've been fortunate in this respect. And I do feel sorry for other writers who don't have the same access. But I'd be a fool not to use this opportunity and privilege. Every human being wants to look his or her best. It's a very natural desire. Why would I want to look like a dog on my book jackets when there's an obliging cousin who makes me (and every woman he photographs) look like a goddess?

I remember a journalist colleague taking a pot-shot at me in print for being methodical about my publicity. There was much sniping regarding my preparation before attending a book-signing session in another city. 'She travels with a set of photographs, book jackets and posters,' the woman had written. Absolutely. If I don't do it, who will? Why should I allow myself to be photographed by some amateur clicking

away with a box camera, when in fact I have taken the trouble
to put publicity stills together? I have run magazines. I know
how convenient it is for editors and art directors when they
have photographs of a high quality to work with. Why take
chances with crummy, out-of-focus, blurred images that may
not reproduce at all when you have shot a special portfolio
for a new book?

The truth is that most people criticize 'cheap publicity'
till they get some themselves. Once they see their names in
print, they want to see it in lights. Once they get public
recognition, they want to perpetuate the moment. Once they
sign their first autograph, they never want to stop. Very few
individuals are honest enough to say so. Amitabh Bachchan
chose to be honest when he admitted as much on a TV
interview recently. I've seen it happen even with the most
reticent of them, genuinely shy people. I've seen them blush
and bloom under the spotlight, still insisting they were
uncomfortable with the attention, but praying hard for it to
not disappear. Those who've shrewdly taken the other route
('I'm a recluse, I detest publicity') have benefited the most
from it. 'Committed' commentators who mock the
'champagne journalists' do so until they have their first sip of
bubbly. Once they get on to those much-coveted party lists,
they learn to boogey in a hurry. And don't stop till they die
on the dance floor.

On a recent visit to Mumbai, V.S. Naipaul posed for
Jitendra Arya. He did so with all the flair of an ageing
Hollywood star—a John Wayne who can spell. I'm sure he'd
have been pretty disappointed had his visit gone unnoticed or
unrecorded. He may have been selective about his interviews,
but he certainly didn't refuse them. In my experience, that has
been true of every single, self-declared 'recluse'. It is one way
of keeping the market up. Create an aura of exclusivity,

pretend to shun publicity, and have the media chase you. Very often such people end up with more of it than those who are more upfront. It's rather a clever ruse, especially when the person doesn't have very much to sell besides an ambiguous and enigmatic persona.

Writers in India are just about beginning to discover the narcotic that fame is. And from all available evidence, they can't get enough. Anybody who has put pen to paper now actively seeks celebrity status. Many meek pen-pushers have discovered the power of a well-taken photograph . . . and they aren't about to let go. I've monitored this transformation in people I know closely. I've seen them dealing with write-ups and pictures in the initial stages, pretending they're deeply, horribly embarrassed . . . watching your face for reactions. Then, if the publicity continues, they're less embarrassed but they feign indifference. Nonchalance soon follows. But these very people make sure each clipping is carefully pasted, dated and filed. 'I'm doing it for my mother—she loves showing off in front of relatives.' 'I couldn't care less . . . but my wife gets a kick out of it.' 'God! Can you imagine—one appearance on television and people hound you at functions.' 'The other day I was recognized at the traffic lights—Jesus, that was weird.' I've had friends who pretend to be publicity-phobic calling up to say, 'Oh, was there something about me in the Mumbai papers last week? Do you think you could locate it and pop it in the mail?'

Most times, people who claim to 'shun' publicity need to rephrase their views. What they actually mean is they don't really mind publicity, so long as it's positive. Give them one adverse comment and they go ballistic. Their skins turn to rice-paper and they can't stop talking about how 'irresponsible' the press is. Publicity that stokes their egos is taken for granted, even as they exclaim, 'Can't they find other

362

people to write about?'

With the full-blown case of 'society writing' that's on at present, complete non-entities are deluding themselves about their status. I overheard a dubious 'businessman' saying coyly to his girl companion, 'I have to be careful these days. People like us who are in the limelight become easy targets because we are so recognizable.' This man would require a placard with his name in neon around his neck for anybody to know who he was. But he genuinely believed he'd arrived because some obscure columnist had mentioned his name in her columns for being the owner of a couple of snazzy cars. Even here, his thrill was premature since he didn't actually own those cars but had merely leased them for a short period—and the same columnist exposed that fact too, subsequently. But while the man was on a publicity high, nobody in his circle dared to shatter his illusions—they couldn't afford to. He paid all their bills.

I'm often asked how I dealt with the early reviews—the really, really nasty ones. The truth is, badly. First, there was shock ('How could they?'). Then disbelief ('No . . . this can't be about me. My precious book'). Then rage ('I'll fix them'). Finally resignation ('Forget it, keep writing'). I think what upset me the most was the tone rather than the content. Then I reminded myself of the fact that I'd written in exactly the same mocking manner myself, often without considering how it must have affected the person I was criticizing. I forced reason to set in. I argued with myself for months. 'If you can dish it out, you must learn to take it on the chin when it's your turn.' My rational self accepted the argument, but emotionally I was shattered.

Dilip would always make light of the whole thing, and successfully blunted the edge of the unrelenting attacks. When I look back, it couldn't have been easy for him—husband of a woman the entire critics' community had dubbed a pornographer. There must have been times when acquaintances came up at the club bar and tried to get a rise out of him. It must have happened at dinner parties or even at business meetings. If it did, he never told me about it. And if someone tried a cheap shot in my presence, he deflected it cleverly—but always with a broad smile. Had he reacted any differently, I doubt that I would have found the motivation or even the courage to carry on.

At the time the reviews were at their strongest, my children were far too young, so they escaped any potential embarrassment the write-ups might have caused. My parents lived in a different world even though their home was a five-minute drive from mine. Besides, my father is an unusual person with an amazingly contemporary outlook. Like my husband, he didn't find anything obscene about my books—and he wasn't pretending. Only once, I heard him asking my mother in the kitchen in a puzzled sort of way, 'My dear . . . how does Shobha know so much about sex?' My mother, ever the blunt pragmatist, responded, 'You are forgetting she is a forty-year-old married woman with children. She may be your youngest offspring, but she is not a child.' That satisfied him and he never wondered again.

Only recently, he called me up at 11 p.m. one night to say, 'I've been unable to find an answer to something that's been troubling me. Maybe you'll be able to throw some light on it. I've noticed that in surveys about sexual attitudes, it's always the men who are asked questions on frequency—how many times a week? A month? A year? Women are rarely asked this. Why is that?'

I gave him a ten-minute dissertation on the subject, and he listened most attentively.

'Thank you, my dear,' he said politely. 'I have learnt a lot tonight.'

That alarmed me. I hastily added, 'Baba, I'm not an expert on the subject.'

But he'd got the answers he was looking for.

*

I don't particularly enjoy 'discussing' my books, and discourage all attempts to do so. In the early years I would find myself gritting my teeth and putting up with all manner of ridiculous questions, mainly sexual. There was one particular politician-businessman who'd phone right after a new title had appeared, to dissect it. Much as he tried to intellectualize the discussion, it was easy to see that all he wanted was to talk dirty. Once, I happened to be present at a journalist's home when he decided to initiate a 'civilized conversation' (his words) on sex. I scrupulously stayed out of it since I'd guessed his motive (how else could such a repressed, unattractive fellow engage the attention of a lively group of women?).

Unfortunately, a voluble (and equally gullible) editor fell right into it by talking about women's sexuality and how misunderstood it is by men. The gleam in the man's eye was unmistakable, his tongue was all but hanging out. He goaded her on as she naïvely and candidly blabbered away. It was the sort of conversation he could never have had with his dull, uneducated wife. The only way he could have been a part of something like this would have been through dialling an international sex-line. And here he was getting it for free from a respected, respectable and reputed woman. Several times that evening he tried to make eye contact with me and to bring up my writing, quoting key passages from the latest book. I ignored him and refused to be drawn into the debate even

365

when the woman doing all the talking tried her best to get me to contribute. After that, I stopped taking the man's calls altogether. He was shrewd enough to know he'd be wasting his time.

Something similar happened over dinner after a book-reading in a southern city. The invitees had turned up in droves, with well-dressed, bejewelled women outnumbering the men. This was for *Surviving Men*, and I'd chosen the passages with care, avoiding those that had any explicit references to sex. We were in a conservative place and I wasn't there to shock anybody or hurt local sensibilities. The reading went smoothly. What started off as a few nervous giggles soon built up into hearty laughter, even applause. Came question-time and a pompous fellow in the front row got up and tugged at his suspenders. He announced, 'I wore these today . . . just in case. You know . . . I wasn't sure I'd still have my pants on after the reading.' Nobody found that funny. He carried on with a few more such remarks. A woman booed. Some others joined her. Finally, it became a chorus.

The other men present thought it wiser to leave quietly. One man stayed behind. He approached me hesitantly, and the intensity with which he spoke rather startled me. 'I need five minutes alone with you,' he pleaded. We were at the pool-side patio of a five-star hotel. There was a formal sit-down dinner to follow. I was travelling with a good friend. She and I exchanged quick looks. I told the man I'd be with him soon. He waited quietly on the sidelines while I finished signing copies and 'performing' for those who wanted to talk, take pictures . . . the standard post-reading hoopla.

After half an hour I drew up a chair and asked him to sit down. Without ceremony he said, 'My wife has left me. I love her very much. I don't understand it. Will she come back to me? I don't want to lose her. I'll kill myself if she doesn't return.' There were tears in his eyes. He was clutching a copy of my book. He looked desperate, crazed. I asked him a few questions about his marriage. It was obvious she'd fallen in love with somebody else. As it often happens, the other man was his best friend. It was equally obvious she had never loved him. There was no way this woman was going to come back—not even for the sake of her two little boys. I didn't have the heart to tell him that. He was asking me for solutions. Me, a total stranger. That's how overwrought he was. I couldn't lie either. Or reassure him that everything was going to be okay. I tried to tell him that he should consider his own priorities and options, keeping in mind the possibility that he may have to raise his children as a single parent.

He burst into tears. 'I love her. I can't live without her,' he wept. In another, more open society, I would have reached across and hugged him, comforted him like I would a child. It pained me to have to keep my hands firmly in my lap and coo inadequate words of false hope. People were beginning to stare. He got up abruptly and strode off.

I went in to dinner, very disturbed by his obvious agony. What had I done to make him feel better about himself? Why had he asked me for an answer I did not have? Or maybe I did—but how could I tell a broken man that his wife was never going to share his life again? And he'd come to the glamorous evening after reading about me in the hope that a worldly-wise, experienced woman would be able to provide insights and instant solutions. That I'd be a Ms Fix-it who'd give him advice that would bring his wife back to him. I felt awful. And helpless. I wasn't in the mood to be gracious and charming to the hosts who'd laid on a banquet. I couldn't swallow even a mouthful of kakori kebab, even as the chef was summoned to hover around and explain the age-old art behind the delicacy.

I was wondering how I'd be able to endure the rest of the evening with its countless courses and inane conversation, when a voice to my right asked, 'Madam, is it true that women in India do not experience real pleasure . . . you know what I mean . . . and that they fool their husbands by pretending? What, according to you, is the percentage of ladies who . . . who . . . experience real pleasure?' I wanted to fling the plate of fragrant biryani at his smug face. Just who the hell did he imagine I was—a sexologist with statistics at my fingertips? Someone who'd conducted a study on female orgasms? I saw the expression in my friend's eyes. She was silently telling me to calm down and not react. While I was playing for time by sipping water slowly, the entire table had laid down their knives and forks and was waiting for me to speak. There was the kind of hush that precedes a stormy discussion. I noticed the perfumed socialites seemed more tense than their paunchy spouses. How many times had they faked it? Was I going to expose them by revealing everything? Would I let the side down in such obviously ignorant and foolish company? Would the husbands go home that night, pounce on these women and ask at the end of it, 'Was that real pleasure you were experiencing, or were you cheating again? According to Shobha Dé ninety-nine per cent of women pretend. How do I know you don't belong to the majority?'

Fortunately, my friend took over the proceedings very smoothly. She's the kind of woman men feel very comfortable with. She looks 'homely', if you get the picture. And therefore non-threatening. She said I was very exhausted . . . readings can be most tiring . . . and then all those questions that followed. The subject was very vast and needed a different forum to discuss thoroughly. Maybe on another visit? Some other time? But definitely not now—not tonight.

The knives and forks went back into metallic action. The

socialites started breathing again. And the men looked completely cheated, dejected.

I excused myself pleading tiredness—my friend had laid the ground so perfectly. We went back to our room and I was livid. The audacity of the fellow, I fumed. She calmed me down. These men never get the chance to talk to 'bold' women, she explained. He must have been looking forward to this evening for months.

After I'd cooled off I understood what she was saying—that dinner was a pathetic statement, an accurate reflection of our society where men and women do not talk openly, where husbands and wives lead compartmentalized lives devoid of any real communication. I felt sick anyway. As I've done ever since my first book was published and I started receiving strange mail. I hoped—believed—the seekers of cheap thrills would disappear a decade down the line. No such luck.

Just a few months ago, after a mass-circulated Hindi weekly carried a glossy profile, I was inundated with letters. Some of them were proposals of marriage from men who'd included passport-size pictures of themselves along with bio-datas and other relevant details ('no encumbrances or liabilities. Of sound health and mind.'). One particularly unattractive gentleman had enclosed a poem which he felt summed up his feelings—'we are soulmates,' wrote the unemployed former bank clerk, 'destined to spend our lives together.' Right.

For every such misguided attempt, there are other charming ones that never fail to touch me. My husband and I were coming back from Kochi a few weeks after *Surviving Men* was published. That very day we'd walked into the small bookshop at the Taj Malabar and discovered my interview in *Newsweek*. It was a special moment in a special location. As it frequently happens with international news magazines, the publication of my piece had been postponed a couple of times since the world was waiting for a legend to die—Chairman Deng had been hanging on precariously for weeks. Several China experts had been interviewed, the last page kept ready, printing schedules kept on hold. If Deng died midweek, I'd be dumped and one of the experts would run. As it turned out Deng did die. *Newsweek* ran a comprehensive cover story—and I still made it to the interview page. That must have angered all those China experts—but did I care?

I'd never been to Kerala and had often talked longingly about it. My husband had planned this short break as an anniversary present. Lulled into a languid frame of mind and mesmerized by the beauty of the backwaters, we were still basking in a warm, romantic haze at the airport lounge when we noticed a young man with a copy of the book. Once the aircraft had taken off I fell into a light sleep, but not before noting that he seemed to be reading avidly and with keen interest. Even so, I pretended to be sound asleep when he walked over to our seats—whatever it was he wanted to convey, my husband would deal with it. If he was planning to punch me, that was fine too—he'd be pulped in return.

I heard him say softly to my husband, 'Please ask missus to autograph my copy.' He handed the book to Dilip and waited while I was gently tapped as if to awaken me from deep sleep. While I feigned disorientation, my husband said lightly, 'It's a fun book, don't you think?' And the young man replied spiritedly, 'No sir . . . it's a very serious book. Your wife has made some important points in it.'

Relieved that there wasn't going to be a major scene and that my honour was intact, I signed with a flourish. The man took the book and hesitated . . . 'You are a great man, sir,' he said to my amused husband. I wonder what that was supposed to mean? I think I do know. People like to believe living with someone who writes controversially requires exceptional qualities . . . that my husband must go through daily hell while I slay dragons and take on the world. Alas, the reality of our life together is far less dramatic. But I hate to disappoint people who wish to fantasize. 'You are a great man, sir,' is a double-edged comment. It implies, 'My god! How have you managed to survive this woman?' It can also mean, 'Hats off to you. A lesser man would have crumbled.'

Funny, but that's not how I've seen either myself or my writing. I'm frequently asked whether my books are designed to shock. The answer to that is an emphatic 'no'. I wouldn't know what else, how else, to write. These are the books within me—sorry, no apologies. It's all right if you hate them, rubbish them, appreciate them, even ignore them. Really. What I find gauche and terribly irritating is when some idiot walks up to me to say a dumb thing like, 'Oh . . . I really loved your *Cosmo* article. It was so inspirational. Now I must get around to reading your books.' Don't bother brother, I'm tempted to drawl. But I can't be bothered to say even that.

There is a variation: women who gush at parties, 'We love your columns, yaar. But we have yet to read your books.' Take your time, darlings. No hurry. By then, I'll have written ten more . . . and you'll be wearing dentures. Do I say that? Nope. I smile and waste my time murmuring, 'It isn't mandatory by law yet . . . it's okay. You won't he dragged to jail for the offence.' Silly. Childish. But I don't know how else to tackle it.

It's worse when an obvious *anpadh* comes up for a quick spot of chamchagiri. 'Madam . . . I loved your book . . . what is it called . . . uh . . . uh . . . yes, yes . . . *Starry Evenings*—no? Am I right?' Absolutely, I assure the person, glad you liked it. There are shopkeepers whose wives watch *Swabhimaan*, who ask me innocently, 'You also write books, don't you?' And I nod sheepishly before getting the subject back on track.

*

Being a writer has its amusing moments too. When I went to London on a book promotional tour, I was hardly prepared for the kind of questions that were put to me. Where on earth had the reporters got all those weird notions from? It was Nari Hira who finally enlightened me. His London office had also received a press release from the publicity division of my publishers (Simon & Schuster). The publicists, in turn, had relied on a grossly inaccurate, thoroughly malicious profile written by a wimpish English writer for *The Sunday Times* a few years earlier. Without checking the facts with me, the over-enthusiastic publicists had added their own colourful details, painting such a distorted picture of my life that I could only gasp. It was too late to recall the offensive press releases. I'd have to swing it somehow . . . reverse the damage if possible.

The first few interviewers weren't prepared to meet someone like me at all and who can blame them? They'd been primed to encounter a monster—an outrageous oriental lady who spoke dirty, wrote dirty and lived dirty. Sorry, but that was not the person sitting across the sofa. So, they'd ask me in utter bewilderment, 'What happened? How come the publicists wrote what they did? Weren't you shown the press release? Didn't you approve it?'

In hindsight I realize what a liability inexperience is when dealing with something like this. I wasn't even aware of the contents of that release when, in fact, I should have exercised complete control over it. Over radio, on television, in print, so many precious minutes were wasted setting the record straight. I was in London for precisely eight days and most of those were invested in an entirely avoidable exercise. On a popular breakfast show, the radio host made a production out of tearing up the press release, rolling it into a ball as noisily as possible and throwing it into a wastebin.

'This is complete rubbish,' he informed his listeners. 'This lady isn't anything like her CV. I'm chucking that away and starting from scratch.'

I could have kissed him with gratitude. If only all the others had been that open and generous. My big regret was the time and effort thrown away in correcting the misleading information when I could have employed both more productively to talk about my books, not the publicists' version of my life.

I was on a learning curve. And I learnt very quickly. Publicists can be dangerous and damaging. Almost irreversibly so. They are there to sensationalize your persona, dramatize your experiences. In a crowded, competitive field, they recognize the publicity value of a juicy scandal, a risqué story. They are also aware of the attention span of the editors they deal with. Give them a story with enough controversy to make the piece, and you're home and dry. Or else, why would anybody be interested in a book by a woman writer from India who is hard to categorize? It took me a while to cotton on, but once I did, I decided to play ball and have one myself.

At one such TV shoot, I found a strange looking creature whom I did not recognize either by name or face. She turned out to be Britain's number one writer of horror fiction—she looked the part too. We were in adjoining make-up booths having our faces fixed by gum-chewing kids talking incessantly over our heads. The woman in the next chair glared malevolently at them while puckering up her over-lipsticked mouth to ensure the colour hadn't run. It was a young TV station with a crazy crew. Most of the people working there were in their early twenties. The director wore bright yellow patent leather shoes. His assistant, an attractive black girl with every conceivable body part pierced by silver rings, literally skipped around the sprawling set, talking non-stop into a walkie-talkie. I was enjoying myself. The publicist, a rather glum lady with a permanently downcast gaze, sat stiffly in a high-backed chair, worrying about our next appointment. I asked her whether the British writer had undergone a sex-change operation. I could have sworn she'd been a man till quite recently. The publicist seemed genuinely shocked as she informed me about the woman's well-known children. Oh, well. Jan Morris has fathered some too. So what?

Yellow Shoes came up to me and said cheerily, 'Time to mug for the cameras, luv.' Right, I performed on cue. By now I knew what was expected of me—it was the novelty of hearing a demure-looking, saree-clad woman from the East talking provocatively about the sexual attitudes of the natives (Brits are obsessive about sex). It would have been sickening had I decided to abandon my sense of humour and taken the entire road-show seriously. It was a new experience, and I was picking up valuable tips. The publicist assigned to me had survived two high-profile international authors before I arrived—Carrie Fisher, who'd brought her hair dresser, personal trainer, bodyguard, children and their nanny with her, and Kurt Vonnegut who'd brought a chronic case of depression along for the trip. Compared to them, I was a welcome break, she told me. Give me a few more years and their kind of success, I chuckled to myself.

It was a tough week for unknown authors waiting to get noticed in London. Maggie Thatcher had come and gone. Joan Collins' latest effort was everywhere—its garish plastic pink jacket painted on London buses doing the Piccadilly Circus routes. Between five to ten new titles by international big names were being aggressively promoted daily, with literary soirées getting as much coverage as film premières. Simon & Schuster needed all the masala they could get out of my short visit. Who would be interested in a book-signing session by an unknown Indian at Harrod's?

In the final analysis I did rather enjoy the whole experience. The publicists had let me down, some interviewers were hard to take and the schedule was hectic but it was all softened by the comforts on offer—a fabulous, well-appointed apartment in central London, very attentive, affectionate publishers, and most evenings free. I was touched by the small, thoughtful gestures—well-picked flowers in the living room with a 'welcome' card, two of my books discreetly displayed on a book-rack, the refrigerator stocked with foodstuff we'd enjoy—a range of cheeses, marmalades, jams, teas, breads; international magazines strewn around the living room, extra pillows on the bed. A great deal of thinking had gone into making our stay comfortable and I appreciated that very much. I felt pampered, and more importantly, respected. Since some of the interviews were to be conducted in the flat, the publishers had made sure there were enough cookies, coffee and nibblies besides a well-stocked bar, to keep the interviewers well-fed and happy. The trip would have ended on a high note had I not missed my step on an escalator at the BBC office the night before we were to fly to Amsterdam.

I had reported for a midnight interview on a programme appropriately called 'Up All Night'. The producer (a woman) organized our security passes and escorted me to the studio upstairs. My husband stayed back with a couple of local friends when I convinced him it would be yet another routine interview and that he needn't waste his time holed up in a sound-proof room while the recording was on. Reluctantly, he decided to take a short walk with the two friends who'd also made up their mind to wait for me. Normally, I'd have been out in twenty minutes. On the way to the studio, I remember thinking how dark and dingy the corridors looked with most of the lights switched off.

Once inside the studio booth, we went through the predictable frothy, chatty banter, wound up the show and started walking back towards the escalators which were stationary. I was wearing high heels and a saree, which made me extra cautious while negotiating my way down the metal steps of the steel contraption. We were in the new wing of the old Bush House Studios, and the producer explained to me how the two buildings were connected. No wonder the gradient of the escalator seemed so strangely angled, I recall thinking, when, god knows what really happened, but I found myself slipping down those steel steps with such velocity, I could see the ceiling whirling crazily above me as my body crashed violently against the sides of the escalator. I cried out in sheer terror as my grip on the railing loosened, and I felt my torso twisting unnaturally while my feet continued their rapid slide downwards. It has to be my level of fitness combined with the remnants of the old athletic training that made me lunge desperately towards the slippery railing for the last time in an attempt to break the fall. My hand found something to hold on to, even as I felt hard, metallic claws tearing through my right knee and then, as my body spun around once again, my lower back. Suddenly it was over. I wasn't dead. But I wished I had been. Never before in my life had I experienced such a raw sense of terror, panic and pain. Those few dizzying seconds when the pattern of the escalator grid swung crazily all around me, there was just one image in my mind, I understood just one thing, I thought of just one person—my mother. And the physical pain she'd stoically endured for three decades. And how I hadn't experienced any myself and could never have imagined the intensity of the sensation. I thought how brave she'd been and I, how insensitive. I thought this was God's way of teaching me a lesson, opening my eyes to another's suffering, making me learn the hard way. In that one excruciating moment, I became my mother's pain. And wept like one of my own young children.

I could barely hear the producer wailing from the top of the escalator, summoning help. I kept repeating, 'I want my husband. Please get my husband.' Four or five security guards ran up the escalator and examined my bleeding back and knee. There was no ice on the premises. Not even a well-stocked first-aid kit. No stretcher either. I couldn't move. My saree was ripped through, my face swollen. Through my puffy eyes I could see my husband running towards me, and I couldn't stop the fresh flow of tears.

What amazes me now is how coolly those present in the offices of the BBC reacted to the emergency. Perhaps they were too scared of a law suit to get involved. So they tried to underplay the accident and get rid of us as fast as possible. A cab was hastily summoned and we were told to go to the nearest hospital, after a makeshift bandage was clumsily tied on. The producer kept repeating she was sorry. But I figure she was more nervous than sorry. Nervous that we'd get tough and ask for compensation. Why were the lights so low in a public area? Why had the escalator been switched off? Why was there no emergency procedure, no doctor or nurse on the premises, not even para-medical staff? How were interviewees expected to negotiate their way in the dark?

I still believe the BBC was liable. But I had neither the energy nor the will to pursue the matter, even though several

English friends advised us to. The accident could so easily have cost me my life. What if my skull had been fractured during the fall? What if I hadn't managed to break the speed at which my body was hurtling down? The whole nightmare could have been far, far more serious. And who would have been responsible? Not the BBC? Not the producer?

An American in my position would have called a lawyer within minutes. Yes, even in that dazed state. Not a doctor. A lawyer. Claimed damages and won them too. My only concern was getting back home to the children. I didn't want to spend an extra minute in England after that. I have been back since. Sensibly, I have forced myself to get over my escalator phobia.

When we returned to Mumbai, *Society* carried a story about my near-fatal accident. I was awfully touched by the response. Complete strangers from all over India wrote to express their sympathy. One card in particular amused and flattered me. It said simply, 'There are thousands of escalators in the world. But only one Shobha Dé.' It could only have come from an award-winning copywriter—Freddy Birdy.

The next time we went abroad, I told myself I wouldn't over-react at the sight of those steel caterpillars climbing up and down shopping malls. Yet, I couldn't control my overwrought response when I caught sight of my two younger children chasing each other on an escalator in a San Fransisco toy store. At that moment, all I could see was the sight of one of them missing a step, getting an errant lace caught in those claws and hurtling down the way I had with nobody to hold on to, and me watching helplessly from a distance.

I rushed after Arundhati and Anandita blindly, insane with anxiety, uncaring how the sight of a deranged Indian woman chasing two small children must have appeared to others in that crowded store. I was screaming like a harridan as I commanded them to freeze, stop their foolish game and wait for me. Once I caught up with the two, I smacked the older one square across her face. Bystanders stared at me aghast and in complete horror. I was sure someone would summon the cops and I'd be hauled in for child abuse. I didn't care. I didn't care. My heart had resumed beating. It was thudding against my rib-cage. My children were safe. They hadn't hurt themselves. They hadn't fallen. They hadn't gone through what I had. That's all that mattered.

As my stung daughter hung her head in shame (not for what she'd done, but the humiliation of having been smacked in public), I continued screaming. I reminded them of my accident and how I could have died. I told them how dangerous their game was. I shook the little one a few times and hollered, 'How many times have I told you not to run on escalators? Not to play games when you are riding on them? Why don't you listen to me?' I was in tears. They were in tears. My husband, I think, was in hiding behind the store's largest teddy bear, too ashamed to own up that he was a member of this tear-streaked, hysterical group. I didn't care. I noticed the strange looks we were getting. The stares. The whispered comments. I marched my kids out of the store. No Dalmatians. No Pocahontas. We were going straight back to the hotel, I barked.

A group of cops, menacing, big-bellied and pig-like, was standing at the corner. My daughter's head had reached her knees by now. She wouldn't stop crying. I was feeling wretched. I had lost control totally. I'd behaved abominably. I was a lousy, crazy mother. Oh god, it was horrible. We walked miserably past the Hard Rock Café. We wouldn't be going there today, that was for sure. No ice-cream treats either.

It took me hours to wind down. My mind kept replaying

the scene. Two happy little girls taking the escalator two steps at a time, their eyes shining with mischief, their minds on the next prank, oblivious, completely oblivious to the danger. One wrong step . . . and . . . and . . . No. I had to stop that. I was going nuts. I sat them down on a bench across a busy park. A street car trundled noisily past us. I hugged them both. I squeezed them and kissed them. They exchanged glances. Mother has lost it again, the look said. Yes, Mother had temporarily lost it. But as I wept some more, this time with relief, I felt I'd freed myself of the horror. It was a clear, beautiful afternoon. The best time to celebrate life . . . childhood . . . innocence. This moment wouldn't come again. I held my daughters' hands and we ran through the park looking for an ice-cream stand. The Dalmatians would follow. So would Pocahontas. They were alive. I was alive. That's all that mattered.

*

So what do I feel about the writing game now that I have some perspective on the whole business? For starters, I believe it is part of my responsibility as a writer to create as much awareness as possible when a new title is published. The criticism that follows comes with the territory and it doesn't affect me in quite the same way. Let's say I expect it and prepare myself psychologically to deal with the assault when it appears. I think even the critics are getting a bit tired of flogging the same old lines. Nothing has really changed—it's still a similar refrain. But the venom has diminished. Another generation of bright young writers has appeared on the scene. Critics have found new targets and new subjects to write about. It is a relief. I have moved on and so have they. There is no official truce—not yet—but an uneasy détente.

Meanwhile, an omnibus has appeared, other titles, several 'erudite' papers on the books. I receive weekly letters from universities in various parts of India. The head of an English department seeks co-operation for the thesis he's working on. The subject? 'Woman as portrayed in the novels of Shobha Dé'. Translators phone to seek rights. The president of the Royal Shakespeare Society of India wants to conduct an all-India seminar on my work. It's a good feeling.

I continue to write at the same manic pace employed for *Socialite Evenings*. I wouldn't know how else to do it. And I'm not sure I'd write any differently were I to slow down or change the technique. This is my natural rhythm. This is all I know. It's best I stick with it and take my chances.

I cannot predict which direction the writing is going to take . . . I'll go meekly down any path it points toward. I strongly believe in the power of intuition and have always followed my instincts even when they seemed absurd. I'm not even sure I'll continue writing. This much I know—I'll stop the day it ceases to excite me. There are a few promises I'd like to keep, mainly to my children. The younger ones want teenage romance stories. And I've discovered I enjoy making them up to amuse Arundhati and Anandita. This year, Arundhati turns thirteen. I wish I could give her the one birthday present unavailable in any shop—a specially bound volume of teeny-bop tales, some old, some familiar, some new. There are a few months left. Maybe I'll still do it.

Anandita wants a kiddy-book with lots of colourful pictures, crammed with imaginary creatures. She deserves that too. I look at her drawings which are unlike any I've seen. Her face is a study of deep concentration. When I ask her to tell me what she's drawn, she always has a vivid story to narrate and I begin to see the quantum leap her quiet mind has taken and marvel at the innocent complexity of a child's world—the one I left behind far too long ago and no longer have access to. I can never hope to improve on her fables, but I'd like to try, if only to test my own story-telling skills . . . and maybe impress her a little, before she too moves on and away into the inescapable trap of adulthood.

Strange, when I look back over my writing years—all twenty-eight of them—I can't quite believe so much time has passed and so many words. I continue to suspect myself ('what am I doing here?'), continue to think of it as a half-way halt (to where?), continue to believe this is a transitory phase before I move on to my real vocation, whatever that may be. There are writers who 'know' they are writers. That's all they are, that's all they want to be. I have never really 'known'. I have not 'chosen'. Writing has happened to me. Like so many other, very important, wonderful, unexpected things in my life. Certainly, I have enjoyed the experience. Tremendously so. I cannot think of another that even compares. But then again, I have not been acquainted with anything else quite as intimately. If writing has happened by default, I'm not complaining. Something far worse could have befallen me.

But now, with the wisdom that hindsight often provides, if I were to come up with an alternative, maybe it would be a career in hotels. I find hoteliering very exciting, very challenging. When Camelia Panjabi, the legendary lady of hoteliering in India, once told me that she actually 'saw' future properties developing in her dreams, down to the last detail, I believed her. Great hotels require that special vision, and she obviously has it. For me, monotony is death. And writing has kept me alive and tuned in. I'm sure a career in hotels would have provided a similar stimulus. I can sit in a lobby for hours, just watching people checking in, checking out, wandering around. I can fantasize about their lives, their reasons for being in that particular destination, what they'd probably do in the privacy of their impersonal hotel rooms. What they'd eat, how they'd shower, where they'd go next.

I love residing in hotels myself. I don't find the experience claustrophobic or boring. I don't miss the space or comfort of home either. So long as the bathrooms are clean, there's room service and a TV set, I have no complaints. I'm happy to flop on a springy bed, remote control in hand, a sandwich on the side-table, some chocolates close by, and zap channels to my heart's content. It's very rare that I'm by myself in a strange room, but on the few occasions that I've travelled without a family member, I've revelled in the complete sense of aloneness and privacy a hotel room provides. No phone calls. No intrusions. A sense of calm. A sense of my own space, never mind that it's hired.

Most women are rarely by themselves—entirely by themselves, that is. They forget what it feels like. Some panic when they're forced into a situation that isolates them. Others cherish the luxury. When I think of it, the only time during the past twenty-two years that I've been left alone has been at the hospital after my deliveries. I was never in a rush to pick up the babies and get home. I wanted to enjoy the long hours of absolute solitude between feeds and visitors, and make the most of uninterrupted reading time. Luxuriate in the unforced rest, be guilt-free about remaining in bed with large, fluffy pillows propping me up, with hot meals on heavy trays being served on the dot. Even being sponged or bathed by soft-spoken nurses with names like 'Sunny' or 'Shiny'.

I'd stay a week when most others took four days. I'd tell myself I'd earned it. One glorious week of being pampered before the reality of sleepless nights and soiled diapers set in. One precious week without someone (generally children) knocking on the bathroom or bedroom door and demanding plaintively, 'May I come in? How much longer? Finished?

Open the door . . . please . . . just open the door.'

Writing is another way of gaining solitude. It's just you and the paper. No intruders. No third person. People think of it as a lonely experience. I suppose it is that. But I like that kind of loneliness. It doesn't depress me. When I'm absorbed in my work, nothing else matters, even if I am physically dealing with several domestic chores simultaneously. In my mind, I shut the door firmly and no one is allowed in till I'm ready to receive visitors.

Often, real-life visitors do turn up when I'm in the midst of a crucial passage. No matter. I put my pen down calmly and look deeply interested. But I'm not really there. And people who know me well, like my husband, instantly recognize the glazed expression in my eyes and stay away. Phone calls, vendors, children's demands, other commitments—no problem. No sweat. I handle them with a tight, controlled smile. The writing process continues in my head, regardless. It's only a question of putting it down on paper at the first opportunity.

Maybe I've trained myself to do this. Maybe I'd have written very differently had my life been simpler. Maybe I wouldn't have written at all. Who knows? The point is, this is it. This is how the ground lies. I have to deal with this, and not something that doesn't exist for me. This is my reality. I have chosen it. I don't particularly want anything to change. Yes, there are times when I yearn for more undisturbed hours, but even that wistfulness is sweet rather than bitter.

There may be more books still waiting to get out. I don't really know or care. Perhaps I'm finally growing up, even if the childish, petulant, self-indulgent self does surface sometimes. Its appearance is less frequent now, and I perversely mourn its demise. One side of me continues to be the defiant schoolgirl who rang the fire alarm and risked being rusticated. So what? Life would be dull without these irrational urges. When critics continue to ask whether I write to provoke, the honest answer is, 'Maybe'. But it's not just that. When I wrote *Sisters* or *Strange Obsession*, I was testing the limits, but not consciously so. These were unabashedly commercial books. What are often labelled sex-and-shopping novels crammed with exotic labels and frantic, fevered couplings. Popular fiction at its most brazen. I knew that when I decided to write them. It's possible I was saying 'Check this out', and waiting for the howls of outrage I knew would follow. Childish? Definitely. I've recognized it for what it was, the equivalent of a kid sticking his or her tongue out at the class teacher and awaiting the reaction. This juvenile game turned out to be a very time-consuming and expensive one, but there's nothing that can't be undone or fixed if there's a genuine will to do so. I had my fun, my little thrills, and I moved on. It's the critics who refuse to.

*

I went to a self-consciously 'literary' soirée earlier this year. A middle-aged single woman had written a deeply personal book that dealt with her sexuality. Written in explicit terms, the book handled the subject in a searingly frank manner. Inevitably, the writer was asked the one question all women writers face: 'How much of the book is about your life, and how much is fiction?' She told me it was a question that revolted her. I nodded in a knowing way ('Been there. Heard that.') and suppressed a smile. But no one called her a pornographer. And no one will. Her carefully staged 'event' was not the target of jibes and the word 'hype' was not used even though a glamorous film star had been roped in and several 'names' invited to jazz up the occasion. Despite the lack of these demoralizing factors, the writer was unhappy with the reception she had been accorded and feared what lay ahead.

I sat with the tormented first-time novelist and held her hand. I had nothing against her or her book. I've always maintained I don't believe in taboos. She'd written a sensitive account of her fears . . . but the subject was the same—female sexuality. I assured her she'd get a sympathetic, positive press even if not a single reviewer actually read her book. The lady was shy but she had the right connections in the media. She'd sail through brilliantly . . . as she deserved to.

It was fairly late in the night when the literary soirée ended. My husband and I drove silently past the beautiful bay shrouded in late winter mist. I wasn't feeling cynical—far from it. Nor was I resentful. I had done what I'd wanted to on my own terms, and the critics had responded on theirs. Neither side could afford to point accusing fingers or talk churlishly about the fairness or unfairness of anything. A writer is a product of his or her immediate environment. Ten years ago, the ball game was different. India was just about waking up and discovering its place in the international context. Everything was new and a little alarming—including my books. Girls from 'good' families did not write risqué novels. Money was perceived as an evil, not an aphrodisiac, the big economic boom had still to happen. So had Harshad Mehta and the scam era. Urban society faked a sophistication it did not possess. Writers in English were still struggling to find that special 'voice' that only genuine confidence can provide.

In such an ethos, my books stuck out and so did I. It must have been the incongruity of it all that confused people. Had I been a streaker during my adolescence, or at least a card-holding member of the Sixties' counter culture, perhaps the books would have been viewed as some sort of dubious 'statements'. But here I was, and here the books were, without a ·convenient pigeon-hole to accommodate us. We'd shifted the goal-posts. Changed the parameters. Tch. Tch. How very inconsiderate and inconvenient.

Moving Images

After *Second Thoughts*, I decided to give myself a small break from fiction. I did begin another novel soon after, but my heart wasn't in it. I wrote fifty pages and realized it wasn't going anywhere. I could very easily have hammered out another three hundred—I had a strong story-line, but the effort wasn't worth it. Besides, I was enjoying writing *Swabhimaan*, the daily soap on Doordarshan.

As with writing and many other developments in my life, my introduction to script-writing also happened in the most unexpected fashion. I had known of and disliked Mahesh Bhatt for years. I found him a bit too brash, a bit too overwhelming. I had discovered to my utter astonishment that we were the same age. I should have guessed as much from his 'hippie' talk. But he looked and seemed older. I'd knocked him in print several times and generally stayed away, recoiling at his in-your-face attitude and sensational quotes ('I'm a leper who sells his wounds.'). I'd enjoyed two or three of his early films and wondered how a man this crass in person could come up with such sensitive subjects (adultery, old age, alienation, illegitimacy) and handle them so deftly. We'd met a few times and circled each other warily.

So it was with some surprise that I answered a call from Amit Khanna, Mahesh's partner and friend, and the head of Plus Channel. He asked me whether I'd be interested in writing a script for a television soap. I said I would. But I didn't have the slightest notion about script-writing. 'Nothing to it,' said Khanna. 'All you need is a strong story. Think about it. Mahesh and I will come over after a fortnight and we'll take it from there.' I said 'Fine'. And set about thinking.

I thought of several potential subjects. Nothing sounded right. They would have worked fine if I had pushed, but the concept wasn't making the right music in my head. The days were ticking by. Nothing to narrate. No flashes of inspiration. And then, one morning in my shower—it happened. The entire story-line appeared as if by magic on my mind's screen. That I'd met a fascinating, foxy lady in Bangalore the previous week was partly the explanation for the miracle. I saw her swimming in my imagination—and I had my central character. Once she got fixed, the story followed. I could see her so clearly—sexy, voluptuous, sharp, ruthless, a survivor. I rushed out of the shower, grabbed a laundry bag, the only sheet of blank paper I could spot, and wrote out the outline for what was to become *Swabhimaan*. My working title was 'The Mistress'. That's how I saw this woman, though she was respectably married to a renegade tycoon. I just knew we'd hit it.

When Amit and Mahesh came home for the meeting, all I needed to say was that one crucial word, 'Mistress'. Amit's response was guarded. 'What about her?' he asked. I explained shortly. 'Her life.' Mahesh jumped up. 'We've got it.' Amit seemed interested but hadn't yet bitten. I elaborated on the plot, fleshed out some of the supporting characters. At the end of fifteen minutes, Amit pulled out a cheque. 'We're in business,' he said. I looked at it and smiled. So my story narration had been nothing more than a pantomime? They'd come prepared to sign me on. Blind. Or else why the cheque? I should have been flattered. Instead, I was disheartened. It was the name they'd just bought. Like a so-called art lover booking a blank Husain canvas. What the hell. We were in showbiz. They knew how things worked far better than I did. If my name made good business sense to them, why was I cribbing? Here was an opportunity that had literally walked in through the door. It was entirely up to me what I chose to do with it. I was getting a crack at learning on the job—a new craft, a new discipline. Here were two people willing to pay for the experience. I'd be a fool not to make the most of it.

Amit got down to brass tacks once I'd accepted the cheque. 'We'll need a detailed outline, plus the break-up of the first twenty-five episodes, by the end of the month.' I said, 'Wait a minute. I really don't know how this thing works. How long is an episode? How many scenes make up one segment?' Amit smiled, 'You'll be able to do it. I can see you have the hang of it already.' This on the basis of a few stray scenes (the dramatic opening with the tycoon, Keshav Malhotra's funeral) and scraps of dialogue I'd written and read out to both of them.

Mahesh was far more effusive. 'You've got it. We've got it. This is going to be a hit.' Encouraged but terrified at what I was taking on, I smiled back nervously. I knew I was putting my foot into unexplored territory. This was going to be big. And different. Another ball game altogether. There was a lot of money riding on it, unlike in book publishing, where if a title flopped the publisher didn't have a fortune to lose. I didn't know the first thing about writing scripts. It was time to ask questions. To learn. I did just that.

I discovered quickly just how much went into a single telecast of twenty-three minutes. Each episode had to be carved up into seven or eight fast-paced scenes. Each scene needed to end on a zinger. And each line of dialogue had to emerge crisp and punchy. Those were the basics. Someone said, 'Think of it as an enormous shawl you have to embroider. Remember all the stitches that have gone into it and then pick them up later, when you need to embellish the pattern.' Dealing with such a large cast of characters, this was an important piece of advice especially when I forgot we'd introduced someone in an earlier episode and left him or her dangling with nowhere to go. By the time I finished the first twenty-five episodes I was mentally and physically exhausted. The length of each episode ran into twenty or more pages. I began maintaining a rough word-count. This was insane. I'd end up writing *Gone with the Wind* several times over by the time we were through with the serial. Exciting as the process was, I was feeling burnt out and needed a break.

The phone calls from the unit would come late into the night. 'Is the next one ready?' I'd wake up in a cold sweat feeling guilty about a missed deadline. I was writing till my fingers nearly fell off. I called Amit. He used the soothing words and calm manner of a doctor giving a pep talk. Amit's bedside manner, I discovered, was impeccable. We worked out another, more reasonable system whereby I'd work with a co-writer who would flesh out the outlines I provided—and we've been adhering to it since.

The thing that happened with *Swabhimaan* was that I discovered a new audience and the new audience discovered me. Since the serial was one of the earliest Indian soaps on the national channel, the potential audience for it was enormous—and eager for something new. When we started telecasting, all of us were worried about the theme. This was no goody-goody soap featuring wonderful, well-mannered, virtuous folks. *Swabhimaan* revolved around a beautiful woman named Svetlana (of all names). 'The Mistress'. And she was no sweet little thing. A fiery divorcee with one legitimate son and two other children fathered by her mentor-lover, Keshav Malhotra, Svetlana was out there at the barricades, fighting for the rights of her two bastard children and taking on a powerful family (the other Malhotras) in the bargain.

How would middle India regard her? If she was seen as a witch, a vamp, the serial would collapse. Chances were she'd be damned for being 'immoral' ('*Hai Ram. Kitni buri aurat hai*'). And we'd be asked to take the serial off the air. Nothing of the sort happened. Soon letters started pouring in from all over India—and viewers declared their unqualified love for Kitu Gidwani's Svetlana. Phew. That was a close call.

The reaction surprised us all, especially when the same viewers expressed their rage too. Their target? Keshav Malhotra's widow, played by Anju Mahendroo.

For me, a new window had opened up thanks to the serial. And I realized that whenever I stepped out of my comfortable, complacent cocoon of urban living and into the great unknown. Just about any destination in India was linked by Doordarshan. Those unfamiliar with my name as a novelist or columnist would come up and start discussing the story-line of *Swabhimaan* with a level of involvement I found puzzling. Others would suggest changes or comment on the behaviour of the characters, as they might have about the conduct of their own family members. 'Really, madam, Rishabh should not have behaved so irresponsibly. Didn't he realize how badly he had hurt Medha?' or 'That man Mahen—he is not at all good to his wife. No wonder she is misbehaving.' My initial reaction was to laugh and say lightly, 'It's only a television programme.' I soon understood it was far more than that for the viewers. And they were innocently and completely immersed in the lives of our characters. I had no right to bring them back to earth and reality. I stopped joking about *Swabhimaan* and listened very attentively whenever I was accosted by an enthusiastic fan of the serial. I learnt much along the way.

Mahesh Bhatt, I also discovered, was not the superficial loudmouth I'd dismissed him for. Behind that abrasive, almost uncouth, façade was quite a character—an intense, passionate, unconventional man who revelled in breaking rules. This obviously gave him a schoolboyish kick, and I soon came to understand his rough mannerisms and devil-may-care charm. It's easy to pass judgement on a man like Mahesh. But it's equally easy to be entirely disarmed by his apparent boorishness. Mahesh has energy levels that are positively scary . . . he just keeps going . . . and going, pushing his mind and body to the very limits, but I guess he doesn't know any other way of living . . . and would be miserable slowing down. It can get on anybody's nerves. And does. It's tiring being around this seemingly tireless fellow, fuelled by nothing more than a gargantuan appetite for life.

I began looking forward to our meetings, when the *Swabhimaan* team would show up at 11 a.m. and we'd settle down for a script discussion. Mahesh, like a little boy with a new toy, would hang onto his cellular phone, displaying great excitement at each ring. And he'd be watching keenly. Once when my frisky boxer (he was a pup then) refused to leave us alone and seemed hell-bent on sharing the chocolate doughnuts on the table, I got up and chased him around the living room. Mahesh found the scene most amusing. 'For once, Shobha Dé is looking flustered. Good, very good,' he said with undisguised glee.

It was my turn to catch him off-guard a month later. We'd just returned with sandesh from Calcutta. I decided to serve it along with the tea. Mahesh had a couple of bites and then asked innocently, 'Where did you get these laddoos from? They're great.' Everybody laughed as I explained they weren't 'laddoos' and that my husband would be aghast to hear sandesh thus described. 'Anyway . . . whatever it is, laddoo or sandesh, let's have some more.' It became a standing joke—each time we met at our place, Mahesh would ask impishly, 'Any more laddoos?'

Three years went by, with *Swabhimaan* holding its own. All of us got pretty good at playing God. Vinod, the person I co-wrote the serial with; Anand, the dialogue writer; others from the unit—we felt awesome as we decided on the fate of our characters. 'Send him to Toronto.' 'Kill him off.' 'Divorce.' 'Death.' 'Illness.' 'Accident.' 'Memory loss.' 'Heart attack.' 'Suicide.' We could do what we wanted with these people and did we feel great! Someone throwing tantrums on the sets? Banish the person. Someone else with a hard-to-take attitude? Knock out the character for the next three months. Weight gain? Drop her or him. Lack of co-operation? Cut the role. It was a good learning experience. Today, I feel confident about tackling another script. The thought doesn't daunt me. It's a craft that has to be mastered the hard way—and mistakes are horribly expensive. Ratings determine everything, and one can't afford to let them slip. Unlike a book, the reaction is immediate.

At one time *Swabhimaan* was being dubbed in Bengali and Tamil. Travelling to Calcutta or Madras meant long discussions with fans of the serial, often in a language I wasn't entirely familiar with. 'But you've written the story,' they'd point out. 'Yes. In English,' I'd be tempted to say. But it was wiser to keep quiet and leave them to their illusions. The response overwhelmed me. Most of these people knew of me only in the context of *Swabhimaan*. They had no idea I wrote columns or books, or even that I had a life outside the serial. In Kolhapur, at a prestigious awards ceremony, the compère emphasized my *Swabhimaan* connection several times over for the benefit of the large audience, shrewdly figuring that few of those present read English in any form. After the function, I was gheraoed by several women telling me that they didn't miss a single episode.

It happened again when I went to visit the public wards of the Tata Memorial Cancer Hospital in Mumbai. A middle-aged man undergoing chemotherapy tried feebly to greet me with folded hands when I was introduced to him. His wife rose from her chair, eyes shining when she heard the magic word *Swabhimaan*. 'One of our biggest regrets in this ward is that there's no television here and we have to miss our favourite programme.'

I couldn't believe I was hearing this under the circumstances. Here I was, shaken by the sight of so many people in that daunting situation, battling for their lives, some of them unaware of the grim reality of their diagnosis. That two people could forget the tragedy that had struck them even for those brief five minutes, and discuss an escapist soap with such involvement and enthusiasm, struck me as being bizarre, practically surrealistic. Maybe that was *Swabhimaan's* function after all—to lull the audience, five afternoons a week, into believing there was such a world out there, where tempestuous love affairs took place against exotic backdrops, and beautiful women were so empowered they didn't need anything more than sharp dialogue and false eyelashes to take them soaring to the top.

Other requests to script for television followed. So far I haven't bitten. Either the money was too low or the set-up seemed shabby. By now, I had established such a positive rapport with Mahesh and Amit, I really couldn't see myself dealing with run-of-the-mill entertainment-world types. Meetings at home were another inhibiting factor. I felt uncomfortable allowing all kinds of strangers from this business to walk in with dubious proposals. *Swabhimaan* had taught me several lessons. For one, it is crucial to work months in advance and get pre-production details out of the way. Amit had decided to stay ninety days ahead of the schedule before a single shot was canned—and this was the discipline the unit maintained. For a soap to make financial sense, it's important to stay on top of it and shoot an episode a day. Easier said than done, as anybody who has had any experience of the medium in India will tell you.

The lack of planning is notorious. What's even worse is the absence of commitment or professionalism. Even though the scope for star tantrums is limited in the TV business, there can be one or two troublemakers in a unit who slow things down for the others. Disciplinary action rarely helps unless the producer means business—which is to throw the star out, no matter what the consequences. It works, as I found out during *Swabhimaan*. And that's where the three-month leeway really helped. Nobody could threaten to quit in the hope and expectation that the serial would collapse overnight. We had three long months before telecast to work things out, get a fresh character or fix the story-line so that the non-co-operative actor's abrupt exit wouldn't create continuity problems.

I rarely met the unit people, other than the directors, dialogue writers, production staff and my co-writer. But I watched the serial faithfully, afternoon after afternoon, and to me the characters became far more real than those enacting them. I'm ready to confess shamefacedly that I didn't even know their off-screen names. This led to several embarrassing situations. Once I received a call from a fine actor in a secondary role. The voice said, 'Good morning, madam. I'm Masood Akhtar.' I paused before saying, 'Who?' The man was witty enough to say, '*Ji, main Shankar aapka driver bol raha hoon—Swabhimaan ka driver.*' We both laughed heartily as I apologized for my ignorance.

The only time I made it to the sets in distant Film City, I was accompanied by a Japanese film crew. They were in Mumbai to make a half-hour documentary on my life and the director seemed fascinated by the subject of the serial. It was decided we'd go and cover an actual shoot. When I walked onto the sets, every single thing seemed so familiar to me—I could recognize the smallest detail: the cheap paintings on the cardboard walls, the bookshelf with plastic curios, the artificial flowers in an ugly vase—I felt entirely at home. Watching Rohit Roy, Anju Mahendroo and Chenna Ruparel go through a particularly emotional scene involving chunks of dramatic dialogue was an experience in itself. None of them muffed a single line. That was discipline and dedication on display. Unlike the spoilt brats of the film industry, here were seasoned actors turning up five days a week, eight hours a day, and working in perfect sync. It made me feel very proud to see their level of commitment under conditions that were far from comfortable. I couldn't have done it.

*

I find my own modest ambitions shrinking as I move on. What do I dream of 'achieving' these days? Small things really. I keep putting off my big project—to take driving lessons, get behind the wheel of a car and zoom off into a glorious sunset. It's been an unachievable dream ever since I first took a shot at it at fourteen. At that time, I thought my reflexes were awful because I was far too young to be experimenting on a borrowed car. It was guilt combined with nervousness that became my alibi (I backed a friend's car into a stone wall at 60 kmph and totalled it). I wonder how he explained it to his father (it was a company car). Over the years, I made several attempts. Each one was a disaster. I put it down to a lack of aptitude. It was when the children started to mock me ('Mother, everybody in the world knows how to drive but you.') that I decided to make it my special project. Alas, that's where it still remains.

Not knowing a basic skill like driving in today's times seems shameful—as my children constantly remind me. I know I'll end up stepping on the accelerator when my foot ought to be pressing down firmly on the brake. This is depressing. I so long to be able to pick up the car keys, twirl them around confidently, saunter down to the parking lot, get behind the wheel, reverse smoothly and shoot off in style. Each time a woman driver passes me, I trail her car with my eyes—but for my lack of mechanical co-ordination, there go I, I sigh. Mastering motoring is not likely to happen now. I've given up. But not my kids. They point to various driving schools in the neighbourhood. 'We won't laugh,' they say. But I know they will. The younger ones in particular fantasize frequently. 'Our friends' mothers drop them to school . . . why don't you take driving lessons during the summer holidays? Imagine—the first day of the new term and Mama driving the car.' It would be easier to oblige if they asked me to take a crash course in deep-sea diving—despite my water phobia and the fact that even when I swam during my school-days I wasn't a very good swimmer.

It's like the tango lessons I keep threatening to take. Easiest thing in the world actually. An old friend from my modelling days conducts classes in the complex where I reside. My daughter Arundhati considers herself an expert after three years of regular lessons. I tell myself, 'Next month, go for it, Dé. Enrol. It's only Salomé. And it will be such fun.' It hasn't happened yet, but I haven't given up. Indeed, the power of this particular rhythm over me is something else altogether. I don't know when or where it took me over, but I only have to hear the first few bars of a tango—any tango—for me to go weak in the knees. I can (and do) watch *Scent of a Woman* and *Valentino* over and over again only for the tango sequences. Once, when my husband and I were in London for just two days, I found out that *Tango Argentino* was playing for a limited run at the West End. We called the theatre—naturally all performances were sold out. Undeterred, we sought the help of our resourceful concièrge. The scalper's rates were obscenely high. Never mind, I argued. I'll go without fancy meals for the next few days. We made it to the show and I sat through those two-and-a-half hours completely spellbound.

If it's the tango, it has to be Argentina. Travelling to distant, unknown, exciting destinations continues to be a heady experience. I take a childlike joy in the anticipation. I must be amongst the very few frequent travellers who actually enjoy airports and the sight of those big beautiful birds on the tarmac. There are so many places still to discover. But the one that tickles my fantasies the most is Buenos Aires. I'd also love to dip my feet in the mighty Brahmaputra someday. Note, I didn't say I'd like to take a dip in the legendary river. That's because of my latent fear of water. I have yet to overcome it and I doubt if I ever will. But I continue to dream wistfully about a day when I shall be able to dive into the deep and mermaid my way through the pool—back and forth, back and forth, twenty, thirty, forty lengths, using a powerful stroke, with my children watching from the sidelines and gasping, 'Wow! Look at that. Mom can swim.' I don't even enjoy soaking in a tub, straining to keep my neck above the waterline. Perhaps that's why I didn't like the *Titanic* all that much. I couldn't see beyond the rising water, with my own deep-seated fears of drowning triggered off by those terrifying images. Someday I'll take the plunge. Someday.

.Just as someday I shall overcome my suspicion of all electronic gizmos and become computer literate. Since I can't type and have always written in longhand, this will be a real leap into the modern world. Till such time, my stiff, overworked fingers, rigid with calluses where I grip the pen, will have to do. See what I mean about shrinking ambitions?

There is one, though, that I share with my husband. We both dream about a time when we'll be free of major responsibilities, free to drop out, climb off the tread mill, leave the lives we've known behind, and become earnest, avid students again. We talk about it all the time. In his case, there is grim determination. In mine, just longing.

We discuss the courses we could take, the joys of campus life we'd experience, the going back to our curtailed academic lives. I know it's an experience we'd cherish. I get the feeling this is a project that will happen, more because he'll make it possible and I'll happily go along. Strolling through Oxford a few years ago, both of us had small knots in our hearts—I call them missed opportunities, he prefers 'future projects'. I'm willing to compromise. I'd love to teach . . . anything to be on campus once more.

I don't long for anything grand. I don't covet possessions—someone's diamonds, another's villa. I love the good and beautiful things of life without actually craving for anything. It makes me feel free and light. No mountain peaks to conquer. Nothing to prove. As for writing—it will always be there, in one form or another. Like a comfortable quilt to draw around myself when there's a chill in the air. I used to think I'd be paralysed without a pen to wield. Not so. There is life after and beyond writing. A life filled with music, laughter and great food. I've experienced it. I know.

Getting Personal

One of my all-time favourite fantasies involves duplicating the life of a friend called Sunita. Years ago, when I used to visit her in Delhi, I'd envy her uncomplicated, stress-free lifestyle. There she'd be, seated in her garden, enjoying Delhi's mild winter sunshine, sipping tea, crocheting or knitting, her hands busy, her eyes sparkling after a long, relaxed sleep. What were her main concerns for the day? Let's see . . . Whether or not the masseuse would show up on time, whether her regular hairdresser would be at the salon to trim her hair, whether the tailor would deliver the saree blouse she was looking forward to wearing that night, whether her cook had remembered to thaw the meat, whether the maid had stocked enough apples to make jam out of, whether the driver had remembered to mail her letters and fetch avocados for the dip she was planning to whip up for cocktail hour.

I'd watch her chatting relaxedly with friends, knitting pullovers for her children, hanging up new curtains in the master bedroom, colour-coordinating her bangle-rack, and I'd vow to myself: someday you too shall enjoy the same degree of leisure. Have nothing more significant on your mind than a nephew's wedding. You too will have a kitchen garden to spend long hours in. You too will peel oranges under a winter sun and keep a cow in the backyard.

None of this ever happened. Today, we have a farmhouse

and a garden, but very little time to enjoy either. I fear I have joined the ranks of die-hard workaholics. I need the pressure deadlines provide. I experience guilt when time gets 'wasted'. And I positively suffer when I'm forced to give up my writing schedules for something I consider a waste of time. When I am 'at it', I don't need anyone or anything. A writer never stops writing. Indeed, my definition of a writer is simply a person who writes. Regularly. Ideally, every single day. That's all it takes to make you one. Call yourself one. When youngsters come up to me to say, 'Ma'am, I want to become a writer', I always ask, 'So . . . what's stopping you? You want to write? Great. Go ahead and write.' It requires no 'investment'. No capital. It's cheap. It's as easy, as painless as you want it to be. You can do it anywhere. Anytime.

I rarely allow anything to disrupt my schedule. Especially when I'm 'heavy with book'. I really do not possess a convincing answer for my father when he asks with ill-disguised exasperation, 'When will you stop writing and make some time for other things?' I don't know. I'm not sure I even want to. Anything or anybody who cuts into this precious priority gets to sample my impatience. Not a pleasant trait, I know, and annoying too. Even to myself.

Since both my sisters live overseas, it's hard for us to co-ordinate time differences, work through time zones and arrive at a mutually comfortable hour for a sisterly chat. It happens all too often that they call when I'm in the middle of an article or busy with an interview. Sensing the edge in my voice they keep it short, and disconnect. Neither of us feels good with an unsatisfactory call like that. Complaints are routed through our father and there's never any doubt as to whose side he's on. One day, after a particularly abrupt conversation, he asked me why I wrote as much as I did. Was it just for the money? I answered thoughtfully (and truthfully) that money was certainly one of the incentives but not the main one. There wasn't enough of it in this profession. Then he enquired, rather delicately, how much I earned in a month and helpfully provided a figure which was embarrassingly low. I could have nodded in a non-committal way and left it there, but I decided to tell him by providing a ballpark figure.

He was quiet for a while before saying, 'You are earning enough . . . but why doesn't it show in your lifestyle?'

I asked him where I was failing according to him. What signs and symbols was he looking for? How was I supposed to live in a way that would reflect my income (not high by today's standards at all, but high enough for a former government officer to feel impressed by)?

He suggested I should buy a brand-new car—one of the fancier new models. I pointed out that I rarely used even the cars we already possess since I didn't go out all that much.

'But if you had a car waiting for you downstairs round-the-clock, you'd find places to go to . . . there are so many exhibitions in the city,' he insisted. I protested mildly that even with ten cars standing by, I wouldn't be able to make time for exhibitions.

'You don't live lavishly, you don't throw weekly dinner parties or wear grand clothes. What's the point of working hard, earning well and not showing it?'

I was a little surprised by his observations. I thought I lived well enough. And it was perfectly true that I didn't have the time to stage extravagant dinner parties on a weekly basis or go traipsing around town from one gallery to the next. As for not dressing grandly, that's just the way I prefer to look. Had I earned five times as much I now do, I doubt that would have changed. I can't see myself sitting around the dining table with my manuscripts, cheap pens and even cheaper pads, weighed down by diamonds and pearls, clad in priceless, off-the-master-weaver's-loom sarees. I am and shall remain a working woman, at heart and in practice. This must disappoint my father, who has a far more aristocratic vision of life. In his view, I should be spending my days like Sunita—only more luxuriously. And I should appear unambiguously wealthy.

It's a view Sunita endorses as well. I remember her telling me a few years ago, 'At our age we should only be seen in really, really expensive clothes and jewellery. Our accessories should be exclusive and hand-picked, our watches the best, our shoes custom-made. We've earned all these goodies. We deserve them.' I was very amused by her observation and told her so, while she adjusted the strap of her diamond-studded gold Rolex, touched the solitaires in her ear-lobes for comfort and gazed fondly at her diamond-encrusted bangles—her 'everyday' wear, as she put it.

I cannot be my father's version of 'rich', a bejewelled pampered *grande dame* sliding diamond rings up and down her hard-worked fingers. I can see the disappointment and disapproval in his eyes each time I visit him in jeans. He would like me to pull out all the stops, deck up and impress his neighbours with my 'wealth'. Sometimes I feel like obliging him, indulging him, pleasing him. But I just end up feeling resentful and ridiculous on the rare occasions I do make the effort. How different my mother was in this respect.

My sister recounts an incident when Aie was lying in bed, very ill and very frail, waiting for my car to drive up and take her and my father a short distance. My father, looking out of the window, announced proudly, 'The Mercedes has arrived.' She mumbled under her breath, 'Yes. But why boast about borrowed feathers?' He didn't hear her, or pretended not to.

He's very particular about my TV appearances as well. He takes the trouble to record them and often plays an interview back for my benefit to point out where I had erred—not so much in what I'd said but in the manner in which I had dressed.

'Look at yourself, my dear. You should stop dieting and start eating. A woman should be well filled out. You should give the impression of being a prosperous person. You dress far too casually. Why do you insist on wearing silver and not gold jewellery? Your make-up is hopeless. You should not apply lipstick. It doesn't suit you.'

I nod my head miserably, specially if I haven't found that particular TV appearance all that awful.. I've stopped telling him I do not diet—never have, never will. I love food far too much to deprive myself. He points to many photographs of my pleasantly plump mother at the same age I am at present and says, 'Now . . . here is a true beauty. See her cheeks. They aren't sunken . . . she didn't diet. She ate well. She was happy and relaxed.'

Maybe he has hit it there. Happy and relaxed, that was it. Nobody is 'happy' in that sense any more. As for relaxation, I hardly know what the word means. If the stress shows, it shows. There's little I can do about it.

Sometimes it worries me that my family seems so overly concerned about appearances—my appearance, in particular. I have one daughter (Arundhati) whose scrutiny is hard to escape. So are her critical comments. Like my father she never tires of remarking on every aspect of my personality. Like him, she strongly objects to my indifference, particularly when she has her young friends over and they catch me in what she witheringly refers to as my 'home clothes'. God help me, too, if I turn up at school functions dressed down by her exacting (almost punishing) standards.

There are times when I resent this level of interest in my appearance and defiantly ignore all requests to change. On another level, I find it touching that my family should feel so protective. I don't mind being seen as a slob, especially on days when I'm slumming. Obviously my kids don't share that view. Often, they walk into an interview or a photo-shoot and are horrified to see me sitting there, my face devoid of make-up, my hair carelessly combed. Once or twice, my finicky daughter has been alarmed enough to rush to my dresser and rush back after grabbing a pair of earrings to slip to me quietly with hissed instructions: 'At least wear these for the photographs. Have you seen yourself in the mirror?' This is the same child who I'm certain will grow up to become a fastidious art director with an obsessive interest in getting the details right.

I was at a Channel 4 shoot a few years ago. The anchor was Nikki Bedi. We were at an overcrowded outdoor location in Mumbai. The light was rapidly fading and the crew was tired and restless. We were about to roll when my daughter, who was studying the TV monitor closely, came up to me and whispered, 'There isn't enough light on your face. The other lady is looking much better.'

By then I'd learnt never to take her observations lightly. I asked the cameraman to swing the monitor around so I could see it. Sure enough, the lighting balance was slightly off since it was designed for much paler skin—it did nothing for me, and I said so. The crew agreed, and we managed to fix it. I don't see her conduct as being precocious, rather it's the instinctive and very intense desire of an unusual child to ensure that her mother is seen in the best possible light—in this case, literally.

Exasperating as this can be occasionally, there have been countless times I've actually thanked God for my family's deep and genuine involvement in my life, even when it has led to small arguments and minor fights. I like the fact that they take me and what I do so completely for granted. For my part, I try and include them in all aspects of my world. Whenever I meet somebody new, a person who leaves an impact of any sort, I come home and share the experience with the family. Now that it has grown and my sisters live overseas it isn't as easy as it used to be, especially since there is just so much one can convey through letters—no matter how long or how newsy.

We are all enthusiastic letter-writers—or used to be, till ISD intruded. The temptation to dial and chat has to be actively fought. When Kunda calls (as she does every week) to swap notes, she tells me little stories about her life in Muscat, and everything is so vividly described, I can visualize it perfectly. The same for Mandakini and Ashok. My mother was particularly adept as a raconteur, with an astonishing memory for the smallest detail ('Did you notice Raju's hankie?').

Whenever we sisters and brother get together, the occasion turns riotous with each one imitating someone we've all known . . . or even strangers we've all seen. These little performances aren't really cruel, but they are so accurate that one can recreate any enacted scenario perfectly. This rather naughty talent runs in the extended family too—I can clearly remember my maternal aunts and cousins doing take-offs on unsuspecting family members and family friends, with exaggerated accents and mannerisms that would have us falling about with laughter. Perhaps to an outsider this might appear malicious and mean. It was never that.

Unfortunately, a pattern was established and it soon became impossible to narrate an incident without acting it out in the protagonists' own voices. It has become a reflex action to the extent that we find ourselves doing it even in the presence of newcomers to the family fold—strangers who look alarmed for the first couple of hours, unsure whether they're expected to join in and contribute, or suppress their laughter and pretend they haven't understood. We urge them to let their hair down—and they often do. The danger lies in the possibility that younger children will unwittingly expose the family's penchant for mimicry. It has happened a few times in the past with one of the kids innocently letting on that a certain individual was being taken apart by the rest, but mercifully nothing terribly damaging has transpired thus far, nothing that couldn't be salvaged.

These days, I miss not having my sisters in the same town. I miss not being able to share our experiences on a daily basis. It's a very reassuring feeling to be able to talk freely as adults, to trust and be trusted. To know there are other individuals besides your own immediate family who can be counted on at all times, individuals whose minds and integrity one respects, whose instincts one trusts, whose judgements are in sync with one's own. Even though we do communicate far more frequently than most scattered families, we experience a sense of frustration at the time lapse between the events and developments in our individual lives and the reactions to them.

Perhaps it's because I belonged to a large family that I decided to have more than one child myself. When I see my children today, I feel they'll value each other's presence far more in the future, even if they don't recognize that fully right now. I was never lonely as a child. And I've never been lonely as an adult. The family has always been there to lean on . . . talk to . . . laugh with . . . even cry with (though tears were never encouraged, not even when we were children). Out of habit and conditioning I scolded Arundhati recently when she was weepy. 'Do I ever cry?' I asked her indignantly. Quietly, the child said, 'Maybe you should. Everybody needs to cry.

I'd never stop you.'

*

I'm often asked about friendship. In an early television programme, I said, truthfully enough, that I didn't invest too much of myself in friendships—the emotional need was simply not there. My life was crowded with family and I preferred it that way. I don't trust people all that easily and good friendships are based on trust (even if it is often betrayed). The interviewer was determined to interpret that to suit her own opinion. The frank remark was presented as an admission of loneliness. It was anything but. I feel very contained and complete within the family fold. I no longer have the time to nurture new relationships, nor the desire to do so. I frequently meet people who fascinate me, interest me, but never enough to work on that initial feeling and allow it to blossom into a long-term relationship. I do not have the reserves or resources to cultivate new friends. Perhaps it is my loss, but I'm not so sure.

As I grow older and more cynical, I find myself increasing the distance, sticking only to those people who don't drain me physically or emotionally. I see women around me reeling from soured relationships, shell-shocked at the breakdown of friendships they've given to generously for twenty years and more. They're puzzled and angry that the other person has waltzed away indifferently, leaving them to cope with the loss on their own. I don't think I could deal with that level of hurt. It's hard enough staying on top of what already crowds my life—I don't need excess baggage.

It's not that I lead an isolated existence. I do make time for the few people I care about. But there is always a tiny barrier, an invisible rope that says 'this far and no further'. It is understood that nobody, but nobody, just 'drops in'—and that includes family. I wouldn't do that to them either. We are all connected by phone—all it takes is a short call. And yet, friends of my friends have a far more informal attitude in their relationships. They go over unannounced, stay the night if the hour is late, share clothes and confidences, holiday together and know one another's movements on a daily basis so closely, it scares me. The concept of privacy is absent in their closeness. I cannot understand that.

They find it strange that I prefer my little island with its deep moat. I see how easily they share their laughter, their tears and their bed with others and I wonder whether I'm far too finicky. Even when I'm visiting my sisters' homes, I wouldn't go lolling around on couches without first checking. Just as I wouldn't invade their bedrooms and bathrooms without seeking permission. It's the same in my father's house. I rarely sit on his bed when I visit, preferring a conveniently positioned chair instead.

It was the way we were raised, with a degree of formality and reserve even amongst members of the family. It's too late now to unlearn all of that, even if I have eased up (just a little) with my own children. I am so accustomed to this way of life, it always jolts a little when I see two generations on back-slapping, buddy-buddy terms.

Friends of mine—ladies I have known for twenty years—recently complained that their young daughters had been snubbing their attempts at closeness. One girl had 'accused' her mother of being less of a mom and more of a girlfriend. The mother was shattered by the harshness of the outburst. 'I thought we were like soulmates,' she cried as we sat at my dining table over a late lunch. I remembered all their jaunts and outings together, nights spent at various city discos and pubs, dancing with acquaintances who easily bridged the gender-divide. I also remembered the giggly, conspiratorial exchanges detailing party flirtations and clandestine phone calls, the common wardrobe and shared make-up, the frequent trips to the jeweller to buy pieces both could wear, late-night movies cuddled in a comfortable double bed with the man of the house reading in an adjoining room. They looked like they were onto a good thing—a great thing. Such bonding, such trust . . . and such fun.

What happened, I asked my friend, whose eyes were puffy with tears.

'She left last night—can you imagine? She wants to live on her own. She said such awful things to me—I can't believe it.'

I could. Believe it, I mean. I'd watched them a few times myself as they danced together at parties—a very attractive mother-daughter couple. Provocative too. Perhaps my friend was entirely unaware of the conflict that was brewing within the young girl who could not handle the kind of attention her mother was receiving from her peer group. From being her best friend, the mother had become a competitor. The younger woman cracked first. It could so easily have been my friend instead. Devastated by what she saw as her daughter's ingratitude, my friend closed the doors on her. They haven't talked for a few months now. If they don't make up soon, the rift could be permanent.

The other friend's daughter finds it traumatic to deal with her mother's many sexual adventures, some of which she has been a part of, if only as a helpless voyeur. Now, at a turning point in their troubled relationship, the daughter has shaved off her hair. Partially, it's to conform to the current fashion trend, but there is also an in-built rebellion in the act—and the young girl says as much.

'My mother used to keep nagging me to fix my hair . . .

411

my clothes . . . my make-up . . . my life. I got sick of it. One day I went and shaved my head. When I came home she screamed. I told her, "Now at least leave me alone when your friends come home. Don't show me off to them like a decorative object you've created . . . or worse . . . picked up somewhere."'

Since the head-shaving incident, the daughter has chosen to live on her own. She glumly accompanies her mother if she's compelled to, but her resentment is obvious. It hurts my friend terribly.

'What did I do to her? I thought we were closer than any two human beings could be. I thought we understood each other. Why does she behave like she hates me?'

Because she probably does—not forever, but during this awful transitional phase when she herself is dealing with her ambivalent feelings towards her mother and experiencing great guilt.

Raising daughters isn't easy—but it doesn't have to be this traumatic either. Women of my generation find it difficult to come to terms with ageing. There is a tremendous resistance to growing old, far more than what our mothers experienced. At fifty my mother had gracefully joined the ranks of senior citizens. She wasn't troubled by a few crow's feet here or a line there. She wasn't obsessive about her weight or silhouette either. She was happily fat and ready for grandmotherhood. My father loved her that way. We loved her that way, too. She seemed so comfortable, so 'motherly', so easy in her own skin. There was no pretence involved, no pressures to look a certain way, behave in a particular manner, be anything other than herself. Looking back, I envy her supreme confidence—she was so clear about her priorities and goals: family and home.

By the time she was fifty, her children had found their

feet and settled down, leaving her free to get on with her life at her own pace. It seemed such an uncomplicated life, and it showed on her face: the clear, frank gaze, the ready smile and a manner so completely natural, it was impossible to resist. The question of her 'competing' with any of her three daughters did not occur to either her or us. She accepted our differences just as we accepted her, which is why when I see women of my vintage desperately fighting to keep their toe-hold in the seduction stakes, I feel exceedingly sorry, especially if they happen to be women I'm fond of.

Like my friend whose daughter turned her back on her, there are countless others who innocently believe the only way to get the love of their kids is to act like one of them. Women confide delightedly about how they share bras and jeans with their growing daughters, how people mistake the two for sisters, how the daughters' boyfriends often call up for them, how much fun it is to knock back tequila shots at local pubs with the kids, or go to a nightclub with them when the dads are away. It is great fun, it can be relaxing, and it is one way of keeping up with the next generation. But it is also addictive and could have unintended consequences.

What had happened to both my friends was that they'd integrated so smoothly into the lifestyles of their children, they no longer identified with their own. Both mothers kept up with the aerobics classes, the hair-streaking sessions and the trendy clothes fixation, way after the daughters had outgrown the novelty of partying with their moms. They couldn't understand the changed status and refused to accept it. It didn't take much time for the young girls to move on and find their kicks elsewhere. That left two very devastated mothers trying hard to come to terms with a feeling of abandonment. The disco scene didn't seem as funky any more, not when the average age at the table was forty-plus, and the man asking them for a dance had thinning hair and a pot-belly. Where were the young, six-pack-gut admirers? Those impossibly fit college boys who knew all the groovy moves? It took a few candid talks for the mothers to realize the game was over—no matter that they'd successfully whittled their waists down to a size ten or that in the dimly-lit interiors of a swanky club, they often got mistaken for their daughters—especially when they'd raided the younger person's closet and worn a favourite sequined crop top to better display the 200-stomach-crunches-a-day belly—flatter than a hard-board, even after bearing those kids.

I fear for my generation of women—they really are like danglers, neither here nor there. They definitely don't want to be like their mothers (why not, I ask you?) and they desperately want to switch places with their daughters (what for, I ask you?). We talk of options, opportunities and choices—sure we have them. What do we actually do with these goodies? We earn, we travel, we splurge . . . and we weep. Has it been worth those extra tears our mothers never felt the need to shed? So, all right, they didn't get to swill champagne cocktails at snazzy international bars, or travel first-class to Budapest and present a paper on ecology there . . . but they didn't have permanent lines creasing their brows either. They slept soundly at night, they awoke feeling cheerful and fresh, they had time for themselves, time for their families, time to savour the small pleasures of life—do I sound like I'm filled with an unfulfilled longing to swap places with my mother?

No, I guess I just sound like I'm growing old. Over-romanticizing my mother's reality. Maybe she wasn't all that blissed out. Maybe she did resent not having had a more exciting, fulfilling existence. Maybe she got a vicarious thrill out of my adventures. Maybe she felt she'd missed out on a lot of stuff that happened to me. Oh . . . I don't know. We never really got around to articulating any of this. I didn't think of asking. And now it's too late.

*

As a young girl my secrets were shared only with my sister Kunda—there was nothing I wished to hide from her. Nothing I ever did. And she never snitched. Not even when her own neck was on the block on account of me (which was often enough). I needed to turn forty before I could speak freely to my father and behave like an adult, if not his equal. Even today, he thinks nothing of reprimanding me when he feels the need, sometimes right in front of my children, who, I suspect, love to see their mother being cut down to size. And yet, even now I never take 'undue liberties' (his words) with him. I rarely speak out of turn (that isn't his version), or voice my irritation / impatience / annoyance. My siblings, even less so. They tell me they're frequently shocked by my daring to question our father . . . or even joke with him. The shift has taken place more easily for me . . . but in their case, it's much too late.

When my sisters visit, my father makes it clear to these ladies (one in her late fifties, the other in her early sixties) that he will be calling the shots during their short stay. He monitors it all—everything from their diet to the time they get home from an outing.

'So long as you are staying under my roof, you are my responsibility . . . and answerable to me. This is my house, you must abide by my rules.'

He enforces them too, often phoning at midnight to check why they aren't back yet. If they mind, they hide their resentment and indulge him. I'd do the same in their place.

415

Whenever I go over, I behave and am treated like a naughty schoolgirl. I invariably come away feeling slightly guilty about some unnamed transgression I may have inadvertently committed. It's hard to shake off old guilt.

I never ever saw my own parents embracing. After I grew up, I wasn't hugged by either of them. Which is why I must have startled my father on his eightieth birthday when I kissed him on the cheek as the band in the restaurant we were in broke into a cheerful 'He's a jolly good fellow.' When I had kids of my own I vowed to be a more 'touchy-feely' parent and I'm glad I've broken though my own inhibitions. For years I couldn't get myself to utter those three magical words ('I love you') even in romantic relationships. Today, I can say them easily to my children and mean every word. I accept their love. And I'm training myself to deal with their outbursts of hostility too. Yes, they come, often without any warning. And I have to be ready when that happens. I am glad they feel free enough to express their feelings—positive and negative. We didn't have that choice. I think it's far healthier to say it out loud and confront it than bottle up resentment for decades.

It took Aditya and Avantika more than ten years to ask me why their father and I divorced. I had been anticipating the moment for years, preparing for it, dreading it. When it arrived I was taken off-guard (we were driving back from a visit to a doctor's rooms). I was conscious of the driver's presence, our outburst of sudden emotionalism, the rush-hour traffic. Even more conscious of the time we had spent tiptoeing carefully around the very subject that had altered our warm, secure world so irrevocably. Even though the divorce itself had been 'civilized' (as the glossies would say) and devoid of acrimony, in the minds of the children there was nothing 'civilized' about the separation and the pain. Aditya and Avantika were fortunate (strange word under the circumstances) to have been raised in a loving, cossetted, attentive environment by doting grandparents, and their father, Sudhir (who married a fine lady, Smita, a year or so after the divorce). It had turned out to be anything but the clichéd horror story riveting TV soaps are made of.

After the divorce and during the months preceding, I continued to be in touch with my in-laws on a daily basis with an on-going dialogue revolving around the children's activities. My former in-laws are wise, enlightened people who recognized the futility of fostering a negative attitude, especially in the minds of young children. I speak to my former mother-in-law and to Smita regularly, and am glad there is not only participation but a sense of deep involvement in the lives of those we jointly love—the children were spared the trauma of fights, arguments and recriminations. But it would be absurd to say they weren't puzzled or hurt at the time. My sole comfort was the knowledge that they were protected, cherished and adored in their paternal home. There was nothing I could give them at that stage in my life—besides the reassurance that I was only a phone call and a few miles away. Always, always accessible and unconditionally theirs. I had no money, no home and no idea of my future. I had asked for nothing—just freedom. It would have been selfish, even cruel, to draw Aditya and Avantika into my turbulent unsettled world. There was little I could have offered them at that point—not even my undivided attention. And yet I was so certain, so completely certain that we'd come out of it with our bonds intact, our love unquestioned. It would take time—years perhaps. But it would happen. And it did. The foundation was rock solid. They would know my reasons for the decision when they were ready to understand and accept them. It was the interim that would be crucial.

And I needed the whole-hearted support of my former

family to provide it. They did. I'm deeply grateful to them for that—and more. Not once was I bad-mouthed. Not a single harsh word was either said to me or spoken against me. As Indumatiben, my ex-mother-in-law stated late one afternoon, as I sat with her in the bedroom of the bungalow that would soon cease to be my home, 'You will always be their mother. Nothing can change that. If I don't respect you, your children will never respect me.' How many mothers-in-law would have the grace and sagacity to figure out something as obvious, as simple, and stick to it?

I was happy when Sudhir decided to marry again, a few months after my marriage to Dilip. His wife Smita's position was the least enviable. And yet over the years she has established the strength of her character in marvellous ways, under highly delicate circumstances at that. Once when Aditya had to undergo minor surgery at the Breach Candy Hospital, Smita and I found ourselves waiting anxiously right outside the operation theatre. There was no strain or awkwardness between us. Strangely, neither of us has ever felt it. When Aditya was wheeled out after half-an-hour or so we could hear him groggily calling out for me as the anaesthesia's effect faded and he found himself emerging from the fog. I held on to his hand tightly. He was no longer an eighteen-year-old with a deep voice and a heavy stubble. He'd become a plaintive child longing for his mother. Smita stood to one side, a quiet, dignified presence, as Aditya's insistent cries ('Mummy? Are you there? Mummy . . . don't leave me') filled the ante-room. A few minutes later the surgeon emerged to check how the superficial wound on my son's forehead was doing. He lifted the taped bandage and a geyser of blood spurted out. Unable to stand the sight, my head reeled, my heart stopped, and I fainted. The first person to reach me and hold on was Smita. I could hear her instructing the nurses.

'Get her a black coffee. Quick. She must lie down somewhere.'
Sudhir was next to her in an instant, summoning help. It was
a moment I shall never forget. The magnanimity and
graciousness of two people who could have been (justifiably)
indifferent if not downright cussed was something not easily
forgotten. But then they weren't average individuals—why
was I forgetting? This was breeding and training at its shining
best. As I re-focused, I could see Smita smiling, 'Are you all
right? Don't worry about Aditya. I've checked with the
doctor. He's fine. You relax . . . here . . . sip some coffee.'

Another emergency. An earlier year. A few short months
after I began my new life, living on my own. It would be the
first Diwali I'd be spending without my children. Without
lights. Without sweetmeats. Without celebration. But why
break an established tradition? Why not maintain a sense of
continuity? I always took the kids Diwali-shopping around
the crowded central Mumbai area where the old bungalow is.
The ritual never varied. First stop: a ready-made clothing store
where we'd buy new clothes for the gurkha's children who
accompanied us. Next stop: shopping for miniature paper
lanterns to string at the entrance of the bungalow. Followed
by rangoli powders, earthenware diyas, laddoos for the
domestics, fragrant bath oils and crackers. As always, I had
a brood of children hanging on to me. We stopped for various
small purchases. Avantika was clutching eight colourful
lanterns in her hands (she was no more than six years old).
Aditya was excitedly showing off his bombs and rockets. I
spotted an old woman selling a particular rangoli pattern
book. I bought it from her and left the children's hands briefly
to dig for some change in my handbag. This couldn't have
taken more than thirty seconds. When I turned around for the
standard head count, one child was missing. Mine. I couldn't
see Avantika in that dimly-lit, ridiculously crowded by-lane

crammed with eager Diwali shoppers. I asked the gurkha's son, '*Baby kidhar hai?*' He shrugged and said. '*Pata nahi. Abhi idhar thi.*'

I couldn't let go of all the other little hands I was holding in my own. Neither could I risk leaving these kids unattended on a busy street-corner. Wild-eyed, and with my heart thumping furiously, I literally dragged them along as I desperately enquired of every hawker, '*Aapne chhoti ladki dekhi? Uske haath mein kandeel the?*' Most nodded and said, '*Us taraf gayee,*' pointing into the far distance. Impossible. That was impossible. How could a six-year-old have travelled so far in those brief seconds? Yet everybody I asked the question of replied with absolute certainty—'That way.' I rushed into my regular jeweller's store and bellowed, 'My daughter . . . Have you seen my daughter?' Men from behind glittering gold counters shouted back, 'Yes. She did come in . . . but she isn't here now.' I could see that. If she wasn't here—where was she? Still accompanied by my rag-tag band of kids, I ran down a filthy, narrow strip of pavement calling out her name. It must have presented quite a sight—a crazed woman trailed by half-a-dozen kids hanging on to her dupatta, rushing around yelling 'A-VAN-TI-KA'.

Fifty metres down the road, two men stopped me.

'Are you looking for a little girl with lanterns?'

'Yes,' I shouted.

'She has gone home,' they said calmly.

'How do you know? Who are you?'

'We saw her crying and stopped her. One of our lady volunteers brought her here and asked her name and address. You live close by, don't you? She showed them a short-cut to the bungalow through that alleyway. Don't worry—she's safe. They accompanied her home.'

At that moment, I died. I'm sure of it. My heart stopped

beating with relief. Avantika, my beloved, darling daughter was all right. Home. Safe. Nothing else registered or mattered. I licked my parched lips. They tasted salty. I asked again, 'Who are you?' The men replied, 'We are from the local Shiv Sena Shakha.' I don't care what anybody thinks of the Sena. I owe them one. A big one. I'm deeply, deeply grateful. And indebted for life.

I had been dealing with my children's questions (as forthrightly as possible) without getting into too many nitty-gritties or apportioning blame. Today they are young adults capable of figuring things out for themselves. I merely provide the framework for them to do so. It's very important that they know that both Sudhir and I have their best interests at heart. I'm confident they believe we do. It's even more important for them to feel free enough to ask whatever they want to—the whys, hows, whats of that period. Nothing is hidden. Nothing needs to be. We love them. That's all that counts. I don't want to suppress or dress up anything. They will remember forever, that blindingly bright day their mother took flight literally as well as metaphorically to Delhi . . . never to come back to their home. Brutal enough. That's a scar even I don't have the power to obliterate. The only compensation? The divorce happened when it happened. Before a marriage on the skids degenerated into an ugly battle. It never reached that stage. We didn't let it. No slanging matches. No slug-fests. Only withdrawal and silence. Lethal, for sure. But still preferable.

My own parents had their share of arguments, and as children we dreaded those dark moments. Most times they settled their differences in the bedroom, but it was impossible not to know that Father and Mother were 'katti'. As a child this frightened me—I couldn't believe adults fought, stopped talking or cried. It made me uneasy. It also made me guilty, like in some convoluted way I'd been the cause of their disagreement.

It's always been tough being a parent but today, more so than ever. The other day Avantika was getting ready for her first television shoot. Everything was set up including a make-up person. Yet, half an hour before reporting time, she hit the panic button. I saw a semi-weepy little girl with a bad case of nerves. In her anxiety she'd broken out in hives, her eyes were puffy and she was obviously miserable. 'Mother, you do my make-up. I don't want a stranger to touch my face,' she insisted. At that moment, she wasn't a 'cool' nineteen-year-old but an uncertain kid who was terrified at the prospect of facing a camera. I was touched that she had sufficient faith in my abilities to make her look her best under the circumstances. I tried to camouflage my own nervousness by wise-cracking and being completely casual about the whole thing. When I looked into her stricken eyes I could clearly see myself at her age. And that's when I realized my mother couldn't possibly have seen herself reflected in mine. We belonged to entirely different worlds. She was always a far, far older person, from another generation. None of my experiences or adventures could have coincided with hers.

My dreams weren't her dreams. My thoughts remained with me. It was as impossible for her to enter my universe as it was for me to build a bridge to hers. Yet, I believe she understood, and accepted me unconditionally, flaws, warts and all. The age difference between my mother and me is almost exactly the same as the one between my daughter Avantika and myself. Yet, because of my crowded life and the times we live in, I can (and do) switch places with whatever she's going through and connect with her anxieties completely—I have been there myself. I have done what she's doing—made the same mistakes. I understand. How could my mother have known anything at all about make-up tricks and camouflage contours? About boyfriend trouble and motorbike rides? Or moonlight dates and mushy poetry? Or split ends and pre-menstrual zits? Here was a woman who'd never felt the need for cosmetics or 'dressing up'. She'd never 'dated' anyone—not even the stranger she married at nineteen. Nobody had written poetry for her, to her, not even my father. As for motorbikes, in her world they were ridden by car mechanics and *mawalis*.

The only cream that came into our house was a jar of Hazeline Snow. This she applied on her face for fear of incurring my fastidious father's wrath. 'Look at you, my dear. Your skin is so dry, go and apply some snow on it.' Her generous use of an all-purpose talcum powder (Cuticura) was equally governed by my father's views on the subject. The talc went on her face as well, even after we grew up and told her it wasn't the best use to put it to. A bright red powder kumkum dotted her broad forehead. And her hair style (a plaited nape bun) remained unchanged throughout her life. Even the curved aluminium hair-pins that held the bun in place were the same ones she'd started out with. And yet, she didn't look 'dated' or 'unfashionable' ever. She was just herself—a proud, self possessed lady, unembarrassed about her extra kilos or limited wardrobe. During most of her youth she owned precisely two 'good' sarees—one silk (black-printed Kashmiri variety in peacock blue) and one Coimbatore cotton. She wore a white cotton blouse with both, a white cotton petticoat underneath. These two garments took her from the lawns of the Rashtrapati Bhavan to the governor's pavilion where all the other women in far finer clothing preened vainly around the venue.

The one piece of jewellery my mother craved, and the only thing she ever asked my father for, was a pair of diamond kudis (a circlet of diamonds, much coveted by middle-class Maharashtrian ladies of a certain age). One of her own sisters (married to an ambitious man) got her pair at a far younger age and my grandmother made a point of rubbing the fact in. 'Can't your important government officer husband give you even that? Have you seen how many tolas of gold your sister possesses?' My mother's unruffled reply to the taunt was, 'My husband earns his salary honestly. He'll give me the kudis when he can afford them.' If there was an implied slight or insinuation in that comment, my grandmother obviously thought it wiser to ignore it.

Even now, whenever my father speaks of my mother (and it's very often) he recalls her contentment the most. He says she never complained. And he boasts as if it all happened yesterday, 'Whatever she wore, she still managed to steal the show from all the other memsahibs.' That's easy to believe. There was a luminous quality to her beauty. It was the expression in her eyes—trusting, childlike, open, and the amazing quality of her skin. If she looked radiantly beautiful, it was because she was a complete natural—and I'm not talking about make-up. My mother was herself at all times—fearlessly so. Nothing and nobody intimidated her. Her attitude to people never varied, whether she was at a boring government 'At Home' or a stuffy official function talking to my father's senior colleagues, without ever feeling the need to flatter their egoes or suck up to their priggish wives.

I like to believe it's one quality I've inherited from her. I cannot recall anybody—and I mean anybody—who has overawed me to an extent that I have felt the need to alter my natural behaviour and pretend to be someone I am not.

Of course, I often play games with people—but I do so consciously and I do it largely for my own amusement.

Whenever I'm tempted to put on a mini-show, I think of my mother and how she'd have handled the situation, adopting nothing more complicated than a direct take-it-or-leave-it, no-nonsense stance. I figure if it worked for her, it should work for me. I'm wrong, of course. My life does not resemble hers, alas. There are times I wish it did.

I recall one occasion when she was arguing with my brother. This, when she was frail and sick but not so weak that she couldn't muster up the energy to put her only son in his place. My brother Ashok and she shared an easy, loving, informal relationship with plenty of mutual teasing and friendly banter. One evening, he went on and on about her middle-classness, till finally, she decided she'd had enough. Tucking her saree pallu into her waistband, nostrils flared, eyes shining, voice rising, she fired back spiritedly, 'I agree I'm a middle-class person. But what on earth gives you the idea you are an aristocrat?' Mother was like that. Blunt, no-nonsense and honest to the core. Diplomacy and tact were strangers to her, even though she never wilfully hurt anybody's feelings. Unlike my father who chose his words with greater care (although he was forceful and direct when he needed to be), my mother was far too guileless and transparent. It simply did not occur to her to camouflage her opinions if they were asked for. And she had the uncanny ability to reach out instinctively to people at all levels. Her approach, way of speaking and demeanour remained the same whether it was a *jamadar* she was dealing with or a minister.

My own children take far too many things for granted. They know no other life. I shouldn't expect them to place the same value on everyday conveniences that I grew up thinking of as unattainable luxuries. These children are privileged, I wasn't. Even though I never felt that way. Never. There were far better-off girls at my school, close friends who arrived in chauffeur-driven cars, had hot lunch brought to them by docile ayahs, wore school tunics made out of expensive blended fabrics, not rough drill, lived in beautiful seaside homes manned by four or five servants, holidayed abroad and enjoyed a lifestyle that was clearly far more affluent than my own. I noticed it all. The differences, I mean. And yet, I don't remember suffering from any feelings of deprivation on account of what they possessed and I didn't. Finally, it was never an issue. Not now. Not then. There are countless people in our immediate circle of friends with far more wealth, women with priceless jewels, unlimited shopping budgets, phenomenal travel plans to exotic destinations. But to date, I have not actively coveted anything they may have flaunted, not a thing. Admired it, gasped. Wondered about the price tag. But not felt the urge to go out and acquire it for myself.

On my infrequent visits to the homes of my school friends I'd take in all the details almost automatically, but with a sense of detachment. Something like 'Oh yes. Well-tuned piano there.' Or 'lovely linen', 'fabulous crystal'. Everything, but everything, would register. The uniformed bearers serving fish meunière at lunch, the elegantly dressed mothers in flowered chiffons supervising the menu, the constant phone calls . . . yes, the phone calls for the mothers did intrigue me. My own rarely received any, except from her nephews and nieces. Certainly no social calls from the ladies of the kitty-party set. I'd listen avidly to my friends' well-groomed mothers making fake conversation, tinkling laughter interspersing the inanities, and somewhere I'd thank God my Aie was not like these superficial brittle women. That she was just 'Aie': strong, simple, easy to figure out, easier still to slot—a mother. Every mother. My mother. I would like to be such a mother to my children, even though I know my vision is unrealistic

426

and foolish. Why should I burden them with my ridiculous 'image'? What right have I to allow that to be imposed on their dreams? When I'm being particularly harsh on myself, I think, maybe I'm wrong. Maybe I'm being presumptuous. Maybe they wouldn't have wanted an anonymous, conventional mother. How would they know the difference, anyway? I'm the only one they have, take it or leave it. Then I console myself with memories of occasions I remember as being special for me and my kids. And I feel okay again. Not for too long though.

While driving past Churchgate station, I point it out to my incredulous younger children—a shabby but important landmark from my childhood.

'This was my station. This is where I'd take a train to school. And this the bus stop I'd walk from.'

They find it hard to believe as they watch the crowds pouring out or rushing in. 'Weren't you scared? Wasn't Aji afraid to let you travel like that?' they want to know.

No, I wasn't scared. Nor was she. In any case, what other options did I have? I took a train to Grant Road station, jumped off and walked the remaining kilometre to school. On the way home, after netball/ throwball/ basketball practice, I walked the remaining kilometre to another bus stop at Nana's Chowk, got into a double-decker, got off near Eros theatre, and sprinted home. For years and years my lunch was a packed sandwich. My allowance? Rarely more than the exact bus-fare with maybe an additional 25 paisa. Even so, there wasn't a single regret. No sense of missing out on anything at all.

My children are always chaperoned to and from school. They've never used public transport, never had to. Except my older daughter, Radhika, who goes to work in a distant office and has chosen to commute by bus. Their lives are cushioned and a bit too comfortable, according to me. I boast that I was part of the real world by age twelve. On my own, left to my devices, free to figure things out for myself. I knew all the bus routes, I knew train time-tables, I knew most of the by-lanes of this vast and crowded city. I could get around without escorts, ayahs or chauffeurs.

It was a toughening-up process and I appreciate its value today. It didn't desensitize me, however. I learnt to deal with people at all levels, look out for my own safety and become reasonably self-sufficient . . . even resourceful. Though my sisters and I weren't 'allowed' any outings unless accompanied by a parent, we still managed to have fun, even on the regular picnics to spots outside the city, when we'd sneak away briefly to giggle and gossip, while our parents napped lightly under the shade of a gulmohur tree. We travelled exclusively in their company. Long trips by car to distant cities, with stopovers in dak-bungalows en route. How can I ever forget the taste of what the rest-house khansama called 'chicken curry' but which must have been pigeon or crow in an oily gravy. These were our uncomplicated adventures—safe and thrill-free.

Even when I became a 'working woman', I continued to be pampered by those around me. It was a soft life. I woke up, got dressed, went to work, came home, went out, went to bed. Family and home were taken for granted, especially all the small comforts and conveniences—telephones, hot meals, running water, laundry, a bed with fresh sheets, ironed clothes, packed lunch, money if I ever ran short. In return, I gave nothing at all—neither my time nor my attention.

Yes, I may have had a few weekend duties—minor chores, really. Vegetable shopping, ironing, rolling out chappatis, frying fish. I grumbled through those as well. But largely, home was a hostel with free boarding and lodging,

428

plus a matron with a smile on her face, who occasionally kissed me . . . for being me. Amazing, that my mother never cribbed or grumbled about my indifference. Or even about my lifestyle which must have been so alien to her. Of course, my older sister, Mandakini, had been a bank manager for a decade by the time I started my career, and the other, Kunda, was qualifying to be an ophthalmic surgeon, so they were used to their kids having less time than before to spend with them or help out around the house. Even so, I know of several parents who aren't as generous or accomodating when their children are struggling to find their feet in the outside world.

My mother hardly got to see me during this busy phase. My father, even less so. The time I spent at home was reserved for phone calls. And pursuing my own selfish interests. Weekends were for unwinding, relaxing, going to movies. Even at that stage I had few friends, since I was never a part of any one particular crowd. Some of these people were extraordinarily wealthy—they can still be counted amongst the richest people of this city. I'd go to their dinner parties clad in my older sister's hand-me-downs or some ridiculous outfit left over from a fashion show, without experiencing any feelings of self-consciousness.

When I recall the contents of 'our' cupboard (I shared it with Kunda), they were pretty meagre. Both my sisters, in their generosity, supplemented my wardrobe whenever they had cash to spare—hand-block-printed sarees from Sohan, cotton kurtas from Handloom House, pretty Venkatgiris from travelling salesmen, trinkets from Tibetan refugees, mojris from Janpath, chiffon dupattas from Mohta Market—my sisters took a keen, affectionate interest in my appearance. I didn't mind, since at that time I had a limited budget. My own salary went towards buying more clothes and on taxi fare—four trips to the office and back (I came home to lunch). Since I've always enjoyed eating out, dinner would be at any of the small restaurants around Colaba, with Paradise being an all-time favourite.

My mother never asked what time I'd be home. My father had a simple rule—the security chain would be in place after midnight, which meant a latch-key would be useless and I'd have to ring the doorbell. And that wasn't the best option, since it would be my father who'd answer the door . . . not with a 'welcome home, darling' smile, I assure you. Rather than face him, I'd rush from wherever I was to make the deadline . . . or risk being shouted at, at midnight.

The two of them had worked out an interesting formula—they presented a united front before the children, though we knew our mother was not always in complete agreement with our father's far stricter outlook. Often, she softened particularly harsh words from him by privately consoling the child who'd been at the receiving end—but did so very cleverly without letting her husband down. She never said, 'He was wrong and you are right.' But by her sympathetic attitude and patient hearing, she made it obvious that she understood. For me, that was enough. I'm afraid I'm not as wise or considerate when it comes to my own children. When I blow up, I blow up. I tend to talk to them as equals, which is not always the best option. I adopt adult standards and an irritatingly rational approach, where a quieter, calmer, more intuitive one would work far better.

It's important for at least one parent to leave a line of communication permanently open—and in our family it was provided by my mother. Most requests were routed through her—we rarely spoke directly to our father, unless he initiated the conversation. One parent represented authority and discipline, the other understanding and indulgence. The roles were rarely interchanged. Today, in our set-up, that's the one improvisation we've introduced. The bad guy sometimes becomes the fall guy. Or, when I'm in a non-receptive mood, my husband plays 'mummy' and soothes ruffled feathers. I find he's often far more simpatico about issues I tend to be rigid about. In my time deadlines were sacred. These days they're impossible to enforce. And there's no point losing sleep over it. He's also more in tune with today's changed social environment. While I tend to get preachy, he prefers to talk. Man-to-man. Man-to-woman. I think the older children respond to this approach far better.

And the man who once inspired such fear in me has today become a confidant—my father. I guess I needed to grow up a great deal to apreciate all that he's done for his family—all that he and my mother did without, too. Four growing children to feed, clothe, educate and entertain—on a government official's modest salary. It's only now, as a parent myself, that I can marvel at their equanimity during those difficult years, when my father would quietly borrow money to pay off fees or settle the local merchant's grocery bills.

Today, at ninety, he's a proud, courageous man who lives a life of great dignity. Everybody in the locality knows him for his generosity and fairness. The raddiwallah down the street comes straight to his door when his mother requires additional funds for hospital care. Similarly, the watchman with a swollen leg does not approach any other 'Saab' in the co-operative housing society in which my father lives. He knows there is one man he can count on for instant help. Recently, I was at his home when a complete stranger rang the doorbell with a convincing sounding hard-luck story. My father is not a rich man. He is a pensioner with enough savings to live a comfortable life, but he certainly does not have surplus funds. I watched him going towards the wooden cupboard and reaching for his familiar, worn, leather wallet.

'Why are you giving money to a man you do not even know?' I asked him.

He looked at me. 'I don't need to know him. He's poor and he needs help. That's all I need to know. What are two hundred rupees? My needs are few. I don't really want anything. I already have too much. If I can give my children and grandchildren expensive gifts on their birthdays, can I not spare such a small amount for a poor man?'

He rarely gets back his 'loans'. He knows he's writing the amount off even as he counts out the notes. And it was always like this, even when he required funds himself. And to my mother's eternal credit, she never once tried to influence or stop him from lending a helping hand, sometimes to ingrates who promptly forgot the favour once the money was in their greedy palms, and failed to recognize the man who'd put it there, when they met accidentally years later.

One story, in particular, touches me each time it's recounted. When my father received his transfer orders to Delhi, he found he owed his landlord (a wealthy merchant) in Satara thirty rupees. Embarrassed by the fact that he didn't have the requisite funds to settle the rent, my father went to him to ask for time. The man laughed. 'It's such an insignificant amount—don't mention it.' The family left for Delhi (I was two years old at the time). We were given government accommodation . . . but the salary-date was still a month away. My father borrowed money against it. And the very first thing he did was to send a money order for thirty rupees to the merchant. Next, he bought basic supplies for his young children—uniforms, text-books and warm clothes for the Delhi winter. Nobody felt the pinch or was made aware of the loan taken.

So often these days, I find myself beseeching my father silently to show me the way through the fog. And he does.

With his robust common sense and practicality, he always points in the right direction. Back then, I was too blinded by my own identity crisis to pay attention to his sagacious advice. What he suggested wasn't in the realm of high philosophy. It wasn't unachievable or remote. His was the way of the pragmatist. Keep your nostrils clean. Pay your taxes. Love your family and country. Do the morally correct thing. Choose the right path. 'A man of character always knows the difference between right and wrong,' he once told me. As a district judge, he was constantly confronted with what to others may have seemed like difficult choices involving conflicting interests. But to him, when he gave his judgements, there was only one way—the fair and just one.

Once, a powerful man who also happened to be his landlord, had to appear in Father's court on serious charges of fraud. Certain that my father would pronounce a favourable verdict, the man swaggered in with his cronies to hear it. 'Guilty,' pronounced my father without the slightest hesitation. The man shot to his feet, his face puffed up with shock and rage. 'I care tuppence about your judgement,' he cried out, even as my father calmly signed the papers. With his influential contacts, the man went on appeal and made sure the judgement was reversed. My father continued paying his rent as a tenant and saw no contradiction in maintaining a civil relationship with his miffed landlord. 'His ego was injured,' says my father, 'I fully understand that. But my own conscience was clear—I was not his tenant in court. He was an accused in mine.' He recalled an invaluable piece of advice given to him by (of all people) Ram Jethmalani many moons ago. 'If you lose a case, make sure you don't lose your client. If you lose the client, don't lose the judge. But if you lose even the judge, don't lose your conscience.' Mr Jethmalani may have forgotten his own words of wisdom . . . but not my father who has lived by them. Over and over again he demonstrated to us, his family, that 'character building' wasn't just an empty slogan to be tossed around carelessly. I didn't see its import then . . . but I do now. Especially when I can see his credo in action even today. Faced with any sort of moral dilemma, I frequently and instinctively turn to him. His advice never wavers from the path of truth, as he perceives it. During the '98 elections when certain politically active individuals approached me, I narrated our conversation to him, with particular reference to their insistence on my declaring my religious allegiance. 'Just tell them firmly, "I make no distinction between man and man." That should be your only reply,' he counselled. Not that I was taking any of the kite flying seriously. But that simple line made it so much easier for me to say 'no' the next time I was accosted.

Did he never ever compromise? Never experience conflict? Was he never tempted? Yes, just once. At least, to my knowledge. And he has no regrets. My mother used to be acknowledged as the prettiest girl in her locality. My father's niece went to the same school as her (St. Columba's) and their families were known to one another. At the time a proposal of marriage arrived from the Pandits (my mother's family) for the youngest Rajadhyaksha son, my father was a briefless lawyer, entirely dependant on the largesse of his eldest brother. He was also rather diffident about his own looks ('Though I had regular features and a good height, my teeth were far too prominent and I wore spectacles. But I was very particular about personal hygiene and grooming'). My father could not believe the gods had favoured him. He'd noticed the sixteen-year-old Shakuntala walking to school and had lost his heart to her. And now, here was the middleman bearing a formal proposal. The question of my father's views on it did not arise. The decision was left to 'tatya', his autocratic older brother (seventeen years his senior). 'Let the horoscopes be matched first and then we shall see,' he said. A tension-filled week passed. Finally when the horoscopes were returned it was with the regrettable news that the stars did not favour the alliance. My father decided to change the stars, such was his determination to wed the petite, fair, long-haired, dark-eyed eldest daughter of the Pandit family. He sought out the priest and persuaded him to take a second look at their charts. In order to facilitate the process, he offered him a small inducement (in cash) for the extra effort involved. Sure enough, the priest contacted the middleman to admit he'd gone wrong in his earlier calculations—the horoscopes matched perfectly after all. They were married soon after—a marriage that only grew and blossomed over the next fifty-nine years. He chuckles at the memory now. They were so looking forward to celebrating their sixtieth anniversary in December '95. They nearly made it, falling short by seven months. My mother passed away in May, with that all-important landmark in their life regrettably unreached.

I still have the photograph (disastrously colour-tinted) taken on my parents' twenty-fifth wedding anniversary, which shows the two of them dressed in their absolute best—my mother in a printed Kashmir silk saree with a mismatched artificial silk blouse, and my father in a brown wool suit. She looks radiantly happy and entirely natural, my father appears ill-at-ease and stern (he has never approved of his own photographs). Their four children, posed formally around them, look . . . look what? A little embarrassed, perhaps. I remember my own outfit—a figure-hugging checked salwar-kameez with a matching dupatta, one of the highly prized items from my wardrobe. The photograph is a sweet and telling portrait of a family that, despite varying individual temperaments, managed to hang together rather nicely . . . largely because of the 'superglue' that held this precarious structure together—my mother.

When she passed away on 7 May, 1995, I wasn't there. This fact has begun to haunt me in a strange and disturbing way. I wasn't there. I should have been there. I could have been there. I ought to have been there. But the tragic fact still remains—I wasn't there. So . . . where was I? Not too far away, actually. Relaxing with my husband at our farmhouse across the harbour. It's easy for me to say, 'Oh well . . . she wasn't critically ill. She wasn't hospitalized. She was frail and old, as she had been for years. I couldn't possibly have seen the end coming that suddenly. Not that very night itself. I wouldn't have been able to save her life anyway. Besides . . . it was just as well. Best to let her go . . . free her of the constant, wracking pain of chronic lung congestion and debilitating rheumatoid arthritis she lived with so bravely.' These are merely empty words that provide little consolation. I wasn't there. That's it. Only my father was. And an impersonal, inefficient hired hospital help who couldn't have cared less in any case—to her my mother was probably just another patient who'd died.

I find it difficult to recreate the scenario. There is far too much guilt and shame involved. I had not been a 'good' daughter during her last few years. Not nearly sympathetic enough. I'd often displayed impatience, even exasperation, over her obvious discomfort. I hadn't been able to understand why she was no longer the woman I knew and loved as my mother. I resented the change that had come over her—not physically but mentally. She seemed distant, disoriented, disinterested, whereas all that while, when I was getting angry and impatient with her for not paying attention, her brain was struggling to keep functioning, deprived as it was by a depleted oxygen supply that her poor lungs were no longer capable of producing even as the heart struggled to go on pumping, refusing to give up long after it had lost most of its capacity to perform normally.

Why wasn't I able to accept these elementary, easy-to-understand explanations even after they'd been made crystal clear to me? Why did I think she was feigning or exaggerating her condition? It's a sorry admission, but make it I must—I failed her during those final years and not once did she express her sorrow or disappointment at my abominable conduct. There was too little compassion, far too much censure, against a helpless woman whose systems were gradually giving up, reducing her body and spirit to nothing more than a hollow, shrunken frame. I watched her waste away—and yet felt nothing at all, except a peculiar rage. Why was she behaving this way? Why did she look so different? I wanted my beautiful mother back—a selfish, childish need. Not this lady, unrecognizable, distant, morose, who stared abstractedly into space, tapped her fingers obsessively, ate very little, spoke very little and seemed supremely indifferent to us all. I felt strangely let down, as if someone was playing a cheap trick on me. I'm certain my mother sensed my withdrawal and was hurt by it. Even in that slightly hazy state her instincts remained as sharp as ever. She knew when a domestic was playing truant, how much food was being wasted, whether or not the day's washing had been hung up to dry. All her life, she'd devoted her energies towards being an efficient homemaker. She wasn't going to allow her neat home where every little object had its specific place, to be overrun by a hired help who placed no value on our family's sentimental belongings—the elegant fruit bowl, the pastry forks, the special English crockery from way back, all the souvenirs from foreign trips presented by the children. She was too frail to go looking for dust on the bookshelves, but she could tell from glancing around her if a single paperweight had been shifted.

Too weak to move around even within the flat, she'd still make the effort to take her place on the sofa every evening to watch the news on television. My father, reclining on the divan, one eye on his beloved wife's breathing pattern, another on the small screen, would try to engage her in an animated conversation on current affairs. Her participation and involvement were quite amazing, considering her lack of actual exposure to the events being discussed. She'd supply the names of obscure ministers and disgraced bureaucrats when even my father with his remarkable memory couldn't recall them accurately. And she'd wait like a child for my sisters' frequent calls, often chattering on like she was on a local line, quite forgetting the hefty phone bills they'd have to settle.

My infrequent visits must have caused her a great deal of anguish, but she never pulled me up, choosing instead to make excuses for my absence. 'Poor Shobha. She has so many other responsibilities—a large family, all the writing she takes on . . .' These convenient alibis would make me cringe—but not enough to take me to her bedside. When I did visit, I'd get impatient to leave, impatient with her manner, impatient with the slow 'progress' she was making. And I'd be insensitive enough to show it. My siblings would wonder what had got into me. I was, after all, her favourite child. The one who'd received the maximum amount of attention and love. The one she had 'spoilt', encouraged and indulged. Had I forgotten all those incidents? No, of course I hadn't. I wanted them back. I wanted it to be like old times. I wanted to place my head in her lap and be caressed by warm, supple fingers, not by this bony hand with its misshapen joints. Maybe she understood my need. I don't know.

About a year before she died, she was hospitalized briefly. Fortunately, my doctor sister was in Mumbai then and took the decision to move her. The timing was awful. For me, that is. I was to leave for a short vacation with the children. It was a long-promised summer break and one which the children had been looking forward to for weeks. I would gladly have stayed behind, but my children would have none of it. If you can't come, we aren't going, the younger ones stated flatly. They were at the age when a holiday meant much more to them than any old lady (even their granny) lying in a hospital. 'She'll be okay. Maushi and the others are there to take care of her,' they pleaded. I was at the hospital when the specialists arrived. 'It's hard to say . . . touch-and-go . . . at her age and in her condition, anything could happen,' they informed the family. Our bags had been packed for a week. Every little detail, down to the red plastic beach bucket and spade, had been taken care of. We were to leave the next morning. In the hospital room, I watched as my sister instructed the nursing staff. The rest of the family waited outside. At one point my mother managed to open her eyes. Noticing me, they lit up. It was akin to a stab straight into my cold, unfeeling heart. I explained the peculiar situation to her—the kids, their disappointment, all the bookings and reservations. She whispered hoarsely, 'You go. Be with your family.'

My sister stared incredulously as I conveyed the decision to my father and brother. They must have been aghast at the thought that I could even think of 'enjoying' myself at a time like this. The specialist had disapproval written all over his face. I'd like to believe it was only she who understood my dilemma, when she gave me the go-ahead to get on that plane with my family. She'd done so without the slightest reservation. It had been a wholehearted decision—such was the magnanimity of that moment. And I'd gone with the absolute certainty that she'd be back home within the week—and she was. While feeding her some soup earlier, I'd sensed in her the will to go on. She wasn't ready to give up the fight just yet. She lived for another year . . . but that extra lease of time could not have brought any additional happiness into her life, where each step was painful, every breath an effort.

One lapse I still cannot forgive myself for involved, of all things, a tandoori chicken. This was about a week before she passed away. I received a call from my father asking whether I could arrange for the chicken since my mother had been demanding it with the persistence of a petulant child. 'Make sure it's from Delhi Durbar,' he instructed, while I absently made a note of it on my date-pad. In my mind, a chicken is a chicken is a chicken. I didn't think it would make any difference to either of them where it came from. But it obviously did. I ordered the dish from the nearby club we are members of, believing it would be more hygienic and convenient. My mother took one look at it and turned away. How could she tell it wasn't from the restaurant of her choice? From its presentation.

The club chicken came neatly diced, whereas the chicken she fancied was served whole. She was deeply disappointed and didn't touch the one I'd sent over. That puzzled and irritated me—and I said as much. My father tiredly said, 'My dear, you don't understand. Your mother's appetite has all but gone. She wouldn't have been able to eat the Delhi Durbar chicken either—but it would have made her very happy to see it the way she remembered having relished it in the past when she was healthy and happy.' I could have kicked myself. It had been such a small request. It was also one of her last. I'd failed her yet again.

The night she died, I'd spoken to her in the morning, as

I usually did. Coincidentally enough, all the children had gone across to meet her that afternoon and reported the visit to me over the phone in Alibag, where I was to spend the weekend. My youngest daughter sounded puzzled when she said, 'Aji didn't recognize me today. She thought I was didi.' That should have rung a few alarm bells, but didn't. I called from the farmhouse at 6 p.m. and spoke to my father. He said bleakly, 'No change. She's all right. We're watching television. The night woman has not arrived so far.' Normally, I would not have spoken to them till the following morning. But something made me phone back, just to check whether the woman attendant had shown up. She was an unreliable, unfeeling person I didn't like or have much confidence in. I wasn't sure I'd be able to get through from Alibag, since the telephone exchange functioned erratically, often frustrating all attempts to reach Mumbai, a mere fourteen miles away as the crow flies. I was hoping against hope I wouldn't get yet another recorded message from the telephone exchange by a woman with an atrocious accent.

My father picked up the phone at the second ring.

'Baba? Everything all right? Has the woman turned up? How's Mother?'

'She's gone.'

'What? You mean she didn't turn up at all?'

'Your mother . . . she's no more. She just died . . . a few minutes ago. Aie is dead. She's gone.' I believed him. It was stated coldly, matter-of-factly.

What I mean is, I didn't launch into 'What? It can't be true . . . Oh no . . . Tell me it isn't so. How could it be possible? She was fine a few hours ago. What happened?'

And I hated myself.

For not being there.

For having been so callous and hard-hearted with her.

441

For being the one child out of four who could have been of some help during the crisis, but was, instead, on a distant farm, preparing to eat a gourmet dinner. I said quietly, 'I'm starting back right now.' And turned to my husband. He knew, I didn't have to explain.

'Let's hire a car,' he suggested. It was a practical, sensible suggestion. Alibag is across the bay from Mumbai and there is no boat service during the monsoons. And in any case, the ferry doesn't ply after a certain hour. He was in no condition to drive himself—my parents were the parents he no longer had. Within half an hour we were on the road. I don't know what I felt during the first few moments, besides overwhelming guilt. It wasn't a sense of sorrow or loss. After all, she'd been ailing and the family was prepared for the inevitable.

It was the image of my father left to cope by himself at a moment like this, alone in his flat, with a sour-faced stranger who could only have been planning her next night shift at some other, equally helpless patient's home. None of his four children was with him to share his insurmountable grief and offer solace. All of us were far too busy with our own lives, our own families, our own preoccupations, our own priorities. The woman who'd brought us into this world was lying dead on her bed, with a fragile eighty-seven-year-old man, her beloved husband, by her side in a dimly lit bedroom of a modern high-rise whose neighbours were merely familiar faces across the landing. There was no one to lighten the burden of this lonely man's sorrow. What use were we—had we been—to these two proud individuals we called parents? What had I ever done for them? How much joy had I brought into their lives through deeds that were performed for them alone?

I had never felt this wretched, this selfish, this small before.

The road to Mumbai was long and circuitous. On a good day it was possible to make the journey in three hours. This wasn't a good day. There was a monumental traffic snarl at a busy junction, with two hundred trucks piled up on both sides of the highway. This looked like the breakdown of breakdowns, with traffic at a total standstill. It had started to rain, which meant a further slowing down of highway patrols—that is, if there were any traffic policemen on duty in the first place. We waited in one spot for two straight hours, in silence. I couldn't speak. There was nothing to say. I concentrated on the slushy countryside, watching the rain, and thought of the tears I wasn't shedding. I was strangely cold and switched off. It was my practical self that was functioning—when would the funeral be? Who'd be home when I got there finally? Would Father have finished dinner? Did Mother die before or after he'd eaten? If it was before, he'd be awfully hungry (and my father is like a child when his stomach is growling). Would my brother and sister-in-law Moyna have arrived? Or were they away at a dinner party and therefore unreachable? The calls to my sisters—would Father have been composed enough to make them, or would . I have to do that? We'd need an ambulance or a hearse—which would it be? Other relatives would have to be told. Mother's only living sister, the one she spoke to every week—someone would have to inform her. Flowers, garlands, agarbattis, ice, a change of clothes . . . what about the ritual bath—would I have to give that? Mother's jewellery—her two mangalsutras, diamond kudis and bangles, I'd have to remove those and replace them with fakes. It had always been Mother's great desire to die a saubhagyawati—a married lady whose husband was still alive. She'd want all the symbols of that—her kumkum, bangles, mangalsutras and a green or red saree to be cremated in. Which one should that be? One of her favourite silks? Had Father discussed the funeral details with her? Unlikely, knowing them. That would have been inauspicious and morbid. Which meant my brother and I would have to make those decisions between us, and fast.

The details of her last moments were not known to me. I didn't want to know either. She was dead. Would Father want to recreate the tragedy, describe what exactly happened? Did I need to relive those gory last seconds and torture myself reconstructing the visuals?

She was dead.

Five hours later, as the white Maruti van took a sharp right, I caught a glimpse of my parents' bedroom window. The light was on. So was the light in the living room. I could see two silhouettes in the balcony—my brother and Moyna. I passed this road each time I left my home. And I always looked for that light in their window. Only this time, it was close to 3 a.m. and I'd have preferred darkness. A dark window would have told me they were both well and fast asleep. Tonight was one night when that light seemed satanic and evil. When light and not darkness represented death.

I walked straight into my parents' bedroom after greeting my brother and his wife briefly. It was a short walk from the entrance—one which I'd taken countless times in the past. Twenty-odd paces past a passage, a bedroom, the kitchen and two bathrooms. I noticed my mother's 'home' saree left on the clothesline to dry. Everything looked exactly the same, smelt the same: of her talcum powder, hair oil, soap. Even when I finally saw her in her usual place on the bed, I found it impossible to believe she wasn't alive. Or that my father, lying quietly on his bed next to hers, was in fact lying beside his wife's corpse and not merely her sleeping form. She looked so calm, peaceful and radiant in death. The frown of pain was missing. Her mouth seemed more relaxed, freed of

444

the strain. Her hair was neatly combed as usual, her bindi in place.

My father's behaviour was in keeping with her appearance as well. For years he'd maintained a silent vigil by her side, alert to the slightest alteration in her breathing pattern, falling into light sleep from time to time, one eye on the clock for her medication, the other on her visible discomfort. It was the same today. He didn't speak, as if afraid to disturb her deep sleep—one she so desperately needed after decades of shallow, wheezy breathing.

I sat by her side. Stroked her forehead. Bent down and kissed her cheek. An unnatural calm prevailed in the room. I asked him how the end came. Suddenly I needed to know. Or maybe I sensed he needed to tell. He narrated it without breaking down, almost clinically. As if he were giving a detailed account as an involved witness. He'd been helping her eat a little dinner. Persuading her to take one more mouthful. Her head was low . . . too low for him to get the spoon of khichdi into her mouth neatly without the contents dribbling down her chin. One arm was around her thin shoulders, as he urged her to raise her head and open her mouth wider. She made a valiant effort to do so and then fell backwards on the bed—dead. He tried to shake her . . . to say . . . come on, sit up . . . you haven't finished the khichdi yet. There was no response. He knew. He called for the woman attendant. She knew. Probably far better than he did. She'd seen a lot of deaths in her time. They went differently—but go they did. The signs were there for her to recognize. But . . . but . . . my mother had spoken to him only minutes earlier. Watched TV, gone unescorted to the bathroom. Washed her face. Said her prayers. Dead, said the woman, she's dead. And that's when my second call came to my father. Dead, he said tonelessly, echoing the woman. She's dead. Your mother is no more.

She was no more. Snuffed out, just like that. I went outside to consult my brother. He said, 'We were waiting for you. Let's get on with the cremation. Electric, of course. Now. Right now. Before daybreak.' Nobody was to be informed except my two sisters. That's the way my mother had wanted it. No priests. No rituals. No prayers. No ceremonies. No mourning.

My father spoke. 'I'd like her to be taken away before dawn. Not in front of the curious, impersonal eyes of neighbours and strangers. Why wait? Call the ambulance. No hearse. I want a smart, new, well-painted, well-maintained air-conditioned ambulance for her last journey.' My eldest daughter Radhika was there by then. She'd been very close to her grandmother. We decided to change my mother's clothes together. Remove her jewellery. Radhika did it as if it was the most natural gesture in the world. Without a sense of horror or revulsion at touching a cold, lifeless body whose limbs had begun to stiffen. As I removed the mangalsutra and diamond kudis and replaced them with cheap imitations, I felt how sad it was to strip this lady of the few possessions that had meant the world to her, had been symbols of her married state and a reflection of her husband's position in life. Even the bright green saree with a simple gold border, which my brother had bought as soon as he heard the news, was awful compared to her naturally good taste in clothes.

It was time to go. With my husband's and brother's help, we managed to place her on the stretcher. I was against her being tied onto it, even though I knew they'd find it difficult to climb down five flights with an unsecured body on the stretcher. Tying her down would have been the final indignity. My brother and I disagreed on this. We argued. I was adamant. He reminded me she was his mother too. Finally, we didn't strap her on.

My father turned to me. He was not going to accompany his wife on her last journey to the electric crematorium but he expressed a desire to go downstairs to where the ambulance was waiting. I was staying back with him. It was close to 5 a.m.

'I cannot see her off dressed like this,' he said with anguish, pointing to his well-ironed, neatly laundered kurta-pajama. 'I need to dress for her.'

We waited while he carefully got into his formal clothes—pinstriped trousers, belt, fine shirt, shoes and socks. We escorted him downstairs. My brother and my husband were seated by the stretcher.

'I wish to pay my last respects to my wife,' said my father, and walked proud, tall and unaided, to the ambulance. He folded his hands in a namaskar, bowed his head, shut his eyes and prayed.

That done, he said, very formally, almost curtly, 'You may leave now.' The ambulance door was shut with a loud, hard bang. The sky was getting light. People were just about starting to stir. The vehicle moved away swiftly, as I held my father's hand and watched it leave the compound. He was still standing tall. We walked back into their room—his room from then on. He lay down on his bed tiredly. I reclined on the next one—hers. The pillow still carried the imprint she had left on it. We didn't speak. He fell into a light sleep. The sky was pink and flushed as I looked out of the window. The morning star was visible just outside, luminous and glowing brightly, fairly high on the horizon. I lay back on my mother's bed and stared at the star's beauty for a long time. Of course that was her. The morning star was my mother. There was no mistaking that. As I continued to stare I saw her face . . . a flash and it was gone. That sad dawn, I was strangely comforted by the distant star that, steadfast and beautiful, seemed to have appeared out of nowhere just for me. I sought to superimpose my mother's image on it and succeeded. It made me feel stronger by its quiet presence in the firmament. And I knew she was okay. She'd be all right, she was free. And most importantly, she was there. I would find her whenever I needed to, merely by looking up, searching through the bright clusters in the sky, till I came across the brightest one—Mother.

*

Sometime ago, I was enjoying a late lunch with an older daughter at a local club, when I noticed a tall, paunchy man with greying hair and paan-stained teeth. He was buying shaving cream at the counter of the club shop and hadn't noticed us. I studied him for a good five minutes. My God. I was back to my childhood, hurtling down a memory chute. I could see him clearly as he was in those far-off days—a dashing cadet in sparkling white. Shy, slow of manner, charming and definitely handsome. I must have been fourteen, and he sixteen. For years and years, we did not speak to each other. By the time we got around to saying 'hello', it was time to move on. He to his career, me to college and my career. Suddenly, he looked up, spotted me and smiled a hesitant smile of recognition. He signed a slip and walked over. I noticed his stride had suddenly changed. He was holding himself taller, there was even a jaunty spring in his walk. He'd become, visibly and magically, the awkward young adolescent who'd invariably quicken his pace at the sight of me.

He was at our table now, his eyes shining with excitement. 'Shobha . . .' he pronounced softly and with some deliberation. I introduced my daughter. He asked us both, very politely, 'Mind if I sit down for a few minutes?' I asked for some coffee. There was no tension, none at all. No self-consciousness either. I asked about him, his family. He asked about mine. It took just a few seconds to reconnect. 'I'm a grandfather now—can you believe that?' he laughed, indicating his shopping bag crammed with chocolates, cheese and toilet articles meant for kids. I guess he wanted me to shake my head in utter disbelief and say, 'Rubbish. It can't be true, you—a grandfather? Come on . . . you have to be joking.' I did and said just that. My daughter looked funnily at me and raised her eyebrows. He looked pleased. It was such a sweet and pleasant encounter.

He asked after my parents—my father in particular, recalling how terrified he used to be of him in those days, how he didn't dare phone when he knew my father was at home, how he'd hang up if anybody else answered. And I immediately thought how easy it was for my own sons, not just to phone friends of the opposite sex, but chat easily with their daddies too. How the boys, Ranadip in particular, often play squash or go swimming with the fathers of girls they're dating, how their mothers invite them over for meals and chats when the girls are away. None of this was possible in my time, at least not in my family. My mother, who was definitely more approachable as compared to baba, dared not 'encourage' such friendships since she knew she'd incur her husband's wrath.

So . . . it was time to say goodbye—and we said it quickly. Mercifully, I wasn't asked for my phone number. There was nothing left to be said, really. The man got up, collected his parcel and shuffled off towards the exit. This time, he didn't even attempt to bring the old jauntiness into his gait.

My daughter looked at me in the way young daughters do—with amusement and curiosity. 'Mother . . . really. I mean . . . poor chap,' was all she said. Why poor? He seemed happy enough.

It's not just old friends I'm sentimental about. I feel that way about letters, too. It's hard to throw any away. It seems somehow insulting to the sender. Funny. Often I don't know the person who's written to me and yet, I can sense his or her reproachful presence as I reluctantly crumple the sheet and toss it into the nearest dustbin; I visualize my own efforts receiving similar treatment at indifferent hands. At our other home across the harbour, there's an enormous aluminium trunk crammed with letters, some of them thirty years old. I've never found the time to read any of them again, but I like the thought that they're still there.

Receiving witty, warm letters from family or friends provides one of life's big thrills. Even today, when the mail is delivered, I tear open the envelope with the most familiar or most interesting handwriting with such eagerness and a sense of anticipation, my children find it hilarious. More often than not, there are several mailers but no letters, but the day I spot an envelope with writing I recognize, I pounce on it and devour each word. It's been said before, but who says it can't be said again?

The art of letter writing has all but disappeared. My children prefer e-mail, my sisters long-distance calls, my friends face-to-face meetings—nobody writes on a regular basis. Nobody misses it either . . . but me. I'm not happy with the substitutes. I can't store calls in old trunks. I can't reach out and recall the exact conversation even fifteen days later. In that ugly, shiny trunk of mine lie several important turning points chronicled in words that at different stages of my life meant everything to me. Most letters are scattered, unnumbered and randomly stored, others, neatly tied with ribbons and preserved in a chronological sequence. There are cards, photographs, memos, telegrams (how quaint those seem now), diary entries, hastily scribbled notes, poems, scrapbooks. So precious. Too precious.

Perhaps the reason I don't dive in and start to devour the treasure is my own fear of how those letters will affect me now. I dare not read some of them—especially those from people I'd deeply hurt and walked away from, kind, good people who to this day are generous enough not to hate me, who continue to talk to me with love and affection, even as I cringe at the memory of how cruelly I'd treated them. Yes, cruelly. Often I'd been knowingly cruel, which makes it even worse. Youth may be a weak excuse, but it still doesn't cover all the ground. I shudder when I recall past transgressions, my rough methods, harsh words and contemptuous dismissals. How could I have behaved so abominably, so arrogantly, especially with people who were trusting, loving and loyal at all times? I now think they forgave me all too easily—assuming they really did so. When I meet friends from those long-ago days and search their faces for signs of anger and hostility, I see instead, just deep understanding, even affection. That's when I console myself with the thought that perhaps I've exaggerated my lapses. Surely there must have been moments that redeemed me sufficiently in the eyes of these very people who are treating me so civilly, decades later.

I'm also quite sentimental about music . . . but not old clothes. I can throw out just about any garment without the slightest regret. But there is one outfit I've hung on to—an inexpensive and rather unattractive salwar kameez that stays in its own special corner of my badly organized cupboard. It's the one I was wearing when I first met my husband. He remembers it a bit too clearly as well, and laughs at the memory. I haven't worn it since that fateful day (11 Aug) and I suspect I never will. The kameez is shocking pink, the salwar golden yellow and the dupatta, emerald green. If it sounds horrendous, that's what it is, only I didn't think so that night. I've kept most of my honeymoon clothes too since they represent our first joint venture. My husband had taken an exceedingly keen interest in acquiring that particular set of clothes, and even though they're sadly out of style, I can't get myself to throw them away. I particularly like the pin-tucked white shirt I wore in Vienna and still think it's the best shirt I've ever possessed.

Music affects me in strange ways. Ravel's 'Bolero'. Oh God. It hurts to hear it. Hindi film music from the Sixties. Early Ravi Shankar. The Beatles. Elvis Presley. Dave Brubeck. Edith Piaf. Simon and Garfunkel. Bade Ghulam Ali. Bhimsen Joshi. It is often the trigger that unleashes long-buried memories—scraps of conversation, an outing, a person, some occasions. It helps 'fix' a period, but even more than that, it facilitates nostalgia. I'd never heard of a smarmy piano player called Richard Clayderman till I met my husband. The first time his soft tinkling got to me was during a long car drive to Juhu. I turned to my husband to ask him to identify the music. He replied shortly, 'Clayderman. It's Clayderman.' We were at that stage of our relationship when it wouldn't have looked too smart to ask, 'Who dat?' or so I feared. I kept quiet and continued to listen. This was awful, I thought, wretched muzak, nothing more. And yet, I didn't want the tape to end. Throughout our short courtship, it was Clayderman and another equally smarmy musician called Lionel Richie with his velvety 'Hello', who kept the fires of our new romance efficiently stoked.

So many years later, when I happen to hear a snatch of either (while passing a record shop, or in a hotel lobby), I catch my breath, overwhelmed by the power exerted over me.

I'm transported . . . leaning my head against the back rest of a white car, gliding along smoothly, with an attentive, gallant stranger by my side. There is so much hope and promise in the air. And tension too. The music is soothing, undemanding. It fills our silences as we tentatively explore each other's worlds—so intimidatingly different, and attractive for that very reason.

There used to be a book I cherished a long, long time ago. A thick, bound book of nursery rhymes, neatly inscribed to 'Shobha Rajadhyaksha', given by my school in Delhi for winning an elocution competition when I was six years old and could barely lisp the chosen poem, such was my terror at being summoned to the principal's office for an impromptu competition. But I can recall the poem I picked very clearly. And recreate the moment of absolute fright as I faced three stern-faced judges and a principal I only recognized as being the second most important being after God. 'I'm busy, said the sea . . . I'm busy, think of me.'

Tears had rolled down my cheeks as I lisped on, wondering what this new form of punishment was . . . what awful thing had I done? At the end of it, I bowed—not out of respect but as a sign of surrender. Do with me what you please, that humble gesture said. It took the jury a few minutes to give me the prize. I brought it home, not quite clear whether it was an extension of the original punishment. I must have been really diffident—and dumb. It was only after my father read out the inscription that I accepted the fact I'd been given a book in recognition for something I'd done—something good and positive. It still puzzles me that a bunch of adults should have summoned such a young child from a classroom in progress, without any explanations, and expected her to recite on command. I continue to regard it as a somewhat cruel and insensitive act. The seeds for my future fear of public speaking, public appearances, public anything, were probably sown then. The fear of authority too.

I'm glad I've succeeded in licking at least one of those bogeys—opening my mouth in public. It was an act that used to paralyse me in the past. The thought of addressing a gathering of more than ten people would give me sleepless nights. I'd agonize over my 'speech' (even if it didn't exceed five simple lines), and freeze on the podium. One day I said to myself, 'This is absurd. In the coming years, you may be required to speak from a platform. The time to start getting used to that fact is now.'

I began by addressing small, non-threatening groups. I discovered I was far better at winging it than reading from a prepared text or committing a speech to memory. Since I had zero experience of acting on stage, I was unable to memorize lines and would expend far too much energy concentrating on getting the words right without skipping any. I was far more relaxed improvising, I could think better on my feet. Soon my confidence grew sufficiently to be able to get on to a stage without my knees buckling or voice cracking. The first few times were traumatic, especially the start, when the sound that emerged from my constricted throat was unrecognizable to me as my own voice. It sounded forced, unnatural and peculiarly pitched. This couldn't be me talking, I thought, my mind split on two levels—one part listening closely to alien-sounding words emerging from my larynx, another focusing on getting them out. It was weird. But I was determined to get over my phobia—and did. Now it hardly matters whether there are fifty or two thousand in the audience. It's between me and the mike. I've trained myself to perform on cue and not care about the applause (or its absence). That I think is the key—do your homework, go prepared, take your time if you have to, don't rush through it like an express train. Pause between sentences, emphasize key words and enjoy the experience. One more thing—stick to your own subject. Don't shoot your mouth off on a topic you know nothing about—the first people to see through the bullshit will be your audience. And then you'll be in trouble. Big trouble.

The book, with its ice-cream pink jacket, remained on my father's bookshelf for several years. It was only when my family moved from a flat at Churchgate to the one they now occupy at Cuffe Parade, that several reminders of my past got cast away, sold to the raddiwallah for a few rupees, by individuals who could not possibly have known how important they were to me. And that includes my Elvis Presley scrapbooks with neatly pasted pictures of my hero, and funny captions that tell their own story.

Elvis Presley was the only real teenage crush I had, the only celebrity I sought (and received) an autograph from, the only male who captured my romantic spirit and had me under a spell that lasted more than five years. Not before, and certainly not since, have I fantasized about an unknown, distant stranger, with as much fervour and passion. Sensing my state, it was baba who expressed his disapproval and disgust in terms that today I find very harsh and a bit too exaggerated. He termed my obsession 'a sign of perversity' and made me feel overwhelmed with guilt about a phase that was entirely pure in its innocence. What was so terrible about loving a hip-swivelling singer in distant California? *Loving*? Absolutely. It was love—unambiguous and true. And I wasn't afraid to express it. I didn't feel stupid or silly about my fixation either.

As always, it was Mother who instinctively understood my feelings and respected them. She never mocked this special love, even though she couldn't possibly have connected with its force. I felt free to talk about it to her, and she'd listen gravely while going about her domestic chores, her dark eyes alert and shining. Sometimes I wonder whether she lived vicariously through our lives. Married off at seventeen, a mother at nineteen, the only world she knew was the one her husband defined for her. Yet, her natural curiosity and keenness to observe, absorb and learn were so ferocious, there wasn't an area of our lives that didn't interest her, including schoolgirl gossip involving friends she wasn't ever likely to meet. Not only did she listen most attentively, she remembered long after we'd forgotten. Which, I now think, is a little sad. For us, it wasn't of any consequence at all. For her, it had become a window to another reality—one she had no access to. It went beyond mere amusement or entertainment. She obviously used our ceaseless prattle as a source of comfort, something she could recall during those long hours we were away, absorbed in our lives where there was little room for her. She quickly picked up our slang, our terminology, our quirky lingo. We picked up hers—Marathi phrases and figures of speech that were unique to her side of the family, a secret language she shared with her mother and sisters. Today, I've passed on most of it, pretty intact at that, to our daughters. We sisters and our brother lapse into it when we meet, and our children use it too. I love the sense of continuity it provides. Silly, childish words that don't mean anything to anybody else, but when we bring them into our conversation, an instant bond gets created, a bond that excludes 'outsiders'. Given that we've all chosen to marry outside the community, Marathi is something we cling to fiercely, afraid of letting go . . . it is one of our few and fragile links to the past, when we lived together as a family and communicated in a common language.

*

I'm always slightly testy when my older children merely inform us about their plans. The question of seeking permission does not arise. I suppose we ought to be grateful we are told at all. Some of our contemporaries complain they don't have the slightest idea where the kids are or even whether they'll be home for the night. Does that make us lucky? Special? Favoured? I don't know. I continue to be uneasy about this new liberalism with children breezing in and out of the home like it's a luxury hotel with twenty-four-hour room service, with no real responsibilities. Above all, I worry about their safety. There are far too many crazies out there now. My parents never worried—not about my getting to school and back, at any rate. Today, I find myself in a tizzy if the children don't ring the bell when I'm expecting them to, even when I know there is a morcha en route and the driver has been caught in the ensueing traffic snarl. Once again, it's a sad reflection of the times—our children are not safe on the streets. They aren't all that safe in the home either, without constant supervision. I remember being out for hours during hot afternoons in the Delhi summers, running around the sprawling colony, going from one friend's home to the other while my mother napped peacefully in Delhi's searing heat, curtains drawn, fan whirring. I can't recall whether or not there was a phone in the house; and if there was one, it certainly wasn't meant for my use. I have no memory of actually dialling someone till the age of twelve or thirteen after we'd settled into our South Mumbai existence.

Today, my family teases me about my 'phone fixation'. My kids say the telephone acts like my security blanket—so long as I know it's there, and someone I want to reach is a few digits away, I feel fine. In touch with the world. I respond a trifle defensively that given my self-imposed isolation by day (I rarely stir out of the house, often not making it past the main door for weeks), I need the periodic breathers a phone provides. I need to feel a part of the outside world, hear an adult human voice as opposed to the background score of assorted children's high-pitched conversations. I call it my only indulgence—and I'm not all that wrong. I love the phone. If I had to grab one object before fleeing from the house during an emergency, it would be the phone—not my modest jewellery collection, not any of my well-loved, well-worn sarees, not old photographs, not even a manuscript. My husband occasionally grumbles at the phone bills (I think he feels obliged to), but I self-righteously point out to him that those are the only bills I run up. I'm not a club-goer, I don't gamble nor do we eat out at fancy restaurants all that much. I'm an erratic and indifferent shopper, rarely splurging on anything obscenely expensive. I pick up all my own bills, don't splurge on redecorating the house compulsively, hardly ever use the car . . . my needs are really boringly limited. So, if the phone bills are on the steep side I think a concession ought to be made. The other day, I was listing my daily quota of calls—people I dial because I wish to speak to them every single day. They numbered five. Some of them I talk to twice a day. That takes the 'fixed' calls to ten. The others are mainly work related and I don't make them. Fifteen to twenty outside calls are received by me between 10 a.m. to 6 p.m. After which, I refuse to be on call for anything 'official'.

Unfortunately, in these days of instant quotes and overnight journalism, reporters think nothing of phoning at 11 p.m. to ask for a quotable sound byte, which naturally appears in an unrecognizable, mangled form the next day. I never go along with these ill-mannered people, especially the kind who phone to ask without a preamble or introduction, 'What are your views on homosexuality . . . infidelity . . .?' Or worse, questions on larger issues that require a well-researched book, not a two-liner to comprehend. I'm astonished at and enraged by the effrontery of it all. Do they imagine people are waiting by the phone, dying to provide saleable 'copy'? Maybe I'm wrong and they're right, maybe there really is a bunch of publicity-hungry people willing to rouse themselves from sleep and talk about a subject they may not know anything about, so long as their mugshots are carried in the papers the next day.

When cell-phones were just introduced, a reporter called to ask my opinion. I gave her my standard reply, 'Sorry, but I don't give dial-a-quote interviews.' There was a pause before the woman said in an exasperated tone, 'You don't understand. This is a new technology that doesn't require any dialling as such.' I hung up without explaining.

Other than these calls, I take them all, crank ones included. I consider myself an expert at disguising my voice, speaking in different accents and taking down messages to myself! What I hate, though, is being 'caught' on the phone by the family. I'm sure I have a guilty look on my face if the call has gone beyond ten minutes, especially if the caller happens to be a stranger.

As a young girl, I remember there were two things my father would object to vociferously—unending phone calls and sleeping late. For someone who enjoys both (perhaps as a reaction to earlier strictures) these habits are hard to break. I'm convinced there are two types of individuals—those who enjoy the dawn and employ great economy with words, and those like myself, who come alive after sunset and thrive on conversation. One of my big reservations about travelling in India is the unearthly hours planes leave at. Much as I enjoy airports, it's the thought of getting out of bed at some ghastly hour that discourages me. In effect, I end up staying awake all night. My husband is convinced I'm going to miss a flight someday because of my penchant for getting to the airport minutes before the counter shuts. So far that has not happened, but I've come pretty close to it.

*

A strange thing has happened over the past ten years. I've started lapsing into Marathi without considering whether the person I'm addressing understands or speaks it. And when I actually meet Marathi-speaking people, I can't seem to stop conversing in a language that for years and years, I'd all but deserted in favour of my glamorous adopted ones—Gujarati and Bengali, both of which I attempt to speak with some amount of fluency.

This happens most with Maharashtrian film stars like Madhuri Dixit or Nana Patekar or Urmila Matondkar or Kajol or models like Madhu Sapre and Milind Soman. Maybe because they are in spheres that have been dominated by non-Maharashtrians, mainly brash Punjabis, in their professional lives they don't get to speak their mother tongue, just as I don't in mine. When we run into each other at glamorous events, Marathi becomes our embrace. We revel and delight in those few short moments when we can be ourselves, stripped of the artifice and alien communication our public lives demand.

One of my big regrets is that I cannot read or write Marathi, unlike my siblings for whom it remains the primary language, thanks to their early schooling in various remote districts of Maharashtra where Marathi was—and still is—the medium of education. My brother still counts in his mother tongue, my sisters dream in it. As for me, it has become just another language I can get by in, my accent slightly off, my vocabulary rather shaky. Even so, I soldier on at every opportunity, even if I'm frequently rebuffed by say, bank clerks, policemen, shopkeepers, who take one look at me and decide arbitrarily (and rather unfairly), 'This woman couldn't possibly be one of us—she isn't a Maharashtrian. Surely not.' Each year, I go to one particular mithai shop at Thakurdwar, a Maharashtrian stronghold, during Diwali, to buy laddoos and assorted sweetmeats. And each year, I'm faced with the same silly question: 'How come you speak Marathi so well, madam?' These days I reply airily, 'Oh, I learnt it in America.' That, I notice, goes over far better than my old standard explanation. 'But why shouldn't I speak it? I'm a Maharashtrian after all.'

Each time I visit Goa, we make a trip to the four-hundred year-old Mangeshi temple that houses the Rajadhyaksha family deity. The visit transforms me, even if the fervour doesn't last beyond a day. When I wear a nine-yard saree, fast in the morning, and present myself to the family priest for inspection and approval, I feel different. I feel Maharashtrian. So what if hours later, I'm back on the beach clad in a casual sarong? That moment is real. And honest. One morning while waiting for our turn to worship, I felt someone tap me on the back. I turned around to see an old lady. She pointed to my forehead and said, 'No bindi? Where's your kumkum?' My hand flew up to check. It was true. The stick-on bindi had fallen off. She indicated that I should wait. Within seconds she was back with red vermillion on her middle finger. I bent down while she created a bindi for me. It was an unforgettable moment. We'd connected wordlessly through a timeless gesture that bound us culturally, emotionally, through gender, tradition and religion. So many levels in one small act.

In '98, we were back for our annual darshan. This time the temple was filled with Saraswat families offering Maha-Rudra Yagna. I was mesmerized by the spectacle—it enveloped all the senses. The reverberations made every sinew in my body respond as priests chanted in unison, their voices sonorous as they echoed off the ancient stone walls of the temple. The air was filled with incense. The fragrance of *bel phool* mixed with the sharp smell of burning camphor. Bells clanged, drums sounded. The chanting continued. I shut my eyes. I could sense the vibrations in every cell of my being. It was primal and deeply moving. This is how it must have been for centuries. This is how it was . . . it is. I wanted to share it with my children. Expose them to their 'Maharashtrian' halves—the ones they were strangers to.

Feeling Great

When I recall the rather extraordinary circumstances of my marriage to Dilip I'm reminded of how a determined suitor can challenge destiny and win. This is a longish story that requires a preamble. In the summer of 1983, Kunda spotted an announcement in a local paper in Muscat where she works as an ophthalmic surgeon at the Royal Hospital. It was an advertisement issued by Reuters, the international news agency, inviting applications for an attractive fellowship. She felt I met the requirements—the candidate had to be under thirty-five years of age, with at least ten years' working experience in journalism. It was designed as a mid-career sabbatical that would provide a ten-month break to the recipient at a college either in Oxford or on the campus at Stanford, California. No strings attached. This period could be used to write a book or a paper or to take a few courses. The terms were extraordinarily generous with a comfortable allowance included. Kunda mailed it to me with a persuasive letter urging me to apply. Why not? she asked. What does it involve besides a few hours of your time? That was true.

The application was to be sent along with two short essays stating why you were interested in the fellowship and how you intended to use the period it covered. Three clippings of published articles were to be attached as well—clippings the applicant thought best represented his or her work. My own life was in limbo at the time. Sudhir and I had filed for divorce by mutual consent. I was assessing future options, unsure of which path to take. I was uncertain about the choices I was making, unsure of what I wanted. Egged on by Kunda and with my customary 'what the hell' attitude, I sent off the application and forgot all about it.

That summer, I was taking a much-needed break in America. *Celebrity* had changed hands. And I didn't like the hands. I needed time off. And took it. I was hoping to unravel the mess my life was in, hoping to find some immediate answers. Late one afternoon, the phone rang and a person with a very 'propah' British accent asked for me, saying he was calling from London. I wondered who could have tracked me down and the first thing I asked was, 'How did you know where to find me?'

After a pause the man said, 'It wasn't that difficult—we called your home.'

Confused and wary, I asked testily, 'So . . . what's this about?'

He said, 'Congratulations. You have been awarded the Reuters Fellowship for the year and we want to know whether you are in a position to accept it.'

I didn't understand. What was he talking about? I'd all but forgotten about the application. My life was being lived roller-coaster style. What fellowship? Why was he congratulating me? Who was he? I thought it was a mistake, or worse, a joke. Some one's idea of a silly gag.

I asked seriously, 'Is this a crank call?'

And he said, 'Oh no. Not at all. You can call us back on these numbers if you wish. We need to know your decision. And by the way—you are the first Asian woman to have won this fellowship. Congratulations again.'

Oh hell! The timing was awful. How could I take ten

months off just like that? What was I supposed to do now? Temporarily alienated from my family, I couldn't ask my parents for advice. Besides, I was thousands of miles away from home. I was scheduled to fly to London shortly and then on to Cannes before heading back to Mumbai. I told the person I'd be in London in ten days' time and would let him know then. 'Do visit the office. Call on arrival,' he said and rang off.

This would mean a major shift in my shaky plans. I'd have to reorganize my life dramatically. Explain to my young children that I'd be away for close to a year. It didn't seem right. It didn't make sense. Bewildered and flattered at the same time, I flew to London.

The appointment was fixed for mid-morning. I walked in wearing a silk saree. The man who greeted me cheerfully said, 'Right. So you are the latest fellow. How jolly. Let me introduce you to everyone.' We went from cubicle to cubicle meeting people. Each time the gentleman said 'Meet the latest fellow—from India', I squirmed. Was he really referring to me? Me? A fellow? A Reuters fellow?

I was given a few days to decide on whether or not I was going to accept. I talked to my sister Kunda. ('Take it. Take it. Don't think.') So, I said, yes, I'd be happy to accept the fellowship—my choice was Stanford. Everything was set in motion. I cancelled Cannes and flew back to Mumbai, a wild-eyed, thoroughly mixed-up woman. I didn't want to leave my children. And yet I knew this was my big opportunity, perhaps the last one. If I didn't grab it, I'd have to make my peace with staying on in a familiar rut. I was restless and bored. Demoralized and depressed. The other option was to try and make another life, in another country with another man. I wasn't convinced about that either.

Winding up was far more traumatic than I'd anticipated.

There were far too many loose ends, far too much unresolved stuff. My children couldn't understand what was happening to their mother, why their lives were likely to be shaken up yet again. I was wracked with self-doubt and guilt. I wasn't being fair. I wasn't doing the right thing. I was being selfish. I would regret the decision. I'd have to pay for it someday. I would lose the love of my children. My family would disown and despise me. I was a bad woman, only thinking of myself and my future. As I prepared to leave, my heart was not in the planning. I went about it robotically, mechanically. There was no real enthusiasm. There was nothing to look forward to. I was submerged in bleakness.

My flight (a metaphorical one, too) was at dawn on 16 August. I met Dilip on the night of the 11th. It was a meeting that altered my life—and gave me the answer I was so desperately looking for. The circumstances could not have been more bizarre. The few days before my departure were packed with informal farewell parties organized by colleagues. At one such, when I arrived at my hosts' home, I was told airily by the hostess that they'd been invited to a dinner at a friend's home and they were sure I wouldn't mind accompanying them. I was aghast. What a ridiculous suggestion.

'Don't worry, we won't stay long. Just a drink and then we'll take you out to dinner.'

But that hadn't been the original plan. I'd assumed they were hosting a small party for me at their home, not asking me to tag along with them to a stranger's. I said I was sorry but I didn't go uninvited to parties.

'Oh, don't worry. It isn't like that. He's a good friend of ours. Stop being such a snob. Besides, it's only for half an hour. Come on, don't be a spoilsport.'

'Call him,' I suggested, 'tell him you'd like to bring a

friend. Check whether it's okay.'

'Stop it. Of course it's okay. It's a big dinner for over seventy people. It really won't matter.'

'No, I'm sorry. Phone first.'

The hostess made a few half-hearted attempts and gave up.

'Come on. Just half an hour. We are already late.' They were at the door.

'Fine. Half an hour,' I said sullenly as I picked up my bag and followed them to the elevator. 'By the way, whose house are you taking me to?'

'Oh, his name is Dilip Dé. You'll like him!'

And that was all I knew as I stood outside the door of my future home. We were going to Mr Dilip Dé's house. And he was a nice man I'd 'like'. Too embarrassed to follow my hosts into a stranger's residence, I lingered at the door. When I looked up, a well-built man in his forties was walking towards me. Dilip Dé.

'Please . . . do come in, welcome, welcome. This is quite an occasion,' he said, not bothering to hide his delight.

I followed him into a large living room where I spotted several familiar faces. 'What shall I get you to drink?' he asked in an old-fashioned boxwallah kind of way. I noticed his strong Bengali accent and recognized the subtle aftershave. I didn't like his blue T-shirt.

'I don't drink,' I answered stiffly.

Undeterred, he added, 'How about champagne?'

I smiled. 'Why not? I never say no to champagne.'

If this is sounding like a smarmy, cheesy film script, I'm sorry, but that's exactly how the lines went. Exactly. I haven't forgotten a single word. It is on instant recall—every bit if it, every detail, every nuance. We relive each moment, each fragment periodically, and it remains as fresh, as vivid, as poignant today as it did when it occurred on that incredible, unplanned night that brought two strangers together and transformed them forever.

I don't know what might have happened to me had I dug in my heels and refused to go to the party. I don't know what made me attend it either. How was I so easily persuaded to gatecrash a dinner at an unknown individual's home? I've always scoffed at words like 'destiny', 'karma', 'pre-ordained'—but I haven't found a more convincing explanation so far. Why did I walk those twenty paces down a long corridor and into my future husband's life and home? What were the forces that compelled me to say 'yes' to my hosts' absurd suggestion? Why didn't I opt out of the evening and go home instead? I could have insisted on doing just that. Why didn't I remind the couple that this was meant to be my evening—a farewell for me, not a walk-in affair to an open-house? I'd never done something as ill-mannered before—not even as a gauche teenager. And here I was, a thirty-four-year-old woman, blithely floating into a formal evening without so much as an invitation to call my own. Not done.

My husband too marvels at the way in which everything happened that night. Nobody had ever walked into his home without being asked—it simply wasn't a practice he endorsed or encouraged. Nobody dared. He'd made an exception. And so had I. How come? Would an astrologer provide some explanations? Maybe even a few answers?

By any standards it was an unusual encounter—one that I might have been able to put behind me (very reluctantly) had the sequence of events been any different. But my husband 'knew'. He just did. He can't explain it either. He wasn't looking for a wife at that stage in his life (he'd been a widower raising two growing children for a little over two years then).

And I wasn't in search of a husband. If anything, I was in the process of finding my own feet as a single woman again and rather enjoying the experience—frightening though it definitely was. And yet, he was certain about our entwined fates, and he didn't take more than a few minutes to tell me so. His manner was amazingly direct and sure. There wasn't the slightest hesitation when, within moments of joining me on a sofa, he asked, 'So . . . when can I meet your parents? Tomorrow?' Of course I didn't take that seriously—which woman would? I treated his comments lightly, laughing them off, trying to distract his attention, while all the time my heart was saying, 'Is this man serious? Does he mean a word of all this? Is he giving me a corny line? If so, I don't like his sense of humour.'

The man was serious. Very serious. Like I said, Dilip recognized something—something very deep and precious—intuitively, instinctively. He knew very little about me. We'd never met. I knew nothing about him. And yet, that night he was one hundred per cent certain we'd spend the rest of our lives together. How? I don't know. Neither does he.

Today, when I reflect on the defining moment of that incredible night of dramatic turning points and tough decisions, one single image stands out. Just one. While the party whirled around us—over sixty people moving freely and easily between the rooms, chatting, laughing, flirting, drinking, Dilip and I had sat riveted to the sofa, almost like we'd been nailed down to it. At one point he'd asked me whether I was interested in art—more specifically, in miniatures. I'd answered indifferently that I didn't know too much about them. 'I'd like you to see something,' he'd said firmly. Dilip's the kind of person who doesn't wait for acquiescence. He stood up and expected me to follow. I'd thought idly, 'Oh well, here's a new variation to the old "come up and see my etchings" line.'

I'd walked behind him into the bedroom which was filled with people talking noisily and obviously admiring something rare and wonderful in a frame. But the only thing that caught my attention in that large room overlooking the sea was the sight of two tousled heads in the middle of a king-sized double-bed. I didn't have to be a genius to figure out their identity. I don't know why, but that single image broke my heart. I didn't care about the damned miniatures being passed around. I didn't notice other details (the sort that usually never escape me). All I could see were two very young children sleeping trustingly on their father's bed while insensitive, loud-mouthed guests moved around, not bothering to put out their cigarettes or step out and allow the two to dream in peace. I found that shocking. And said so.

Dilip looked at me and said, 'They are used to it . . .' Long pause. '. . . now that I'm alone. My children often sleep in the room with me.'

That sentence said it all. It stated far more than just the obvious—that the kids were motherless. And that he was horribly lonely and needed the comfort of their presence. It also told me a few more things: that they weren't being raised by a series of efficient nannies. That they weren't meant to be invisible or kept out of sight. That Dilip didn't lead a life of dissipation with assorted women traipsing in and out of his bed. That he was a caring father who tried sincerely to fill the void the children's mother had left. In my eyes all these things made him an honourable man, no matter what else his faults may have been.

That night, I went home to my parents' flat, a few metres down the road from Dilip's, a very confused woman. Of course I'd been flattered by his attention (he'd ignored everybody else—legitimate guests—at his own dinner and

470

concentrated on a gatecrasher). But it wasn't as if this sort of attention was new to me. The confusion was created by his obvious earnestness and the passion he packed into his simple words. There were no masks, disguises or smart lines. This man was saying very simply, 'I am interested in you. I'd like to see you again. And if things work out, I believe we should get married.' Sounds crazy? Absurd? Maybe. But then again—not everything spins around logic.

He'd said he'd call the next day. He knew three things about me: i) my age ii) my community iii) my marital status. I was sure that in the cold and sober light of day he'd kick himself and say, 'God, what an ass I must have made of myself. Damn. Now . . . what was her name again?'

I wasn't expecting his call. And it didn't come. Not till twelve noon. The voice over the phone was wonderful but businesslike. And terribly formal. No jokes. No warm greetings. 'Is it still on for tonight?' he asked, and I stammered, 'Well . . . yes . . . yes . . . that is, I can only make it after ten . . . . I'm umm . . . busy till then . . . I mean . . . I'm expecting a call, and . . . so . . .'

He didn't let me finish. Almost curtly he said, 'All right then. I'll be there at ten past ten.'

I turned in a panic to my mother. 'He's coming,' I announced, flushed and excited.

She nodded in a knowing sort of way, like she'd known he would (I'd 'confessed' over tea in the morning). My father looked indifferent as if fatigued at the thought of yet another complication in my already complicated life. I gave them the time of his arrival.

My father huffed, 'Women from decent families do not receive men at such a late hour. It's completely unacceptable.' I knew he wouldn't meet him, the official reason being: 'Once I remove my dentures after dinner I only put them on again

471

in the morning.' If my father wouldn't meet him for whatever reason, it followed my mother wouldn't either (he'd construe it as an act of complicity).

It was left to my sister Mandakini (visiting from New York) to size up the man who'd decided to become her new brother-in-law. She opened the door for Dilip (it was a wet and stormy monsoon night), asked him to sit down and came rushing into my parents' bedroom to report, 'Bengali. Uttam Kumar type. Probably wears a wig. The hair seems unnaturally thick.' So much for sisterly solidarity. I was dressed in my sole French chiffon (black) and feeling like a schoolgirl on her first date.

'Fondue,' announced Dilip, 'I hope you like it. I've booked a table at the Café Royale—there's a fondue festival on.' I nodded dumbly. He wasn't asking for my opinion anyway. It had been taken for granted that I'd have no objections to fondue. I didn't.

That evening I barely got to open my mouth. Dilip spoke incessantly, persuasively, passionately, like his life depended on what he had to convey to me in those few hours. He kept back nothing. The narration was impassioned and honest-sounding. Here was a man saying, 'This is me. This is my life. Take it or leave it. But mainly—take it.' He didn't ask me a single question. Just as well. There would have been no time to answer it. By the time he was through, it was 2.30 a.m. And we hadn't so much as touched the fondue (presented twice over by the bewildered staff). We hadn't touched each other either—physically that is. Not even a handshake. And yet, what we'd shared had been immeasurably intimate.

The countdown had begun. The clock was ticking away infuriatingly. And I still didn't know—stay or go? Stay or go? Marry a stranger and take my chances? Stay back, not marry, and see where the relationship took us? Maybe nowhere.

Once again, Dilip knew exactly how to pitch it. He helped me arrive at my decision by not pushing me to take one. He'd obviously made his. But he refrained from using any pressure tactics. He let me be. There were roughly thirty-six hours left to go before I boarded that flight to New York. If he was conscious of the passing minutes, he didn't show it. I didn't understand his calm—it was unnatural. But he understood my fear.

It was Hariprasad Chaurasia who helped me make that fateful decision—even if he doesn't know it. Dilip had bought tickets for his concert. So had my father and his brother. Oops, I thought to myself. How's Dilip going to handle that? Expertly, as it turned out. We met them during the interval. Dilip was gallant and correct without falling all over them. He fetched cold coffee (the Tata theatre serves the best) for us all and escorted them back to their seats. He was respectful but not deferential. It was hard to fault him. Harder still for me to resist an invitation back to his home—perhaps for the last time.

We sat in the study outside his bedroom, conscious at all times of the presence of a young child sleeping a few feet away from us. Once again Dilip chose to speak. This time his voice was steady, his words well considered. He reasoned with me about the benefits of the Reuters fellowship and what it might mean down the line—a smart career move. If that. Then he talked of what our future together would mean—stability for our children. Lifelong love and companionship for us—if we worked at it and valued the commitment. 'It's up to you. The decision is yours. I'll respect it whichever way it goes.' It was one of the toughest calls of my life. I tried bargaining. 'I'll go for a year and then if we still feel the same way, we'll take it from there.' 'No,' said Dilip firmly, 'it has to be decided tonight. This is the moment. If you go, it's goodbye. If you stay, we share our lives together . . . starting now.'

Our wedding ceremony was idyllic—the way I'd always visualized it since my childhood. The way I'd always wanted it—small, pretty and meaningful. We'd decided to do it our way this time around. No interference from anybody. In any case, who would have dared—or cared, for that matter? We were much too old to let someone else take the decisions.

Such a contrast to our passive participation during our respective first wedding ceremonies, where we'd been puppets dancing to the tune of well-meaning but overwhelming family members determined to make super productions of the events. Isn't that how it is in most traditional Indian homes? Mine had been beautiful, each detail perfectly executed. But I'd felt alienated from the grand proceedings, dressed up in finery I wasn't accustomed to or comfortable wearing. Weighed down and feeling suffocated, all I'd been acutely conscious of during the prolonged marriage rituals was the sharp pain in my scalp caused by extra-long, lethal-looking pins that were holding up my elaborate hairstyle. I couldn't wait to rip off my heavy Benarasi saree and tear my hair free. There was no question of my exercising control over the arrangements or even expressing an opinion. I'd gone along in a bewildered haze, kept my head bowed, my eyes modestly lowered, while nearly spraining my lower back with all the bending and feet-touching. It shows in the photographs. My smile is a tight, polite one, my eyes expressionless, my posture uncharacteristically stiff. All that extravagance . . . all that enthusiasm . . . all that effort. How sad. Compared to that, the divorce itself was easy—almost too easy. And just for the record, officially speaking, I was a divorcee for precisely one and a half hours. Now that's a story. Since our divorce was by mutual consent, we had nothing to contest. After our first appearance in court to file the papers in July 1984, our lawyer,

Anand Grover, had suggested tea and butter biscuits at a nearby Irani restaurant. The three of us had walked over and chatted briefly. After Sudhir left, Grover turned to me and asked, 'I hope you aren't planning to remarry. What's there in marriage, anyway?' I turned to him, rather amused, and asked, 'How come you're married?' We joked about the subject for a while, before I answered truthfully and seriously—'I happen to like being married. I believe in marriage. I enjoy being a wife. I don't want to spend the rest of my life on my own.' Grover shrugged. He seemed surprised.

The divorce came through at 11.30 a.m.

I married Dilip at 1 p.m.

Touch and go.

That pretty much sums up the way my life has been.

My family was astonished by my decision. Or maybe they weren't. It was at a stage in my life when nothing I said or did surprised them any more. My father assumed his stoic, stony face. My mother looked visibly apprehensive. It was a big step—perhaps the biggest I'd ever taken. It was going to affect not just my own life but the lives of four young children—his and mine. In hindsight, I suppose my parents might have eventually approved of our marriage but we wanted to spare them possible embarrassment by involving them directly in the arrangements. Dilip's parents were dead. That left our children (far too young) and a handful of friends. Perfect. I'd dreamt of a wedding ceremony performed in a temple courtyard open to the sky, with towering trees forming a protective canopy—a setting steeped in benevolent forces, exuding positive energy and charged with spiritual vibrations. We found exactly such a setting in the historic Laxmi Narayan temple in central Mumbai. I'd very much wanted a priest to recite Sanskrit shlokas he'd be able to explain to us in a language we understood—we found him. And I'd wanted to be surrounded by family and a few people who loved us, accepted and understood our special situation—they were there to share our joy.

Stripped of artifice and any unnecessary displays, our wedding was charming in its minimalistic beauty. This time, I was dressed in a red cotton chanderi saree, my hair flying free in the afternoon breeze. Dilip was wearing a traditional Bengali dhoti, an angavastram covering his bare chest. There was laughter and there were tears. Above all, there was a sense of dignity and solemnity about everything. It was a do-it-yourself wedding organized personally by the groom and bride, without fuss or frills. It was a strong affirmation of both fate and faith as we walked around the holy fire, watched by those we respected and cared for: my family, Dilip's younger brother Arjun (our big regret was that Dilip's parents weren't alive to bless us) and a few, very few friends.

While seated in the pretty mandap, I looked up and saw my parents as they watched the ceremony, frowns of concentration creasing their brows. I wondered what was going on in their minds. I'm certain they were apprehensive—but beyond that? It was remarkable how broad-minded they had been. Not one of their children had married within the closed Saraswat Brahmin community we were born into. Mandakini wed a Parsi, Cyrus Tata; Kunda was Mrs Srinivasan; Ashok had fallen in love with Moyna Mukherjee, a Bengali. And here was the youngest opting for the second time to tie the knot with a non-Maharashtrian. If they had any reservations on this score, they kept them to themselves. They hadn't interfered in any way. Nor had I asked for help. Dilip had singlehandedly organized the small celebration, not skipping a single step. He had personally selected my sarees, going to the trouble of locating my tailor and having matching cholis stitched. He bought jewellery to match. 'Why should you be short-changed because my parents are not alive to organize what is traditionally given to the bride?'

It couldn't have been better. We felt responsible for ourselves and our decision, without anybody attempting to manipulate us or telling us what to do, how to do it and when. Unlike traditional Indian weddings where the bride and groom are rarely consulted and are often the least important participants in the proceedings, which are rudely hijacked by insensitive 'elders' of the families. Most importantly, Dilip and I enjoyed every moment of our wedding—and why not? We'd organized it down to the last detail—practically picked the flowers from the fields ourselves, as it were.

While the ceremonies were going on, I looked at Dilip's expression as he listened intently to the priest's chanting. This was the man I was going to spend the rest of my life with. Seeing the determination on his face, I knew I'd be able to count on him, no matter what came our way. I saw Dilip's children (Ranadip and Radhika) wilting slightly in the heat as they innocently shuffled a pack of cards to kill time, waiting for the 'boring' ceremony to end, perhaps oblivious to the major shift that was about to take place in their world. They had had 'Daddy' to themselves for two years. And Daddy was getting married. A near-stranger would be sharing their home. The new 'Mrs Dé'. They'd be entrusting their young lives to my care henceforth. Would I be up to it?

A late lunch had been organized at my new home, which was discreetly decorated with specially ordered rose-and-jasmine garlands. The lady who welcomed me with an aarti was not a relative but perhaps something more—a loyal maid called Bijoli Debi who seemed genuinely happy about the new developments in her employer's life. A traditional wedding feast followed for family and a few friends. I overheard one of the children talking to a friend on the phone. Said Ranadip, unable to disguise the excitement in his voice, 'I'm sorry I can't come and play just now . . . you see, I'll have to ask my mother's permission first.' It was the way he uttered that word 'mother'—with pride—that reassured me more than any speech or gesture might have. There was such heartbreaking trust in that single word. This shy, awkward little boy was calling me 'mother' so ungrudgingly, unquestioningly. It terrified me.

Over the next few weeks it was to be repeated several times by both the children. 'My mother says . . .', 'My mother won't allow . . .', 'I'll have to ask my mother . . .' For two years they'd been deprived of a child's most basic right—to call out to a 'mother'. Now, having regained it, they obviously couldn't get enough. Each time I heard them using that word, I felt my heart doing a flip-flop. In those early months, it wasn't me, the person, who mattered, it was me the figurehead, the 'mother'. I worried about what would happen when the novelty of repeating the 'mother mantra' wore off, and they discovered they were better off without the stranger—me—in their midst? What if they rejected me and my tentative overtures? What if the frequency and monotonous utterance of that magical word 'mother' ceased to have any significance in their lives? And what of my own biological children who didn't enjoy the same access to me—their 'real' mother—at the time (more due to logistics than anything else)? Would they start to resent the presence of two—no, three—new entrants in my life? So many complications. So much 'newness' to deal with. What if—horror of horrors—I failed them all?

Enough 'well-wishers' had predicted failure. The reactions to the 'news' were many. Most, negative. 'Friends' would sidle up to us individually and whisper, 'My God! I hope you know what you're doing . . .' To Dilip they'd say, 'She's a very self-willed woman. Far too strong-headed.' And to me they'd coo, 'Well . . . we're happy for you, of course. But he does have two kids, you know.'

The general verdict? It's never going to work. There was a great deal of speculation and gossip. Some of it hurt. The rest we laughed at. Dilip decided to introduce me to his hometown, Calcutta (just before our wedding). I'd been there several times but this time it was going to be dramatically different. 'Watch out—snakepit ahead,' a friend warned me, as I walked into the first of several dinners in our honour. There was curiosity mixed with scepticism. I could sense the women sizing me up and the men getting that particular look in their eyes. The kind men get when another man dares to take a step they themselves don't have the courage for. The expression registers several emotions—envy being the most apparent one. I must have been thoroughly dissected and shredded after the trip. I didn't know any of these people. We didn't have a common past, there were no overlapping reference points. But there was enough shared history within those groups for them to regard me as an intruder invading their turf. Just as well we weren't planning to shift there, I thought thankfully. I might have been eaten alive or swallowed whole. Like the little fish (chhoto maach) Bengalis deep fry and devour.

Dilip's relatives were far more welcoming. They greeted me warmly and took me into the fold without hesitation. I met as many mashimas and pishimas as was possible during our short stay, and felt entirely at home. Everything was alien to me—the language, the food, the mannerisms. And yet there was enormous affinity at important levels. I felt I belonged. I felt comfortable . . . even when I heard Dilip being addressed as 'Gopal' (his 'dak naam') or 'DK' (as his friends call him).

There was a lot we had to find out about one another—I was just about starting. No sweat. No hurry. We had years ahead of us.

I decided to begin at the most basic level—food. I must confess, so many years later (we are in the fourteenth year of our marriage—incredible), I still love my man but can't get myself to love mustard oil. I speak a version of Bengali—enough to get by. And have learnt to appreciate and acknowledge the superiority of fresh-water fish over the sea variety. I can't bear Rabindra Sangeet (it sounds like a dirge), nor do I salivate over an earthen pot of mishti doi. My Maharashtrianness or 'Indianness' stays intact. I am and will die a true 'Bombaywalli'.

Funny thing is, I have never once regretted that frightening decision to stay back and reinvent my life. We've had our rough moments, bumpy patches, arguments, disagreements and fights. There have been tears, accusations and recriminations. But no real regrets. The parameters of our relationship have been drawn by Dilip. Initially I chafed at some of them. Now I know it was his more mature, more experienced voice redefining marriage for me. We never ever discussed 'space', and I still don't understand what couples mean when they state proudly, 'Our marriage works because we give each other a lot of space.' My parents weren't troubled by such problems. And neither am I.

The need for 'space' makes marriage sound like a tenancy in a crowded block. Marriage means being together, even at times when the sight, smell and sound of the 'other' drives you crazy. 'Space' connotes escape, but maybe I'm wrong. Space also obliquely refers to a strong desire for privacy, for expressing one's individuality, for putting up invisible barriers around oneself. It's a modern-day invention I don't fully appreciate or understand. Marriage to me connotes commitment and surrender. Merging with, blending, overlapping, combining. It is a symbiotic relationship where one feeds on the other, depends on the other, needs the other. There is no room or requirement for 'space'. It's a misleading and mischievous concept that has led to several modern-day marriages breaking up—perhaps because the two people have misconstrued its true interpretation (whatever that is). Individuals in search of vast and unlimited space are better off single—they can have any amount of it staying on their own.

I still believe that marrying Dilip and basing my decision on nothing more than a gut-feeling, a strong impulse which said 'You are doing the right thing', was one of my smarter choices, if not the smartest. He was right. What might my life have been after Stanford? It's impossible to speculate, but I can hazard a good guess. I'd have been on a high while on campus, enjoyed every moment of the fellowship, met several interesting people, experienced great exhilaration . . . and eventually packed my bags and come home. To what? Uncertainty. Insecurity. Alienation. From family, friends and colleagues. Would it have been worth the experience? Who's to say? All this is in the realm of conjecture—I've never wasted time wondering. All I know is, I'm glad I listened to my heart and stayed. I'm grateful that I met Dilip. And overjoyed that we decided to expand our family and have two children of our own.

Taking Stock

Today, Dilip and I have six wonderful children, and I say that as an exceedingly proud and clearly prejudiced mother. Each one of them is special. Each one has enriched our lives even if they don't know it. Funnily enough, they'd worked out their own equations a long time ago and without any parental prodding. It helped that Dilip's two, Ranadip and Radhika, and my two, Aditya and Avantika, grew up together in the same school, with Radhika and Aditya sharing a classroom since age eight. The four of them knew one another before Dilip and I did. I wonder how the 'yours, mine and ours' scenario might have worked out had the two sets of children been forcibly thrown together and instructed to 'be friends'. It never works. What if the ones I 'inherited' (Ranadip and Radhika) had turned out to be absolute brats? What if they had conspired to give me a hard time—and had succeeded? Mercifully, nothing like that occurred. They were good children—even docile. Life fell easily into a domestic pattern. I was never asked to arbitrate. The question of taking sides never arose.

By modern standards, we share a fairly formal relationship with our children. And a quaintly old-fashioned one between ourselves. We never address each other by our respective first names. I call him 'Dé' in public. He simply says 'she'. In the privacy of our home, he calls out, 'where are you?'

when he needs me, while I find it easier to just go up to him and start talking. Strangely, it was the same with my parents. My mother said 'A-ho' to my father. He responded with 'A-ga'.

Today, if the children fight, they sort it out amongst themselves. When they make up, they do so on their own terms. I stay out of their dynamics, even though I am an overly concerned, overly curious mother who'd ideally like to be consulted and involved in every single aspect of my children's lives. They do not hesitate to tell me where to get off, even if they're considerate enough to do so obliquely and gently. That's all right by me. I sometimes forget to acknowledge the fact that they are adults now (well, four of them qualify) and capable of handling their own lives. I tend to interfere, maybe because I want so much to be a part of their day-to-day developments. Crazy. Unrealistic, too.

I often find myself wondering what the children make of their rather unusual set-up. Do Rana and Radhika torment themselves with the thought of how different their lives might have been had their mother been alive? Do Aditya and Avantika actively miss my presence in their home—a home we once shared? Do the four of them, occasionally at least, resent what is after all a highly artificial situation? I suppose I'll never really know. We've all had to adapt and accommodate and train ourselves to respect the circumstances.

The girls have had their teenage crushes and 'serious' boyfriends. The boys—oh hell, men—theirs. I have 'disapproved' of each and every person, much to the children's exasperation and wry amusement. They've sulked. Stormed off. Defied. Coerced. Rebelled. Held out. Raged. In other words, they've taken the same route I took in my twenties. I tend to forget that. They never fail to remind me.

483

The two little girls, Arundhati and Anandita, have been the lucky recipients of their siblings' unstinted love. My only prayer to God is: 'May it always be this way. May the six of them stay close and supportive of one another. May they be friends in their later years. May their children love one another. May they wish each other well always.' That's all I really want today. Peace and joy within our family. Heaven knows that's hard enough to achieve in a 'normal' set-up. It's harder still for those of us who have chosen to tread a less-peopled pathway. I have tried to retain neutrality at all times though I must have failed frequently. The affected children will surely remember. And maybe even forgive . . . but that's a big hope. I can only say that I have tried my best. My methods may have been flawed, but the intentions were always sincere.

Parenting is the single most difficult responsibility in the world—don't let anybody tell you otherwise. But as Dilip reminds me when I'm at my lowest regarding something I've said to one of the children or they've said to me, 'Don't give up. We can only try hard, do our best. The rest is up to them.' And yet, their power to affect my sense of being remains undiminished. Very recently, when Aditya said to me quietly and with obvious remorse, 'There were times when I was younger when I felt jealous of my friends. Jealous of the fact that they had a mother to go home to and share things with, jealous of their constant interaction,' I felt my heart contract painfully. I can never make up for that loss. Never. Of course, it hasn't been easy on either set of children. My own must have mourned my absence as deeply and silently as I mourned theirs. While Dilip's children must have equally strongly mourned an even more poignant absence—Rita, their biological mother, a lady I never knew but would like to have known. I could have understood her precious offspring better.

I didn't try and replace her in their lives, I merely attempted to take care of them to the best of my ability, raise them in a manner that would have made her proud.

Now that they are both in their twenties, I'm struck by two things—the first being the untamperable, stubborn genetic code we are born with that can resist and withstand all influences—even those unconsciously unleashed by a well-meaning stepmother who, while she hasn't given birth to the children, has nurtured them as she thinks best. Today Ranadip and Radhika are proud individuals in whom I see their mother far more clearly than I can see myself. Initially, it surprised and hurt me to recognize that biology had triumphed over environment, nature over nurturing. I couldn't understand some of their actions or mannerisms—where were they coming from? Why were we out of sync on some issues? Why wasn't it easier to create bridges? After all, I spent far more time with them during their formative years than I did with my natural-born children. I've also spent more years with them than the sadly limited ones they shared with their mother. And yet. Yes, and yet. That poignant, painful 'and yet' that nobody can fully explain.

It's only during the past two years that I've put my own little ego aside and accepted the fact that they cannot possibly take on my colours, values or attitudes—we are and will remain differently wired. With that realization, the disappointment has been easier to come to terms with. Dilip is our primary and vital link in the chain. So long as he understands, so long as he decodes and plays interpreter, it's fine. We are fine.

I feel more competent nowadays. I have taught myself to identify the areas that genes indisputably control, and deal with the children using that knowledge. I no longer wonder why Radhika and I don't laugh at the same things. I know her sense of humour doesn't overlap with mine. I'm not surprised or hurt that our tastes and responses are so diametrically different when it comes to food, clothes, books, films, music. I no longer agonize, 'Why isn't she even a little like me? Why has nothing rubbed off? Why don't we share more in common?' I know better now. Radhika is an intense young woman with a strong focus, an introvert who prefers to spend her spare time with books and music. Her fulfilment lies elsewhere—not in the world I inhabit. My early sense of defeat which turned to resignation has now been converted into acceptance. Of our parallel lives, our obvious polarities. I'm not puzzled any more. She is her own person—very much so. And she carries her own mother within her. And always will. As nature intended. Nurturing may or may not tell—but that's the way the cookie crumbles. Who am I to question or change that which cannot be altered? Instead I remember how bravely she'd defended me in a hostile classroom when I was asked to give a presentation on popular culture to seniors majoring in English literature at her college.

She'd sat through my hour-long lecture with her head held high, unflinching in her support. I wouldn't have wanted to swap places with her that muggy afternoon. Had the situation been reversed I don't know how I would have handled it. Some of the students were decidedly antagonistic, just stopping short of sneering openly. I'm sure she knew the overall sentiments in that stiflingly hot classroom, but she remained a loyal daughter and I shall always respect her for it.

Just as I shall always respect a lesson I learnt thanks to Aditya, when I attended a concert he was performing in while at school. It's always hard for a proud parent to conceal his or her delight at watching a child achieve something—no matter how big or small. Aditya must have been fourteen at the time—that horribly awkward pause between adolescence and adulthood. He was exceedingly self-conscious, a shy, reserved young man. I'd been surprised at his readiness to take part in a musical (*My Fair Lady*) of all things. I waited anxiously for the big moment—his number—which required him to waltz with a few other classmates. It took me a while to recognize him when he appeared on stage. No—was that really Aditya? My son, Aditya? This chap seemed so much older than my little boy. And could that really be make-up on his smooth, whiskerless face? I clapped long and hard after the gig was over. I'd managed to make eye contact with him during the performance and smile encouragingly. He'd blushed and looked away hastily. I decided to go backstage and demonstrate my appreciation still more effusively. I walked into the green room expectantly, found him with his friends, and exclaimed with undisguised glee, 'You were great. Terrific. Congratulations.'

He seemed deeply embarrassed. After a couple of minutes he took me aside.

'Mother, how could you?'

How could I what?

'How could you single me out for praise? All of us were in it together. What about my friends? You didn't bother to congratulate them. They were as much a part of the number as I was. If you had to shower compliments, you should have done so on everybody, not me alone.'

I felt tears stinging my eyes. I felt snubbed and small all of a sudden. Momentarily, I was stunned. It was nothing short of a reprimand, a sharp slap on my face. And I was hurt. I turned away, my body crumpled, when I felt a hand on my shoulder. It was Aditya's. 'I'm sorry, mom. But that's how I genuinely feel.' He was absolutely right. I'd had no business rushing in with my idiotic praise for a group item. My lack of judgement and sensitivity had been the cause of embarrassment for my son. And I regretted my spontaneous but immature conduct. It was a lesson I wasn't going to forget in a hurry.

There have been several such incidents involving our children. Each time I learned a new and refreshing 'truth'. They helped me change, re-evaluate my worn attitudes, reassess my rigid positions on issues that concern us all. I feel thankful to them for having pointed out my mistakes. Some of us get to that peculiar position in life where nobody ever dares to question or condemn any of our actions. It's tempting to succumb to sycophancy—after all, who likes criticism? Yet, after each slip-up I mentally thank the kids for not being dumb, uncritical witnesses, for having the courage to tell me I am wrong even if that means incurring my wrath temporarily. I listen to their unpalatable comments, swallow and digest them reluctantly but also realize how precious they are, how valuable. In the world I occupy, nobody bothers with the truth. What for? It's far easier to lavish compliments and say, 'You are the greatest.' Easier still to believe it all. My children's voices are the echoes of sanity constantly reminding me of my limitations in the healthiest possible way. I hope they never stop telling me when and where to get off—more for my own sake than theirs.

It took a comment from Ranadip to drive home a point, a troubling one. We've had our differences, Ranadip and I, and I'd been feeling of late that perhaps my attitude had been a bit too unbending and harsh, at a time when he was staging his battle for identity and sovereignty over his turf. We'd faced some tense situations, argued about the parental exercise of 'authority' and then settled for a semi-permanent stand-off. Rana is now a careerist with a life of his own. An exuberant, popular extrovert with countless friends the world over, and a social life that would be the envy of any dedicated mover and shaker. It took me a while to recognize his right to be himself. After a couple of uneasy years I'd started telling myself it was time to recognize the fact that he was a twenty-five-year old man and treat him accordingly. A tentative thaw was gradually taking place when, one evening at the dining table, he mentioned a friend's mother, someone known to me.

'She has single-handedly ruined the lives of her children—her son's in particular,' Ranadip commented.

I was surprised by the remark. All along I'd thought this particular woman was his idea of the dream mother—liberal, sporting, friendly, the kind who qualifies for 'cool'.

He carried on, 'She was never a figure of authority. She failed her children by being a bit too buddy-buddy with them. They stopped respecting her.'

Was he trying to tell me something? I'd like to think so. I felt enormously relieved. Years of being unpopular vanished in an instant. Yes, I'd occasionally behaved like an ogre. I'd held out. I'd agonized over being seen as the vamp of the piece—the evil, unsympathetic stepmother. But I'd resolutely refused to compromise my own value-systems, the familiar ones I had been raised with. Through it all, I'd stuck to my guns—and my principles. Refused to buckle under pressure. Maybe, just maybe, the gamble had paid off.

For every small pinch, for every harsh word, the children have touched me with their kindness and love in a way and manner that conveyed its own special message, its own deeper lesson. I know I can count on each and every one of them when push comes to shove. That's saying a lot already.

I detested the word 'discipline' as a young adult. How can I expect my children to love it? They don't. Aditya has been away for over four years but I haven't entirely given up trying to enforce rules for him to live by. Most times, he just laughs and does exactly as he pleases. In Avantika I see a mirror-image (figuratively and physically). It makes it that much harder. I persevere regardless. Something is bound to stick. Recently, my husband and I were leaving on a fortnight's trip abroad. The younger children's summer vacation had begun. They desperately wanted to accompany us. There would have been no real point in taking them on what was going to be a hectic business trip. To mollify them I'd spent ten days in Goa before our London trip and explained why we wouldn't be able to travel together this summer. There was obvious disappointment but no voicing of resentment.

The two little girls clung to me and cried the evening before our flight.

'We'll miss you,' they whimpered. 'We'll miss seeing you writing at the dining table . . . we'll miss Daddy watching TV in his room.'

Predictable responses. We sat down to dinner unable to eat very much. It was going to be a very long and guilt-ridden fortnight.

As I indifferently pushed some food around in my plate, Arundhati came up to me carrying a hand-made card (a family tradition). Along with it came a surprise—a cassette.

'Listen to it in the car on the way to the airport,' she said shyly.

Anandita had painstakingly drawn yet another set of her unique, quirky, magical pictures saying 'Have a blast. Have fun. Safe journey.' I felt still worse. It was the tape that did me in—carefully recorded, thoughtfully put together, it featured sweet words of love and encouragement from Arundhati, interspersed with some of our favourite music. A lot of time and trouble had gone into putting it together.

Dilip kept it safely in a drawer next to his bed and we left. When Arundhati called us in London the next day, her voice registered great disappointment.

'You left my tape behind,' she said softly.

'We didn't want to lose it,' I explained.

'But . . . I wanted you to have it with you there,' she went on.

'I know, darling. But it was far too precious for us to risk misplacing it somewhere,' I tried to reassure her. And hoped desperately that she understood.

On our return at some unearthly hour, we found a large poster stuck on our bedroom door. It said, 'Welcome Home Parents. We really missed you.' Inside the room were two carefully positioned cards—one for me, one for Dilip. How very generous of them, I thought to myself, not to have grudged us this badly timed (from the children's point of view) break, not to have demanded anything (fancy gifts) by way of 'compensation', and to have had the goodness of spirit to say, 'We hope you had a great time', 'remember us', and what was more, to have meant every word of it.

It reminded me of my fiftieth birthday party, planned with such precision and care by the entire family. When I entered my room after dinner at my father's home, I found the place imaginatively festooned with flowers, balloons, paper windmills and messages on the mirrors. 'Happy Birthday Mom' was written with flowers on our bed. Charming presents followed. Aditya gave me a panda of my own: 'Since once I heard you say that nobody gives you soft toys any more.' Another (Avantika) produced entwined silver hearts inside the famous blue box from Tiffany's—more to demonstrate how grown-up and sophisticated she herself now was, a signal that we were finally equals in a universal women's club. Rana designed a card with 'cool copy', perfectly in keeping with his status as a senior copywriter in a large advertising agency. Radhika created another, using her newly-acquired skills as a computer graphics whiz.

But what broke my heart (besides Dilip's meticulously executed surprise dinner party for family and a few close friends) was the odd assortment of gifts Arundhati had bought with her hoarded pocket money. It consisted of a tea cup—no saucer—(because 'you love your morning tea and you like nice cups'); a mud pack—imported ('I overheard you telling a friend you hadn't used one in months after the last one ran out'); a teething ring ('because even mummies should be treated like babies sometimes') and a plastic kitchen set for kids ('you always say you like playing with toys but you don't have any of your own'). These were no ordinary gifts. These were a sensitive child's carefully observed offerings of love and deep attachment.

I felt I didn't deserve any of it. Kunda had handpicked each lily and gerbera that went into a beautiful arrangement of flowers artistically arranged in my mother's buttermilk churner—a ceramic container I'd once said I wanted since I associated it with her and my childhood. She had supervised it all, even the floral 'toran' strung along the entrance to my father's home. I was made to feel far more special than I really was. And for what? Arriving at a humdrum milestone? Millions made it without any fuss or notice. It's a memory I shall cherish forever, made possible by dearly beloved people I'm blessed to have in my life. Even though I do not believe in reincarnation, at a time like this I tell myself it has to have some connection to good deeds performed in a previous birth. In this one I have been selfish, impatient and far from likeable. Despite that, I've received a disproportionate amount of love. It doesn't figure. But then, very few things actually do. Somehow, it all pans out . . . or does it?

Dilip often reminds me of the fact that he is eight years older. 'I have lived in this world longer than you. I have seen more of it. Between the two of us we have a century plus of experience. Remember just one thing—people make mistakes when the tide is either very high or very low. That's when the panic sets in. The trick is to wait out those periods. Wait for a calmer sea. Answers and solutions automatically follow.' I recall these words whenever I need to take crucial decisions.

The other day I received a call from my former mother-in-law. She was wondering whether I had Aditya's horoscope with me. I said I'd look, and in case I didn't have it, I'd arrange to get a new one cast.

'Do you remember . . . he was born at eleven at night on Gauri Visarjan day. When the doctors saw him they commented, "Only Gauris have been born in the nursing home since morning—seven of them. At last we've got a Ganapati."'

Both of us laughed at the memory. Aditya was her first grandchild—a very precious one. He was my first child, and I'd been bewildered. Not because I was all that young, but I do believe nothing and nobody can 'prepare' a woman for childbirth—no amount of reading on the subject, no amount of sharing with other women, no reassuring grandmother's tales, no sympathetic doctors, not even a spouse who is with you all the way. The first time a woman gives birth, she explodes. And the shock waves that follow leave her reeling—for months, years, sometimes forever. It has very little to do with the physical pain—which, by the way, is definitely for real and definitely crippling. It is deeper, more visceral. Her life changes irrevocably from the moment of conception. She will never again be the same person.

When I discovered I was pregnant, I'd taken it entirely in my stride. Of course I was pregnant. I was meant to be. All young married women get pregnant. I took it for granted and went about preparing for the event in a calm, organized way.

I didn't think beyond practicalities—the baby's crib, nappies, whether disposable ones or the traditional cotton triangles, massage oil, baby soap, baby clothes and booties—you know, the usual lists. I chose my own gynaecologist, a wonderfully gentle, refined, articulate lady called Dr Tara Rama Rao, and I surrendered my body and the unborn baby's fate to her care. That I had a relatively rare blood group (O-Rh-negative) was a source of concern, but when my doctor assured me it wouldn't affect the first born, I believed her and enjoyed my pregnancy without the slightest anxiety. For the first time I felt I 'belonged' to the world around me—the world of experienced elderly ladies who'd seen umpteen childbirths over the years in the extended family I was then married into. They knew all there was to anticipate and do. I merely had to carry the child. Everything else was taken care of.

I bloomed briefly during the pregnancy—which was seen as an ominous sign. 'If a woman glows and looks wonderful while carrying, it means she'll have a daughter,' I was told. I stopped blooming. Unconsciously the pressure of producing a son got to me. I began worrying—what if it was a girl? Would I disappoint the eager family? I was engulfed by charming superstitions whereby for months, till I actually started showing, the fact of the pregnancy was kept under wraps ('Why attract the evil eye?'). I was taken regularly for my check-up, and the necessary injections to counter the blood-group factor were flown in from Switzerland. My doctor, composed and unhurried in all things and at all times, was made aware of the special status of the baby ('we haven't had a child in the family for over thirty years').

I wasn't weighed down by the burden, mainly because I

remained active and busy through it all, working at *Stardust*, writing from home, going out in the evenings. I exercised regularly, climbed stairs briskly, ate like a horse and yet didn't bloat grotesquely. I'd been told by other women that a time would come when I'd hate the sight of my misshapen body and resent the whole idea of motherhood. That didn't happen either. Of course, I was bigger than a tub and astonished at the size of my distended belly. I could not have imagined that skin could stretch so tautly over a surface without bursting. I was delighted, as all mother are, with all the 'firsts'—the first kick, the fist hiccup, the first vigorous movement. But at no point was I alarmed by the newness of the experience, nor discouraged at what lay ahead.

When I went into labour, I was prepared for a long wait—but not an interminable one. Dr Rama Rao assured me it was common for primies to take upto thirty-six hours, even longer. Since my water bag had burst, it was felt that induced labour would work better and accelerate the process. Well . . . I guess Aditya wasn't in a hurry in there. He took his time to arrive.

I was determined to wait it out and resisted a C-section even when I was exhausted to the point of collapse and didn't believe I'd have the energy to push even a pingpong ball out of my fatigued womb. But when the moment arrived, I discovered not just animal strength in those toned-for-the-job muscles, but impressive lung power as well. I don't recall yelling, but my mother who was right outside, along with some of the other members of the family, told me I nearly brought down the roof of the OT.

The first thing I did when I saw the infant was to count his fingers and toes and check for a cleft palate while instructing the nursing staff to note the time of his arrival on a piece of paper. I was far too tired to exult. All I wanted was a hot dinner and some sleep (I didn't get either). Right outside my room several raucous, rowdy processionists carrying Gauri to her immersion in the sea, and beating enormous drums while chanting Ganapati Bappa Morya, were making sure I couldn't catch up on my lost sleep. I knew I ought to have been feeling differently. I knew I should have been telling myself, 'You are a mother now. Do you get it? A mother. You have a son. Another life that was growing inside you all these months. Think about it. Everything has changed—your life, your priorities, your thoughts.' Instead, my mind was drifting, I was thinking of hot chocolate and cookies, of my own comfortable bed back home, of a much needed shampoo, a long, relaxing bath—creature comforts. No 'higher' thoughts. No noble feelings.

The next day there was much celebration within the family. I recalled the seventh-month ceremony at my parents' home and felt a little sad at its implications. I suppose that's the way it was in the old days when the mortality rate during childbirth was so frightfully high—the mother or the baby. It was always the baby that won, which was why the mother-to-be was given what was a grand send-off, just in case she didn't make it. She'd be dressed in a fine bridal saree, her hair held back with flowers, her body bedecked with jewellery. Women from the family would offer gifts, and her favourite dishes would be cooked, like for the last supper. Maybe I'm being morbid in interpreting this charming ceremony thus, but that was an explanation someone gave me, and I believed it.

Now that mysterious, silent presence in my womb was a reality. Narcissistically I looked for traces of me in the tiny, screwed-up face when the nurses brought Aditya to me in the morning. My little Ganapati had come into the world with a stamp on his forehead that said, 'I am me—unmistakable and unswappable'; I leaned over and kissed the slightly raised birthmark adorning his brow. The question of finding a name for him didn't arise—I'd already decided it was to be Aditya, the first name of Sürya—the sun. On the way home from the hospital, we stopped at a temple to seek the Almighty's blessings. I was carrying my son, my first born, in my arms for the first time in public, and it felt wonderful, just wonderful, to be able to cradle a tiny, warm, compact body close to my bosom, hold a finger under his nose and feel his breath, kiss the tender, peeling skin of his cheeks, trace my finger along the outline of his face and ask, Is there anything of me in this little being who, till recently, was an energetic tenant residing inside my body? Surely he is more a piece of me than of anybody else, even his father? I carried him, I nurtured him, I brought him into the world. I have every right to be a part of him . . . surely he knows that? Irrational, childish desires of establishing ownership. I wondered if all mothers felt this way, so possessive and proprietorial! Aditya was mine. I could not bear to share him. I couldn't bear to share the experience either. I found it hard to discuss what I'd felt or been through with anybody. But I knew without a doubt that giving birth had been the most significant moment of my life. One that I would cherish till my last breath. Too precious to dilute through conversation . . . even thought.

People talk of how 'primal' the process is; I suppose they are right. But it's much more than that. Every fibre of a woman's being is involved while bearing a child. It envelops everything on every plane. It covers all dimensions—physical, emotional, cerebral, and moral. It is like nothing you've known before, an emotion so strange, so alien and so powerful, there is just one thing to do—surrender to its might. Hand yourself over, body and soul.

There wasn't a single aspect of pregnancy, delivery or

motherhood that I grudged or resented. I loved it all. Enjoyed every bit of it—bloated belly included. Which rather surprised me. I had never been one to coo over other peoples' babies or grab every passing kid and slobber over it. Babies . . . children . . . had not interested me in the least. I didn't particularly like them, their smells, their baby talk, their intrusions, their demands. I'd wonder how mothers coped with grubby little creatures crawling all over them. Unlike other little girls who played 'doll-doll' and cradled plastic babies in their arms for hours, crooning gentle lullabies, I'd preferred rougher, sportier games, often hanging out with little boys and kicking a ball around rather than setting up a 'kitchen' with discarded pots and pans. Even during my first pregnancy, I didn't think too much about motherhood or how it might transform me. I was merely walking down a conventionally-approved route—you marry, you produce children.

Now, suddenly, I was becoming aware of my own changed perspectives and priorities. I discovered that nothing mattered so much to me as being with the little fellow, watching him for hours on end, monitoring each change, recording it faithfully.

Two-and-a-half years later, I became pregnant once again—this time older, wiser, more in control, and actively overjoyed. I desperately wanted a daughter, and got one. Avantika was born with a beauty spot on her left cheek—she was pink and pretty, delicate and feminine even at birth. Her name was in my mind as well, even though the 'nakshatra' at the time of her birth suggested another one starting with a 'U'. Well, she was called both—Uttara and Avantika. But it was the latter that stuck. By now, I was confident and prepared—even if I had been warned by Dr Rama Rao that chances of the second baby being affected by the Rh-negative factor were high. Aditya had inherited my blood-group, diminishing the possibility of the next child being affected by anti-bodies, and to our delight, Avantika was Rh-negative too. To me it meant just one thing—great, now I can have a third without worrying. And with luck, a fourth and a fifth and a sixth too.

Of course, I had to wait for over eight years before Arundhati was born. By then, medical science was much more advanced, and Dilip and I discovered the miracle of sonography (Arundhati was a comparatively late baby even for a third child and Dr Rama Rao didn't want to take any chances). When we actually saw our yet-to-be-born daughter floating around inside my womb like an astronaut in space—weightless, out of control, limbs moving spasmodically, when we heard her heart-beat over an amplifier, sounding much like the hooves of a galloping horse, it was hard to believe our eyes or ears. It was like a sci-fi trip. A trance. Momentarily I forgot all this was taking place inside me. It was as if we were watching a fascinating movie on the 'Discovery' channel. In a way, the mystery and mystique of birth was robbed of its magic at that moment. The unbearable suspense of finding out whether it would be a boy or a girl, normal or . . . That delicious edge of tension and uncertainty was gone. We knew we were welcoming our Arundhati into the world and I was ready for her.

This time I was flying solo—no in-laws to fuss over me, no infrastructure to absorb the anxiety of those early days back at home when a mother and child uneasily get used one another. No one to say, 'Don't worry. If you're tired, I'll sit by the baby . . . you relax.' Nobody trustworthy to leave the little one with, even for a few hours. I was that much older. Mental preparedness was one thing, physically I did feel the strain. And yet, each time I looked at Arundhati or held her close to me, my softest, most vulnerable side would instantly respond. I didn't mind the 'night shifts'—even though sleep deprivation does affect me a great deal. I didn't resent being completely and totally tied down for months together (I didn't trust maids, no matter how efficient) and I revelled in every activity associated with mothering, from nursing the baby 'on demand' to bathing her in the traditional way, after a vigorous oil massage administered while she lay face down over my stretched out legs, her head between my calves, her feet pointing towards me.

I'd done that for the other children too, but with help and supervision provided by a veteran bai—that marvellous breed of women specializing in post-delivery massages. Once the child had been taken care of, the bai would turn her attention to me. This was one of the big luxuries—being pampered with an hour long massage myself, and bathed in water close to boiling point. Her strong, gnarled fingers would pummel every sinew till I could almost feel her rough hands on my bones, and I would collapse later on my inviting bed and sleep the dead sleep of the Gods along with my infant who'd received similar ministrations earlier. There was no such 'perk' this time around. And I doubt that I'd have had the patience to lie for an hour and more on a straw mat, being kneaded like so much pliable dough. It was easier to get back into my own exercise routine at a time convenient to me, often between those unending feeds.

None of the babies gave me a hard time or cause for worry. Of course, like all nervous, overwrought mothers, I overreacted to every twitch and spasm, but I was also that much calmer. It sounds like a cliché but the arrival of Arundhati was crucial to my relationship with Dilip. What sort of father would he make? Would he be able to cope? He was forty-five and at the peak of his professional life. How would he take being saddled with a wet and whimpering bundle at this stage—a demanding, overactive baby cutting into our time together, taking away the attention a new wife generally reserves for her husband? I knew he wasn't the most patient man on earth. Would Arundhati try his limited quota still more? And if he resented her presence in our lives, if he found it intrusive, how would I handle it? Get hypersensitive? Withdraw? Feel unnecessarily aggressive?

It took some time for both of us to adjust to altered schedules. I must have resembled an ill-tempered cow on some days, when I was far too frazzled to bother to change out of my caftan or even run a comb through my hair. I'd been determined not to turn into a slob during those dreadfully oppressive post-delivery months, but I'd slipped up often enough. There were times when I caught myself gritting my teeth and going through a long day and unending night with the resolve and determination of a Scout Master. This wasn't the way it was meant to be. I wanted the experience to be joyful. I wanted to be in a permanent state of bliss. I wanted to be the perfect mother and wife. The best. Nothing less. And here I was getting irritable and short. Walking around the house with a frown, snarling at the domestics, being snappy with Dilip.

Meanwhile, the baby's demands were increasing. A familiar saga. One day I sat down and wept. How I wept. I felt deflated and defeated. The dream wasn't following the script. I can't tell you how much better I felt after that long hard cry. It was obviously overdue. Too many unresolved issues had remained unexpressed and bottled up for far too long. I'd tried to come to terms with a hundred disparate things—a new marriage, a new set of children and now a new baby. I'd been trying too hard. It wasn't possible. It wasn't feasible. It wasn't worth the strain. I decided to relax, unwind and be truer to myself and to my instincts. There were no prizes to be won, no certificates I was striving for. As for approval—it was there. Dilip expressed it constantly and in different ways. He knew we'd both undertaken an unusual responsibility. But he was confident we'd be up to it—if not immediately, then in the future when we were better prepared. He was right. The moment I made up my mind to go with the flow and not push myself quite that hard, everything gradually fell into place.

By the time Anandita arrived, I was like the smiling Buddha. I was sure it would be a cakewalk this time—and it was just that. Three hard shoves and she was out. It had been an effortless delivery. As for the name, we were undecided. Aparajita? Mrinalini? Ahilya? One of our friends, the painter Prafulla Dahanukar, was at the hospital to greet me and she intercepted Dilip as he was marching off to fill in the municipal form announcing the birth. 'What are you going to call her?' Prafulla asked. 'Shobha is keen on either Anandita or Mrinalini,' he said a bit uncertainly. 'Call her Anandita,' Prafulla instructed, 'Mrinalini is . . . is . . . I don't know . . . Mrinalini. I prefer Anandita. It's so musical and sweet.' So Anandita—the giver of joy—stayed.

Someone foolishly asked me, 'Did you plan another child because you wanted a son?' No. We decided to have Anandita because we wanted her. Despite my age (I was forty-one when she was born), despite everything we were told ('It's insane. And so risky'). We also wanted a companion for Arundhati. The older children would marry and leave. Who would Arundhati have then? No sibling to call her own. When I watch them together now, I know I did the right thing even if it was rash.

The older children unconditionally accepted the new entrants to the family and showered love and attention on them. It might have been a different story with a less happy ending, had they at any stage displayed insecurity, jealousy, hostility, indifference or rage.

The two little sisters became the focus of their existence. I knew I could count on the older girls, Radhika and Avantika, to help me organize birthday parties and entertain kids with ten-second attention spans. I didn't expect them to do night shifts or change nappies, all I wanted was their tacit support, and I got that in spades. I can't honestly recall a single nasty incident involving the sets of siblings. We've travelled together extensively and in its own crazy way it has all come together. I am no 'Supermom' even if I do have a T-shirt hailing me for being one. I'm not a 'super' anything for that matter. I am just a middle-aged woman who has tried to make some sense of a life some might think of as unconventional. I suppose it has been that. Funny, I never think of it that way.

*

I often wonder whether the kids would have preferred a 'regular' mother—someone pleasantly plump, homely, complacent, easy-going, anonymous. Completely anonymous. Are they embarrassed by me? By what I write? What I represent? Most times, they seem pretty proud—at least that's what I'd like to believe. They say so too. It's only at school functions, college affairs, or when their friends' mothers are also around, that they notice I'm a little different. And maybe they long for a more conventional motherly mother. Even though I'm always home when they get back from school, I fear I'm not entirely as attentive when they go on and on about what happened in class, who said what, who did this, who lied, who cheated, who won, who lost.

My preoccupied air gives me away even if I'm pretending

to listen closely. The kids know it. They can sense it. And I'm sure they resent it, even if they don't come right out and say so. I get the hint when my middle daughter Arundhati scolds the youngest one during exam time, 'Come on . . . do your spellings. Nobody is going to take them up. Mama is writing. She has to finish her book. And I have my own exams . . .'

I cringe and die a little at such moments. It's unfair, I tell myself, really unfair, for such young children to 'understand', 'make allowances for', 'accept'—why the hell should they? Why should they accommodate me? Shouldn't it be the other way around? It's as if a demon possesses my soul when I'm working on a book (which for the past ten years has been most of the time). I hate cutting away. I hate interruptions. And God knows I have enough of them without sitting at the desk of a third-grader going over 'Krishna and Sudama' for the twentieth time.

And yet, these same kids are conscious of how I'm perceived by the outside world—and very protective about my image (minor-league as it is). Walking into a prestigious saree store with my daughter Avantika one day, we ran into a heavily perfumed, perfectly coiffeured, frighteningly well-dressed group of ladies from Lahore, who happened to recognize me. My daughter shrank with shame once the ladies had finished with their cooing and innumerable 'inshallahs' and 'mashallahs'. She marched me off to the nearest mirror (the store is lined with them), an accusatory finger pointed at a miniscule haldi stain on my white cotton kurta. 'Mother—just look at yourself. It's disgraceful. Fine, don't get all dolled up if you don't want to, but must you go out in stained clothes?' She had a point—not that it altered anything, even though I pretended to feel penitent at that moment.

It happened again, more recently, when my husband and I got off a train at Pune station and had a photographer jump out at us from the shadows. There I was, bleary-eyed and practically sleep-walking down the long platform, my hair mussed up, a bottle of mineral water in one hand, a baseball cap in the other. The suddenness of the act woke me up all right. But as luck would have it, the same photographer was assigned by his paper to shoot me during my stay in Pune. This time I made sure I had my face on. At least my eyes were open and my hair neatly brushed. After he'd finished the session, I asked him about the other pictures. He looked crestfallen. 'Something went wrong with the roll. The rest of the photographs on it came out fine—only yours were blank. It has never happened before.' I knew whose side God was on that morning. I resolved never again to travel looking like something the cat had dragged in. My husband chuckles at the memory and each time we are setting out for the airport or station at some ghastly hour, he points to my make-up. 'Put some on . . . comb your hair . . . remember Pune?'

I'm touched. But also worried. The pressure to resemble, talk and behave like 'other' women gets to us all. This was more than evident when I was to get up at 4.30 a.m. to drop my youngest, Anandita, to the station. It was going to be her first camp—first time away from home. I knew she wouldn't sleep a wink that night, I was equally sure I'd have to sacrifice my sleep too. Instead of dressing in the dark, I decided to 'sleep' with light make-up on, just in case she disapproved of a bleary-eyed mummy in shabby clothes coming to the station while all the other mothers were smartly turned out. I'd carefully picked out a dull green jacket and beige trousers. The effort was worth it. Her eyes shone as much with gratitude as appreciation as she held my hand proudly while approaching the tour group.

Even for today's kids it must be something of a pressure to have their parents live up to a certain preconceived image.

With the older children (affectionately referred to as my censor board) constantly monitoring my every move, sometimes it becomes a bit of a pain. My husband has recently started smoking cigars. I have the occasional puff, more for a lark than anything else. At a media party where the kids were present, they pounced on me when they spotted the stogie held between my fingers. 'Stop it, mother,' my daughter admonished, swooping down and snatching the cigar out of my delicate grip. 'I'm just having some fun,' I said weakly. 'Think of something else to amuse yourself with,' she replied frostily. Out went the cigar.

It's difficult meeting children's critical standards. Kids are most embarrassed by the prospect of parents making fools of themselves in public. They find it hard to accept that parents too can have their odd moments and off-days, or that they are allowed to let their hair down occasionally, maybe even act foolish. I live in horror of putting my children in a spot and am on my best behaviour all the time in their presence, almost to the point of stiffness. Once Radhika asked Dilip and me why we never hugged or kissed in front of them. I was stumped for an answer. She added, 'Children like to see their parents showing affection.' Later when Dilip and I talked about her remark, we resolved to be more affectionate in future. These days we attempt an awkward clinch or two, but it's just that—awkward.

However hard I might try, it's not always possible to be on my best behaviour. When I'm under extreme pressure, I tend to regress and behave like a spoilt child—literally so. A couple of years ago, I was invited by *Society* magazine to attend their annual 'Society Collections'—a prestigious event at which craftspeople from all over India display their spectacular wares. They usually invite a movie star to inaugurate the show. That year it happened to be Juhi

Chawla, a friendly, confident, sunny young woman with a great smile. I was happy to be there and to meet up with ex-colleagues. But after a point I started feeling restless and slightly bored. After a short tea-break in the conference room, I strolled into the area where the public address system was. I cannot resist picking up a phone, any phone, if it's next to me, so when it rang, I did just that. It was an irate security officer who wanted to page the drivers of illegally parked cars in the lot downstairs. Instead of passing the mike on to the woman in charge of such announcements, I decided to handle it on my own, adopting a wide variety of accents (I'm quite good at them). The *Society* staffers dissolved into a fit of giggles, which spoiled my act somewhat, but by then I was having such a wonderful time, I didn't want to stop. In retrospect, I wonder what those impressionable young journalists made of my atrocious conduct. But at that point I was beyond caring.

I often man the phone lines at the video parlour next door when I'm looking around for films to view. Sometimes the callers happen to be regulars of the library who demand to know whom they're speaking to—and I tell them. Other times, they're friends of my children who recognize my voice and start an extended conversation. To me, this seems like harmless fun at that moment. It's only later that I rue my silly behaviour.

My kids have begun to recognize the signs and they physically restrain me from making an ass of myself. 'Mother,' one of them invariably cautions, 'don't, just don't. Take it easy, okay? Relax.' That's warning enough, though nothing in the world can stop me from dancing on the spot if a favourite song is playing. It could be in a crowded shopping arcade, an airport cafe, a record shop or a hotel lobby. That's when my children get totally paranoid. 'Everybody's looking,' they plead, even when the place is empty. 'Let them,' I say blithely, while my feet shuffle. These are the few remaining pleasures of life. Simple and innocent. I don't hurt anyone. I don't think my kids should mind all that much. It's a strain being sensible, mature and well-behaved all the time. I too need a break. Need to let my hair down. Regress. It's a release that frees me from the burden of adulthood. I love it.

The only concession they make in this regard is dancing in Goa. I'm 'allowed' to let down my hair during our bi-annual holidays, but within limits—their limits. They sportingly take turns indulging my passion and taking to the dance floor with me—the older ones with pained expressions, the younger ones, unselfconscious and free (they don't know they're supposed to act like mama's police force yet).

This very passion (dancing in Goa) can sometimes lead to potentially tricky situations, as a dear friend of mine and I found out while strolling to dinner past a lively Goan band playing the irresistible 'Lambada' for a private party. It was far too tempting—an empty dance floor, a crowd of morose-looking guests standing around wondering what they were doing at a beach resort (other people must have wondered too, given the heavy, formal city clothes this lot was wearing), and a young, high-spirited band wasting all that hot Latin music on this sorry lot.

My friend Judith and I decided to show them a step or two—while our younger children clapped on the sidelines, she and I did a pretty neat version of the Lambada, much to the delight and suppressed giggles of the crummy group. We were having fun till we spotted the slimy fat man working his video camera from a dark corner. He'd got it all—our abandoned spirit, our hot moves, and my friend's generous display of leg. The sight of that and the evil little red eye indicating the camera was on, froze us mid-step. We glared at the man—who kept shooting. We requested him to stop at once. He only laughed. 'Madam . . . what's the problem? Holiday *hai—sab chalta hai,*' he shrugged. We wondered whether or not to inform hotel security and retrieve the tape. Finally we agreed to let him keep the only recording in existence of an impromptu performance neither of us regretted. To each his or her own cheap thrills. The next morning, the heavy pinewood door of the unisex sauna cubicle at the health club swung open—and there he was, the beast himself (no camera) wearing ill-fitting nylon trunks, leering in our general direction. We all but ran out. As we ducked into an icy shower, our one consolation was the thought of the beast's trunks melting in the 85° heat of the sauna and causing permanent welts in all that ugly flesh. There was justice in the world after all.

It amazes my friends when they discover how terrified I can be of my children and their opinion of me. 'It ought to be the other way round, surely?' they laugh. Maybe, maybe not. As a parent, I know one thing very clearly—I never want to hurt, consciously embarrass or disgrace my kids. It has probably happened a few times, but entirely inadvertently. I listen to them because I trust them and have absolute faith in their judgement. I know they'd be truthful with me even if it offends—how many outsiders would do that? I also know they have my interests at heart just like I have theirs—they have nothing to gain by misleading or flattering me.

'Open Days' and 'PTA' meetings at school are great levellers. I remember when the older children were teenagers, they'd tell me to present myself on these occasions decorously clad in a saree. 'Don't wear fancy sunglasses. Don't wear jeans. Don't tie a top-knot. Don't wear jewellery. And don't use lipstick,' they'd caution. I understood their reservations perfectly when I overheard their sharp comments about some 'mothers' who regularly arrived for these meetings like they were auditioning for a fashion show. The children's scorn was doubled if these ladies tried to look half their age by squeezing themselves into a pair of too-tight jeans, borrowing their daughters' T-shirts and painting their faces excessively. 'Did you see that auntyji? She looked a riot. Poor Sonya . . .' they'd sympathize. I never wanted their friends to say that about me . . . or pity my children.

At a dinner party we hosted, a particularly obnoxious corporate man was busy leching at all the women present while his young son watched TV with our son Ranadip in the bedroom. Someone asked the teenager, 'Which one is your dad?' And he replied, 'The jerk who's making the biggest ass of himself outside.' When my children repeated this to me, my heart went out to the boy. It must have been pretty awful for him, and his mother, to watch the head of the family getting snubbed and being shunned by all our female guests on account of his slobbering, disgusting behaviour. That was ten years ago. Today, that sensitive young boy has grown into a sensitive young man, living in New York, alienated from his parents, desperately seeking an independent identity in the arms of a much older lover—a well-connected mentor who appears to adore and understand the troubled youth.

*

It's true that at some stage in a woman's life, a very sweet role-reversal takes place. Very recently I ran into Dimple at a smallish dinner. I knew I'd said the wrong thing the moment I opened my mouth and expressed my mild shock over her dramatically altered appearance. Back from London with a stylish hair cut, Dimple's signature mane was missing. With all that hair gone she was difficult to recognize—still ravishing, of course, but not the same woman whose luxuriant auburn tresses gave the impression of having an independent life of their own. She was defiant and defensive about her decision. 'What the fuck,' she repeated several times. She was right. What the fuck. She wanted to take it all off, she took it off. It wasn't anybody's business. Certainly not mine. She explained how the 'new look' was affecting people—her fans and family. I was more interested in what her daughters had said to her when they first saw their transformed mom. Twinkle, the older one, had said, 'It's okay, Mom. You look great. Don't let anybody get to you about this.' The younger one Chinky had been equally supportive.

I then told her my own experience when at age forty I'd gone to a salon at the spur of the moment and asked my regular hair person to cut my long hair off. She'd refused. Just like that. 'No, I'm sorry. I can't do this. Please get one of the other girls. It's a crime, if you ask me.' I was determined, crime or otherwise. The lady manager told me gently to go home, sleep on it and come back the next day. 'No way,' I'd insisted stubbornly, 'it's now or never.'

It was 'now'. And it was awful. I crept home, hoping I wouldn't have to meet anybody I knew en route. My husband's face fell (my freshly cut hair was about the length he wore his) but he swiftly rearranged his expression to say cheerfully, 'It's . . . it's . . . smart. Different. You look . . . young.' The younger children were more honest. 'It's horrible. Terrible. Yuck. When will it grow back?' The teenagers, Radhika and Avantika, were still more crushing. 'Mother . . . it's all right . . . I suppose. It's just that you look so . . . so . . . ordinary. Like any other woman on the street.' One of the boys, Aditya, looked and looked away, without saying a word. The other, Rana, merely shrugged. I threw my head back jauntily. 'Well . . . I wanted to do it. Love me, love my

511

short hair. Is it me or my long hair?' The answer was pretty evident. I promptly decided to grow it back. It took nearly four years and even then it wasn't the same, but it had to do.

Dimple's experience was similar, and she wasn't enjoying it at all. In her case, I could see how it worked—the hard-to-escape beauty trap she's caught in. The first night after she'd cut her hair, just as she was about to leave her home, her movie-star daughter had stopped her. 'Wait, wait, wait. Let me fix your hair. It isn't falling right. I'll put in some lighter highlights.' Dimple seemed genuinely touched by the concern. 'Twinkle brought out an expensive Christian Dior product and worked it into my hair,' she said proudly. 'She also examined my face and asked, "Where are your eyes? Your cheeks? You need more shadow, darker blush-on."' Dimple smiled, 'Funny, isn't it? Now I've become her daughter and she my mother. The amount Twinkle fusses over me . . . worries constantly about my well-being, it's scary. And it isn't fair. She's so young. Why should my problems become hers? But she is so mature. I was a fool at her age. I didn't understand anything. Today she advises me, and I listen. Yet, I feel so guilty. Especially when she says, "Mom, don't worry about a thing. I'll take care of you. You go ahead and enjoy your life. Do exactly what you want. I'm earning. Leave it all to me. You don't have to accept some stupid serials or lousy films because of financial tension. It's not your problem any more, it's mine."'

While narrating this, her eyes filled with tears. My own were moist too. I shared a few experiences of mine with my own daughters with her. It was a good moment between women—mothers. On the ivory sofa at the other end of the living room was Goldie Hawn, sexy, svelte and dazzling at fifty-two. Earlier we'd spoken about her children—a son aged twenty-one and a daughter about eighteen. 'They are just so beautiful,' she'd said completely naturally. It wasn't a boast. It wasn't even mere motherly pride. Hers was a professional assessment—both kids are in showbiz. I cribbed (indulgently) about my daughters raiding my wardrobe. There's nothing I can call my own any longer—not my clothes, shoes, accessories or jewellery.

She threw back her head and laughed knowingly. "It's exactly the same at my home—half my stuff is missing. My daughter is all over my things."

That night, I couldn't wait to get back home and see the sleeping forms of our own younger children in our room. It is one sight I don't think I can get enough of or ever get over. We walk in and observe the two little girls fast asleep, hair tousled, brows uncreased, fists curled up under their chins. Sometimes they stir, open their eyes and smile sleepily. In that half-dopey smile there is such trust, it breaks my heart. I want to hug and kiss them in their deep sleep, stroke their soft cheeks, enter their dream world stealthily and stay there. The image of children—any children—sleeping, affects me deeply. I've often wondered why. Perhaps it takes me back to my own placid, secure, warm childhood when I shared my parents' room and sensed their presence through the night. And to the time when Kunda and I roomed together.

I have never entirely understood the Western mode of child rearing where infants are studiously placed in their cribs across the landing, the lights switched off, the door firmly shut, with only a baby alarm serving as an early warning system and a few teddy bears for company. I do believe very young children need their parents every minute of their lives—even in deep sleep. They move out when they're good and ready to. One just has to wait for the signal.

In our home it's an easy, flexible arrangement. We take our cues from the children. If they'd rather spend the night in their room, that's all right by us. If they want to camp in on mattresses spread out on the carpet next to our beds, that's fine too. So far it has worked out rather well. And I haven't had to turn to my well-thumbed Freud to figure out its long-term effects. I find this arrangement far more natural and mutually fulfilling than the other, more practical one of marching kids off to their beds at 8 p.m. whether or not they're ready to sleep, then patting yourself on the back for instilling a sense of discipline. Kids aren't puppies who need training. Even puppies love crawling into their owners' beds to be hugged and cuddled. It's not even the assumed kiddie deprivation I'm thinking of—it's the pleasure we'd be depriving ourselves of. I am selfish. I need the kids . . . whether or not they need me.

I remember a 'live' interview for a ticketed audience at the Melbourne Writers' Festival. The woman conducting it was a formidable TV anchor with a huge following. The auditorium was packed, more for her than me, I'm sure. I was slightly late and terribly flustered since I'd just finished a radio interview at a station down the road and had walked briskly to this venue, losing my gold earring somewhere along the way (I found it later, still lying on the deserted asphalt I'd walked over two hours earlier. Says something? Either Aussies are extraordinarily honest, or the road was extraordinarily deserted). The woman, who had an impressive reputation as the Barbara Walters of Aussie television, and an equally impressive on-view cleavage, greeted me frostily and we began even before I could catch my breath. The interview went well enough till she came to the question, 'When do you have time exclusively to yourself?' And I said, truthfully enough, 'Never.' 'What about when your children are asleep? They don't need you then.' And I replied spontaneously, 'I hope they do. I want to be a part of their dreams . . . just as they're

514

a part of mine. The need never ends.' She got a little testy at that but concluded our session on a charming note.

After we were through and I'd walked out for a coffee and cookie break, about half a dozen women came up to say how touched they were by what I'd said. I didn't think I'd said something all that emotional. One woman grasped my hand and whispered, 'You are a courageous lady. It takes a lot to admit something like that in public.' I honestly didn't get it. What had I said that required 'courage' under the circumstances? I was baffled by their reaction and said so.

'My dear . . . very few Australian women would admit to such a need in these times—they'd be damned for making a politically incorrect remark. People would mock them. But we loved you for saying it out loud. A lot of us feel exactly the same way. We dare not show it.' Their remarks have stayed with me. How sad that society can exert such pressure on expressing one's love for one's own children.

When mine called the same night for their regular little chat, I could barely speak coherently. They sounded so cheerful . . . so generous about my absence. I asked the little one, Anandita, what she wanted from Australia. She said very carefully, 'Three-coloured pasta and Parmesan cheese. That's all.' I thought it a most unusual request for a six year old. She explained she'd been eating it at a friend's home and loved the taste. The very next day I went in search of the pasta and cheese. It wasn't hard to locate. But each time I see the dish on a menu, I can hear her sweet voice over a long-distance line making that request and sounding so grateful when I phoned back to say I'd found it.

I often agonize over the vast age-gap between me and my youngest daughters. When Anandita was around four years old, she'd asked me in all seriousness, 'Mama, were there dinosaurs on earth when you and daddy got married?' She wasn't being cute. Then she'd sighed deeply as is her habit and said, 'You are so-o-o-o old. When will you die? And then, what will happen to me?' That made me do a double-take. I often wonder whether they're being short-changed by a mother who can contribute all of her mind to their young lives but rarely her body. I no longer have the energy to plan weekend picnics, visits to the planetarium, trips to the zoo, excursions to distant spots. I barely survived 'Disneyland' in the summer of 1997 and thanked my stars I wasn't in a wheelchair after my kids had dragged me from one ride to the next as I gasped, spluttered and panted in sheer exhaustion.

I watch the mothers of their friends—young, vibrant women with fit, well-toned bodies and inexhaustible reserves. On 'Open Days' at school we squeeze into kiddy-chairs and scrutinize our children' art works. The other moms are in their twenties. They could be my children. And then my eyes fall on a painstakingly written composition, suitably illustrated with crayon pictures. 'The Person I admire most.' Anandita's characteristic left-handed scrawl goes all over the page as she states, 'The Person I admire the most in the whole world is my mama. She is very kind. She has brown eyes. And long hair. She takes care of me. She loves me. And I love her . . .' I fight back my tears. I don't deserve her admiration at all. When was the last time I put my pen down, packed away my papers and said, 'Come on, kids. Let's go find some sea shells'?

My children cut me down to size whenever they think I'm about to start flying into the stratosphere. I like that. I like their honesty and courage in speaking their minds. God knows I lacked both with my parents. There was no question of speaking my mind as a young person. I was free to talk about myself—my small triumphs, my anxieties, my desires, mainly with my mother who was always attentive, invariably interested. But I never felt I could cross that invisible line and tell either of them what I really felt deep down, even though ours was an exceptionally communicative family. Children were taught their place early in life. Later, as adults, on a more equal plane, we still suffered from innumberable inhibitions that prevented us from telling it like it was. Parents were parents—beyond approach or reproach.

That's not how my kids view us. With me, they are alarmingly informal. When my son Aditya described his experiences in some of New York's hottest new clubs, I said half-jokingly, 'Maybe you could take me with you the next time we are there together.'

He looked at me witheringly. 'But Mother, they won't let you in.'

Won't let me in? Why? Pat came the reply: 'You are too old. Besides, you have to be really, really good-looking.'

Oh dear. Temporarily crushed, and I confess, a little shocked by the bluntness, I asked plaintively, 'So . . . where do old and ugly people go if they want to have some fun?'

'Nowhere,' he said teasingly. 'They stay home.'

He made it worse by saying a little later, 'The DJs in these clubs are real sensitive. If they don't like the crowd, they just pack up and go home. If someone like you walked in the music would stop. The bouncers are pretty tough too. You've got to have the right look.'

Days after this rather cruel remark, while I was still brooding over its implications, he saw me all dressed up on Dusshera day. After surveying me critically, he admitted slowly, 'Well . . . maybe if you came dressed like this in a gorgeous saree, you'd be let in. But you'd have to come in with a group of hangers-on. Then they'd mistake you for a diva . . . or an exotic transvestite.'

Thanks a lot, son, I said to him, I think I'll just stay home and count my gray hair.

517

Was this the same boy who years ago had spent most of his modest holiday allowance in Singapore buying me an expensive flaçon of *Poison*, the newly-launched perfume, because he thought it suited my 'exotic personality'? The same boy who, when he saw me on television for the first time, tuned away disappointedly saying, 'What is all this? Just talk, talk, talk. Why can't you sing and dance like they do on *Chitrahaar*?'

The evening of Aditya's transvestite remark, my husband and I walked into a newly opened, very happening bar the kids had told us so much about. We took one look at the twenty-something crowd at the counter and tried to slink away as inconspicuously as we'd entered. Unfortunately, we were spotted by the manager and before we could make our great escape, we were dragged right back in. My son's words were still echoing in my ears. He was right . . . we were too old and too out of it.

When I recounted my conversation with Aditya to a few women my age, the more self-assured ones were amused by the exchange, the others, offended on my behalf. 'My God! Didn't you feel like killing Aditya?' Frankly, I didn't. I appreciated both, his humour (hell, I hope he was being at least half-funny) and his brutally frank comments, even if he hadn't meant them literally. Let's face it, at fifty there are loads of interesting things one can do, but traipsing around trendy bars which only come to life at 1 a.m. isn't an option any more. What I failed to convey to my son when I enthusiastically volunteered to go clubbing with him, was the fact that as always, the journalist-voyeur in me was hungry for the experience. I hadn't even thought of it as an evening on the town. I'd wanted to be a fly on the wall, an invisible observer checking out a changed scene, getting a sense of the buzz in such places—places whose existence I wouldn't have known about, places I wouldn't be in a position to access, without the help of someone like him.

I'm constantly surprised by the power the children have over me. My evening can be totally ruined by a critical look, comment, exchange. I will brood for hours, examine it from all sides, draw absurd conclusions, suffer, feel guilty, angry, suffer some more. Agonize, agonize, agonize till we make up· and are back to our original closeness.

I wonder if they realize just how strongly their comments affect me. Especially the younger childrens'. It's almost absurd. Once while leaving for a Brian Lara dinner (he was being honoured at a local hotel) I dressed hurriedly in a sequined chiffon saree . . . the kind I rarely wear. I needed instant approval and went off to seek it. My daughter Arundhati was in the shower and summoned me into the bathroom. I pleaded. I cajoled. I needed her to look me over and pronounce judgement. She refused—and rightly so. I explained to her (yelling over the noise of the shower and her own lusty singing) that if I walked in and got wet even a little, the chiffon would shrink and shrivel up. No problem, she crooned, angle yourself in such a way that I can view your reflection in the mirror. I did precisely that, adjusting my position several times so as to accommodate her. One quick look was all she needed to say witheringly, 'Sorry, you look awful.' That was it.

I would have changed my saree, but we were already late. My evening was effectively ruined. A few people actually showered lavish compliments, but I knew they were lying, or even if they weren't, I preferred to believe my daughter. Kids don't lie to you about yourself—they lie about themselves, and only if they have to. They are merciless when it comes to letting you know what they think of you. It's the same when it comes to my columns, books, interviews. My children don't spare me.

How can I forget a particularly devastating moment while I was checking the final proofs of *Surviving Men*? Radhika was observing me as I sat nose deep in the loose pages.

'Is that the new book?' she asked.

I grunted in the affirmative.

'May I read it?'

Flattered and a little flustered (it was the first time any of the children had asked to go through a proof), I handed it over proudly. She must have flipped through a few chapters the same night. It was back on the desk the next morning.

'Finished it?' I asked eagerly, dying for a pat on the back, an enthusiastic response.

'Most of it,' she answered truthfully.

'And . . .?'

'It was fun. Interesting,' came the laconic reply.

I was crestfallen, till I reasoned that the book was far too cynical for someone her age—a young girl in love (which she was then) at that. Even so, I resolved never ever to show my proofs to anybody—not even to one of the kids.

It's a funny thing with children, though. They need approval from their own peer group for parents to look better in their eyes. In the summer of '98, my son Aditya was visiting friends in Italy. 'Give me the Italian edition of *Starry Nights*,' he said a trifle guardedly. 'Maybe I'll present it to the people I'm staying with.' I didn't really expect him to. But not only was the book given to the girlfriend of his host, her feedback (she said she loved it) was conveyed to me by him. Oh well—if that's what it took to look good in my son's eyes . . . With the younger children, it's always, 'Mama, my friends think . . .' I've stopped interrupting them to demand, 'Never mind what your friends think. What do you think?' I'm scared of the answers.

When *Time* magazine profiled me in 1990, my children reacted to it as just another write-up. One desultory look and that was it. One of the boys asked in all innocence, 'Just a single page? Why not the cover?' Yeah, sure. The excitement was shared only by my husband when he called from the office to announce gleefully, 'You've made it. You're on this week.'

The profile was important to me at that stage of my writing career. It didn't matter what the correspondent had written either about me or my book, what counted was the fact that I'd made it to a one-pager in the international edition of the world's number one newsmagazine. I wasn't blasé about it then and I don't feel blasé about it now. It remains a moment that mattered, no matter what else followed.

*

My son Aditya said to me recently, 'Mother, you work far too hard. Slow down. Have some fun. Splurge on yourself. Lead a luxurious life. What the hell. You only live once. Enjoy yourself, dammit, what's the point? Every time I see you, you're writing. Answering mail, making calls, slogging. Forget it. Just be. Look at other women your age. Nobody functions like this. The trouble with you is you're so bloody middle class in your attitude. You really don't know how to let go . . . relax.' He made me think. I tried it. It didn't work. I couldn't let go. I couldn't relax. The more I forced myself the more it knocked me dead. I wasn't enjoying myself at all. I was suffering. Middle class I was. Middle class I shall remain.

In the summer of '97, the entire family had gone to America to attend Aditya's graduation. It was an expensive trip and I was very conscious of the tab. On our last day in

New York, I was walking down Fifth Avenue with Kunda, who was there for her daughter Lakshmi's wedding reception. Knowing my weakness for sunglasses, she encouraged me to walk into a store specializing in the latest designs. Within the first five minutes I'd spotted a smashing pair, tried it on and returned it to the owner with visible regret. 'Much too expensive.'

Kunda took me aside. 'Buy it,' she said.

'What?'

'Buy it, go on. Spoil yourself just this once. You deserve a present. And the shades look great on you.'

'But . . . but . . . do you know the price?'

'The price be damned. Don't think. Get them.'

I did. It was an extravagant purchase. I felt a little guilty . . . but above all I felt elated as we walked back to the hotel. My children couldn't believe that I'd splurged. I couldn't believe it either. But each time I wear my snazzy shades, I recall that moment in the shop when I said decisively, 'I'll take them', and a small shiver of pleasure and guilt travels down my spine.

It was only after I'd bought those 'JPG' sunglasses that I understood Aditya's thrill on hiring a Porsche Boxer for twenty-four hours as a graduation gift to himself. When he roared up to collect me for dinner, he was another person—a man in control of a very sophisticated machine. As I slid into the bucket seat next to him, I was affected by its plushness too. I could relate to my son's sense of awe as, with a light touch of his fingertips, the two-seater took off smoothly and we headed for a posh seafood restaurant where Aditya had made a booking.

On the way, several people yelled out, 'Hey graduate, that's quite a car.'

Aditya would nod, smile, wave and say airily, 'Sure is. A

graduation gift from my mom.'

Dream on, boy, I thought to myself. He'd spent a ridiculous amount of money for a momentary, fleeting pleasure. I would never have done that. Never. Then again, I would never have experienced the undiluted, sensuous pleasure of driving around in one of the world's spiffiest cars, listening to hot tracks on a great sound system and being next to someone I was finding hard to recognize as the once reticent, intense, soulful-eyed adolescent I used to build sand castles with. I caught a glimpse of his dreams that night. I hope he works hard to fulfil them.

I'm constantly astonished by the children's cavalier attitude and say so. Not that it changes anything. Where have they got it from? 'It's the age, Mother,' they mock affectionately, 'we belong to an era of undisguised greed—and we love it.' Their world is different, very different. And for my own sanity, I should get used to it. I remember when Ranadip was given a car of his own on his twenty-first birthday, he accepted the gift most naturally. 'My kids will have this and more,' he grinned, 'it's called the trickle-down effect. We work less but maximize our returns.' How's that for an argument? There was nothing I could say.

But the comment has stayed with me. Ranadip is probably right. Why should I impose my own standards or even ideals on the children? They belong to another age. They don't value what I value. It's for me to reorient myself and see things their way—the younger generation is never going to alter its vision. It's the parents who are sensible enough to accept the irrevocability of this basic premise who manage to strike some sort of an equation with their offspring. I'm learning, I'm learning. But don't let anyone tell you it's easy when twenty-year-olds start teaching you about the phenomenon known as the 'trickle down' effect—and you're the one stuck with fat bills.

*

All this was playing on my mind as Dilip and I drove back one night after a night out on the town. 'Gypsy kings' was playing on the car stereo. I watched the lights of Marine Drive—it is a sight I never tire of. There was a lovely, post-Eid crescent dangling precariously over the skyline, the night air was cool. We were both unusually quiet. No post-mortems. No comparing notes. No gossiping. We drove along silently. I leaned back in the seat. From that angle I could see the tops of the Art Deco buildings we were driving past, familiar silhouettes I'd seen thousands of times. What was I looking for? What did I really want? My husband was in a mellow, reflective and relaxed mood himself. I could tell from the angle of his neck, the tap-tap-tap of his fingers. I looked at his profile as he drove with calm concentration, his hands steady on the steering wheel.

It was easy that night to predict a few things—constants that followed a reassuring pattern. I knew that when we got home we'd be greeted sleepily by King Tuts wagging his stump of a tail half-heartedly. We'd open the door of our bedroom quietly, very quietly—the two youngest ones, Arundhati and Anandita, would be sound asleep on their makeshift beds on the carpet. We'd tip-toe past them so as not to disturb their sleep, put away our watches, fold our clothes and get ready for bed. My husband would consult the clock and raise his eyebrows. 'Nearly one o'clock—did you realize it was this late?' I'd nod while hanging up my saree. 'Have to wake up early tomorrow morning,' he'd whisper and sure enough, one of the girls would awake. She'd open her eyes, rub them and open them wider. They'd shine with joy and relief—Mother

and Father were back. Now she could really really sleep. I'd
lie down beside her for a while, playing with the silky strands
of her stray hair, rubbing her ear lobes, kissing her cheeks
softly. I'd reach across and stroke the other one's arms, notice
how tall she'd grown in the past month. So tall, her feet were
sticking right out of the mattress, her toes freezing without
the blanket covering them. I'd have to replace her favourite
baby quilt with an adult-sized one very soon. I'd stare at the
rapidly changing contours of her face—the nose that was
beginning to look more like my own, the cheekbones which
were jumping off her oval face now that the baby fat had
melted away, the glossy hair she'd forced me to cut only last
week and which looked like it had already grown an
impressive inch. I'd remove her alarm clock with its 'Lion
King' face to a safer place. I'd shift the bottle of water. I'd
pick up her funny earrings, the silver ones with the wonky
'Nike' logo, and put them in a drawer. Readjust the pillows
to prevent her from rolling under our bed at night and hurting
her head against the edge. I'd take one final lingering look at
her and her sister's sleeping forms and reluctantly switch off
the light.

This and this alone was all that mattered. That has ever
mattered. What difference did anything else make? Here was
where my happiness was. Here was where I felt warm, loved
and secure. There would be other things in life. Other
triumphs. Other glories. But for me that night, only one reality
counted. As I got under my Jaipuri razai, I felt enveloped in
a strange kind of warmth. I put my head down on my
extra-large pillow that's a family joke, and looked up at the
ceiling, which is unremarkable as ceilings go . . . but right
then, it resembled a softly lit sky. I didn't want to stir. I didn't
want to breathe. I didn't want to destroy the serenity of the
moment. It was perfect. Too perfect.

This was heaven. It had to be.

Epilogue

I didn't think I'd ever write this book. But then, I had never thought I'd write any book. See? Who can tell? All memory is selective. Most of us use it as a screen. We recall what we want to, blank out what we don't. Or at any rate, when one undertakes an exercise like this book, what finally makes it in is that which is shareable. There are choices involved. A window opens, but often the light only falls on a few specific artefacts inside. I have chosen to carve up my life into those segments I have no reservations about revealing and serving up to readers. It isn't lapses in memory I'm hiding behind. Rather, it is my conscious decision to exercise control over those aspects of my life I'm not ready to make public. Those that are precious and private to me. It's all about 'readiness', isn't it? Some people can do it (reveal all) without any reservations and even fewer regrets. I cannot. And have no desire to.

Selective Memory, as the title itself suggests, provides an overview of a journey. I've experienced much in these years, met a great number of interesting people, raised a large family, tried hard to lead an integrated life. Today, I'm prepared to provide a peep into the past without indulging in a voyeuristic catharsis. The one word that has inhibited me all along has been 'indulgence'. Self-indulgence. A detailed chronicling of one's own life seems the worst kind of narcissism, with its in-built assumption that there are people out there who are at all interested in you.

Now that the book is over and done with, I can honestly say I enjoyed writing it. When I started, I wasn't sure it was such a good idea. Especially since it was very clear to me right from the start that it wasn't going to be a 'bare-all-dare-all' shocker. I didn't want to lay everything on the line. What for? On the other hand, I could also recall my conversations with friends, when I'd scoffed, 'Nobody in India has succeeded in writing a real honest-to-goodness, no-holds-barred autobiography.' True enough. But I wasn't about to play pioneer.

I read somewhere that what one chooses to forget is often as significant as what one actually remembers. In my case, it's slightly different. I haven't forgotten all that much. On the contrary, I remember more than I care to. I selected what would go into the book without hiding behind the smokescreen of a convenient memory-loss.

The woman you meet in *Selective Memory* may not be the woman you think you know. But it's me all right. Dates, times, events, places . . . I've tried to get them right. But the book is not about chronological correctness, it has more to do with perceptions and feelings. I wasn't working with files and papers, just emotions and textures. It's possible I've got sequences jumbled up and a few vital facts hopelessly scrambled. However, I've sincerely tried to marshal as many relevant, significant details as it was humanly possible to recall while writing the memoir. If there are any lapses or errors in the narrative (as there are bound to be), I appeal to your better nature to overlook them. What's more important is the telling of the story and that I can assure you has been completely upfront, well-intentioned and truthful.

It's never easy to 'chapterize' a life. I've lain awake several nights in a row, prodding my mind to remember, waking up frustrated, going to the table in a dark mood and leaving it in a rage. Not that it helped. All I know is, at this stage in my life, the one thing I don't need is regret. There has been a great deal of 'coming to terms' during the past year. And in a way the writing of the book has been responsible for it. I've looked back and discovered areas I didn't know existed—either within me or in the people I thought I understood so well. Ten years ago, these discoveries might have unhinged me . . . but what is it they say about turning fifty? It's true. Every bit of it.

On the eve of my fiftieth birthday in January 1998, I sat down in this very chair and wrote the word 'Fifty' fifty times over. I stared at the page for a long time . . . waiting for it to sink in and make sense. Fifty? Who, me?

I knew I was meant to feel different, somehow transformed, wise and calm. But here I was excitedly wondering what my family had planned for me the next day.

But something happened during the night. It was a miracle. When I awoke, I did feel different. Bloody hell—I felt fifty. And wonderful.

By then, the book had reached its mid-way mark. After the morning's celebration, I went to take a look at what I'd written the previous day. A few pages later, I put the manuscript aside. There was a great deal in there . . . and much more still left to chronicle. My mood was slightly smug and complacent. I told myself in a pleased sort of way, 'It hasn't been too bad a life, has it?' And it really hasn't. I folded my hands in prayer and thought: God has been most kind. I didn't forget to touch wood . . . as an additional safety measure.

I went back to my room. The house was quiet, as it generally is at mid-morning. I stared at the calmness of the sea outside my window for a long time and felt the same calmness enveloping me. It was the 'turning fifty' syndrome all over again. I'd heard people talking about it and never quite believed them. What nonsense. Forty-nine can't be all that different from fifty. But it was. It is.

There is a sense of acceptance today that didn't exist previously. This is who I am. No tricks. No games. No camouflage. Life is about going on . . . and that's just what I'm doing. Slow and easy, one day at a time.

*

Sunday afternoon. BBC is showing part II of its tribute to Frank Sinatra. I can predict how it will end. With the legendary crooner belting out 'My way'. Sinatra was fortunate. He'd written his own epitaph years before his death. As I listened to the lyrics, my eyes filled with tears (there must have been millions of moist eyes at that very moment all over the world).

> I've loved. I've laughed and cried
> I've had my fill
> My share of losing
> And now as tears subside
> I find it all so amusing
> To think I did all that
> And may I say, not in a shy way
> Oh no! Oh no! not me
> I did it my way.

Thus sang the man disparagingly described by the commentator as a lounge-bar crooner. Yet, it took a lounge-bar crooner to touch the lives of countless people over forty years of a controversial career. 'My way' was everyman's anthem. It spoke for all those individuals who'd chosen to stick their necks out for different reasons at different times, and paid the price for doing so. I searched my mind desperately for an anthem, an epitaph to call my own. Something that would sum up, howsoever clumsily, all that I'd experienced during the past fifty years. Nothing came up on the blank screen. Nothing. And I called myself a writer. Some bloody writer, I thought wryly.

I remembered my response to an interviewer who'd asked the standard question: 'How would you like to be remembered?'

I'd said airily, 'As someone who dared.'

Dared what? Thankfully, I wasn't asked or I'd have been stumped for an answer. I was no female Frank Sinatra, alas. Just an ordinary woman who occasionally took her chances.

I turned to Arundhati in sheer desperation. 'How would you describe your mother?' I asked. I was practically pleading.

She thought for a bit and replied, 'Traditional'.

Now I'd heard it all. Really, really heard it all. I smiled a private smile. I'd finally met someone—a canny twelve-year-old—who knew me. Who had guessed my secret. Identified the demon. Understood. I felt naked. I felt good. Everything began to fall into place. Frank Sinatra was on his last bars. I hummed along with him. His way, huh? And mine too. Yes, most definitely mine too.